A·N·N·U·A·L E·D·I·T·I·O·N·S

Mass Media

Twelfth Edition

EDITOR

Joan Gorham
West Virginia University

Joan Gorham completed her undergraduate work at the University of Wisconsin and received master's and doctoral degrees from Northern Illinois University. She is currently associate dean for academic affairs in the Eberly College of Arts and Sciences and a professor of communication studies at West Virginia University. Dr. Gorham is the author of *Commercial Media and Classroom Teaching* and has published numerous articles on communication in instruction. She has taught classes dealing with mass media and media literacy at the high school and college levels, as well as for teachers throughout the state of West Virginia.

McGraw-Hill/Dushkin
2460 Kerper Blvd., Dubuque, IA 52001

Visit us on the Internet
http://www.dushkin.com

Credits

1. **Living With Media**
   Unit photo—© Getty Images/Ryan McVay
2. **Covering News**
   Unit photo—© Getty Images/Alan Pappe
3. **Players and Guides**
   Unit photo—Photograph courtesy of the Federal Communications Commission
4. **A Word From Our Sponsor**
   Unit photo—© Getty Images/Larry Brownstein
5. **The Shape of Things to Come**
   Unit photo—© Steve Cole/Getty Images.

Copyright

Cataloging in Publication Data
Main entry under title: Annual Editions: Mass Media. 2005/2006.
1. Mass Media—Periodicals. I. Gorham, Joan, *comp.* II. Title: Mass Media.
ISBN 0–07–321754–9   658'.05   ISSN 1092–0439

Twelfth Edition

Cover image © Jason Reed/Getty Images and Cartesia/PhotoDisc Imaging/Getting Images
Printed in the United States of America   1234567890QPDQPD0987654   Printed on Recycled Paper

Editors/Advisory Board

Members of the Advisory Board are instrumental in the final selection of articles for each edition of ANNUAL EDITIONS. Their review of articles for content, level, currentness, and appropriateness provides critical direction to the editor and staff. We think that you will find their careful consideration well reflected in this volume.

To the Reader

In publishing ANNUAL EDITIONS we recognize the enormous role played by the magazines, newspapers, and journals of the public press in providing current, first-rate educational information in a broad spectrum of interest areas. Many of these articles are appropriate for students, researchers, and professionals seeking accurate, current material to help bridge the gap between principles and theories and the real world. These articles, however, become more useful for study when those of lasting value are carefully collected, organized, indexed, and reproduced in a low-cost format, which provides easy and permanent access when the material is needed. That is the role played by ANNUAL EDITIONS.

According to the U.S. Department of Commerce, in 1999 the average American spent 3,405 hours—the equivalent of 142 days or 85 40-hour work weeks—consuming mass media messages. Between 1996 and 2002, the average consumer added 45 minutes of media time per day, 274 more hours in 2002 than in 1996. In September 2003, the number of U.S. Internet users passed 150 million, over half of the national population, for the first time. Along with school, the church, and the family, mass media has a great potential for shaping American society. And, just as schools and families have been blamed for a variety of society's ills, these media have taken their fair share of criticism.

The mass media are a part of the fabric of American society. Learning how to evaluate media messages critically—asking who created this message? What is its intent? How objective is it? How does what I am seeing or hearing reflect and/or shape real-world realities?—is a part of being literate in today's society. The organization of these readings reflects this media literacy perspective. Unit 1 offers commentary on mass media use and content, and its impact on individuals and society. Unit 2 explores media as sources of news and information. Unit 3 introduces perspectives on media ownership, regulation, and ethics. Unit 4 addresses relationships between the content and financial sides of media enterprises. Finally, unit 5 takes a look ahead at the shape of tomorrow's media.

You will find that the writers included in this collection frequently use television as a reference point in describing how mass media messages are shaped and interpreted. This is a reflection of the media focus of the public press and of television's rapid acceptance and continuing presence as the "massest" of mass media. Most of the articles, even those that are primarily descriptive, include an editorial viewpoint and draw conclusions or make recommendations with which you may disagree. These editorial viewpoints are more frequently critical than they are complimentary. They are not necessarily my opinions and should not necessarily become yours. I encourage you to debate these issues, drawing from the information and insights provided in the readings as well as from your own experiences as a media consumer. If you are an "average" American, you have spent a great deal of time with mass media. Your own observations have as much value as those of the writers whose work is included in these pages.

The articles selected for inclusion in this twelfth edition of *Annual Editions: Mass Media* reflect three issues of particular concern at the beginning of the new millennium. The first is the extent to which the U.S. government and legal system should rightfully be involved in regulating either media messengers or media messages. The second is the ongoing debate over how news is selected and packaged, ethical practice, and coverage of war and terrorism. The third is a heightened awareness of a media landscape profoundly altered by corporate mergers and technological change.

As always, those involved in producing this anthology are sincerely committed to including articles that are timely, informative, and interesting. We value your feedback and encourage you to complete and return the postage-paid *article rating form* on the last page of the book to share your suggestions and let us know your opinions.

B. Gorham

Joan Gorham
Editor

Contents

UNIT 1
Living With Media

The concepts in bold italics are developed in the article. For further expansion, please refer to the Topic Guide and the Index.

UNIT 2
Covering News

The concepts in bold italics are developed in the article. For further expansion, please refer to the Topic Guide and the Index.

UNIT 3
Players and Guides

The concepts in bold italics are developed in the article. For further expansion, please refer to the Topic Guide and the Index.

UNIT 4
A Word From Our Sponsor

The concepts in bold italics are developed in the article. For further expansion, please refer to the Topic Guide and the Index.

UNIT 5
The Shape of Things to Come

The concepts in bold italics are developed in the article. For further expansion, please refer to the Topic Guide and the Index.

The concepts in bold italics are developed in the article. For further expansion, please refer to the Topic Guide and the Index.

Topic Guide

This topic guide suggests how the selections in this book relate to the subjects covered in your course. You may want to use the topics listed on these pages to search the Web more easily.

On the following pages a number of Web sites have been gathered specifically for this book. They are arranged to reflect the units of this *Annual Edition.* You can link to these sites by going to the DUSHKIN ONLINE support site at *http://www.dushkin.com/online/.*

ALL THE ARTICLES THAT RELATE TO EACH TOPIC ARE LISTED BELOW THE BOLD-FACED TERM.

Television

War reporting

World Wide Web Sites

The following World Wide Web sites have been carefully researched and selected to support the articles found in this reader. The easiest way to access these selected sites is to go to our DUSHKIN ONLINE support site at *http://www.dushkin.com/online/*.

AE: Mass Media 05/06

The following sites were available at the time of publication. Visit our Web site—we update DUSHKIN ONLINE regularly to reflect any changes.

General Sources

General Communication Resources
http://www.uiowa.edu/~commstud/resources/scholarsdesktop/

An encyclopedic resource related to a host of mass communication issues, this site is maintained by the University of Iowa's Department of Communication Studies. It provides excellent links covering advertising, cultural studies, digital media, film, gender issues, and media studies.

The Media and Communications Studies Site
http://www.aber.ac.uk/~mcswww/Functions/medmenu.html

Many Internet resources covering everything from advertising to the impact of the media on perceptions of gender, ethnicity, and class can be found here. Access the home page of the Association for Media, Communication, and Cultural Studies, a British organization, and the online International Journal of Media and Communication Studies.

Netcomtalk/Boston University
http://web.bu.edu/COM/communication.html

The College of Communication at Boston University presents this multimedia publication site for daily perusal of a wide variety of news items and topics in media and communications. Click on "COMNews Today" for the latest happenings in mass media.

NewsPlace
http://www.niu.edu/newsplace/

This site of Professor Avi Bass from Northern Illinois University will lead you to a wealth of resources of interest in the study of mass media, such as international perspectives on censorship. Links to government, corporate, and other organizations are provided.

Resources for Journalists
http://www.usu.edu/~communic/resources/links.html

This list of online resources for journalists covers general sites and includes a site of the week and helpful Web pages that reporters in the technological age should know about. Web search tools, outline style guides and writing assistance, and career guidance and jobs are also available here.

Writers Guild of America
http://www.wga.org

The Writer's Guild of America is the union for media entertainment writers. The nonmember areas of this site offer useful information for aspiring writers. There is also an excellent links section.

UNIT 1: Living With Media

Children and the Media Program
http://www.childrennow.org

Children Now's site provides access to a variety of views on the impact of media on children. Public opinion surveys of young people, independent research on television and print media, industry conference proceedings, and more are available. An Internet resource list is included.

Freedom Forum
http://www.freedomforum.org

The Freedom Forum is a nonpartisan, international foundation dedicated to free press, free speech, and free spirit for all people. Its mission is to help the public and the news media understand one another better. The press watch area of this site is intriguing.

Geocities
http://www.geocities.com/Wellesley/1031/#media/

This site presents a negative perspective on how the media portray women. By clicking on its many links, you can find such varied resources as an archive on misogynistic quotes and a discussion of newspeak and doublethink.

National Coalition on Television Violence
http://www.utexas.edu/coc/journalism/SOURCE/j363/nctv.html

This page will lead to definitions of the problem of television violence, explanations of how it affects people and what can be done about it, a bibliography, and a list of related organizations.

UNIT 2: Covering News

Cable News Network
http://www.cnn.com

CNN's interactive site is considered to be an excellent online news site.

Fairness and Accuracy in Reporting
http://www.fair.org

FAIR, a U.S. media watch group, offers well-documented criticism of media bias and censorship. It advocates structural reform to break up the dominant media conglomerates.

Organization of News Ombudsmen (ONO)
http://www.newsombudsmen.org

This ONO page provides links to journalism Web sites. ONO works to aid in the wider establishment of the position of news ombudsmen on newspapers and elsewhere in the media and to provide a forum for the interchange of experiences, information, and ideas among news ombudsmen.

Television News Archive
http://tvnews.vanderbilt.edu

By browsing through this Vanderbilt University site, you can review national U.S. television news broadcasts from 1968 onward. It will give you insight into how the broadcast news industry has changed over the years and what trends define the industry today.

UNIT 3: Players and Guides

The Electronic Journalist
http://spj.org

This site for The Electronic Journalist, an online service of the Society of Professional Journalists (SPJ), will lead you to a number of articles having to do with journalistic ethics, accuracy, and other topics.

www.dushkin.com/online/

Federal Communications Commission (FCC)

http://www.fcc.gov

The FCC is an independent U.S. government agency whose mission "is to encourage competition in all communications markets and to protect the public interest." Access to information about such topics as laws regulating the media is possible.

Index on Censorship

http://www.indexonline.org

This British site provides information and many international links to show "how free speech affects the political issues of the moment."

International Television Association

http://www.itva.org

The home page of the International Television Association, which describes itself as "the premier association for video, multimedia and film professionals," is useful for links to other media resources, discussions of ethics topics, explanation of such issues as "fair use," and debate over the impact of the Internet.

Internet Law Library

http://www.phillylawyer.com

Featuring abundant resources in communications law, this site includes the most recent developments on this subject.

Michigan Press Photographers Association (MPPA)

http://www.mppa.org

Ethical issues in photo journalism are featured at this site sponsored by the MPPA.

Poynter Online: Research Center

http://www.poynter.org

The Poynter Institute for Media Studies provides extensive links to information and resources on media ethics, media writing and editing, visual journalism, and much more. Many bibliographies and Web sites are included.

World Intellectual Property Organization (WIPO)

http://www.wipo.org

Click on the links at WIPO's home page to find general information on WIPO and intellectual property, publications and documents, international classifications, and more.

UNIT 4: A Word From Our Sponsor

Advertising Age

http://adage.com

Gain access to articles and features about media advertising, such as a history of television advertising, at this site.

The Cable Center

http://www.cablecenter.org/history/index.cfm

This site will provide information as to how and why cable television was started. To view milestones in the cable industry, click on a decade in the Timeline menu.

UNIT 5: The Shape of Things to Come

Citizens Internet Empowerment Coalition (CIEC)

http://www.ciec.org

CIEC is a broad group of Internet users, library groups, publishers, online service providers, and civil liberties groups working to preserve the First Amendment and ensure the future of free expression. Find discussions of the Communications Decency Act and Internet-related topics here.

Educause

http://www.educause.edu

Open this site for an e-mailed summary of info-tech news from various major publications and for many other resources meant to facilitate the introduction, use, access to, and management of information resources in teaching, learning, scholarship, and research.

We highly recommend that you review our Web site for expanded information and our other product lines. We are continually updating and adding links to our Web site in order to offer you the most usable and useful information that will support and expand the value of your Annual Editions. You can reach us at: *http://www.dushkin.com/annualeditions/*.

UNIT 1
Living With Media

Unit Selections

Key Points to Consider

- Kristin Anderson and Donna Cavallaro examine the influence of media on children's choice of heroes and role models. Who have been your role models? Do your choices align with Anderson and Cavallaro's findings?

- In your opinion, has society become more violent because media have become more violent, or have media become more violent because society has become more violent?

- Do you agree with criticisms of media portrayals of women, men, and minorities? What positive examples of each can you think of?

- Does media content primarily reflect social reality or does it significantly shape social reality? Should it do otherwise? Why or why not?

- Why is it so difficult for research to definitively resolve media effects questions?

 **Links: www.dushkin.com/online/**
These sites are annotated in the World Wide Web pages.

Children and the Media Program
http://www.childrennow.org

Freedom Forum
http://www.freedomforum.org

Geocities
http://www.geocities.com/Wellesley/1031/#media/

National Coalition on Television Violence
http://www.utexas.edu/coc/journalism/SOURCE/j363/nctv.html

The media have been blamed for just about everything from a decrease in attention span to an increase in street crime to undoing our capacity to think. In *Amusing Ourselves to Death* (Penguin, 1986), social critic Neil Postman suggested that the cocktail party, the quiz show, and popular trivia games are reflections of society's trying to find a use for the abundance of superficial information given to us by the media. Peggy Noonan, a former network writer and White House speechwriter, has observed that experiences are no longer "real" unless they are ratified by television (which is why, she says, half the people in a stadium watch the game on monitors rather than the field). Marie Winn's memorable description of a child transfixed by television—slack-jawed, tongue resting on the front teeth, eyes glazed and vacant (*The Plug-In Drug*, Penguin, 1985, 2002)—has become an oft-quoted symbol of the passivity encouraged by television viewing. We, as a nation, have a distinct love-hate relationship with mass media.

Questions of whether or not, and to what extent, media influence our behaviors, values, expectations, and ways of thinking are difficult to answer. While one bibliographer has compiled a list of some 4,000 citations of English-language articles focusing just on children and television, the conclusions drawn in these articles vary. Isolating media as a causal agent in examining human behavior is a difficult task.

Media messages serve a variety of purposes: they inform, they influence public opinion, they sell, and they entertain—sometimes below the level of consumers' conscious awareness. Children watch *Sesame Street* to be entertained, but they also learn to count, to share, to accept physical differences among individuals, and (perhaps) to desire a *Sesame Street* lunch box. Adults watch crime dramas to be entertained, but they also learn that they have the right to remain silent when arrested, how (accurately or inaccurately) the criminal justice system works, and that the world is an unsafe place.

Nicholas Johnson, a former chairman of the Federal Communications Commission, has noted, "Every moment of television programming—commercials, entertainment, news—teaches us something." How such incidental learning occurs is most often explained by two theories. Social learning (or modeling) theory suggests that the behavior of media consumers, particularly children, is affected by their imitating role models presented via media. The degree to which modeling occurs depends upon the presence of *inhibitors*, lessons learned in real life that discourage imitation, and *disinhibitors*, experiences in real life that reinforce imitation.

Cultivation theory holds that media shape behavior by influencing attitudes. Media provide a "window to the world," exposing consumers to images of reality that may or may not jibe with personal experience. *Mainstreaming* effects occur when media

1

introduce images of things with which the consumer has no personal experience. *Resonance* effects occur when media images echo personal experience. For example, recent research has found that knowing someone who is openly gay or lesbian is the single best predictor of tolerance of same-sex marriage, but seeing likable gay characters on shows such as "Will & Grace" also has significant effects on attitude. In one study, anti-gay perceptions in students with little personal experience interacting with gay men decreased by 12 percent after viewing ten episodes of HBO's "Six Feet Under." This is a mainstreaming effect. Heavy media consumers are more likely to be affected than light consumers, since they spend more time absorbing information from media. Television viewers who have had real-world experiences similar to those seen in a TV show may find that watching the show reinforces their beliefs (resonance). However, viewers who have had personal experiences that differ from the images portrayed on television are not as likely to believe what is on television over what has been observed in real life

The readings in this unit examine media use, media content, and media effects. "A Defense of Reading" focuses on how the brain processes different types of media messages. "Parents or Pop Culture? Children's Heroes and Role Models" examines social learning and cultivation effects of media role models, acknowledging also the significant role parents play in modeling behavior and values. "Media Violence and the American Public: Scientific Facts Versus Media Misinformation" and "The Whipping Boy" take differing views on a long-standing concern with effects of media violence. "Crime Scenes: Why Cop Shows Are Eternal," "Black Angels," and "Spirit TV: The Small Screen Takes on Eternity" focus on explicit and implicit lessons in entertainment media. "The Triumph of the Image" looks at mainstreaming, resonance, and politics in an era of shortened attention spans and splintered media audiences.

The writers whose views are included in this section acknowledge increasingly complex interactions among media producers, owners and distributors, consumers, and regulatory agencies. They share concerns with media influence on daily living and on society, but differ in conclusions regarding direction and degree of responsibility for mitigating undesirable effects. Some take a *feedforward* perspective, holding media accountable for shaping changes in public attitude and behavior. Others argue a *feedback* viewpoint, in which controversial media content simply reflects changes in social reality and what media consumers choose to make popular.

A Defense of Reading

MARIE WINN

Television's impact is undoubtedly greater on preschoolers and pre-readers than on any other group. Until television, never in human history had very young children been able to enter and spend sizable portions of their waking time in a secondary world of incorporeal people and intangible things, unaccompanied by an adult guide or comforter. School-age children fall into a different category. Because they can read, they have other opportunities to leave reality behind. For these children television is merely *another* imaginary world.

But are these imaginary worlds equivalent? Since reading, once the school child's major imaginative experience, has not been seriously eclipsed by television, the television experience must be compared with the reading experience in order to discover whether they are, indeed, similar activities fulfilling similar needs in a child's life.

What Happens When You Read

It is not enough to compare television watching and reading from the viewpoint of quality. Although the quality of the material available in each medium varies enormously, from junky books and shoddy programs to literary masterpieces and fine, thoughtful television shows, the nature of each experience is different, and that difference significantly affects the impact of the material taken in.

Few people besides linguistics students and teachers of reading are aware of the complex mental manipulations involved in the reading process. Shortly after learning to read, a person assimilates the process so completely that the words in books seem to acquire an existence almost equal to the objects or acts they represent. It requires a fresh look at a printed page to recognize that those symbols we call letters of the alphabet are completely abstract shapes bearing no inherent "meaning" of their own.

Look at an "o," for instance, or a "k." The "o" is a curved figure; the "k" is an intersection of three straight lines. Yet it is hard to divorce their familiar figures from their sounds, though there is nothing "o-ish" about an "o" or "k-ish" about a "k." Even when trying to consider "k" as an abstract symbol, we cannot see it without the feeling of a "k" sound somewhere between the throat and the ears, a silent pronunciation of "k" that occurs the instant we see the letter. A reader unfamiliar with the Russian alphabet will find it easy to look at the symbol "ш" and see it as an abstract shape; a Russian reader will find it harder to detach that symbol from its sound, *shch*.

That is the beginning of reading: as the mind transforms the abstract symbols into sounds and the sounds into words, it "hears" the words, as it were, and thereby invests them with meanings previously learned in the spoken language. Invariably, as the skill of reading develops, the meaning of each word begins to seem to dwell within those symbols that make up the word. The word "dog," for instance, comes to bear some relationship with the real animal. Indeed, the word "dog" seems to actually possess some of the qualities of a dog. But it is only as a result of a swift and complex series of mental activities that the word "dog" is transformed from a series of meaningless squiggles into an idea of something real. This process goes on smoothly and continuously as we read, and yet it becomes no less complex. The brain must carry out all the steps of decoding and investing with meaning each time we read. But it becomes more adept at it as the skill develops, so that we lose the sense of struggling with symbols and meanings that children have when they first learn to read.

But the mind does not merely *hear* words in the process of reading; it also creates images. For when the reader sees the word "dog" and understands the idea of "dog," an image representing a dog is conjured up as well. The precise nature of this "reading image" is little understood, and it is unclear what relation it bears to visual images taken in directly by the eyes. Nevertheless images necessarily color our reading, else we would perceive no meaning, merely empty words.

The great difference between the "reading images" and the images we take in when viewing television is this: We create our own images when reading, based on our own experiences and reflecting our own individual needs. When we read, in fact, it is almost as if we were creating our own, small, inner television program. The result is a nourishing experience for the imagination. As psychologist and writer Bruno Bettelheim once noted, "Television captures the imagination but does not liberate it. A good book at once stimulates and frees the mind."

Television images do not go through a complex symbolic transformation. The mind does not have to decode and manipulate during the television experience. Perhaps this is why the visual images received directly from a television set are strong, stronger, it appears, than the images conjured up mentally while reading. But ultimately they satisfy less.

The perfect demonstration that a book image is more fulfilling than a television image is available to any parent whose child has read a book before its television version appears. Though the child will tune in to the TV program eagerly, hoping to recreate the delightful experience the book provided, he or she invariably ends up disappointed, if not indignant. "That's not the way the mother looked," the child will complain, or "The farmer didn't have a mustache!" Having created personalized images to accompany the story, images that are never random but serve to fulfill some emotional need, the child feels cheated by the manufactured images on the screen.

A ten-year-old child reports on the effects of seeing television dramatizations of books he has previously read:

> *The TV people leave a stronger impression. Once you've seen a character on TV, he'll always look like that in your mind, even if you made a different picture of him in your mind before, when you read the book yourself. The thing about a book is that you have so much freedom. You can make each character look exactly the way you want him to look. You're more in control of things when you read a book than when you see something on TV.*

It may be that television-bred children's reduced opportunities for "inner picture-making" accounts for the curious inability of so many children today to adjust to nonvisual experiences. Twenty years ago, a first-grade teacher who bridged the gap between the pre-television and the television eras reported:

> *When I read them a story without showing them pictures, the children always complain "I can't see." Their attention flags. They'll begin to talk or wander off. I have to really work to develop their visualizing skills.... They get better at [it] with practice. But children never needed to learn how to visualize before television, it seems to me.*

Today reading specialists have begun to examine the phenomenon of "aliteracy," a condition that seems to be increasing among American schoolchildren. One of their findings about this large cohort of kids who have mastered the skills of reading yet do not choose to read for pleasure is relevant to a discussion of television's impact on reading: aliterate readers "need help visualizing what they are reading."

Losing the Thread

A comparison between reading and viewing may be made in respect to the pace of each experience and the relative control we have over it. When reading, we can proceed as slowly or as rapidly as we wish. If we don't understand something, we may stop and reread it. If what we read is affecting, we may put down the book for a few moments and cope with our emotions.

It's much harder to control the pace of television. The program moves inexorably forward, and what is lost or misunderstood remains so. Even with devices like a VCR, though a program can be stopped and recorded, viewers find it hard to stop watching. They want to keep watching, so as not to lose the thread of the program.

Not to lose the thread... it is this need, occasioned by the relentless velocity and the hypnotic fascination of the television image, that causes television to intrude into human affairs far more than reading experiences can ever do. If someone enters the room while we're watching television—perhaps someone we have not seen for some time—we feel compelled to continue to watch or else we'll lose the thread. The greetings must wait, for the television program will not. A book, of course, can be set aside, reluctantly, perhaps, but with no sense of permanent loss.

A grandparent describes a situation that is, by all reports, not uncommon:

> *Sometimes when I come to visit the girls, I'll walk into their room and they're watching a TV program. Well, I know they love me, but it makes me feel bad when I tell them hello, and they say, without even looking up, "Wait a minute... we have to see the end of this program." It hurts me to have them care more about that machine and those little pictures than about being glad to see me. I know that they probably can't help it, but still.... "*

Can they help it? Ultimately, when we watch television, our power to release ourselves from viewing in order to attend to imperative human demands is not altogether a function of the program's pace. After all, we might choose to operate according to human priorities, rather than yielding to an electronic dictatorship. We might quickly decide "to hell with this program" and simply stop watching when a friend enters the room or a child needs attention.

We might… but the hypnotic power of television makes it difficult to shift our attention away.

The Basic Building Blocks

At the same time that children learn to read written words they begin to acquire the rudiments of writing. Thus they come to understand that a word is something they can write themselves. That they wield such power over the very words they are struggling to decipher makes the reading experience a satisfying one right from the start.

A young child watching television enters a realm of materials completely beyond his or her understanding. Though the images on the screen may be reflections of familiar people and things, they appear as if by magic. Children cannot create similar images or even begin to understand how those flickering electronic shapes and forms come into being. They take on a far more powerless and ignorant role in front of the television set than in front of a book.

There's little doubt that many young children have a confused relationship to the television medium. When a group of preschool children were asked, "How do kids get to be on your TV?" only 22 percent of them showed any real comprehension of the nature of the television images. When asked, "Where do the people and kids and things go when your TV is turned off?" only 20 percent of the three-year-olds showed the smallest glimmer of understanding. Although there was an increase in comprehension among the four-year-olds, the authors of the study note that "even among the older children the vast majority still did not grasp the nature of television pictures."

Children's feelings of power and competence are nourished by another feature of the reading experience: the non-mechanical, easily accessible, and easily transportable nature of reading matter. Children can always count on a book for pleasure, though the television set may break down at a crucial moment. They can take a book with them wherever they go, to their room, to the park, to their friend's house, to school to read under the desk: they can *control* their use of books and reading materials.

A Preference for Watching

There'd be little purpose in comparing the experiences of reading and television viewing if it were not for the incontrovertible fact that children's television experiences influence their reading in critical ways, affecting how much they read, what they read, how they feel about reading, and, since writing skills are closely related to reading experiences, what they write and how well they write.

Children read fewer books when television is available to them, as reports from so many TV Turnoffs make clear. A child is more likely to turn on the television set when there's "nothing to do" than to pick up a book to read—it simply requires less effort. In a survey of more than 500 fourth- and fifth-graders, all subjects showed a preference for watching over reading any kinds of content. Nearly 70 percent of 233,000 sixth-graders polled by the California Department of Education in 1980 reported that they rarely read for pleasure. Meanwhile, in the same poll, an identical percentage of students admitted to watching four or more hours of TV a day.

In 1992 a government report made headlines by stating that one-third of all students *never* read in their spare time and that one-third of all eighth- and tenth-graders read fewer than five pages a day for school or homework. At the same time, the report noted, while two-thirds of the eighth-graders who had been tested for reading skills and comprehension watched more than three hours a day, those students who watched two hours or less proved to get higher grades on the exam.

Children are often candid about their preference for watching over reading. The twelve-year-old daughter of a college English teacher explains:

> I mean television, you don't have to worry about getting really bored because it's happening and you don't have to do any work to see it, to have it happen. But you have to work to read, and that's no fun. I mean it's fun when it's a good book, but how can you tell if the book will be good? Anyhow, I'd rather see it as a television program.

The mother of boys aged twelve and ten and a girl aged nine reports:

> My children have trouble finding books they like in the library. They seem to have some sort of resistance to books, even though my husband and I are avid readers. I think if they didn't have television available they'd calmly spend more time looking for something good in the library. They'd have to, to avoid boredom. But now they don't really look in the library, whenever I take them. They don't zero in on anything. It's not the ultimate entertainment for them, reading. There's always something better and easier to do. So they don't have to look hard at the library. They just zip through quickly and hardly ever find more than one or two books that interest them enough to take out.

Understandably those children who have difficulty with reading are more likely to combat boredom by turning to television than successful readers are. Television plays a profoundly negative role in such children's intellectual development, since only by extensive reading can they hope to overcome their reading problems. This point is frequently raised by teachers and reading specialists: Television compounds the problems of children with reading disabilities because it offers them a pleasurable nonverbal alternative, thus reducing their willingness to work extra hard at acquiring reading skills.

It's easy to demonstrate that the availability of television reduces the amount of reading children do. When the set is temporarily broken, when a family participates in a TV Turnoff, or when a family decides to eliminate television entirely, there's always an increase in reading, both by parents and by children. When the less taxing mental activity is unavailable, children turn to reading for entertainment, more willing now to put up with the "work" involved.

Home Attitudes

The role of the home environment was the subject of one of many studies looking into television and its relation to children's reading achievement. The researchers centered attention on the various stages of reading development and compared the impact of television viewing at each stage—from a pre-reading stage, through the initial decoding stage, into the stage of increasing fluency, and finally, to the stage in which children can read for knowledge and information.

The authors noted: "If the home environment encourages and enhances reading activities, the child has a better chance of progressing trouble-free through the first three stages. On the other hand, if the home environment has few facilitating mechanisms for reading development, and if it stresses television as the means for entertainment, activity, interaction and information acquisition, then the child's reading development may be impeded." The authors conclude by noting that "age is an important variable in the study of televiewing and reading, and the younger the children included in the study, the higher the probability that effects of the home environment and television viewing on reading behavior will appear."

Lazy Readers

Besides reducing children's need and willingness to read, television may subtly affect the actual ways in which children read, what might be called their reading style. For while children of the television era can and do still read, something about their reading has changed.

Reading specialists sometimes refer to certain children as "lazy readers." They define them as intelligent children from educated families who have never made the transition from learning *how* to read to being able to absorb what they read. They read well enough, but not with the degree of involvement and concentration required for full comprehension.

Critic George Steiner referred to this sort of reader when he noted: "A large majority of those who have passed through the primary and secondary school system can 'read' but not *read*."

Similarly, educator Donald Barr once observed: "Children may pick up and leaf through more books, but what they do looks to me less like reading every year." He, too, connected the deterioration in meaningful reading with children's television experiences. "TV stimulates casting your eye over the page, and that is a far different thing from reading."

Many teachers speculate about a connection between this style of reading and children's television involvement. Concentration, after all, is a skill that requires practice to develop. The television child has fewer opportunities for learning to sustain concentration than the "book" child of the past. Indeed, the mental diffuseness demanded by the television experience may influence children's attention patterns, causing them to enter the reading world more superficially, more impatiently, more vaguely.

Nonbooks

Parents often assuage anxieties about their children's television involvement by maintaining that their children still read. But the reading reported by parents often falls into a category that might be called the "nonbook." The headmaster of a selective boys' school in New York reports.

For as much television as our boys watch I have found no substantial correlation between the amount of television watching and the circulation of books from the library. The important change is in the kinds of books the boys read.... [W]hat is really a new trend, it seems to me, is the great interest children have in reading the 'nonbook' kind of thing. The most conspicuous example of a 'nonbook' is the Guinness Book of Records. *A great deal of the reading the boys seem to be doing these days falls into that category.*

The nonbook seems designed to accommodate a new reading style. It is not the kind of book with a sustained story or a carefully developed argument that is read from beginning to end. It's a book to be scanned, read in fits and starts, skimmed, requiring little concentration, focused thinking, or inner visualization. Yet it provides enough information and visually pleasing material to divert the child who does not feel comfortable with the old sequential style of reading.

For the television-bred child, an important aspect of the nonbook is its instant accessibility. Reading a "real" book can be hard at the outset, as the scene is verbally set and new names and places and characters are introduced. But a nonbook, like television, makes no stretching demands at the start. Composed of tiny facts and snippets of interesting material, it does not change in any way during the course of a child's involvement in it. It does not get easier, or harder, or more exciting, or more suspenseful; it remains the same. Thus there is no need to "get into" a nonbook as there is with a book, because there are no further stages to progress to. But while the reader of a nonbook is spared the trouble of difficult entry into a vicarious world, he is also denied the deep satisfactions that reading *real* books may provide.

Parents and teachers suggest that boys are more likely to turn to nonbooks than girls. Indeed, boys have long been known to be more resistant than girls to any form of narrative fiction. Then, in 1998 a literary phenomenon arrived from across that Atlantic that grabbed girls and boys alike: a mild, bespectacled boy with magic powers named Harry Potter.

What about Harry Potter?

Just when the cause of reading seemed hopeless, something happened to show that all was not lost. Suddenly tens of thousands of kids all over the United States (and the world) found themselves entranced by a series of books that had no tie-ins with any TV programs or movies whatsoever, books that simply stood on their own as a good, old-fashioned read. Harry Potter had taken the country by storm.

Children from the third grade on up through high school (and adults too) became so involved with Harry Potter that they skipped their regular television programs in order to continue reading. Parents and educators were amazed… and delighted. Reading for pleasure among children had been in a long, long decline. Was it possible that today's children were suddenly becoming the sorts of passionate readers once common before televising came into the home?

The Harry Potter books are everything children's literature ought to be; superbly written, filled with suspense and excitement, containing adult characters both exotic and somewhat familiar from the real world, and one of the most appealing cast of child characters ever gathered in a single work. There's an inspiring and yet not too goody-goody boy hero, several girl heroines any feminist would applaud, a couple of deliciously hateable kid villains, as well as a host of imaginary creatures— dragons, hippogrifs, phoenixes, manticores, glumbumbles, basilisks, and more.

In no way is Harry Potter a nonbook. Each volume contains long, complex narratives that require sustained attention to follow. Moreover, there are almost no illustrations, thus requiring much inner visualizing in order to bring the people and fantastic creatures to life.

That a population of video-weaned children were able to fall for the charms of this marvelous, marvel-filled series of books has been one of the most hopeful omens of the television era. It is an indication that skills and abilities like inner-visualizing and following a narrative have not disappeared; they have just gone underground. Under the right circumstances—a great book combined with an international craze—these skills can once again be activated.

As I write, however, the movie version of the first Harry Potter book has just been released. Though the film was criticized (by adult critics, to be sure) for hewing too closely to J. K. Rowling's book, it was a huge success with children throughout the country, who were delighted that the film was so faithful to the story they loved. The movie broke box office records and will surely continue to attract a large audience for years to come. Film versions of the next two Harry Potter books are already in production.

For most of the Harry Potter fans who flocked to see the movie, it was a fine recreation of their reading experience. But from now on great numbers of children will see the movies before reading the books. For them, things will be different. Having seen the film, a boy who then chooses to read the book will never be able to transform the main character into himself as he reads—a deeply satisfying part of the reading experience. Thereafter he will visualize only the movie's version of the bespectacled boy wizard. Similarly a girl reader who admires Harry's friend Hermione will never have the pure pleasure of creating the adorable though sharp-tongued little witch in her own image. Hermione will now resemble the Hollywood version.

Radio and Reading

Before television, children listened with pleasure to radio programs. Now that television has captured the child audience almost in its entirely, people tend to think of radio as simply an inferior version of TV—television without the pictures. But is this indeed the way to look at radio?

During the early days of video technology, psychologist and art theorist Rudolph Arnheim spoke out in favor of "blind broadcasting," suggesting that radio listening provides similar gratifications to reading: "The words of storyteller or the poet, the voices of dialogue, the complex sounds of music conjure up worlds of experience and thought that are easily disturbed by the undue addition of visual things."

Among the thousands of studies of the various media's effects on children, there is little research directed toward the effects of radio listening. But the few studies available go far in confirming Arnheim's hunch, that a visual medium like television will have deleterious effects on a viewer's powers of imagination, while the radio experience will not.

A study at the University of California compared children's responses to a radio story and a television version of the same story. The researchers found that children were able to provide far more creative endings to the audio version than the video one, provoking the inescapable conclusion that radio stimulates children's imagination significantly more than television does.

An example of radio's power to stimulate the imagination appeared in a recent review of a book about the baseball player Joe DiMaggio:

> The beauty of radio is that, unlike television, it puts the listener in the mix. There are no highlight shows, instant replays, or let's-go-to-the-videotape features to show us what happened. Visual images speak to the visceral, while voices heard but not seen allow free play in the cineplex of the mind… "

Many educators believe that radio, an exclusively linguistic medium, has far more in common with reading than with television, a medium relying to a great extent on the visual. Indeed, while television has long been associated with a decline in academic achievement among its heaviest viewers, radio listening may prove to reinforce verbal skills almost as well as reading can. Certainly there is circumstantial evidence supporting such a view, notably, the long decline in SAT scores that began when the first television generation sat down at the test tables. During the heyday of children's radio, on the other hand, when there were great numbers of national radio broadcasts and American children invested almost as much time listening to the radio as they now spend watching TV, there was no equivalent decline; indeed, scores went steadily upward.

While television has displaced radio as an entertainment medium for children (with the exception of teenagers who listen to the radio almost exclusively for popular music), Books on Tape and other companies offer similar opportunities for listening experiences without pictures. The growing popularity of taped books as a source of entertainment for children may be a sign that parents are seeking to loosen television's bondage on their lives. Or, since Books on Tape are mainly used on car trips, it may simply mean that television has not yet penetrated the car market as it has the minivan market. Time will tell.

If You Can't Beat 'Em, Join 'Em

A somewhat desperate attempt to stem the decline in children's free-time reading is seen in the if-you-can't beat-'em-join-'em approach that enlists television itself as a spur to encourage children to read more.

Over the years a spate of television programs have appeared, some sponsored by public funds, others by television networks themselves, all with the much-applauded aim of promoting reading among children. Programs such as *Reading Rainbow* enlist a chirpy, magazine-style format and a TV-star host to stimulate an enthusiasm for reading among children clearly in need of such stimulation—after all, they *are* watching the program, not reading a book.

Other efforts of the past have included the Read More About It project, initiated by CBS with the cooperation of the Library of Congress, which had the stars of a number of TV shows based on books step out of their roles at the close of the dramatization to exhort the TV viewers to go out and read the book now that they have seen the program. NBC too did not fail to plug reading: "When you turn off your set, turn on a book" was the message flashed at the end of a popular late-afternoon children's series. Similarly, ABC joined the reading bandwagon by ending certain children's specials adapted from books with words "Watch the Program—Read the Book."

No one, however, either on public or commercial television, has gone so far as to suggest: "Don't watch the program—read the book instead." And yet, as it happens, that would be a far more effective message. While there is no evidence whatsoever that television exhortations lead to a greater love of reading, there is the considerable evidence from TV Turnoffs organized by schools and libraries throughout the country, as well as from the annual National TV-Turnoff Week, run by the TV-Turnoff Network, demonstrating that when competition from the TV set is eliminated, children simply and easily turn to reading instead.

While efforts to encourage reading via TV programs may be well intentioned, they represent a misguided hope that there is an easy out from a difficult state of affairs. Indeed, the ways to encourage reading are well known, and require time and effort on the part of the parent. An education writer expressed it well:

Future readers are made by mothers and fathers who read to their children from infancy, read to them during quiet moments of the day and read them to sleep at night. Only then does the book become an essential element of life.

Why Books?

Well, what of it? Isn't there something a bit old-fashioned about a defense of reading in the electronic era? The arguments for reading are powerful:

Reading is the single most important factor in children's education. Reading trains the mind in concentration skills, develops the powers of imagination and inner visualization, lends itself to a better and deeper comprehension of the material communicated. Reading engrosses, but it does not hypnotize or seduce a reader away from human responsibilities. Books are ever available, ever controllable. Television controls.

In reading, people utilize their most unique human ability—verbal thinking—by transforming the symbols on the page into a form dictated by their deepest wishes, fears, and fantasies. As novelist Jerzy Kosinski once noted:

> [Reading] offers unexpected, unchannelled associations, new insights into the tides and drifts of one's own life. The reader is tempted to venture beyond a text, to contemplate his own life in light of the book's personalized meanings.

In the television experience, on the other hand, viewers are carried along by the exigencies of a mechanical device, unable to bring into play their most highly developed mental abilities or to fulfill their particular emotional needs. They are entertained by television, but the essential passivity of the experience leaves them basically unchanged. For while television provides distraction, reading supports growth.

MARIE WINN has written thirteen books, among them *Children Without Childhood, Unplugging the Plug-In Drug*, and *Red-Tails in Love: A Wildlife Drama in Central Park*. She has written for various publications including *The New York Times Magazine* and *Smithsonian*, and currently writes a column about birds and nature for *The Wall Street Journal*. Married to the documentary filmmaker Allan Miller, she lives in New York City within walking distance of two young grandchildren. She frequently visits two others in San Francisco and a great niece in England. All five children are growing up (and flourishing) without television.

Parents or Pop Culture?
Children's Heroes and Role Models

What kind of heroes a culture promotes reveals a great
deal about that culture's values and desires.

Kristin J. Anderson and Donna Cavallaro

One of the most important features of childhood and
adolescence is the development of an identity. As children shape their behavior and values, they may look to
heroes and role models for guidance. They may identify
the role models they wish to emulate based on possession
of certain skills or attributes. While the child may not
want to be exactly like the person, he or she may see *possibilities* in that person. For instance, while Supreme Court
Justice Ruth Bader Ginsberg may not necessarily directly
influence girls and young women to become lawyers, her
presence on the Supreme Court may alter beliefs about
who is capable of being a lawyer or judge (Gibson & Cordova, 1999).

Parents and other family members are important role
models for children, particularly early on. Other influences may be institutional, such as schools, or cultural,
such as the mass media. What kind of heroes a culture
promotes reveals a great deal about the culture's values
and desires. Educators not only can model important behaviors themselves, but also can teach about values,
events, and people that a culture holds dear.

Television, movies, computer games, and other forms
of media expose children to an endless variety of cultural
messages. Which ones do children heed the most? Whom
do children want to be like? Do their role models vary according to children's ethnicity and gender? Finally, what
role can educators play in teaching children about role
models they may never have considered?

This article examines the impact of the mass media on
children's choices of heroes and role models. The authors
address the questions posed above in light of results from

a survey and focus groups conducted with children ages
8 to 13.

THE MENU OF POP CULTURE CHOICES

Television and Film for Children

Male characters—cartoon or otherwise—continue to be
more prevalent in children's television and film than female characters. Gender-stereotyped behaviors continue
to be the norm. For instance, male characters are more
commonly portrayed as independent, assertive, athletic,
important, attractive, technical, and responsible than female characters. They show more ingenuity, anger, leadership, bravery, and aggression, and they brag, interrupt,
make threats, and even laugh more than female characters do. In fact, since male characters appear so much
more frequently than female characters, they do more of
almost *everything* than female characters. Also, while the
behavior of female characters is somewhat less stereotypical than it was 20 years ago, in some ways male characters behave *more* stereotypically than 20 years ago (for
instance, males are now in more leadership roles, are
more bossy, and are more intelligent) (Thompson &
Zerbinos, 1995). These gender-stereotyped images, and
the inflexibility of male characters' roles, make for a restricted range of role models.

Parents, educators, and policymakers are also concerned about the aggressive and violent content in children's programs. Gerbner (1993) studied the violent

9

content of children's programs and observed that "despite all the mayhem, only 3.2% of Saturday morning characters suffer any injury"; thus, children do not learn about the likely consequences of aggressive action. In children's shows, bad characters are punished 59 percent of the time. Even more telling, good characters who engage in violence are punished only 18 percent of the time. The characters that might be the most appealing to kids—the heroes and protagonists—rarely feel remorse, nor are they reprimanded or impeded when they engage in violence (National Television Violence Study, 1998). The authors found that 77 percent of the children surveyed watch television every day. Thus, many children may be learning to use violence as a problem-solving tool.

Characters in animated films also tend to follow stereotypes. While some positive changes in the portrayal of ethnic minority and female characters can be noted, both groups often remain narrowly defined in children's animated films. In his discussion of Disney films, Henry Giroux (1997) notes how the villains in the film *Aladdin* are racially stereotyped. The main character, Aladdin, the hero of the film, is drawn with very light skin, European features, and no accent. Yet the villains in the story appear as Middle Eastern caricatures: they have beards, large noses, sinister eyes, heavy accents, and swords. *Pocahontas*, who in real life was a young Native American girl, was portrayed by Disney as a brown-skinned, Barbie-like supermodel with an hourglass figure (Giroux, 1997). Consequently, animated characters, even those based on historical record, are either stereotyped or stripped of any meaningful sign of ethnicity. Fortunately, educators have the power to counter such unrealistic images with more accurate representations of historical characters.

Real-Life Television Characters

While some progress can be seen in the representation of ethnic minorities on television, the late 1990s actually brought a decrease in the number of people of color on prime time programming. In 1998, only 19 percent of Screen Actors Guild roles went to people of color. Roles for African American, Latinos, and Native Americans decreased from 1997 to 1998 (Screen Actors Guild [SAG], 1999). Women make up fewer than 40 percent of the characters in prime time. Female characters tend to be younger than male characters, conveying the message to viewers that women's youthfulness is more highly valued than other qualities. In terms of work roles, however, female characters' occupations are now less stereotyped, while male characters' occupations continue to be stereotyped (Signorielli & Bacue, 1999). This research suggests that girls' potential role models are somewhat less gender-stereotyped than before, while boy's potential role models are as narrowly defined as ever.

From Comic Book to Playground

Superheroes are the larger-than-life symbols of American values and "maleness." Perhaps the medium in which superheroes are most classically represented is comic books, which date back to the 1930s. The role of the hero is central to the traditional comic book. While female superheroes can be found in comics today (e.g., Marvel Girl, Phoenix, Shadow Cat, Psylocke), they represent only a small proportion—about 24 percent of Marvel Universe superhero trading cards (Young, 1993). Moreover, women and people of color do not fare well in superhero comics. To the extent that female characters exist, they often appear as victims and nuisances. People of color are marginalized as well. African American and Native American characters are more likely to be portrayed as villains, victims, or simply incompetent than as powerful and intelligent (Pecora, 1992).

One indirect way to gauge the impact of role models on children is to examine the nature of superhero play. Superhero play involving imitation of media characters with superhuman powers is more prevalent among boys than girls (Bell & Crosbie, 1996). This might be a function of the mostly male presence of superhero characters in comics and on television, or it may be due to girls receiving more sanctions from parents and teachers against playing aggressively. Children's imitations of superheroes in play concerns many classroom teachers, because it usually involves chasing, wrestling, kicking, and mock battles. Some researchers argue that superhero play may serve an important developmental function by offering children a sense of power in a world dominated by adults, thus giving children a means of coping with their frustrations. Superhero play also may allow children to grapple with ideas of good and evil and encourage them to work through their own anxieties about safety. Such play also may help children safely express anger and aggression (Boyd, 1997).

Other researchers and educators express concern that superhero play may legitimize aggression, endanger participants, and encourage stereotypical male dominance (Bell & Crosbie, 1996). One researcher observed children's superhero play in a school setting and found that boys created more superhero stories than girls did, and that girls often were excluded from such play. When girls were included they were given stereotypical parts, such as helpers or victims waiting to be saved. Even powerful female X-Men characters were made powerless in the boys' adaptations (Dyson, 1994). Thus, without teacher intervention or an abundance of female superheroes, superhero play may only serve to reinforce gender stereotypes.

One way to gauge popular culture's influence on superhero play is to compare the kind of play children engaged in before and after the arrival of television. In one retrospective study (French & Pena, 1991), adults between the ages of 17 and 83 provided information about their favorite childhood play themes, their heroes, and the qualities of those heroes. While certain methodological pitfalls common to retrospective studies were unavoidable, the findings are nevertheless intriguing. People who grew up before television reported engaging in less fantasy hero play and playing more realistically than kids who grew up with television. While media was the main source of heroes for kids who grew up with television, the previous generations found their heroes not only from the media, but also from direct experience, friends/siblings, and parents' occupations (French & Pena, 1991).

Recent Media Forms: Music Television and Video Games

Video games and music television videos are relatively recent forms of media. In a recent poll, girls and boys from various ethnic backgrounds reported that television and music were their favorite forms of media (Children Now, 1999). What messages about race/ethnicity and gender emerge from music videos—the seemingly perfect merger of children's favorite two media? Seidman (1999) found that the majority of characters were white (63 percent) and a majority were male (63 percent). When people of color, especially women of color, appeared in a video, their characters were much less likely to hold white collar jobs. In fact, their occupations were more gender-stereotyped than in real life. Gender role behavior overall was stereotypical. Thus, music television is yet another domain that perpetuates racial and gender stereotypes.

In the survey described below, the authors found that nearly half (48 percent) of the children surveyed played video and computer games every day or almost every day. Boys, however, were much more likely than girls to play these games. Of those who play computer/video games every day or almost every day, 76 percent are boys and only 24 percent are girls. Consequently, girls and boys might be differentially influenced by the images represented in video and computer games.

What *are* the images presented in video and computer games? Dietz's (1998) content analysis of popular video and computer games found that 79 percent of the games included aggression or violence. Only 15 percent of the games showed women as heroes or action characters. Indeed, girls and women generally were *not* portrayed—30 percent of the videos did not include girls or women at all. When female characters were included, 21 percent of the time they were the damsel in distress. Other female characters were portrayed as evil or as obstacles. This research points to at least two implications of these games. First, girls may not be interested in playing these video and computer games, because the implicit message is that girls are not welcome as players, and that girls and

women can only hope to be saved, destroyed, or pushed aside (see also Signorielli, 2001). Second, these images of girls and women found in video and computer games may influence boys' perceptions of gender.

In the past few years, a growing number of computer and video games geared toward girls have been made available by companies such as Purple Moon and Girl Games. These games have adventurous content without the violence typical of games geared toward boys. Two of the best-selling computer games for girls, however, have been *Cosmopolitan Virtual Makeover* and *Barbie Fashion Designer*. While these games may encourage creativity, ultimately their focus is on beauty. One columnist addresses the dilemma of creating games that will appeal to girls while fostering creativity and ingenuity:

> A girl given a doll is being told, "Girls play with dolls just like mommies take care of babies." A boy given a computer game is being told, "Boys play with computers just like daddies use them for work." A girl given *Barbie Fashion Designer* is being told, "Girls play with computers just like girls play with dolls." A lucky few might get the message that, as some girls exchange dolls for real babies, others might progress from *Barbie Fashion Designer* to real-life fashion designer, or engineering systems designer, or software designer. But there's a good chance that many will not. (Ivinski, 1997, p. 28)

As more and more educators begin using the Internet, CD-ROMS, and videos as teaching tools (Risko, 1999), they will be faced with the challenge of finding materials that fairly represent a wide range of characters, people, and behavior. Paradoxically, the use of "new" technology, such as CD-ROMs and computer games, implies that a student is going to enjoy a progressive, cutting-edge experience. However, educators must be vigilant about the content, as they should be with any textbook or film. The cutting-edge format of these new technologies does not guarantee nonstereotyped material.

A SURVEY OF CHILDREN'S ROLE MODELS AND HEROES

Whom do children actually choose as role models, and why? The authors surveyed children about their heroes and role models, both people they know and famous people or imaginary characters. Survey questions also addressed children's interaction with television, film, computer/video games, books, and comic books. The children talked about their answers in small groups. One hundred and seventy-nine children, ages 8 to 13, were surveyed from five day camp sites in central and southern California. The ethnic breakdown of the survey sample was as follows: 24 African Americans, 31 Asian

Americans, 74 Latinos, 1 Middle Eastern American, 2 Native Americans, 45 whites, and 2 "other." Ninety-five girls and 84 boys participated. The samples of ethnic and gender categories were then weighted so that each of these demographic groups, when analyzed, reflects their actual contribution to the total population of children in the United States.

Do Children Admire People They Know or Famous People?

The survey began with the following: "We would like to know whom you look up to and admire. These might be people you know, or they might be famous people or characters. You may want to be like them or you might just think they are cool." More respondents described a person they knew (65 percent) rather than a person they did not know, such as a person or character in the media (35 percent). When asked in focus groups why they picked people they knew instead of famous people, one 10-year-old white girl said, "I didn't put down people I don't know because when nobody's paying attention, they do something bad." Another student said, "Some [media figures] are just not nice. Some famous people act good on TV but they're really horrible." Thus, some children employed a level of skepticism when judging the worthiness of a role model.

Figure 1 represents the percentages of role models the children knew versus media heroes they identified. Similar to the overall sample, 70 percent of the African American and 64 percent of the White children chose people they knew as heroes. In contrast, only 35 percent of the Asian American kids and 49 percent of the Latino kids named people they knew. This latter finding seems paradoxical; Asian American and Latino children would seem more likely to choose people they know as role models because their ethnic groups are represented less frequently in mass media than are African Americans and whites. Perhaps Asian American and Latino children have internalized a message that they should not look up to fellow Asian Americans or Latinos as role models, or it may be a byproduct of assimilation. Obviously, further work in this area is needed.

On average, responses from girls and boys differed. While both girls and boys named people they knew as their heroes, 67 percent of the girls did so as compared with only 58 percent of the boys. Since boys and men are seen more frequently as sports stars, actors, and musicians, girls may have a smaller pool of potential role models from which to choose. Another factor might be that the girls in this study reported watching less television than the boys did, and so they may have known fewer characters. Sixty-seven percent of the girls reported watching television one hour a day or more, while 87 percent of the boys reported watching television this amount.

Do Children Choose Role Models Who Are Similar to Themselves?

One feature of role modeling is that children tend to choose role models whom they find relevant and with whom they can compare themselves (Lockwood & Kunda, 2000). Children who do not "see themselves" in the media may have fewer opportunities to select realistic role models. Two ways to assess similarity is to consider the ethnicity and gender of children's chosen role models. Do children tend to select heroes who are of their same ethnic background? Because data was not available on the ethnic background of the reported role models whom the children knew personally, the authors examined only the heroes from the media, whose backgrounds were known, to explore this question (see Figure 2). African American and white children were more likely to have media heroes of their same ethnicity (67 percent for each). In contrast, Asian American and Latino children chose more white media heroes than other categories (40 percent and 56 percent, respectively). Only 35 percent of the Asian Americans respondents, and 28 percent of the Latino respondents, chose media heroes of their own ethnicity.

How can we explain the fact that African American and white children are more likely to have media heroes of their same ethnicity, compared to Asian American and Latino children? There is no shortage of white characters for white children to identify with in television and film, and African Americans now make up about 14 percent of television and theatrical characters (SAG, 2000). While African American characters are represented less frequently than white characters, their representation on television, film, and music television is much higher than for Asian American and Latino characters (e.g., Asians represent 2.2 percent, and Latinos represent 4.4 percent, of television and film characters) (SAG, 2000). Also, fewer famous athletes are Asian American or Latino, compared to African American or white.

Also of interest was whether children choose role models of the same, or other, gender. Overall, children in this study more often chose a same-gender person as someone they look up to and admire. This pattern is consistent across all four ethnic groups, and stronger for boys than girls. Only 6 percent of the boys chose a girl or woman, while 24 percent of the girls named a boy or man. Asian American boys actually picked male heroes exclusively. Asian American girls chose the fewest female role models (55 percent) compared to the other girls (see Figure 3). These findings associated with Asian American children present a particular challenge for educators. Asian Americans, and particularly Asian American women, are seldom presented as heroes in textbooks. This is all the more reason for schools to provide a broader and more diverse range of potential role models.

Figure 1

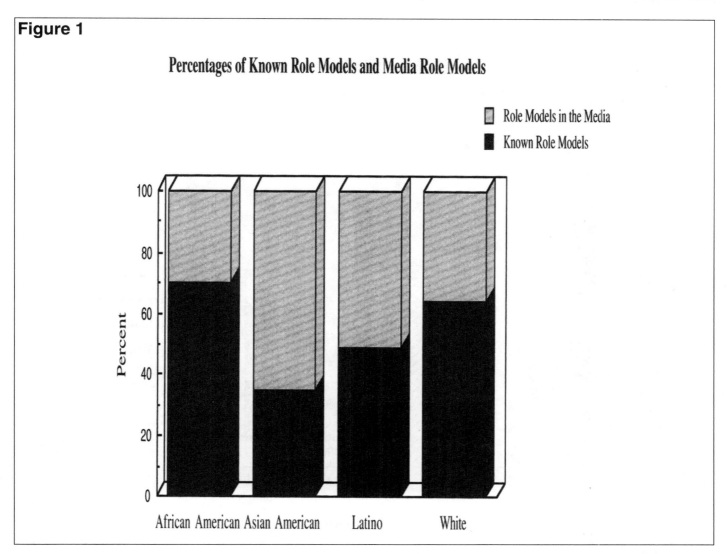

Percentages of Known Role Models and Media Role Models

Legend:
- Role Models in the Media
- Known Role Models

(Chart categories: African American, Asian American, Latino, White; Y-axis: Percent, 0 to 100)

At the same time, it has been reported that boys will tend to imitate those who are powerful (Gibson & Cordova, 1999). Thus, while boys tend to emulate same-gender models more than girls do, boys may emulate a woman if she is high in social power. Therefore, boys may be especially likely to have boys and men as role models because they are more likely to be portrayed in positions of power. It also has been noted that college-age women select men *and* women role models with the same frequency, whereas college-age men still tend to avoid women role models. The fact that young women choose both genders as role models might be a result of the relative scarcity of women in powerful positions to serve as role models (Gibson & Cordova, 1999).

Who Are Children's Role Models and Heroes?

Overall, children most frequently (34 percent) named their parents as role models and heroes. The next highest category (20 percent) was entertainers; in descending or-

der, the other categories were friends (14 percent), professional athletes (11 percent), and acquaintances (8 percent). Authors and historical figures were each chosen by only 1 percent of the children.

Patterns were somewhat different when ethnicity was taken into account. African American and white children chose a parent more frequently (30 percent and 33 percent, respectively). In contrast, Asian Americans and Latinos chose entertainers (musicians, actors, and television personalities) most frequently (39 percent for Asian Americans and 47 percent for Latinos), with parents coming in second place. When gender was taken into account, both girls and boys most frequently mentioned a parent (girls 29 percent, boys 34 percent), while entertainers came in second place. Figure 4 illustrates these patterns.

When taking both ethnicity and gender into account, the researchers found that Asian American and Latina girls most frequently picked entertainers (50 percent of the Asian American girls and 41 percent of the Latinas), while African American and white girls chose parents (33 percent and 29 percent, respectively). Asian American boys most frequently named a professional athlete (36

Figure 2

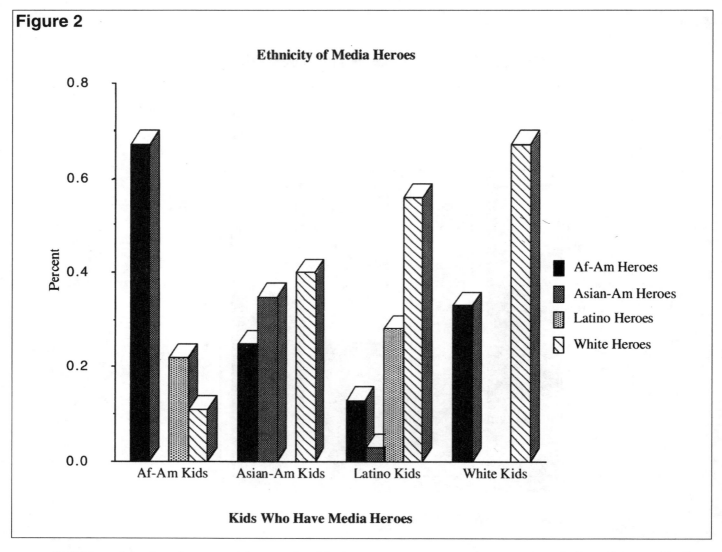

Ethnicity of Media Heroes

Kids Who Have Media Heroes

percent), African American boys most frequently picked a parent (30 percent), Latino boys most frequently chose entertainers (54 percent), and white boys picked parents (38 percent).

What Qualities About Their Role Models and Heroes Do Children Admire?

When asked why they admired their heroes and role models, the children most commonly replied that the person was nice, helpful, and understanding (38 percent). Parents were appreciated for their generosity, their understanding, and for "being there." For instance, an 11-year-old African American girl who named her mother as her hero told us, "I like that she helps people when they're in a time of need." Parents were also praised for the lessons they teach their kids. A 9-year-old Asian American boy told us, "I like my dad because he is always nice and he teaches me."

The second most admired feature of kids' role models was skill (27 percent). The skills of athletes and entertain-

ers were most often mentioned. One 12-year-old white boy said he admires Kobe Bryant because "he's a good basketball player and because he makes a good amount of money." A 10-year-old Asian American girl chose Tara Lipinski because "she has a lot of courage and is a great skater." A 9-year-old Latino boy picked Captain America and said, "What I like about Captain America is his cool shield and how he fights the evil red skull." The third most frequently mentioned characteristic was a sense of humor (9 percent), which was most often attributed to entertainers. For instance, a 10-year-old Latino boy picked Will Smith "because he's funny. He makes jokes and he dances funny."

These findings held true for children in all four ethnic groups and across the genders, with two exceptions: boys were more likely than girls to name athletes for their skill, and entertainers for their humor. Given the media attention to the U.S. women's soccer team victory in the World Cup in 1999, and the success of the WNBA (the women's professional basketball league), the researchers expected girls to name women professional athletes as their heroes. However, only four girls in the study did so. Despite recent

Figure 3

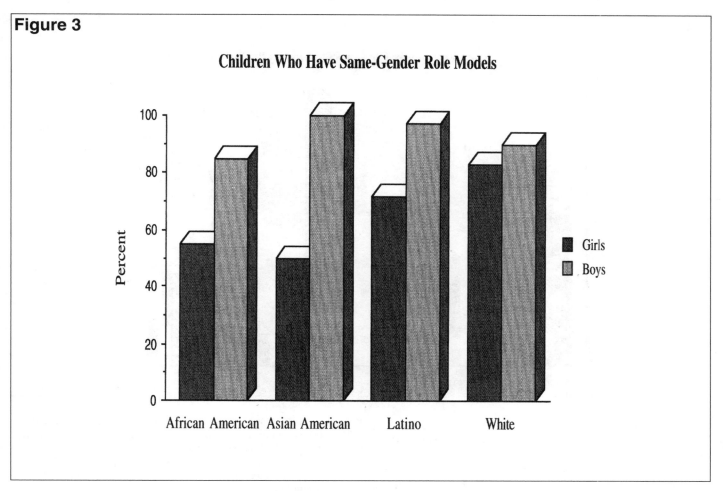

Children Who Have Same-Gender Role Models

strides in the visibility of women's sports, the media continue to construct men's sports as the norm and women's sports as marginal (e.g., references to men's athletics as "sports" and women's athletics as "women's sports").

> ## When children's heroes were media characters, African American and white children were more likely to name media heroes of their same ethnicity. In contrast, Asian American and Latino children tended to name media heroes who were not of their same ethnicity.

Summary and Implications

Whether the children in this study had heroes they knew in real life, or whether they chose famous people or fictional characters, depended, to some extent, on the respondents' ethnicity and gender. Overall, however, the most frequently named role model for kids was a parent. This is good news for parents, who must wonder, given the omnipresence of the media, whether they have any impact at all on their children. Popular culture was a significant source of heroes for children as well. Entertainers were the second most frequently named role models for the children, and the number increases significantly if you add professional athletes to that category. The attributes that children valued depended on whom they chose. For instance, children who named parents named them because they are helpful and understanding. Media characters were chosen because of their skills. When children's heroes were media characters, African American and white children were more likely to name media heroes of their same ethnicity. In contrast, Asian American and Latino children tended to name media heroes who were not of their same ethnicity. Children kept to their own gender when choosing a hero; boys were especially reluctant to choose girls and women as their heroes.

The frequency with which boys in this study named athletes as their role models is noteworthy. Only four girls in the study did the same. The implications of this gender difference are important, because many studies find that girls' participation in sports is associated with a number of positive attributes, such as high self-esteem and self-efficacy (Richman & Shaffer, 2000). Therefore, school and community support of girls' athletic programs and recognition of professional women athletes would go

Figure 4

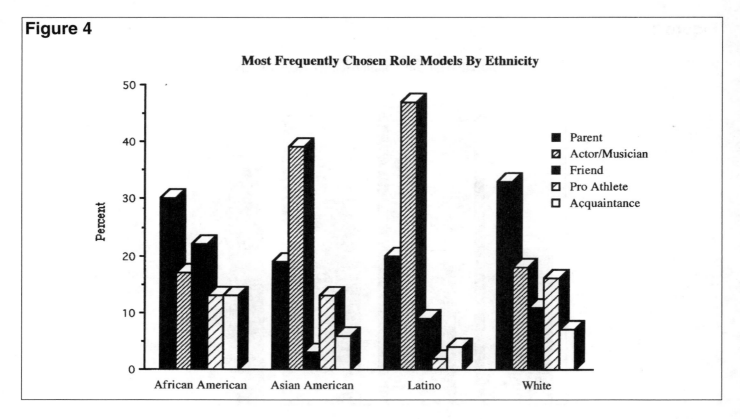

Most Frequently Chosen Role Models By Ethnicity

a long way to encourage girls' participation in sports, as well as boys' appreciation of women athletes as potential role models.

The mass media are hindered by a narrow view of gender, and by limited, stereotyped representations of ethnic minorities. Parents and educators must take pains to expose children to a wider variety of potential role models than popular culture does. Historical figures and authors constituted a tiny minority of heroes named by the children surveyed. Educators can play a significant role by exposing students to a wide range of such historical heroes, including people from various professions, people of color, and women of all races.

Finally, educators could capitalize on children's need for guidance to expose them to a greater variety of role models. Doing so affirms for the children that their race and gender are worthy of representation. A variety of potential heroes and role models allows children to appreciate themselves and the diversity in others.

References

Bell, R., & Crosbie, C. (1996, November 13). Superhero play of 3-5-year-old children. Available: http://labyrinth.net.au/~cccav/sept97/superhero.html.

Boyd, B. J. (1997). Teacher response to superhero play: To ban or not to ban. *Childhood Education, 74,* 23–28.

Children Now. (1999, September). *Boys to men: Messages about masculinity.* Oakland, CA: Author.

Dietz, T. L. (1998). An examination of violence and gender role portrayals in video games: Implications for gender socialization. *Sex Roles, 38,* 425–433.

Dyson, A. H. (1994). The ninjas, the X-men, and the ladies: Playing with power and identity in an urban primary school. *Teachers College Record, 96,* 219–239.

French, J., & Pena, S. (1991). Children's hero play of the 20th century: Changes resulting from television's influence. *Child Study Journal, 21,* 79–94.

Gerbner, G. (1993). *Women and minorities on television: A study in casting and fate.* A report to the Screen Actors Guild and the American Federation of Radio and Television Artists, Philadelphia: The Annenberg School of Communication, University of Pennsylvania.

Gibson, D. E., & Cordova, D. I. (1999). Women's and men's role models: The importance of exemplars. In A. J. Murrell, F. J. Crosby, & R. J. Ely (Eds.), *Mentoring dilemmas: Developmental relationships within multicultural organizations* (pp. 121–141). Mahwah, NJ: Lawrence Erlbaum Associates.

Giroux, H. A. (1997). Are Disney movies good for your kids? In S. R. Steinberg & J. L. Kincheloe (Eds.), *Kinderculture: The corporate construction of childhood* (pp. 53–67). Boulder, CO: Westview Press.

Ivinski, P. (1997). Game girls: Girl market in computer games and educational software. *Print, 51,* 24–29.

Lockwood, P., & Kunda, Z. (2000). Outstanding role models: Do they inspire or demoralize us? In A. Tesser, R. B. Felson, et al. (Eds.), *Psychological perspectives on self and identity* (pp. 147–171). Washington, DC: American Psychological Association.

National Television Violence Study. Vol. 3. (1998). Thousand Oaks, CA: Sage.

Pecora, N. (1992). Superman/superboys/supermen: The comic book hero as socializing agent. In S. Craig (Ed.), *Men, masculinity, and the media* (pp. 61–77). Newbury Park, CA: Sage.

Richman, E. L., & Shaffer, D. R. (2000). "If you let me play sports": How might sport participation influence the self-esteem of adolescent females? *Psychology of Women Quarterly, 24,* 189–199.

Risko, V. J. (1999). The power and possibilities of video technology and intermediality. In L. Semali & A. Watts Pailliotet (Eds.), *Intermediality: The teachers' handbook of critical media literacy* (pp. 129–140). Boulder, CO: Westview Press.

Screen Actors Guild. (1999, May 3). *New Screen Actors Guild employment figures reveal a decline in roles for Latinos, African American and Native American Indian performers.* Press Release. Available: www.sag.org

Screen Actors Guild. (2000, December 20). *Screen Actors Guild employment statistics reveal percentage increases in available roles for African Americans and Latinos, but total number of roles to minorities decrease in 1999.* Press Release. Available: www.sag.org.

Seidman, S. A. (1999). Revisiting sex-role stereotyping in MTV videos. *International Journal of Instructional Media, 26,* 11.

Signorielli, N. (2001). Television's gender role images and contribution to stereotyping: Past, present, future. In D. G. Singer & J. L. Singer (Eds.), *Handbook of children and the media* (pp. 341–358). Thousand Oaks, CA: Sage.

Signorielli, N., & Bacue, A. (1999). Recognition and respect: A content analysis of prime-time television characters across three decades. *Sex Roles, 40,* 527–544.

Thompson, T. L., & Zerbinos, E. (1995). Gender roles in animated cartoons: Has the picture changed in 20 years? *Sex Roles, 32,* 651–673.

Young, T. J. (1993). Women as comic book superheroes: The "weaker sex" in the Marvel universe. *Psychology: A Journal of Human Behavior, 30,* 49–50.

Authors' Notes:

This project was conducted in conjunction with Mediascope, a not-for-profit media education organization. The terms "hero" and "role model" tend to be used interchangeably in the literature. When a distinction between the terms is made, role models are defined as known persons (e.g., parents, teachers) and heroes are defined as figures who may be less attainable, or larger than life. Both kinds of persons and figures are of interest here; therefore, the terms are used interchangeably, and we specify whether known people or famous figures are being discussed.

Kristin J. Anderson is Assistant Professor, Psychology and Women's Studies, Antioch College, Yellow Springs, Ohio. Donna Cavallaro is graduate student, counseling psychology, Santa Clara University, Santa Clara, California.

From *Childhood Education,* Spring 2002, pp. 161-168. Reprinted by permission of the authors and the Association for Childhood Education International. © 2002 by the Association for Childhood Education International.

Media Violence and the American Public
Scientific Facts Versus Media Misinformation

Brad J. Bushman and Craig A. Anderson
Iowa State University

Fifty years of news coverage on the link between media violence and aggression have left the U. S. public confused. Typical news articles pit researchers and child advocates against entertainment industry representatives, frequently giving equal weight to the arguments of both sides. A comparison of news reports and scientific knowledge about media effects reveals a disturbing discontinuity: Over the past 50 years, the average news report has changed from claims of a weak link to a moderate link and then back to a weak link between media violence and aggression. However, since 1975, the scientific confidence and statistical magnitude of this link have been clearly positive and have consistently increased over time. Reasons for this discontinuity between news reports and the actual state of scientific knowledge include the vested interests of the news, a misapplied fairness doctrine in news reporting, and the failure of the research community to effectively argue the scientific case.

I n the movie *Grand Canyon* (Grillo, Kasdan, & Okun, 1991). Steve Martin plays the role of a producer of B-grade violent movies. However, after an armed robber shoots Martin's character in the leg, he has an epiphany. "I can't make those movies anymore," he decides. "I can't make another piece of art that glorifies violence and bloodshed and brutality. I can't contribute another stone to this landslide of dehumanizing rage that has swept across this country like a pestilence.... I'm done, kaput, finished. No more exploding bodies, exploding buildings, exploding anything. No more shit. I'm going to make the world a better place." A month or two later, his friend, played by Kevin Kline, calls on Martin at his Hollywood studio to congratulate him on the "new direction" his career has taken. "What? Oh that," Martin's character says. "That's over. I must have been delirious for a few weeks there." He continues. "There's always been violence, there will always be violence, violence and evil and men with big guns. My movies reflect what's going on; they don't make what's going on."

Modern society is exposed to a massive dose of violent media. What effect, if any, does this exposure have on people? In the 20th century, two major explosions occurred: a mass media explosion and a violent crime explosion. After discussing both, we raise four questions. Does the level of violence in the "reel" world mirror the level of violence in the real world? Is there strong evidence linking exposure to media violence to aggression? How have news reports of the violent-media effect on aggression changed over time? Is there any correspondence between the cumulative scientific knowledge about media violence effects on aggression and news reports about this link? The answers to these questions differ depending on whom is asked. In this article, we consider answers from two sources: the entertainment industry and the scientific community. We also discuss why the entertainment industry and the scientific community often disagree in their assessment of the effect of violent media on aggression.

THE MASS MEDIA EXPLOSION

A mass media explosion occurred in the 20th century. Inventions such as the television set, the digital computer, and the videocassette player forever changed the way people gain information about the world, including information about how violent the world is. Television was introduced to the United States at the 1939 World's Fair in New York. Two years later, on July 1, 1941, the Federal Communications Commission licensed and approved the first commercially available television stations. Because of World War II, however, full-scale television broadcasting was suspended until 1946. In 1950, about 9% of American homes had TV sets. It didn't take long for television ownership in the United States to increase. By 1955, it was up to about 65%, and by 1965, it reached about 93%. Since 1985, television ownership has been about 98% (Nielsen Media Research, 1998). More recent types of electronic media have also become ubiquitous implements in modern society. About 97% of homes with children have a VCR, 90% have a CD player, and

89% have either a personal computer or other video-game-capable equipment (Federal Trade Commission, 2000).

The American public has consumed media as if they were ambrosia. A recent national study reported that consuming media is a full-time job for the average American child, who spends about 40 hours per week doing it (Kaiser Family Foundation, 1999). More than half of this time is spent watching television programs, movies, or videos. One telling statistic is that at 10 a.m. on any Saturday morning, more than 60% of all children in America are watching TV (Comstock & Scharrer, 1999).

Figure 1

U.S. Violent Crime Rate per 100,000 Inhabitants

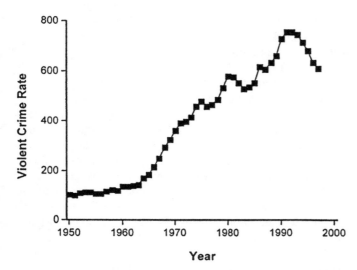

Note. Data were obtained from *Uniform Crime Reports* (U.S. Federal Bureau of Investigation, 1951–1999).

VIOLENCE IN THE REEL WORLD

Violence in drama is as old as drama itself—from ancient Greek drama, through the Elizabethan theater, to modern electronic dramas. In William Shakespeare's play *Macbeth,* for example, Macbeth's head is brought on stage at the close of the play. In 1903, Edwin S. Porter directed a film called *The Great Train Robbery* (Edison & Porter, 1903). This 11-minute film is usually considered the first film ever made to tell an organized story (Turan, 1972). In one scene, there is a large close-up of a cowboy firing his pistol directly at the camera. The first audiences who saw the film reacted by running out of the theater screaming.

Americans get a heavy dose of media violence. A recent content analysis of more than 8,000 hours of programming on cable and broadcast television in the United States found that about 60% of TV programs contained violence (*National Television Violence Study,* 1996, 1997, 1998). By the time the average American child graduates from elementary school, he or she will have seen more than 8,000 murders and more than 100,000 other assorted acts of violence (e.g., assaults, rapes) on network television (Huston et al., 1992). The numbers are higher if the

child has access to cable television or a videocassette player, as most do. Violence dominates the big screen as well as the small screen. The percentage of PG films produced has steadily dropped over the years (Auletta, 1993). Even G-rated films contain more violence now than they ever have before (Yokota & Thompson, 2000). Violence is also frequently found in video games. For example, Provenzo (1991) found that 85% of the most popular video games were violent. Even young children are exposed to many violent video games. Buchman and Funk (1996) found that fourth-grade girls and boys reported that the majority of their favorite games were violent ones (59% for girls, 73% for boys).

One plausible explanation for the media emphasis on violent materials is that violent media are easy to export to foreign markets, perhaps because they lose less in translation than do other types of media. Comedies, for example, often require some knowledge of the popular culture. In time, violent media might become America's most exportable commodity (Hamilton, 1998).

THE EXPLOSION OF VIOLENCE IN THE REAL WORLD

Violence is as American as cherry pie.

—H. Rap Brown

Among industrialized countries, the United States is one of the most violent (Zimring & Hawkins, 1997). Scholars have been investigating media violence as a potential contributor to societal violence in the United States since the early 1960s. One possible reason for the early interest in a link between media violence and societal violence is that violence in the United States began to increase fairly dramatically in 1965, exactly when the first generation of children raised on TV began to reach the prime ages for committing violent crimes (see Figure 1). Indeed, studies of violent crime rates before and after the introduction of television have shown similar effects in several countries (e.g., Centerwall, 1989, 1992).

Of course, such comparisons of demographic trends are not proof of any causal relationship between violent media and violent crime. Numerous factors influence violent crime rates, including simple demographic trends (e.g., changes in age distribution) in the population. Thus, large numbers of empirical studies of media violence have ben conducted over the past 40 years using more traditional psychological research methods. Before examining the outcomes of those studies, we first consider the claim that media violence mirrors what is happening in contemporary society.

DOES THE LEVEL OF VIOLENCE IN THE REEL WORLD MIRROR THE LEVEL OF VIOLENCE IN THE REAL WORLD?

The entertainment industry often claims that violent media simply reflect the violence that already exists in society. Consider the following statements from representatives of the three major television networks. According to Leonard Goldenson of

ABC, "We are presently reaping the harvest of having laid it on the line at a time when many Americans are reluctant to accept the images reflected by the mirror we have held up to our society" ("Fighting Violence," 1968, p. 59). Julian Goodman of NBC agreed. "The medium is being blamed for the message" ("Fighting Violence," 1968, p. 59). Howard Stringer of CBS claimed that the TV industry is "merely holding a mirror to American society" (West, 1993). Zev Braun, also of CBS, said, "We live in a violent society. Art imitates the modes of life, not the other way around. It would be better for Congress to clean that society than to clean up the reflection of that society" ("Violence Bill Debated in Washington," 1990).

However, even in reality-based TV programs, violence is grossly overemphasized. For example, one study compared the frequency of crimes occurring in the real world with the frequency of crimes occurring in the following reality-based police TV programs: *America's Most Wanted, Cops, Top Cops, FBI, The Untold Story,* and *American Detective* (Oliver, 1994). The real-world crime rates were obtained from the U.S. Federal Bureau of Investigation (FBI: 1951–1999) *Uniform Crime Reports,* which divide seven major types of crimes into two categories, violent and nonviolent. About 87% of the crimes occurring in the real world are nonviolent crimes, whereas only 13% of crimes occurring in reality-based TV programs are nonviolent crimes. The largest discrepancy between the real world and the world depicted on television is for murder, the most violent crime of all. Only 0.2% of the crimes reported by the FBI are murders, whereas about 50% of the crimes shown in reality-based TV programs are murders (Oliver, 1994).

According to film critic Michael Medved (1995), the claim that the entertainment industry merely reflects the level of violence in society is a lie.

> If this were true, then why do so few people witness murders in real life but everybody sees them on TV and in the movies? The most violent ghetto isn't in South Central L.A. or Southeast Washington D. C.; it's on television. About 350 characters appear each night on prime-time TV, but studies show an average of seven of these people are murdered every night. If this rate applied in reality, then in just 50 days everyone in the United States would be killed and the last left could turn off the TV. (pp. 156–157)

In summary, there is far more violence in the reel world than in the real world.

IS THERE STRONG EVIDENCE LINKING EXPOSURE TO MEDIA VIOLENCE WITH INCREASED AGGRESSION?

The "Logical" Debate

The television and motion picture industries often claim that violent media have no influence on aggressive behavior. For example, Jack Valenti, president of the Motion Picture Association of America, said, "If you cut the wires of all TV sets today, there would still be no less violence on the street in two years" (Moore, 1993, p. 3007). However, this same industry makes all of its money from commercials, charging hundreds of thousands of dollars for a few minutes of commercial airtime. As former Federal Communications Commission Chairman Reed Hundt said, "If a sitcom can sell soap, salsa and cereal, then who could argue that TV violence cannot affect to some degree some viewers, particularly impressionable children?" (Eggerton, 1994, p. 10).

Sometimes, the entertainment industry goes one step further and claims that violent media influence behavior in a beneficial way. For example, TV scriptwriter Grace Johnson said that violent TV shows "often serve as a release valve for aggressive impulses which would otherwise be bottled up, only to explode later" ("See No Evil?", 1954, p. 8). Similarly, film director Alfred Hitchcock said, "One of television's greatest contributions is that it brought murder back into the home where it belongs. Seeing a murder on television can be good therapy. It can help work off one's antagonism" (Myers, 1999, p. 412).

The first recorded description of this "catharsis hypothesis" occurred more than one thousand years ago, in Aristotle's (trans. 1970) *Poetics.* He taught that viewing tragic plays gave people emotional release (*katharsis*) from negative feelings such as pity and fear. The tragic hero in a Greek drama did not just grow old and retire—he often suffered a violent demise. By watching the characters in the play experience tragic events, the viewer's own negative feelings were presumably purged and cleansed. This emotional cleaning was believed to benefit both the individual and society.

The ancient notion of catharsis was revived by Sigmund Freud and his associates. For example, A. A. Brill, the psychiatrist who introduced Freud's psychoanalytic techniques to the United States, prescribed that his patients watch a prizefight once a month to purge their angry, aggressive feelings into harmless channels (Feshbach & Price, 1984). While serving as chairman of the National Board of Review of Motion Pictures, Brill said,

> You remember that the Greeks spoke of the play as effecting a "catharsis" of the emotions. The movies serve this purpose. So do hockey and football games. People get rid of pent-up aggression when they go to a prizefight, and society approves of this release. Children, too, have plenty of bottled up protest against life's little tyrannies—keeping clean, learning lessons, behaving themselves—and the screen is the great medium for giving the child an outlet for this revolt. (Mackenzie, 1940, p. 9)

The Scientific Evidence

Psychologists have studied the effect of violent media on aggression for several decades. Hundreds of studies have been conducted on this topic. Scientific evidence from a collection of studies, such as those on media-related aggression, can be integrated and summarized in a narrative (qualitative) review or in a meta-analytic (quantitative) review. Both types of reviews have been conducted on the research literature about media violence and aggression, and all have come to the same conclusion: that viewing violence increases aggression (e.g., Hearold, 1986; Hogben, 1998; Huston et al., 1992; National Institute of Mental Health, 1982; Paik & Comstock, 1994; Surgeon General's Scientific Advisory Committee on Television and Social Behavior, 1972; Wood, Wong, & Chachere, 1991). On the basis of such findings, in July 2000, six major professional societies—the American Psychological Association (APA), the American Academy of Pediatrics, the American Academy of Child and Adolescent Psychiatry, the American Medical Association, the American Academy of Family Physicians, and the American Psychiatric Association—signed a joint statement on the hazards of exposing children to media violence, noting that "at this time, well over 1,000 studies...point overwhelmingly to a causal connection between media violence and aggressive behavior in some children "(*Joint Statement,* 2000, p. 1).

One common industry response to the conclusions of such literature reviews is to deny the findings. For example, Jim Burke of Rysher Entertainment said, "I don't think there is any correlation between violence on TV and violence in society" (Stern, 1995, p. 28). Another is to claim that the effects of media violence on aggression are so small or that they affect so few people that the risks to society are negligible and can and should be ignored. For example, a *Time* magazine writer concluded, "While the bulk of published research has indeed found some correlation between watching fictitious violence and behaving aggressively, the correlation is statistically quite modest" (K. Anderson, 1993, p. 66).

But is the effect so small? How is on to judge? This type of question begs for a quantitative answer, and meta-analysis techniques have been developed to help address such questions. In the remainder of this article, we use the correlation coefficient, denoted by r, as the quantitative measure of the effect of one variable (e.g., exposure to media violence) on another variable (e.g., aggression).[1]

Earlier meta-analytic reviews of studies of media violence on aggression have reported average effect sizes ranging from $r = .11$ (Hogben, 1998) to $r = .31$ (Paik & Comstock, 1994). In all cases, the reviews found a significant positive relation. That is, greater exposure to media violence is strongly linked to increases in aggression.

Just how small are these estimates of the media violence effect? Figure 2 presents the results of the largest published meta-analysis on violent-media-related aggression (Paik & Comstock, 1994, included 217 studies in their meta-analysis), along with the results from a number of meta-analyses done in other (primarily medical) domains. All of the correlations in Figure 2 are significantly different from zero. Note, however, that the second largest correlation is for violent media and aggression. Most people would agree that the other correlations displayed in Figure 2 are so strong that they are obvious. For example, most people would not question the assertion that taking calcium increases bone mass or that wearing a condom decreases the risk of contracting HIV, the virus that causes AIDS.

Why, then, do some individuals question the assertion that viewing violence increases aggression? One possible reason is

that people do not understand psychological processes as well as they physiological processes. Another possibility is that people might (mistakenly) believe that the media violence data are merely correlational. A third possibility that we examine in more detail later in this article is that news media reports of media violence research might not be accurately presenting the state of scientific knowledge, much like news media reports on the relationship between cigarette smoking and lung cancer in the 1950s, 1960s, and 1970s seemed to inaccurately portray that research as being weaker than medical scientists knew it to be.

More Logical Analyses

The Smoking and Media Violence Analogy

There are at least six instructive parallels between the smoking and lung cancer relationship and the media violence and aggression relationship. First, not everyone who smokes gets lung cancer, and not everyone who gets lung cancer is a smoker. Similarly, not everyone who watches violent media becomes aggressive, and not everyone who is aggressive watches violent media.

Second, smoking is not the only factor that causes lung cancer, but it is an important factor. Similarly, watching violent media is not the only factor that causes aggression, but it is an important factor.

Third, the first cigarette can nauseate a person. Repeated exposure reduces these sickening effects, and the person begins to crave more cigarettes. Similarly, the first exposure to violent media can make a person (especially children) anxious and fearful (Cantor, 2000). Repeated exposure reduces these effects and leaves the viewer wanting stronger doses of violence.

Fourth, the short-term effects of smoking are relatively innocuous in most cases and dissipate fairly rapidly. Smoking one cigarette has numerous physiological effects that are rarely serious and that dissipate within an hour or so. Similarly, watching one violent TV program on film increases aggressive thoughts, feelings, and behaviors, but these effects usually dissipate within an hour or so (Bushman & Huesmann, 2001).

Fifth, the long-term cumulative effects of smoking are relatively severe. One cigarette has little impact on lung cancer. However, repeated exposure to tobacco smoke, for example, smoking one pack of cigarettes a day for 15 years, seriously increases the likelihood of a person contracting lung cancer (and other diseases). Similarly, watching one violent TV show has little impact on the likelihood of a child becoming a habitual violent offender, but the empirical evidence now clearly shows that repeated exposure to violent media, for example, a couple of hours a day for 15 years, causes a serious increase in the likelihood of a person becoming a habitually aggressive person and occasionally a violent offender (Huesmann, Moise, Podolski, & Eron, 2000).

One final parallel also deserves consideration. In the long fight of medical science against the tobacco industry, the big money interests of the tobacco industry apparently led them to deny publicly that there was any scientific evidence supporting the claim that tobacco products caused lung cancer. Many of the

Figure 2

Comparison of the Effect of Violent Media on Aggression With Effects From Other Domains

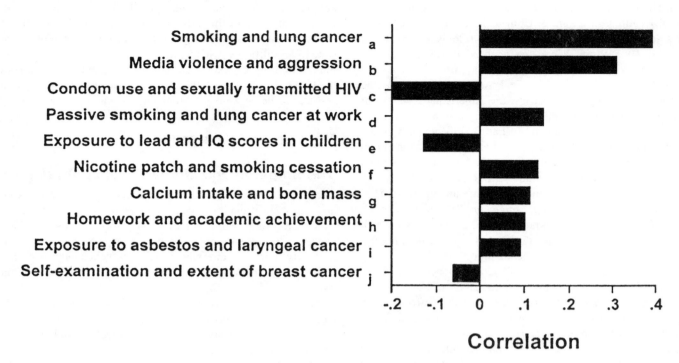

Note. All correlations are significantly different from zero. a = the effect of smoking tobacco on lung cancer, as estimated by pooling the data from Figures 1 and 3 in Wynder and Graham's (1950) classic article. The remaining effects were estimated from meta-analyses: b = Paik and Comstock (1994); c = Weller (1993); d = Wells (1998); e = Needleman and Gatsonis (1990); f = Fiore, Smith, Jorenby, and Baker (1994); g = Welten, Kemper, Post, and van Staveren (1995); h = Cooper (1989); i = Smith, Handley, and Wood (1990); j = Hill, White, Jolley, and Mapperson (1998).

same arguments used in this war of deception have been and continue to be made by the entertainment industry regarding reports that exposure to violent media causes aggression. In both cases, the industry claims that there is no good evidence have persisted long after the scientific data clearly indicated there could be no reasonable doubt about the seriousness of the causal impact. That point in the history of scientific developments in the smoking case was reached quite some time ago: In 1964, the U.S. Surgeon General concluded that the evidence on the harmful effects of tobacco smoke was overwhelming enough to warn the American public about it (U.S. Department of Health, Education, and Welfare, 1974). In the next section of this article, we show that the no-reasonable-doubt point in the data on media violence effects was also reached some time ago: The U. S. Surgeon General issued such a statement in 1972 (Surgeon General's Scientific Advisory Committee on Television and Social Behavior, 1972).

When Small Is Big

Obviously, exposure to media violence does not produce violent criminals out of all viewers, just as cigarette smoking does not produce lung cancer victims out of all smokers. This lack of perfect correspondence between heavy media violence exposure and violent behavior simply means that media violence exposure is not a necessary and sufficient cause of violence. When an ad is shown on TV, no one expects that it will sell the product to everybody. If the ad influences only 1% of viewers, it is considered to be a great success (Medved, 1995). Suppose violent media make only 1% of the population more aggressive. Should society be concerned about a percentage so small? The answer is a resounding "Yes!" Suppose 10 million people watch a violent TV program. If only 1% of the viewers will become more aggressive afterward, then the violent TV program will make 100,000 people more aggressive! Because so many people are exposed to violent media, the effect on society can be immense even if only a small percentage of viewers are affected by them. It takes only one or two affected students to wreak murderous havoc in a school, as demonstrated in recent years in Jonesboro, Arkansas; West Paducah, Kentucky; Pearl, Mississippi; Stamps, Arkansas; Springfield, Oregon; Littleton, Colorado; and Santee and Elcajon, California. (See Abelson, 1985, and Rosenthal, 1990, for example of how small effect sizes can yield large effects.)

It might be that only 1 in 1,000 viewers will behave more aggressively immediately after viewing a particular program, but the cumulative effects may well increase the aggressiveness of most (if not all) of the 1,000 viewers. Furthermore, laboratory experiments have shown that merely viewing 15 minutes of a relatively mild violent program increases the aggressiveness of a substantial proportion (at least one fourth) of the viewers (e.g., Bushman, 1995).

HOW HAVE NEWS REPORTS OF THE VIOLENT-MEDIA EFFECT ON AGGRESSION CHANGED OVER TIME?

Print and TV news reports have a substantial impact on public opinion (e.g., McCombs & Shaw, 1991; Rogers & Dearing, 1988; Strange & Leung, 1999) as well as on public policy (e.g., Jordan & Page, 1992; Page & Shapiro, 1989). Thus, it is important that news reports on scientific findings accurately reflect ongoing changes in the state of knowledge in the field.

To quantify and analyze mass media reports of the effect of violent media on aggression and violence, we coded every newspaper and magazine article we could find on the topic. All forms of mass media were considered (e.g., television, film, music, video games, pornographic magazines, comic books). Six computer databases were searched from the year each individual database started until 2000. The six databases were (a) *Readers' Guide Abstracts* (1890–2000), (b) *Alternative Press Index* (1969–2000), (c) *Access* (1975–2000), (d) *Expanded Academic Index ASAP* (1980–2000), (e) *Periodical Abstracts* (1987–2000), and (f) *National Newspaper Index* (1994–2000). The following key words were used in the computer searches: *violen** or *aggress**, as well as *TV, televis*, film, movie, screen, music, radio, video game, computer game, electronic game, cartoon, comic, pornograph*, erotic*, news, book, magazine, or sport**. The asterisk option retrieves words containing the letter string with all possible endings. The search yielded 636 articles concerned with media violence effects on aggression.

The newspaper and magazine articles were rated using a 21-point scale that ranged from -10 to 10. The scale contained five verbal anchors. The article was given a rating of -10 if it said that viewing violent media causes a decrease in aggression. The article was given a rating of -5 if it only said or implied that parents should encourage their children to consume violent media. The article was given a rating of 0 if it said there was no relationship between violent media and aggression. The article was given a rating of 5 if it only said or implied that parents should discourage their children from consuming violent media. The article was given a rating of 10 if it said that viewing violent media causes an increase in aggression and violence in society.[2]

Each article was rated by one judge. For purposes of assessing reliability, an additional three judges each rated a random sample of 50 articles using the same scale. A different random sample (with replacement) of articles was selected for each additional judge. Reliability coefficients ranged from .77 to .96. Thus, there was a high degree of agreement among judges regarding the portrayal of violent-media effects in magazine and newspaper articles.

The average rating for the 636 articles was 4.15 ($SD = 3.25$), a value significantly less than 5, $t(635) = 6.60$, $p < .0001$. Recall that an article was given a rating of 5 if it merely said or implied that parents should discourage their children from consuming violent media. On average, the mass media acknowledge that media violence is positively related to aggression, although they tend to claim that the relationship is not very strong. Of the 636 articles coded, only 36 (5.7%) stated that media violence was a cause of societal violence. Almost half of the articles (305, or 48%) did not even advise parents to discourage their children from consuming violent media.

Figure 3

News Reports of the Effect of Media Violence on Aggression

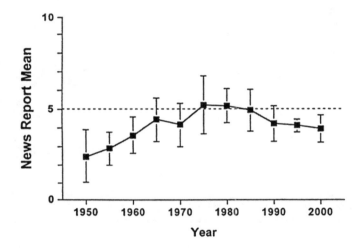

Note. News report means are the average rated conclusions of newspaper and magazine articles. A rating of 0 indicates that the article said there was no relationship between violent media and aggression. A rating of 5 indicates that the article urged parents to discourage their children from consuming violent media. A rating of 10 indicates that the article said that viewing violence caused an increase in aggression. Capped vertical bars denote 95% confidence intervals.

Of more interest is the pattern of news reports across time. Because media violence studies did not exist in the early years of societal concern, one might expect that early mass media reports would on average note that there is little relationship between media violence and aggression. Because the evidence did accumulate in support of the conclusion that media violence is positively (and causally) related to aggression, one might also expect that the average news report would shift over time to the positive end of the 21-point rating scales.

For each five-year period between 1950 and 2000, we plotted the mean article ratings and 95% confidence intervals. These data are depicted in Figure 3. As one can see in Figure 3, the average mass media perspective has generally been that media violence is positively, but only weakly, related to aggression. This view was held even before there were any published scientific studies on the issue (i.e., the 1955 and 1960 data points in Figure 3). There has been some systematic fluctuation over time, with the strongest statements about this effect occurring in late 1970s and early 1980s (i.e., the 1980 and 1985 data points in Figure 3). Unfortunately, in more recent years the average news media article does not even warn parents that they should prevent their children from viewing violent TV shows and movies or playing violent video games. Thus, mass media news reports in recent years have edged away from the already weak message being given to the public in earlier years.

Figure 4
Cumulative Meta-Analysis of Scientific Studies on Media-Related Aggression

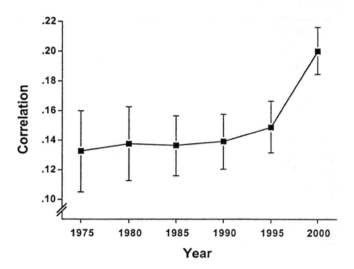

Note. A positive correlation indicates that media violence was positively related to aggression. Capped vertical bars denote 99.9% confidence intervals.

We used polynomial regression analysis to examine the linear and quadratic effects for news reports over time. The linear effect was nonsignificant (even with a sample size of 636), $t(634) = 0.59$, $p > .05$. The correlation between publication year and article rating was .02. However, the curvilinear effect, as modeled by a quadratic term, confirms that the observed increase and subsequent decrease in indeed a statistically significant pattern, $t(633) = 3.98$, $p < .0001$. Furthermore, the mean rating for the 1975–1985 intervals was significantly higher than the mean rating for the 1990–2000 intervals, $Ms = 5.09$ and 4.06, respectively, $t(521) = 2.79$, $p < .01$, $d = 0.31$. Thus, mass media news reports in recent years have edged away from the already weak message being given to the public in earlier years.

IS THERE ANY CORRESPONDENCE BETWEEN THE CUMULATIVE SCIENTIFIC KNOWLEDGE ABOUT MEDIA VIOLENCE EFFECTS ON AGGRESSION AND NEWS REPORTS ABOUT THIS LINK?

To assess the accumulated scientific knowledge about media violence effects, we did a cumulative meta-analysis on empirical studies of the relationship between exposure to violent media and aggression (e.g., Lau, Schmid, & Chalmers, 1995). In cumulative meta-analysis, the scientific studies are arranged in a

chronological sequence, from the earliest study to the latest study. A meta-analysis is performed on the first two studies, then on the first three studies, then on the first four studies, and so on. At each step, the reviewer can test whether the combined effect is significantly different from zero. This allows the reviewer to determine the point in time when enough studies had been conducted to yield a significant treatment effect.

Aggression was defined as any behavior intended to harm another individual who is motivated to avoid that harm. Because several previous meta-analyses did not report detailed results on their data matrix and sometimes included broader definitions of aggression, we conducted an entirely new meta-analysis. We then compared the results of our cumulative meta-analysis of media violence effects on aggression with the news reports of such effects.

Cumulative Meta-Analysis

Literature Search

To retrieve relevant studies, we searched the *PsycINFO* database from 1887 (starting date) to 2000 using the following terms: *violen** or *aggress**, as well as *TV, televis*, film, movie, screen, music, radio, video game, computer game, electronic game, cartoon, comic, pornograph*, erotic*, news, book, magazine, or sport*. We restricted the search to empirical studies involving human participants. We also combed the reference sections of the four previous meta-analyses of violent media and aggression (Hearold, 1986; Hogben, 1998; Paik & Comstock, 1994; Wood et al., 1991).

Criteria for Relevance

Because the mass media news industry has easy access only to published research on the effects of violent media, we excluded unpublished studies. However, the results are virtually identical if unpublished studies are included in the cumulative meta-analysis. Also, publication status did not influence the magnitude of the relationship between violent media and aggression, $X^2(1, k = 262) = 2.70$, $p > .05$. We also included only those studies that examined aggressive behavior. Thus, we excluded studies that examined the effect of violent media on aggressive affect, aggressive cognition, physiological arousal, and prosocial behavior. The literature search resulted in 202 independent samples from published articles concerned with media violence effects on aggressive behavior, with a total sample size of 43,306 participants.

Each research report discovered by the *PsycINFO* search was coded by one judge ($k = 478$). To assess coding reliability, an additional three judges each coded a random sample of 50 articles. A different random sample (with replacement) of articles was selected for each additional judge. The judges coded the year the research report was released, whether the research report was published (e.g., journal article) or unpublished (e.g., doctoral dissertation), sample size, effect-size estimate (if reported), type of study (i.e., experimental vs. nonexperimental),[3] and type of dependent measure (i.e., aggressive behavior, aggressive cognition, aggressive affect, prosocial behavior). If the dependent measure was aggressive behavior, judges coded whether the target was a real person or an inanimate object (e.g., an inflatable doll). There was perfect agreement among judges on the coded characteristics.

Results

All studies combined. The data are plotted in Figure 4 in five-year intervals, beginning with 1975. We started the plot in 1975 because fewer than 30 studies had been published before 1970. By 1975, 80 studies had been published. As one can see from the cumulative effects plotted in Figure 4, the magnitude of the violent-media effect on aggression has increased over time and shows no signs of leveling off or decreasing. To be conservative, we used 99.9% confidence intervals instead of 95% confidence intervals. None of the confidence intervals include the value zero. Note also that the confidence intervals have become narrower over time, as more studies were conducted. Thus, an accurate reading of the research literature over time would be that as time passed, scientific evidence regarding the effect of violent media on aggression increased. Since 1975, the media violence effect has been significantly greater than zero.

From a skeptic's perspective, the data point of most importance might well be the lower boundaries of the 99.9% confidence intervals, because these represent a very conservative estimate of how small the true effect might be. As shown in Figure 4, the lower boundary estimates increased at each interval. Thus, even if news media reports were based on a very conservative reading of the actual scientific state of knowledge, the ratings of news reports should have increased across time; as we saw earlier, the curvilinear trend for news report conclusions was essentially opposite in form.

Experimental versus nonexperimental studies. We also did cumulative meta-analyses separately for the experimental and nonexperimental studies. The results are presented in Figure 5. Four points are particularly interesting from these data. First, the experimental studies yielded average affect sizes that are significantly greater than zero at each time, establishing a causal link early in the history of media violence research. Second, the nonexperimental studies yielded average effect sizes that are significantly greater than zero at each time period, indicating a significant relationship between exposure to violent media and real-world measures of aggression (e.g., assault). Third, the effects are larger for experimental studies than for correlational studies, although this difference has decreased over time.[4] Fourth, the experimental effects did not change much across time, whereas the nonexperimental effects systematically increased.

To further investigate these time-based trends, we used polynomial regression analysis to examine the linear and quadratic effects for scientific studies over time. When all studies were in the model, the linear effect was significant, $t(200) = 6.05$, $p < .0001$. The correlation between publication year and violent media effect size was .40. The curvilinear effect was also significant, $t(199) = 5.82$, $p < .0001$. However, as noted earlier, the

cumulative analyses suggested that this time trend was operative only in nonexperimental studies. We therefore investigated this effect separately for experimental and nonexperimental studies.

Figure 5

Cumulative Meta-Analysis of Experimental and Nonexperimental Studies on Media-Related Aggression

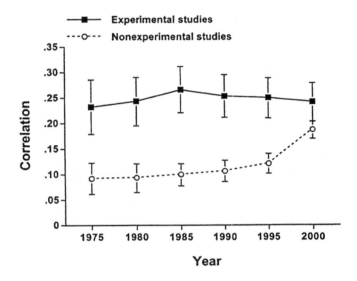

Note. A positive correlation indicates that media violence was positively related to aggression. Capped vertical bars denote 99.9% confidence intervals.

Polynomial regressions confirmed these differential shifts. For experimental studies, the linear and quadratic terms were both nonsignificant, $ts(114) = -1.33$ and -0.06, respectively, $ps > .05$. But for nonexperimental studies, the linear and quadratic terms were both significant, $ts(114) = 6.46$ and 4.16, respectively, $ps < .0001$. Figure 6 displays the best-fitting regression line relating time to the size of the media violence effect in nonexperimental studies.[5]

There are at least four plausible explanations for the recent increase in effect size found in nonexperimental studies. One explanation is that the research methodology in nonexperimental studies has improved, reducing measurement error. For example, better measures of exposure to media violence or of aggressive behavior would tend to produce larger effect sizes, if the true effect is positive. A second possibility is that media consumption itself has increased over time, thus increasing the amount of violent media consumed by some portion of the population and thereby increasing the effect size. A third possibility is that the amount of violence in entertainment media is increasing (e.g., there is more violence in G-rated movies of recent years than in earlier G movies; Yokota & Thompson, 2000). A fourth possibility is that the distribution of violent media consumption changed. Specifically, if the variance (or range) of media violence consumption increased, such that a relatively larger proportion of the population consumed more violent media and a correspondingly larger proportion of the population consumed less violent media, the observed effect size would increase. This could come about, for instance, if one portion of the population believed reports of potential problems and subsequently decreased their own and their children's violent media consumption, whereas another portion believed claims of no effect or of beneficial effects of consumption and subsequently increased consumption of violent media.

Figure 6
Violent Media Effects for Nonexperimental Studies Over Time

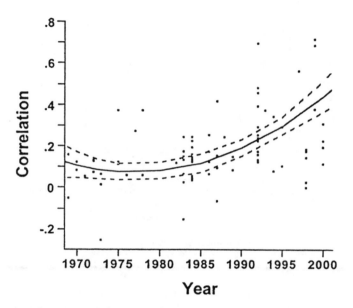

Note. The equation for the curve is $r = -18.93 + 0.0095933 \times year + 0.00069 \times (year - 1983.99)^2$. To reduce multicollinearity, year is centered for the quadratic term. The middle solid line is the regression line, and the upper and lower dashed lines are the upper and lower 95% confidence interval bands, respectively.

We presently do not have data that would allow testing of these possibilities. Such testing is largely irrelevant to the present article, so we end this section by simply noting that there time-based trends are interesting and worthy of additional investigation.

Comparison of Actual Effects to News Reports

To address more clearly the question of whether there is any correspondence between the accumulating scientific evidence concerning media violence and aggression and the news media reports on the same empirical question, we plotted the average ratings of the news reports and the cumulative correlations on the same plot, shown in Figure 7. The discrepancy is disheartening at best, especially since 1985. As it became clearer to the scientific community that media violence effects were real and significant, the news media reports actually got weaker. In fact,

there is a strong negative correlation between the average effect size and average news report rating for the six data points in Figure 7 from 1975 to 2000, $r = -.68$. The correlation is even stronger if the conservative lower boundary estimates of the effect size are used instead of the average effect size, $r = -.75$. In summary, whatever is driving the shifts in news reports over time, it is clearly not the empirical data.

General Discussion

In 1995, *Newsweek* magazine published an article that claimed there was no solid evidence that exposure to media violence increases aggression (Leland, 1995). We wrote a letter to the editor in an attempt to correct this factually incorrect statement. The reply said that they were not interested in publishing our letter. More recently, *The New York Times* published an op-ed article (Rhodes, 2000) that similarly attacked extant media violence research in general and specifically targeted the pioneering and ongoing research of Rowell Huesmann and Leonard Eron (e.g., Huesmann et al., 2000). Despite protests from a variety of sources, including a very thoughtful reply by Huesmann and Eron, no rebuttal, retraction, or reply was ever published (International Society for Research on Aggression, 2001). In an age of multinational, multimedia mega-corporations, perhaps it should not be surprising that truth in journalism has been forced to the back of the bus, as if it is not as important or valuable as profits or a good story. Nonetheless, the *Newsweek* incident was a shock to us, one that instigated the present research. *The New York Times* incident confirms the generality of this problem, as does Figure 7.

Figure 7 reveals a major problem in the public reporting of social science information. Mass media magazines and newspapers have consistently failed to capture the changes in the scientific state of knowledge as research evidence supporting the causal link between exposure to media violence and aggression has accumulated. By 1975, the effect was clear, yet major news sources continue today to suggest to the U.S. public that there is relatively little reason to be concerned about media violence. Indeed, since the mid-1980s, the average news story has actually softened a bit on the media violence problem, even though the cumulative evidence is now more overwhelming in showing that short- and long-term exposure to media violence causes significant increases in aggression.

There are several plausible explanations for this apparently irresponsible reporting pattern. The simplest, perhaps, is that the print news media industry has a vested interest in denying a strong link between exposure to media violence and aggression. There are at least three ways in which such a denial might serve the profits of the news media companies. First, many print news media companies are part of larger conglomerates that directly profit from the sale of violent media such as television and movies. Second, many print news media get a lot of their advertising revenue from companies that produce and sell violent media. For example, almost all newspapers advertise movies. Third, the print news media may fear they will offend their readers by printing stories with which their readers might disagree. Given the large number of people who consume violent media and who allow their children to do likewise, such fears might be legitimate, even though the biased reporting of scientific "fact" is not.

Figure 7

Effect of Media Violence on Aggression: News Reports Versus Scientific Studies

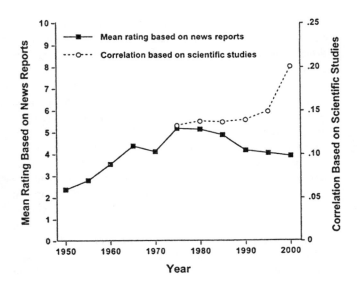

Note. Ratings based on news reports are positive if the article said that exposure to media violence is positively related to aggression. Correlations based on scientific studies are positive if media violence was positively related to aggression.

A second plausible explanation for the apparent misreporting of the state of media violence evidence concerns a misapplied fairness doctrine. There may be a sort of journalistic "fairness" heuristic guiding the reporting of scientific findings that systematically leads to an overemphasis on minority views. Specifically, an attempt to get both sides of the story may itself lead to a final story that puts too little emphasis on the findings and opinions of leading researchers and puts too much emphasis on the few dissidents who can be found on almost any scientific issue. Indeed, a reading of even a small sample of the print media reports on media violence reveals that this fairness doctrine extends even to the public opinions of people who clearly have a monetary interest in befuddling the general public. Of course, the mass media industry has the money and the expertise to hire top guns to create such obfuscations and to deliver them in a convincing fashion, much as the tobacco industry successfully did for several decades.

A third plausible explanation involves the failure of the research community to effectively argue its case. There are at least four contributing factors involved. First, research scientists typically do not see themselves as public policy advocates. It is not normally considered a part of their jobs to take on the task of educating the general public. Second, the scientist role itself includes a very conservative norm against publicly making the kinds of claims that scientists privately believe to be true, especially concerning the generalizability of their results

and the ability to draw causal inferences from their studies. It is deemed more proper to discuss limitations of a particular study, especially if it is a scientist's own study. Third, research scientists do not have the time needed to educate reporters or to respond to the hired guns whose only job is to attack the research base of the undesired findings. Fourth, attempting to educate the general public is very costly in many ways, not just in the amount of time required. For instance, hate mail is one additional cost that must be borne by anyone who appears in mass media sources with an opinion on a controversial issue. The Internet has made such hate mail easier to send and seemingly more prevalent. Also, there are security risks associated with becoming a more public figure. A more mundane yet real cost involves expenses accrued in presenting scientific information to appropriate sources. For instance, as one of us—Craig A. Anderson—recently discovered, the U.S. Senate does not pay travel expenses associated with testifying for one of their myriad committees. In addition, public debates about media violence effects make it more difficult to continue to conduct research on media-related aggression, because the participant pool becomes less naive and more suspicious of the research.

It is likely that all three of the explanations—the vested interests of the news media industry, a misapplied fairness doctrine, and communication failures—are operative, in both the specific case of research on media violence and aggression and more generally. The research community can do relatively little about the first two. However, we believe that the research community can more effectively present the research findings.

One major step would be to realize that the conservative scientist role and the public educator role are two very different roles with different norms. When the U.S. Senate, CNN, *The New York Times,* or the *London Daily Observer* asks researchers whether they believe that exposure to violent media causes an increase in aggression, they are not asking for the overly conservative, self-defensive kind of answer that is appropriate when discussing their latest research projects at an APA convention. They are asking for their opinions, based on their knowledge of the research literature and their general knowledge of their scientific fields. For instance, in recent testimony before the U.S. Senate Committee on Commerce. Science, and Transportation, Craig A. Anderson testified that there is now a sufficient empirical database to state that exposure to violent video games can cause increases in aggression (C.A. Anderson, 2000). This assessment was based on a thorough review of the video game literature, our own recent research on this topic (C.A. Anderson & Bushman, in press), knowledge of the vast TV and movie violence literature, and knowledge about the key psychological processes at work in the media violence phenomenon. This is not to say that scientists should abandon all caution and deliver outlandish, quotable statements. For instance, we also testified that although there are good reasons to expect that the negative effects of exposure to violent video games will be larger than the comparable TV violence effects, there currently was not sufficient research evidence to claim this effect had been demonstrated as a fact. (Of course, many newspaper and Web-based accounts misreported what was actually said.)

One way to decide the proper response for the public education role might be for scientists to ask themselves what sort of actions they are taking in their personal lives relevant to the issue being considered. For instance, in deciding whether to state that they believe that playing violent video games can cause increases in aggression, scientists might ask whether they allow (or would allow) their children to play such violent games. If their answer is "no," and if that answer is based on their knowledge of the research literature, then the proper answer to the question, "Can playing violent video games cause increases in aggression?" would be some version of "Yes, on the basis of the research in the TV literature as well as the video game literature, I believe that exposure to violent video games can cause increases in aggression and that this effect is serious enough to lead me to prevent my own children from playing such games." Admittedly, this is not a great sound bite, but it is appropriate. Additional caveats may be appropriate, of course, but in our view, it would not be appropriate to hide behind the conservative scientist role and deny a belief in the causal role of media violence.

Another major step that researchers can take is to realize that the role of disseminating insights gained from their research *is* a part of their job, along with restructuring evaluation systems so that they explicitly include a public education component. For the typical faculty member at a research university, this suggests that departments need to add a public-education-efforts dimension to the annual performance evaluations (it could be part of the research service or teaching components).

A third step—public education efforts by relevant professional associations—is already being taken to some extent. Both APA and the American Psychological Society have made such efforts. For example, APA's Science Advocacy Training Workshops bring in a group of researchers who are experts on a particular topic, create a forum in which to discuss some of the issues involving the future of research on this topic, and arrange meetings with appropriate congressional staff. A recent report revealed that one such workshop group succeeded in getting language incorporated into a house committee report accompanying the Veterans Administration–Department of Housing and Urban Development bill "urging the NSF (National Science Foundation) to increase efforts to fund research on the impact of emerging media on children's cognitive, social and emotional development" (Kobar, 2000, p. 6).

We believe that more efforts along this line can be made. For instance, when a major news source such as *Newsweek* magazine misrepresents the current state of psychological science knowledge, one or more of the relevant professional associations could take an active role in countering that misrepresentation, perhaps by issuing a press release.

Finally, scientists must be willing to pay some of the unavoidable costs, both monetary and personal, associated with educating the public. Some of the monetary costs can be defrayed by relevant organizations: For example, APA generously picked up some of the travel costs for some of the participants in the Senate hearings mentioned earlier. However, other costs, such as time or having to deal with hate mail, are costs that individual researchers may simply have to pay on their own. We believe that the benefit to society of more effectively communicating to a broad general audience the knowledge gained from psychological research is worth the cost. We also hope that the research presented in this article helps to correct the continuing public misrepresentation of what is known about the effects of exposure to media violence on aggressive behavior.

NOTES

1. The correlation coefficient measures the magnitude of (linear) relation between two variables. The value of a correlation coefficient can range from -1 (a perfect negative correlation) to +1 (a perfect positive correlation), with 0 indicating no correlation between the two variables. In research, however, virtually no correlations are perfect. According to Cohen (1988), a *small* correlation is $\pm .1$, a *medium* correlation is $\pm .3$, and a *large* correlation is $\pm .5$, respectively. According to Cohen, most of the correlations in the social sciences are small-to-medium in size. The correlation coefficient can be calculated between two continuous measures, such as number of hours of violent TV watched per week and teacher ratings of aggressiveness, as well as between one dichotomous and one continuous measure, such as in experiments wherein children are randomly assigned to watch either a violent or a nonviolent TV show (dichotomous variable) followed by a free-play period in which the number of times the child hits another child is recorded (continuous variable). If the correlation is between two continuous variables, it is called the Pearson product-moment correlation coefficient; if it is between a continuous and dichotomous variable, it is called a point-biserial correlation.

2. The same pattern of results occurred when, instead of using these ratings as a continuous measure, we used the percentage of articles stating that viewing violence causes an increase in aggression or the percentage that implied that parents should discourage their children from consuming violent media.

3. In true experiments, the experimenter manipulates the treatment (i.e., violent versus nonviolent or no media exposure) and research participants are randomly assigned to different levels of the treatment. Random assignment reduces the likelihood of any potential confounds, thus allowing much stronger causal statements to be made about the results.

4. There are at least three possible explanations for the relatively large effects in experimental studies. First, experimental studies are more effective at controlling extraneous variables than are nonexperimental studies. Second, the violent media is generally more concentrated in experimental studies than in nonexperimental studies. Third, the time between exposure to violent media and measurement of aggression is generally shorter in experimental studies than in nonexperimental studies. In sum, regardless of preference for experimental or nonexperimental methods, it has been decades since one could reasonably claim that there is little reason for concern about media violence effects.

5. For ease of interpretation, Figures 4, 5, 6, and 7 show correlation coefficients. The analyses, however, are based on Fisher's z scores. Each Fisher's z score was weighted by the inverse of its variance (i.e., n -3). These procedures and the rationale for using them are described in Wang and Bushman (1999).

REFERENCES

Abelson, R. P. (1985). A variance explanation paradox: When a little is a lot. *Psychological Bulletin, 97*, 129–133.

Anderson, C. A. (2000). *Violent video games increase aggression and violence.* [Testimony at the U. S. Senate Committee on Commerce. Science, and Transportation hearing on "The Impact of Interactive Violence on Children"]. Retrieved April 9, 2001, from the World Wide Web: http://www.senate.gove/~brownback/00032land.pdf

Anderson, C. A., & Bushman, B. J. (in press). Effects of violent video games on aggressive behavior, aggressive cognition, aggressive affect, physiological arousal, and prosocial behavior: A meta-analytic review of the scientific literature. *Psychological Science.*

Anderson, K. (1993, July 12). The great TV violence hype. *Time, 142*(2), 66–67.

Aristotle. (1970). *Poetics* (G. F. Else, Trans.). Ann Arbor: University of Michigan Press.

Auletta, K. (1993, May 17). What won't they do? Hollywood decision-makers discuss the social impact of the big screen and the small screen—and where the entertainment industry's responsibilities end. *New Yorker, 69,* 45–53.

Buchman, D. D., & Funk, J. B. (1996). Video and computer games in the '90s: Children's time commitment and game preference. *Children Today, 24,* 12–16.

Bushman, B. J. (1995). Moderating role of trait aggressiveness in the effects of violent media on aggression. *Journal of Personality and Social Psychology, 69,* 950–960.

Bushman, B. J., & Huesmann, L. R. (2001). Effects of televised violence on aggression. In D. Singer & J. Singer (Eds.), *Handbook of children and the media* (pp. 223–254). Thousand Oaks, CA: Sage.

Cantor, J. (2000, August). *Media violence and children's emotions: Beyond the "smoking gun."* Paper presented at the annual convention of the American Psychological Association, Washington, DC. Retrieved November 3, 2000, from the World Wide Web: http://www.joannecantor.com/EMOTIONS2_sgl.htm

Centerwall, B. S. (1989). Exposure to television as a risk factor for violence. *American Journal of Epidemiology, 129,* 643–652.

Centerwall, B. S. (1992). Television and violence: The scale of the problem and where to go from here. *Journal of the American Medical Association, 267,* 3059–3063.

Cohen, J. (1988). *Statistical power analysis for the behavioral sciences* (2nd ed.). Hillsdale, NJ: Erlbaum.

Comstock, G. A., & Scharrer, E. (1999). *Television: What's on, who's watching, and what it means.* San Diego, CA: Academic Press.

Cooper, H. (1989). *Homework.* New York: Longman.

Edison, T. A. (Producer), & Porter, E. S. (Writer/Director). (1903). *The great train robbery* [Motion picture]. United States: Edison Manufacturing.

Eggerton, J. (1994, January 31). Hundt hits television violence. *Broadcasting and Cable, 124*(5), 10–12.

Federal Trade Commission, (2000). *Marketing violent entertainment to children: A review of self-regulations and industry practices in the motion picture, music recording, & electronic game industries—Appendix B.* Washington DC: Author.

Feshbach, S., & Price, J. (1984). Cognitive competencies and aggressive behavior: A developmental study. *Aggressive Behavior, 10,* 185–200.

Fighting violence. (1968, December 27). *Time, 92,* 58–59.

Fiore, M. C., Smith, S. S., Jorenby, D. E., & Baker, T. B. (1994). The effectiveness of the nicotine patch for smoking cessation. *Journal of the American Medical Association, 271,* 1940–1947.

Grillo, M. (Producer), Kasdan, L. (Producer/Cowriter/Director), & Okun, C. (Producer). (1991). *Grand Canyon* [Motion picture]. United States: 20th Century Fox.

Hamilton, J. T. (1998). *Channeling violence: The economic market for violent television programming.* Princeton, NJ: Princeton University Press.

Hearold, S. (1986). A synthesis of 1043 effects of television on social behavior. In G. Comstock (Ed.), *Public communication and behavior* (Vol 1., pp. 65–133). New York: Academic Press.

Hill, D., White, V., Jolley, D., & Mapperson, K. (1988). Self examination of the breasts: Is it beneficial? Meta-analysis of studies investigating breast self examination and extent of disease in patients with breast cancer. *British Medical Journal, 297,* 271–275.

Hogben, M. (1998). Factors moderating the effect of television aggression on viewer behavior. *Communication Research, 25,* 220–247.

Huesmann, L. R., Moise, J., Podolski, C. P., & Eron, L. D. (2000). *Longitudinal relations between childhood exposure to media violence and adult aggression and violence: 1977–1992.* Manuscript submitted for publication.

Huston, A. C., Donnerstein, E., Fairchild, H., Feshbach, N. D., Katz, P. A., Murray, J. P., Rubinstein, E. A., Wilcox, B. L., & Zuckerman, E. (1992). *Big world, small screen: The role of television in American Society.* Lincoln: University of Nebraska Press.

International Society for Research on Aggression. (2001). Editor's note. *Bulletin of the International Society for Research on Aggression, 23,* 5–6.

Joint statement on the impact of entertainment violence on children: Congressional Public Health Summit. (2000, July 26). Retrieved December 4, 2000. from the World Wide Web: http://www.senate.gov/brownback/violence1.pdf

Jordan, D. L., & Page, B. I. (1992). Shaping foreign policy opinions: The role of TV news. *Journal of Conflict Resolution, 36,* 227–241.

Kaiser Family Foundation. (1999, November). *Kids and media at the new millennium.* Menlo Park, CA: Author.

Kobar, P. C. (2000). Policy news you can use: A federal funding update for NSF and NIH. *Psychological Science Agenda, 13*(4), 6.

Lau, J., Schmid, C. H., & Chalmers, T.C. (1995). Cumulative meta-analysis of clinical trials builds evidence for exemplary medical care. *Journal of Clinical Epidemiology, 48,* 45–57.

Leland, J. (1995, December 11). Violence, reel to real. *Newsweek,* 46–48.

Mackenzie, C. (1940, June 23). Movies and the child: The debate rages on. *New York Times Magazine,* 9–10.

McCombs, M. E., & Shaw, D. (1991). The agenda-setting function of mass media. In D. Protess & M. McCombs (Eds.). *Agenda setting: Readings on media, public, opinion, and policymaking* (pp. 17–26). Hillsdale, NJ: Erlbaum.

Meved, M. (1995, October). Hollywood's 3 big lies. *Reader's Digest, 147*(882), 155–159.

Moore, J. W. (1993, December 18). Lights! Camera! It's gun control time. *National Journal,* 3007.

Myers, D. G. (1999). *Social psychology* (6th ed.). Boston: McGraw-Hill.

National Institute of Mental Health. (1982). *Television and behavior: Ten years of scientific progress and implications for the eighties (Vol. I): Summary report.* Washington, DC: U.S. Government Printing Office.

National television violence study (Vol. 1). (1996). Thousand Oaks, CA: Sage

National television violence study (Vol. 2). (1997). Studio City, CA: Mediascope.

National television violence study (Vol. 3). (1998). Santa Barbara: Center for Communication and Social Policy, University of California.

Needleman, H. L., & Gatsonis, C. A. (1990). Low-level lead exposure and the IQ of children. *Journal of the American Medical Association, 263,* 673–678.

Nielsen Media Research. (1998). *Galaxy explorer.* New York: Author.

Oliver, M. B. (1994). Portrayals of crime, race, and aggression in "reality-based" police shows: A content analysis. *Journal of Broadcasting and Electronic Media, 38,* 179–192.

Page, B., & Shapiro, R. (1989). Educating and manipulating the public. In M. Margolis & G. Mauser (Eds.), *Manipulating public opinion: Essays on public opinion as a dependent variable* (pp. 294–320). Pacific Grove, CA: Brooks/Cole.

Paik, H., & Comstock, G. (1994). The effects of television violence on antisocial behavior: A meta-analysis. *Communication Research, 21,* 516–546.

Provenzo, E. F. (1991). *Video kids: Making sense of Nintendo.* Cambridge, MA: Harvard University Press.

Rhodes, R. (2000, September 17). Hollow claims about fantasy violence. *The New York Times,* Sect. 4. p. 19.

Rogers, E., & Dearing, J. (1988). Agenda-setting research: Where has it been, where is it going? In J. A. Anderson (Ed.). *Communication yearbook* (Vol. 11, pp. 555–594). Newbury Park, CA: Sage.

Rosenthal, R. (1990). How are we doing in soft psychology? *American Psychologist, 43,* 775–777.

See no evil? (1954, November 10). *Scholastic, 7–8.*

Smith, A. H., Handley, M. A., & Wood, R. (1990). Epidemiological evidence indicates asbestos causes laryngeal cancer. *Journal of Occupational Medicine, 32,* 499–507.

Stern, C. (1995, January 30). Syndicators say Clinton off base on violence. *Broadcasting and Cable, 125*(5), 28–30.

Strange, J., & Leung, C. C. (1999). How anecdotal accounts in news and in fiction can influence judgments of a social problem's urgency, causes, and cures. *Personality and Social Psychology Bulletin, 25,* 436–449.

Surgeon General's Scientific Advisory Committee on Television and Social Behavior. (1972). *Television and growing up: The impact of televised violence.* Washington, DC: U. S. Government Printing Office.

Turan, K. (1972, June). The new violence in films. *Progressive, 36,* 40–44.

U.S. Department of Health, Education, and Welfare. (1974). *The health consequences of smoking.* Washington, DC: U. S. Government Printing Office.

U.S. Federal Bureau of Investigation. (1951–1999). *Uniform crime reports.* Washington, DC: U. S. Government Printing Office.

Violence bill debated in Washington: Most panelists argued against legislation. (1990, February 5). *Broadcasting, 118*(6), 77–79.

Wang, M. C., & Bushman, B. M. (1999). *Integrating results through meta-analytic review using SAS software.* Cary, NC: SAS Institute.

Weller, S. C. (1993). A meta-analysis of condom effectiveness in reducing sexually transmitted HIV. *Social Science and Medicine, 36,* 1635–1644.

Wells, A. J. (1998). Lung cancer from passive smoking at work. *American Journal of Public Health, 88,* 1025–1029.

Welten, D. C., Kemper, H. C. G., Post, G. B., & van Staveren, W. A. (1995). A meta-analysis of the effect of calcium intake on bone mass in young and middle aged females and males. *Journal of Nutrition, 125,* 2802–2813.

West, W. (1993, July 5). TV's bigwigs are a smash at the Capitol Hill comedy club. *Insight on the News, 9*(27), 40–41.

Wood, W., Wong, F. Y., & Chachere, J. G. (1991). Effects of media violence on viewers' aggression in unconstrained social interaction. *Psychological Bulletin, 109,* 371–383.

Wynder, E. L., & Graham, E. A. (1950). Tobacco smoking as a possible etiological factor in bronchiogenic carcinoma. *Journal of the American Medical Association, 143,* 329–336.

Yokota, F., & Thompson, K. M. (2000, May 24/31). Violence in G-rated animated films. *Journal of the American Medical Association, 283,* 2716–2720.

Zimring, F. E., & Hawkins, G. (1997). *Crime is not the problem: Lethal violence in America.* New York: Oxford University Press.

Brad J. Bushman and Craig A. Anderson, Department of Psychology, Iowa State University.

We thank Colleen Phillips for help with searching for news reports and scientific studies. We thank Kelly Golson, David Kufner, and Colleen Phillips for rating the news reports. We thank Angelica Bonacci, Nick Carnagey, and Colleen Phillips for coding the scientific studies.

Correspondence concerning this article should be addressed to Brad J. Bushman, Department of Psychology, Iowa State University, Ames, IA 50011-3180. Electronic mail may be sent to bushman@iastate.edu.

From *American Psychologist,* June/July 2001, pp. 477-489. © 2001 by The American Psychological Association. Reprinted by permission.

The Whipping Boy

The hidden conflicts underlying the campaign against violent TV

By Jib Fowles

Although television violence has never been shown to cause hostile behavior, its sinister reputation lives on. This is because the issue masks a variety of other struggles. Many of these conflicts are suppressed because they may pose a threat to social order or are considered unseemly topics for public discussion. Hence, we hear only the polite versions of the conflicts between races, genders, and generations, although these struggles roil national life. Because they are denied full expression, such conflicts are transferred into other debates, including and perhaps especially the issue of television violence.

Television violence is a whipping boy, a stand-in for other clashes, real or imagined. As one astute observer put it a few years back during a previous cycle of panic, "The debate about children and media violence is really a debate about other things, many of which have very little to do with the media."

There are several reasons why television violence has become such an exemplary whipping boy. First, it is a large target, present in one form or another in virtually every household in America. Second, if one puts on blinders, there might seem to be some correspondence between the mayhem on the television screen and real-life aggression; both televised entertainment and the real world deal in hostilities. (See sidebar.) Third and most important, television violence attracts no champions; the very idea of defending it seems silly to most people. Even industry representatives rarely get beyond conciliatory statements when they are compelled to address the matter. In one survey, 78 percent of entertainment industry executives expressed concern about the content of the action dramas they helped produce. In 1993 Ted Turner,

perhaps the most conspicuous industry leader at the time, said in congressional testimony that television was "the single most important factor causing violence in America." The object of derision simply stands still and takes all the abuse that can be heaped on it.

What are the real conflicts that are being displaced? Most entail the stronger overwhelming the weaker, but in some conflicts the weaker retaliate through moral exertion. Here is a brief examination of the most important conflicts.

High vs. Low

The attack on television violence is, at least in part, an attack by the upper classes and their partisans on popular culture. In this interpretation, which has been broached repeatedly for a quarter-century, the push to reform television is simply the latest manifestation of the struggle between the high and the low, the dominant and the dominated.

The United States is often regarded as a virtually classless society. Indeed, the overwhelming majority of Americans identify themselves as members of a "middle" class. Everyday experience, however, points in a different direction. Americans constantly make class judgments about one another. They quickly note outward appearances and speech patterns. When necessary, one person learns about the other's occupation and education, where he lives and what car he drives, and locates that person socially. Notions of class rank notoriously crop up in courtship and marriage. Characters in films and television programs radiate class information about themselves to audience members who know precisely how to read such clues.

Perhaps the preeminent living theorist and researcher into matters of class and culture is Pierre Bourdieu. He is best known for his work on the segmentation of society according to preferences in aesthetic taste (for instance, going or not going to art museums). At the center of Bourdieu's work is the concept of *habitus*, an idea similar to that of the English word, *habit*. Habitus is the system of predispositions ingrained in a particular group or social class. It manifests itself in similar thoughts, behaviors, expressions, and leisure pursuits. The shared habitus unites and defines the social entity. Habitus, however, does not shackle individuals; in Bourdieu's scheme, there is ample room for idiosyncratic action.

Another concept special to Bourdieu is *capital*, approximately equivalent to social power. In addition to conventional economic wealth, there are several other kinds of capital in Bourdieu's system. Cultural capital (preferences gained primarily through education), symbolic capital (prestige and honors), and social capital (whom one knows) work together with financial capital to define a person's location in the overall social structure. Social action then becomes a function of class habitus and personal capitals. A final term from Bourdieu's work is *reproduction*, which is the manner by which social classes reproduce themselves and, in doing so, preserve status differences. For Bourdieu, the reproduction of habitus is the key work of a social class.

Although Bourdieu does not discuss television in his magisterial work, *Distinctions* (1984), it does not take much imagination to extend his analysis. He writes in his opening pages that taste (cultural capital) functions as a marker of social class; therefore, different preferences (such as watching television violence or not) can be used to situate a person hierarchically. According to this system, an attack on the most popular medium, on television and especially its violent content, would also be an attack by the dominant class on the habitus of the dominated. To reconfirm social distinctions and maintain exclusivity, members of the dominant class need only profess an opposition to television violence. (Ironically, Bourdieu, mustering all the trappings of a French intellectual, himself attacked television in a series of lectures published in English in 1998, calling the medium "a threat to political life and to democracy itself.")

In the derisive vocabulary of this dominant class, violent content is delivered via the "mass media." This term is used so much that it seems unremarkable, but repetition has concealed its derogatory nature. Programming is not received by an undifferentiated horde; it is received by individuals. In fact, there is no mass, there are no masses. As the cultural critic Raymond Williams wrote in 1958, "The masses are always the others, whom we don't know, and can't know.... Masses are other people. There are in fact no masses; there are only ways of seeing people as masses." When dominant Americans chastise the non-existent phenomena of the "masses" and their "mass medium" of television, with its evil content, what they are really endeavoring is to disparage and suppress the culture of dominated Americans.

The class nature of this conflict is evident in the string of congressional hearings that have addressed television violence. Consider the five such congressional hearings held between 1988 and 1995. Of the 36 non-industry witnesses who testified against television violence, only seven were women. None was black or Hispanic. The 29 white males were identified as presidents, professors, directors, representatives, senators, senior scientists, and other distinguished titles that suggested they were well advanced in their careers. It is this patrician sector of society that for reasons of its own leads the attack on rowdy television violence.

The means by which one enters into society's dominant segment, and in doing so learns to affect reproachful views on television violence, is the academy. The general veneration that greets the academy is a sign of its near-sacred station and of the importance of its role in, as Bourdieu would view it, the reproduction of the dominant class and its habitus. Although the rewards of academics are middling in terms of financial capital, the cultural capital they accrue cannot be surpassed. To have a college degree—only about one-quarter of American adults do—is to have the credential of the dominant; not to have a college degree is to remain forever among the dominated.

Academics strive to regard television with condescension or an affected indifference. "A studied, conspicuous ignorance about television," communication professor Ellen Seiter wrote in 1996, "is a mark of distinction (like all distinctions, it is valued because it is so difficult to maintain)." Professors' general attitude toward television become more pointed when the topic of television violence is discussed; they are quick to assert piously that television is dangerously violent. Among college communication teachers, two-thirds of a 1991 sample of 486 instructors agreed that television "increased aggressive behavior." Of 68 scholars who had published papers or reports specifically on television's effects, 80 percent concurred that television violence produced aggressiveness.

Professors researching television's effects, therefore, seem to occupy a doubly honored position. Not only are they, like their colleagues, performing the crucial service of reproducing the dominant classes, but they also are breathing life into a key issue in the struggle between the dominant and the dominated. They may devote their entire careers to demonstrating the dangers of television violence and are bound to receive approbation from the dominant class as a result. No wonder the position of television effects researcher has proven so attractive.

Yet when a given skirmish over violence has exhausted itself and a lull sets in, members of the dominant class revert to their un-self-conscious viewing of televised mayhem. Even college professors watch TV. During one

Missing Link
The bum rap against TV violence

If there were a causal connection between watching symbolic televised scrapes and the menacing aggression lurking in the real world, then this relationship would surely be reflected in national crime trends.

One could expect that, as television violence proliferated, rates of violent crime would also increase. It does appear that television violence has been slowly growing in volume and intensity since 1950. Even if the networks have been televising fewer bloodbaths in recent years, as some observers claim, there is still more violence available overall because of the expanding number of channels. Moreover, each annual contribution to the mountain of violent offerings may well have had a cumulative effect. We should logically expect a steady increase in national violent crime data during the television era. Conversely, a drop in violent crime rates would cast doubt on any linkage between television violence and antisocial behavior.

Striking testimony to the TV violence-crime wave connection has been offered by psychiatrist Brandon Centerwall. In a 1989 paper, Centerwall examined the increasing incidence of homicide in the United States during th 1960s and early '70s, noting that the trend paralleled the diffusion of television sets approximately 15 years earlier. He then argued that the earlier development caused the latter, with the time lag allowing for indoctrination of the young into the ways of video slaughter and then the years for them to mature into killers. As he wrote in a 1992 paper published in *The Journal of the American Medical Association*, "The introduction of television in the 1950s caused a subsequent doubling of the homicide rate, i.e., is a causal factor behind approximately one half of the homicides committed in the United States." Centerwall cited similar trends for television-ridden Canada and the lack of such high crime rates in South Africa, which had no television until 1975.

But Centerwall's intriguing data are more readily explained in terms of a factor he chooses to slight: the unanticipated surge in births between 1947 and 1964 (peaking in 1957) known as the baby boom. Murders are disproportionately the handiwork of young males, and throngs of them were maturing in the 1970s, producing unusually high homicide rates. It was

shrewd of Centerwall to select Canada as his other test case because Canada and the United States were among the very few countries to experience a postwar bulge in birth rates. South Africa, with its low pre-1975 murder rates, did lack television, but more significantly it lacked a baby boom.

When America's violent crime statistics are extended beyond Centerwall's cutoff date of 1975 and beyond the dates of his publications, the weakness of his causal argument becomes clear. Violent crime in the 1980s remained high, but as the baby boom cohort members aged past their 30th birthdays in the 1990s crime began to decline. FBI statistics show that from 1991 onward the violent crime rates have decreased each year. Moreover, rates for property crimes have been decreasing since 1980. Thus, as more entertainment violence has become available on television, crime rates in the United States have been decreasing.

In any case, television is not a schoolhouse for criminal behavior because, as a rule, televised amusement is not a very good teacher. Viewers turn to entertainment for relief, not instruction. They usually want to get material out of their minds rather than put things into them.

It's not difficult to demonstrate the medium's uninstructive nature. Studies have looked for—but failed to find—evidence that TV watching influences viewers' attitudes or behavior in a range of areas. In terms of violence, for example, there is no demonstrable statistical relationship between a viewer's favorite aggressive television hero—the one with whom the viewer is most likely to identify—and any imitated attitudes or behaviors, according to research by British researchers Dennis Howitt and Guy Cumberbatch. And as university of Toronto psychologist Jonathan Freedman recently told REASON, both the number of published studies purporting to link TV viewing to aggressive behavior and their highly arguable conclusions are routinely exaggerated. (See "Phantom Studies," Citings, December 2000)

As liberal media critic Todd Gitlin has written, "Violence on the screens, however loathsome, does not make a significant contribution to violence on the streets. Images don't spill blood."

—Jib Fowles

lull in the violence debate, a 1982 study found that media professors did not restrict their children's viewing any more than the rest of the population did.

Us vs. Them

Perhaps the most striking conflict concealed in the debate over television violence involves the fabrication and control of "the Other." The best-known treatment of the concept of the Other is Edward Said's *Orientalism* (1978). The Orient, argued Said, was one of Europe's "deepest and most recurring images of the Other." It was "almost a European invention" that served as "a Western style for dominating, restructuring, and having authority over the Orient." Superiority over the Other was one motive for this phenomenon; another was self-definition. "The Orient," Said wrote, "has helped to define Europe (or the West) as its contrasting image, idea, personality, experience."

Thus the Other, the "not-us," is a fabrication used both to regulate those classified as the Other and to distinguish the culture of those doing the classifying. It is also a mechanism for emphasizing differences and disregarding similarities in order to maintain group solidarity. The Other differs conceptually from the mass in that the mass can be a part of "us," even if a discredited part, whereas the Other remains outside.

In the United States, the Other is often primarily a Dark Other—blacks and, to a lesser extent, Hispanics. The Dark Other is the recipient of an undeniable assault that plays out in racially charged terms. One form of the assault on the Dark Other is the War on Drugs. This "war" promotes definitions of legal and illegal drugs that have favored whites at the expense of the Dark Other; alcohol and prescription tranquilizers (both of whose records of extensive abuse and human damage are well documented) enjoy legal protection, whereas drugs associated with black culture, such as marijuana and cocaine (the health effects of which, on examination of the data, appear to be negligible), are proscribed. Of course, there is nothing inherent in these drugs that allocates them to the legal or illegal categories. These allocations are socially determined.

The anti–television violence crusades are part of this same assault. People do not worry about their own viewing of violent shows, and in fact they are so at peace with it that they are less likely to acknowledge the violence at all. They worry extensively, however, about what the Dark Other is watching. As British media scholar David Buckingham noted in 1997, "Debates about the negative effects of the media are almost always debates about other people."

"People like us" project a scenario onto the Dark Other in which viewing entertainment violence leads to real-life criminal behavior. This scenario is false in every detail—there exists no uniform Dark Other, and symbolic violence does not produce aggression—but it is upheld due to the emotional conviction behind it and the handy availability of rationalizing "scientific proof." Fears of the Dark Other—fears of difference, of being preyed on, of having one's culture overturned, of invalidating one's identity—are denied expression elsewhere but are allowed to sneak into the attack on television violence. In this way, the Dark Other, his culture, his viewing habits, and his behaviors are disparaged.

There is a curious twist to all this, however—a complexity revealing much about the intricacies of social life. Whereas whites push off the Dark Other with vigor, at the same time they subtly beckon him back. Cultural theorists Peter Stallybrass and Allon White observe that whatever is excluded and displaced to the Other then becomes an object of fascination and is summoned back. The desire for cultural homogeneity produces instead a heterogeneous mix. Thus whites are fascinated by the music, dance, clothing styles, and behavior of blacks. Whites study black athletes, seeking to learn about the prowess of the Other. Whites welcome black entertainers, even when (or especially when) black actors are involved in violent scenarios.

Old vs. Young

Adults who enlist in the anti-television crusade always insist that it is "impressionable youths" whom they wish to protect. In the guise of shielding youths, however, adults are trying to contain and control them.

This generational conflict emerges in contemporary polls: A 1997 survey by Steve Farkas and Jean Johnson of 2,000 randomly selected American adults found them ill disposed toward both younger children and adolescents. The majority of respondents used harsh terms to characterize 5-to-12-year olds, such as "lacking discipline," "rude," and "spoiled." Two-thirds of the respondents were very critical of teenagers, calling them "irresponsible" and "wild." According to the report, "Most Americans look at today's teenagers with misgiving and trepidation, viewing them as undisciplined, disrespectful, and unfriendly." Six hundred teenagers were also surveyed, however; they viewed things differently. Most felt happy in their lives and in their relationships with adults. These discrepant attitudes indicate much about the essential nature of generational strife—of who deprecates whom.

Antagonism toward the young can be especially strong in an adult population configured like that of the United States—one that is aging rapidly due to the baby boom phenomenon. As subculture researcher Dick Hebdige observes, in the consciousness of adult society, "Youth is present only when its presence is a problem, or is regarded as a problem." Overall, adults feel threatened by the next generation.

Social scientist Charles Acland has argued that "youth's complex relationship with popular culture as a lived and expressive domain is menacing because the uses of culture cannot be policed completely." With adults able only partially to supervise the "menace" of popular culture, children and adolescents turn to their television shows, their movies, their computer games, and their music as an escape from adult restraint. Passing through a difficult stage in life, indeed perhaps the most strenuous one of all, youths turn to television violence for the vicarious release it can offer.

The consumption of symbolic violent content correlates negatively with age. According to a 1993 study commissioned by the Times Mirror Center for People and the Press, age is the single most significant factor in the viewing of television violence: Younger viewers watch much more than do older viewers. Cultural critic James Twitchell suggests that "if you study the eager consumers of vulgarities, you will soon see that this audience is characterized not so much by class (as we tend to assume, due in part to Marxist interpretations of the culture industry) as by maturity."

Youths do not think it probable that there could be any transfer from television's violence to aggression in the real world; of all age groups, they are the least likely to believe there is a connection. Elizabeth Kolbert, a *New York Times* reporter, interviewed three teenage felons on the subject in 1994 and noted, "The three teenagers… all scoffed at the notion that what young people see on the screen bore any relation to the crimes they committed."

Weaker vs. Stronger

There are at least two cases where the anti-television crusade allows a weaker group to mount an attack against a stronger target. The first relates to the struggle between masculinity and femininity. As the male expresses dominion and the female resists it, everything in culture becomes gendered, or has reference to gender. This pervasive rivalry would be expected to find its way into the anti-television campaign as another camouflaged conflict between the dominant and the dominated, but in this instance the thrust is completely reversed. That is, when the struggle between genders enters into the debate over television violence, it does so as an act of resistance by the female against the male—as a small counterstrike.

The power of males is most pointedly realized in the violence some of them direct toward women. Alert to the chance of male animosity, women are prone to feeling wary of violence even in its flattened, symbolic form on the television screen. The figment may draw too close to the real thing, whether experienced or imagined, to permit the degree of unimpeded pleasure that male viewers might enjoy. In surveys females are more likely than males to report there is "too much violence in television entertainment" and have been so since the general question was first asked in 1972. When queried about the amount of violence on specific action programs, women viewers will perceive more of it than will men, presumably because of their awareness of and uneasiness about the vicious content.

The recurring moral crusade against television violence affords women a choice opportunity for retribution. Seemingly untainted by any overt hostility on its own part, the movement to purify televised entertainment, one that all agree is to be rhetorical only, seems to be shielded from any possibility of retaliatory strikes. How much contention against males is bound up in the 1994 assertion of Barbara Hattemer, president of the National Family Foundation, that "as media violence is absorbed into a person's thoughts, it activates related aggressive ideas and emotions that eventually lead to aggressive behavior"? How much gender strife is exposed in the hyperbolic 1996 statement of Carole Lieberman, chairperson of the National Coalition Against Television, that "more lives are damaged or destroyed by the effects of on-screen violence than by any other medical problem"? She has forgotten heart disease, cancer, and other maladies, and she has done so for a particular reason.

The second case of a counterstrike against a stronger group involves religion. Many of the groups organized in opposition to television violence have religious ties. Here, neither the contestants nor their motives are camouflaged. The partisans on the attacking side are explicit and vociferous; they stand for religiosity, conservative beliefs, and "family values," and they are against licentiousness, media excesses, and symbolic violence. Those under attack—the entertainment industries and, by extension, all sorts of permissive people—respond first with incomprehension and then with annoyance, wishing the conservative and fundamentalist contingent would disappear. It would be easy for the political left to ignore the religious right if the latter did not comprise a well-defined and adamant voting bloc.

This cultural axis could hardly be more different from class antagonism. Social classes are stacked from bottom to top. Here, the axis and its poles can be understood as horizontal, stretching from the most conservative to the most free-thinking. Those gathered at the conservative and evangelical pole come from a wide range of social strata, although they are frequently depicted by their opponents as occupying lower-status positions exclusively. Seeking certainty in the literal word of the Bible, often believing in creationism and patriarchal traditions, and adhering to longstanding customs and attitudes, those clustered at this pole are often moved to take issue with the novelties of social transitions and the uncertainties of modern life.

Fundamentalists rail against the expanding, heaving tableau of television violence, and in organized fashion they strike out against it. The American Family Association (AFA), headed by the Rev. Donald Wildmon, has objected strenuously to video carnage. In 1993 Randall

Murphree, editor of the association's *AFA Journal*, wrote: "Violence on the small screen continues to invade America's homes as television offers more graphic murders, bloodier assaults, and general mayhem. And all the while, the dramatic effects on society grow more and more alarming." In 1997 the AFA announced that, by its count, violent incidents in prime time network programs had increased 31 percent from the previous year—an increase far in excess of those measured by other monitors. As an example of the AFA's activities, in August 1997 its "Action Alert" roused its members to contact CBS and "express your concerns about their dangerous agenda of expanding the limits of violence on television through [the cop drama] *Brooklyn South*."

The issue of television violence affords groups such as the AFA the sanctioned opportunity to carry out a cultural attack—to have at their opponents, to condemn immoral depictions and the entertainment industry that produces and distributes them. Doing so, fundamentalism affirms its presence to others through an issue that is allowed to capture media attention and affirms its role to itself as a guardian of traditional mores. Television violence allows conservative forces the opportunity to carry their standard forward.

As religious conservatives react negatively to social changes of greater and lesser profundity, they may be performing an important service for American civilization. American culture is venturing into areas rarely if ever visited before, and never on such a large scale (for example, in matters of widespread individuality or of social inclusiveness). Some sort of conservative movement may prove useful, much like a sea anchor during turbulence, for steadying the vessel of culture.

The Big Lie

The widely held belief that television fantasy violence stimulates aggression in the real world and should be censured is what propaganda experts might call "a big lie"—a grotesque fabrication to which all unreflectingly subscribe. What makes this particular big lie different from the propagandists' is that it is not bestowed on an acquiescent population by some cabal; rather, this is one that we all repeatedly tell one another, duping ourselves as we dupe others. We do this for reasons of convenience: By repeating this uncontroverted big lie with ever-increasing volume, we can easily vent some of our own hostilities regarding other, truly confounding social conflicts. While censure is generally directed by the stronger party toward the weaker, in some instances it flows in the opposite direction. Within the gender wars, and in the in-

vectives of the religious right, condemnations are directed by weaker parties toward stronger targets. But whether the chastising energy flows from the stronger toward the weaker or from the weaker toward the stronger has nothing to do with the actualities of television violence.

Whatever its immediate source, the energy that breathes life into the whipping boy of television violence has its ultimate origins in fear—fear of disorder that, in the extreme, could overturn society. As Charles Acland has written, "A society is always concerned with normalization, with the organization of its order, to assure the continuation of its structures and distribution of power." Although social order is a perpetual preoccupation, at this point in history it would seem to be an obsessive one; witness the outsized emphasis on the containment of crime at a time when crime is on the decline and the reckless hysteria of the War on Drugs. Sociologist Graham Murdock refers to the "fear about the precarious balance between anarchy and order in the modern age." Exactly why this fearful fixation on social order should be occurring now is open to question. Its existence, however, should not be doubted. Indeed, the need to strengthen social controls has a correlate in Americans' increasing imposition of self-controls: Per capita alcohol consumption and cigarette smoking have been on the decline and health club memberships on the rise for most of the past 30 years.

Television is new enough that it is not embraced without reservations, and it has not yet accumulated the social equity that would allow it to be shielded by nostalgia. In addition to its relative novelty, it is enormous, filling up the day (television viewing trails only work and sleep in terms of expended time), and can be menacing on this count. Because everyone has access to television, its use cannot be regulated, and thus for those who want to control it, the medium is believed to be out of control and threatening. The rise of television, observes media scholar Richard Sparks, "has been taken to signify the drift of history beyond willed control or direction. The censure of television bears witness to the fear of the future."

General apprehension about the course of history is in several senses the opposite of video violence—the passivity of fear vs. the frenzy of aggression, the amorphous vs. the detailed, and the actual vs. the symbolic. The two find each other as if magnetized, whereupon the flaying of the whipping boy begins.

Jib Fowles (fowles@cl.uh.edu) is a professor of communication at the University of Houston-Clear Lake. This article is adapted from his book The Case For Television Violence *(Sage Publications).*

Crime Scenes
Why cop shows are eternal.

by Lee Siegel

HE IS THERE, DAVID CARUSO, WEEK after week, with his red hair and narrow eyes and bitter irony, aided by the other *CSI: Crime Scene Investigation* officers, picking up the pieces of incredible violence and following them back, like Hansel in the asphalt jungle—though he follows computerized simulations of entry wounds, not pieces of bread—to the deformative trauma that shattered a life; and there is Jerry Orbach, a nice Jewish actor playing a nice Italian cop, as Lenny in *Law & Order,* who hates the scumbags with matter-of-fact irony and feels for the helpless unlucky guys driven beyond the law to defend themselves; and there is Vic in *The Shield,* brutal, good-hearted, and corrupt, way behind *CSI* in technology, and way beyond *Law & Order* in psychology. And there are a lot of other guys, and also a few women, running around the tube with a badge and a gun. The proverbial complaint that there's never a cop around when you need one may or may not be true, but there's always a cop show around, whether you want it or not.

Here is a sample of the police dramas currently on television, both new shows and old: *CSI, Without a Trace, Law & Order, 24, The Shield,* a new *Dragnet, The Division, Fastlane, Cops, The Sentinel, Streets of San Francisco, True Crime, Boomtown, The Wire, NYPD Blue, Hawaii Five-O, Columbo, Miami Vice, U.S. Marshals, Hill Street Blues, Forever Knight.* At any moment on American television, someone is either committing a crime or getting arrested, shooting or getting shot, chasing or being chased. There is even a show called *Animal Cops,* which—alas—is not about animals empowered by the

CSI: CRIME SCENE
INVESTIGATION
(CBS)

DRAGNET
(ABC)

LAW & ORDER
(NBC)

NYPD BLUE
(ABC)

THE SHIELD
(F/X)

WITHOUT A TRACE
(CBS)

state to pursue and apprehend bad animals ("Up against the wall! Spread your legs! Now spread your other legs!"). This particular brainstorm depicts real cops pursuing and apprehending miscreant schnauzers and so forth.

And in the unlikely event that you tire of any of the countless television series about the police, you can flip between cop movies and cop shows—between *Training Day,* in which a good cop battles a corrupt cop, and *The Shield,* in which good cops become bad cops while battling to remain good; or between the wildly successful black-cop and white-cop teams in *Lethal Weapon* and *Die Hard With a Vengeance* (where Samuel L. Jackson isn't a cop but acts like one) and the current incarnation of *Law & Order,* whose writers have given Lenny a new black partner. The configurations are the same; only the names have been changed to protect against the hypercritical. On the big screen and the small, cops enthrall us the way gods and demigods captured the imaginations of the ancient Greeks and Romans.

Like the demigods of mythological yore, like Achilles with his divinely wrought shield, cops on television—they also have shields—occupy a hybrid, liminal realm. They are half ordinary citizens constrained by laws, customs, and convention, and half divinities, free to exert their will, to thwart someone else's, to punish and to kill, to set matters straight: that is, they are glamorously unconstrained by laws, customs, and conventions. When you sit for an hour in a traffic jam and fantasize about taking the motorcycle away from the guy ahead of you and tearing straight up between the lanes, you are fantasizing about being a cop.

OF COURSE, ALL THE SUBLIMINAL energy packed into the figure of the cop has a strong symbolic dimension. The dramatic, untrammeled doings of television cops appeal to the American self, with its daydream of a dramatic, untrammeled existence: television cops represent the fantastic consummation of the American promise of radical individualism. They seem simultaneously to have their way and to possess the power to keep other people from achieving theirs. The power offered by a plastic card with a big line of credit is half like the power represented by a badge.

The cop who goes too far in battling his conventional or dumb or corrupt superiors, who themselves have gone too far; or who passes beyond legal boundaries fighting a conventional or dumb or corrupt system that has exceeded all legal boundaries; or who slugs it out with bad guys just as unconstrained by law, custom, or convention as he is; or who wrestles with his own demons; or who finds himself lost and ineffectual in that realm where unthinking exercise of the will can alienate the object of desire (the realm of romantic love)—it is not too grandiose to say that the image of the American cop embodies the perpetual American dilemma: how far can individual freedom go before one person's freedom becomes another person's crisis?

That conundrum has a long history. In American pop culture, there was always the good outsider sheriff squaring off against the bad insider sheriff—Wyatt Earp; Gary Cooper in *High Noon*—or the good stranger vanquishing the established authorities that had become villainous, as in Shane (which means "beautiful" in Yiddish—did its Jewish writer do that on purpose?). But though the good outsiders and strangers often had complex natures—like Shane himself, whose noble motives were entangled with his desire for the wife of another good man—they usually remained incontestably good. Film noir, with its morally ambiguous heroes, only occasionally influenced the cinematic image of the Western lawman.

Matters were even more clear cut on television, where after World War II the Western kept bad guys and good guys as distinct from one another as the city was from the suburbs. During the postwar exodus out from the urban centers, morally reassuring Westerns such as *Gunsmoke* and *Bonanza,* meant to be watched by the whole family, catered to the suburban imagination just as all those morally unsettling postwar film noirs, meant to be watched alone in a dark theater, appealed to the urban imagination. The cop shows of the time were even more black and white, as if these police series were as comforting as the sight of their black-and-white patrol cars. Shows such as the old *Dragnet* and *Adam-12* portrayed law-enforcement fig-

ures unobstructed by complex natures or dubious superiors. A comedy police show would be inconceivable now, but back then you had series like *Car 54, Where Are You?*—on cable you can still catch the reruns, which seem like prehistoric cave paintings—and *Mayberry RFD,* humorous cop shows featuring bumbling policemen akin to *West Side Story's* Officer Krupke. Even the serious police dramas of the time, viewed now, seem to have a comic spirit animating their simple divisions between good and bad.

WE HAVE ALL HEARD ABOUT HOW the Vietnam War, and the 1960s, and the race riots, and Watergate, changed popular culture; how they made the movies, and the television, and the songs, and the musicals, more cynical, more ambiguous, more "real" about buried motives and hidden conduct. Indeed, the chief cause of reality television is that in our commercial society people have cynically come to associate artistic pretense with entrepreneurial misrepresentation; and as popular art has absorbed this skepticism of pretense and become more ironic about itself, people have come to suspect any strain of sincerity in actual life. Cop shows belatedly reflected the social and cultural movement toward "the real." In the early 1990s, *NYPD Blue* revolutionized television cops by dramatizing their inner lives and depicting cops torn by anger, and alcoholism, and lust, and infidelity. Though these figures remained for the most part on the right side of the law, they enacted private transgressions that were at the heart of the public crimes they were dedicated to investigating.

It might seem that with this riveting and beautifully done series television cops had become more like real cops, more like actual life. Yet since most people's perception of the police is the simple one of men and women who really are there to serve and to protect, the cardboard cops of *Adam-12* and the old *Dragnet* are closer to real life than *NYPD Blue's* dramatic, exciting, conflicted cops. Even for the black or Hispanic kid who is being brutalized by a cop, the hackneyed simplicity of the good cop gone bad is obviously more real than the romantic image of authority figures tormented by the burden of their jobs. Justin Volpe, the cop now serving time for torturing Abner Louima, is Joe Friday turned on its head.

So rather than bringing the viewer closer to actual cops, with their (to the or-

dinary citizen) obscure and unknowable inner lives, *NYPD Blue* ended up making these half-divine figures of authority—the authority to interrupt a life, or the authority to take a life—transparent and comprehensible. The show simultaneously demystified them and made them unreal. It glamorized sordidness rather than exposing it. And it made the revelation of psychological forces into just another type of information. With its portrayal of cops who are just as screwed up as the rest of us, but who, like the rest of us, still get up in the morning and do their jobs, *NYPD Blue* made mysterious quasidivinities rationally apprehendable.

THREE DIFFERENT TYPES OF POLICE shows grew out of *NYPD Blue.* The first is the simple good guy/bad guy police show like the new *Dragnet,* which is really the old *Dragnet* with more vicious crimes; and *Law & Order,* where the inner lives of Lenny (who, we learn, lost his daughter to drugs) and his partner obtrude tastefully on the plots, which are almost always complex and intelligent and wholly absorbing.

The second type is the gritty police series, which goes even further than *NYPD Blue* in portraying cops torn, conflicted, gone rotten, and in extremis. There aren't many of these: *24* has some raw, ambiguous moments, and so does *The Wire,* and so did *The Beat,* which is now defunct. The raw police show par excellence currently on the air is *The Shield,* a series that has remarkably shorn itself of glamour and romanticism. Interestingly, the "reality" police show, *Cops,* which seems to be on cable twenty-four hours a day, is closer to the old simplistic police dramas than to something like *The Shield,* since its policemen always get their culprit, and we never see corrupt or tormented or brutal cops. What the gritty police shows did take from *Cops* is the shaky hand-held camerawork, which is one of the few romantic elements of *The Shield,* and the most down-to-earth feature of *Cops.*

The other, and far more plentiful, species of cop show took from *NYPD Blue* its style of making the cop, suspended between mortal and immortal realms, rationally knowable. For in the end Andy Sipowicz's drinking, and his violence, and his unhappiness, amplified the perception of him as a figure who could enforce his will despite the obstructions to his will. His weaknesses empowered him; the disclosure of his weaknesses empowered the viewer. The more explicit the revelation of what motivated him, the more familiar and predictable he became as a person. And this psychological omniscience of *NYPD Blue*'s scriptwriters seems to have passed into the minds of *CSI*'s and *Without a Trace*'s investigators, who couple their psychological mastery with technological fluency.

WHEN YOU WATCH *CSI* OR *WITHOUT a Trace* you are enjoying the fruits of *NYPD Blue*'s fantasy of omniscience. There is very little violence on any of these shows, which already distinguishes them from a television universe where a series like Oz, set in a prison, has pushed the boundaries of graphic violence about as far as they can go on television. *CSI*'s cops, though they carry highly visible, oversize guns on their hips—as if to compensate for the show's lack of violence—catch their criminals by means of forensics and various kinds of technology. Such violence as there is the show enacts through the *CSI* investigators' graphic computer simulations of knives penetrating skin, tissue, muscle, and bone. It's where Sherlock Holmes meets Popeye Doyle. Not the least of the show's enthrallments is the illusion it offers that by its imagining and then rationalizing the worst, the worst will never happen.

Without a Trace, in which detectives piece together the puzzle of a life in order to find missing persons, is more cerebral and more subdued, and yet the series also has a consoling faith in the ability of its cops to uncover the truth, always accurately, in this case by deciphering the meaning of a pause in conversation, or a shift in someone's glance. *Law & Order* takes a different tack. In its divvying up of the program into police show (first half) and courtroom drama, which includes the categorization of information about the crime (second half), it offers a complete spectacle of the rationalization of the irrational.

While *The Shield* and the other gritty police shows enact the old drama of the American will enmeshed in its paradoxical freedoms, *CSI,* and *Without a Trace,* have submerged that drama in the world of the video game and the Internet, where the technology-created culture of engaged isolation meets the old-time crime drama. *NYPD Blue*'s moral ambiguities have become the hard new scientific certainties. A gritty, morally shadowy drama such as *The Shield* is really a throwback to a soft bygone humanistic complexity.

And the most significant thing about these shows, particularly *CSI,* is that they fuse the crime drama with the medical drama. The body is the most intimate, and potentially the most threatening, dimension of a person's existence, and in *CSI*'s forensic obsession with bodies—you can also flip to the fact-based series *Forensic Files*—viewers can be held rapt and also reassured that no wound, no invasion of the body, is, in the end, fatal.

For though *CSI* is an innovative (as they say) police show, it has also pushed the medical drama into a new phase. The doctors on ER race to save a person's life. The cops on *CSI,* fiber by fiber, semen stain by semen stain, wound by wound, work to capture the perpetrator of the fatal blow, and thus, by finding the agent of the formative wound, they do not save a person's life—they resurrect a person from the dead. In a similar way, the detectives on *Without a Trace* redeem a person from the ranks of the missing. As American society goes, so goes the American crime drama. If ever there was a show that expressed our solitary, computer-riveted sense of being there but not being there, of being mysteriously injured or depressed yet feeling healthy and optimistic, of being helpless to influence events but feeling strangely that we are powerful enough to do so, it is these raw, entertaining, gripping, utterly delusive fantasies of transparency and control.

LEE SIEGEL is TNR's television critic.

We're Not Losing the Culture Wars Anymore

Brian C. Anderson

The Left's near monopoly over the institutions of opinion and information—which long allowed liberal opinion makers to sweep aside ideas and beliefs they disagreed with, as if they were beneath argument—is skidding to a startlingly swift halt. The transformation has gone far beyond the rise of conservative talk radio, that, ever since Rush Limbaugh's debut 15 years ago, has chipped away at the power of the *New York Times*, the networks, and the rest of the elite media to set the terms of the nation's political and cultural debate. Almost overnight, three huge changes in communications have injected conservative ideas right into the heart of that debate. Though commentators have noted each of these changes separately, they haven't sufficiently grasped how, taken together, they add up to a revolution: no longer can the Left keep conservative views out of the mainstream or dismiss them with bromide instead of argument. Everything has changed.

The first and most visible of these three seismic events: the advent of cable TV, especially Rupert Murdoch's Fox News Channel. Since its 1996 launch, Fox News has provided what its visionary CEO Roger Ailes calls a "haven" for viewers fed up with the liberal bias of the news media—potentially a massive audience, since the mainstream media stand well to the American people's left.

Watch Fox for just a few hours and you encounter a conservative presence unlike anything on TV. Where CBS and CNN would lead a news item about an impending execution with a candlelight vigil of death-penalty protesters, for instance, at Fox "it is *de rigueur* that we put in the lead why that person is being executed," senior vice president for news John Moody noted a while back. Fox viewers will see Republican politicians and conservative pundits sought out for meaningful quotations, skepticism voiced about environmentalist doomsaying, religion treated with respect, pro-life views given airtime—and much else they'd never find on other networks.

Fox's conservatism helps it scoop competitors on stories they get wrong or miss entirely because of liberal bias. In April 2002, for instance, the mainstream media rushed to report an Israeli "massacre" of Palestinian civilians in a refugee camp in the West Bank city of Jenin; Fox uniquely—and correctly, it turned out—treated the massacre charge with complete skepticism. "We try to avoid falling for the conventional liberal wisdom in journalistic circles—in this case the conventional wisdom 'Israeli bad, Palestinian good,'" says daytime anchorman David Asman. "Too often ideology shapes the tendency to jump to a conclusion—something we try to be aware of in our own case, too."

Nowhere does Fox differ more radically from the mainstream television and press than in its robustly pro-U.S. coverage of the War on Terror. After September 11, the American flag appeared everywhere, from the lapels of the anchormen to the corner of the screen. Ailes himself wrote to President Bush, urging him to strike back hard against al-Qaida. On-air personalities and reporters freely referred to "our" troops instead of "U.S. forces," and Islamist "terrorists" and "evildoers" instead of "militants." Such open displays of patriotism are anathema to today's liberal journalists, who see "taking sides" as a betrayal of journalistic objectivity.

Asman demurs. For the free media to take sides against an enemy bent on eradicating the free society itself, he argues, isn't unfair or culturally biased; it is the only possible logical and moral stance. And to call bin Ladin a "militant," as Reuters does, is to betray the truth, not uphold it. "Terrorism is terrorism," Asman says crisply. "We know what it is, and we know how to define it, just as our viewers know what it is. So we're not going to play with them: when we see an act of terror, we're going to call it terror." On television news, anyway, Fox alone seemed to grasp this essential point from September 11 on. Says Asman: "CNN, MSNBC, the media generally were not declarative enough in calling a spade a spade."

Fox's very tone conveys its difference from the networks' worldview. "Fox News lacks the sense of out-of-touch elitism that makes many Americans, whatever their politics, annoyed with the news media," maintains media critic Gene Veith. "Fox reporters almost never condescend to viewers," he observes. "The other networks do so all the time, peering down on the vulgar masses from social height (think Peter Jennings) or deigning to enlighten the public about things that only they understand (think Peter Arnett)." This tone doesn't mark only Fox's populist shows, like pugnacious superstar Bill O'Reilly's. Even when Fox goes upscale, in Brit Hume's urbane nightly *Special Report*, for example, the civility elevates rather than belittles the viewer. For Ailes, Fox's anti-elitism is key. "There's a whole country that elitists will never acknowledge," he told the *New York Times Magazine*. "What people resent deeply out there are those in the 'blue' states thinking they're smarter."

The "fair and balanced" approach that Fox trumpets in its slogan is part of this iconoclastic tone, too. Sure, the anchor is almost always a conservative, but it's clear he is striving to tell the truth, and there's always a liberal on hand, too. By contrast, political consultant and Fox contributor Dick Morris notes, "The other networks offer just one point of view, which they claim is objective." Not only does the Fox approach make clear that there is always more than one point of view, but it also puts the network's liberal guests in the position of having to defend their views—something that almost never happens on other networks.

Viewers clearly like what they see. Fox's ratings, already climbing since the station debuted in 1996, really began to rocket upward after the terrorist attack and blasted into orbit with Operation Iraqi Freedom. "In the Iraqi war," Dick Morris explains, "the viewing audience truly saw how incredibly biased the other networks were: 'Turkey did not let us through, the plan was flawed, we attacked with too few troops, our supply lines weren't secure, the army would run out of rations and ammo, the Iraqis would use poison gas, the oil wells would go up in flames, there would be street-to-street fighting in Baghdad, the museum lost its priceless artifacts to looters,' and now we're onto this new theme that 'Iraq is a quagmire' and that there 'aren't any weapons of mass destruction' and that 'Bush lied'—and all the while, thanks in part to Fox News, Americans are seeing with their own eyes how much this is crazy spin." The yawning gulf separating reality and the mainstream media during the war and its aftermath, Morris believes, "will kill the other networks in the immediate future—to Fox's benefit."

The numbers make clear just how stunning Fox's rise has been. Starting with access to only 17 million homes (compared with CNN's 70 million) in 1996, Fox could reach 65 million homes by 2001 and had already started to turn a profit. A year later, profits hit $70 million and are expected to double in 2003. Though CNN founder Ted Turner once boasted he'd "squish Murdoch like a bug," Fox News has outpaced its chief cable news rival in the ratings since September 11 and now runs laps around it. This past June, Fox won a whopping 51 percent of the prime-time cable news audience—more than CNN, CNN Headline News, and MSNBC *combined*. The station's

powerhouse, *The O'Reilly Factor*, averages around 3 million viewers every night, and during Operation Iraqi Freedom the "No Spin Zone" drew as many as 7 million on a given night; CNN's Larry King, once the king of cable, has slipped to 1.3 million nightly viewers. Cheery *Fox and Friends* has even edged out CBS's *Early Show* in the ratings a few times, despite the fact that CBS is free, while Fox is available only on cable and satellite (and not every operator carries it). While the total viewership for ABC, CBS, and NBC news—more than 25 million—still dwarfs Fox's viewers, the networks are hemorrhaging. CBS News just suffered its lousiest ratings period ever, down 600,000 viewers; 1.1 million fewer people watch the three network news programs today than 12 months ago.

Fox enjoys especially high numbers among advertiser-coveted 25- to 54-year-old viewers, and it is attracting even younger news junkies. As one CNN producer admits, Fox is "more in touch with the younger age group, not just the 25–54 demo, but probably the 18-year-olds." Even more attractive to advertisers, Fox viewers watch 20 to 25 minutes before clicking away; CNN watchers stay only ten minutes. Fox's typical viewer also makes more money on average—nearly $60,000 a year—than those of its main cable rivals.

Not only conservatives like what they see. A new Pew Research Center survey shows that, of the 22 percent of Americans who now get most of their news from Fox (compared with a combined 32 percent for the networks), only 46 percent call themselves "conservative," only slightly higher than the 40 percent of CNN fans who do so. Fox is thus exposing many centrists (32 percent of Fox's regular viewers) and liberals (18 percent) to conservative ideas and opinions they would not regularly find elsewhere in the television news—and some of those folks could be liking the conservative worldview as well as the professionalism of the staff and veracity of the programming.

The news isn't the only place on cable where conservatives will feel at home. Lots of cable comedy, while not traditionally conservative, is fiercely anti-liberal, which as a practical matter often amounts nearly to the same thing. Take *South Park*, Comedy Central's hit cartoon series, whose heroes are four crudely animated and impossibly foul-mouthed fourth-graders named Cartman, Kenny, Kyle, and Stan. Now in its seventh season, *South Park*, with nearly 3 million viewers per episode, is Comedy Central's highest-rated program.

Many conservatives have attacked South Park for its exuberant vulgarity, calling it "twisted," "vile trash," a "threat to our youth." Such denunciations are misguided. Conservative critics should pay closer attention to what *South Park* so irreverently jeers at and mocks. As the show's co-creator, 32-year-old Matt Stone, sums it up: "I hate conservatives, but I really fucking hate liberals."

Not for nothing has blogger and former *New Republic* editor Andrew Sullivan praised the show for being "the best antidote to PC culture we have." *South Park* sharpens the iconoclastic, anti-PC edge of earlier cartoon shows like *The Simpsons* and *King of the Hill*, and spares no sensitivity. The show's single black kid is called Token. One episode, "Cripple Fight," concludes with a slugfest between the boys' wheelchair-bound, cerebral-palsy-stricken friend Timmy and the obnoxious Jimmy, who wants to be South Park's Number One "handi-capable" citizen (in his cringe-making PC locution). In another, "Rainforest Schmainforest," the boys' school sends them on a field trip to Costa Rica, led by an activist choir group, "Getting Gay with Kids," which wants to raise youth awareness about "our vanishing rain forests." Shown San José, Costa Rica's capital, the boys are unimpressed:

Cartman [holding his nose]: Oh my God, it smells like ass out here!

Choir teacher: All right, that does it! Eric Cartman, you respect other cultures this instant.

Cartman: I wasn't saying anything about their culture, I was just saying their city smells like ass.

But if the city is unpleasant, the rain forest itself is a nightmare: the boys get lost, wilt from the infernal heat, face deadly assaults from monstrous insects and a giant snake, run afoul of revolutionary *banditos*, and—worst of all—must endure the choir teacher's New-Agey gushing: "Shhh! Children! Let's try to listen to what the rain forest tells us, and if we use our ears, she can tell us so many things." By the horrifying trip's end, the boys are desperate for civilization, and the choir teacher herself has come to despise the rain forest she once worshiped: "You go right ahead and plow down this whole fuckin' thing," she tells a construction worker.

The episode concludes with the choir's new song:

> *Doo doo doo doo doo. Doo doo doo wa.*
> *There's a place called the rain forest that truly sucks ass.*
> *Let's knock it all down and get rid of it fast. You say*
> *"save the rain forest" but what do you know?*
> *You've never been there before.*
> *Getting Gay with Kids is here*
> *To tell you things you might not like to hear.*
> *You only fight these causes 'cause caring sells.*
> *All you activists can go fuck yourselves.*

As the disclaimer before each episode states, the show is so offensive "it should not be viewed by anyone."

One of the contemporary Left's most extreme (and, to conservatives, objectionable) strategies is its effort to draw the mantle of civil liberties over behavior once deemed criminal, pathological, or immoral, as a brilliant *South Park* episode featuring a visit to town by the North American Man-Boy Love Association—the ultra-radical activist group advocating gay sex with minors—satirizes:

NAMBLA leader [speaking at a group meeting, attended by the *South Park* kids]: Rights? Does anybody know their rights? You see, I've learned something today. Our forefathers came to this country because they believed in an idea. An idea called "freedom." They

wanted to live in a place where a group couldn't be prosecuted for their beliefs. Where a person can live the way he chooses to live. You see us as being perverted because we're different from you. People are afraid of us, because they don't understand. And sometimes it's easier to persecute than to understand.

Kyle: Dude. You have sex with children.

NAMBLA leader: We are human. Most of us didn't even choose to be attracted to young boys. We were born that way. We can't help the way we are, and if you all can't understand that, well, then, I guess you'll just have to put us away.

Kyle [slowly, for emphasis]: Dude. You have sex. With children.

Stan: Yeah. You know, we believe in equality for everybody, and tolerance, and all that gay stuff, but dude, fuck you.

Another episode—"Cherokee Hair Tampons"—ridicules multiculti sentimentality about holistic medicine and the "wisdom" of native cultures. Kyle suffers a potentially fatal kidney disorder, and his clueless parents try to cure it with "natural" Native American methods, leaving their son vomiting violently and approaching death's door:

Kyle's mom: Everything is going to be fine, Stan; we're bringing in Kyle tomorrow to see the Native Americans personally.

Stan: Isn't it possible that these Indians don't know what they're talking about?

Stan's mom: You watch your mouth, Stanley. The Native Americans were raped of their land and resources by white people like us.

Stan: And that has something to do with their medicines because . . . ?

Stan's mom: Enough, Stanley!

South Park regularly mocks left-wing celebrities who feel entitled to pontificate on how the nation should be run. In one of the most brutal parodies, made in just several days during the 2000 Florida recount fiasco, loudmouth Rosie O'Donnell sweeps into town to weigh in on a kindergarten election dispute involving her nephew. The boys' teacher dresses her down: "People like you preach tolerance and open-mindedness all the time, but when it comes to middle America, you think we're all evil and stupid country yokels who need your political enlightenment. Just because you're on TV doesn't mean you know crap about the government."

South Park has satirized the sixties counterculture (Cartman has feverish nightmares about hippies, who "want to save the earth, but all they do is smoke pot and smell bad"); anti-big-business zealots (a "Harbucks" coffee chain opens in South Park, to initial resistance but eventual acclaim as everyone—including the local coffee house's owners—admits its bean beats anything previously on offer in the town); sex ed in school (featuring "the Sexual Harassment Panda," an outrageous classroom mascot); pro-choice extremists (Cartman's mother decides she wants to abort him, despite the fact that he's eight years old, relying on the "it's my body" argument); hate-crime legislation, anti-discrimination lawsuits, gay scout leaders, and much more. Conservatives do not escape the show's satirical sword—gun-toting rednecks and phony patriots have been among those slashed. But there should be no mistaking the deepest thrust of *South Park*'s politics.

That anti-liberal worldview dominates other cable comedy too. Also on Comedy Central is *Tough Crowd with Colin Quinn*, a new late-night chatfest where the conversation—on race, terrorism, war, and other topics—is anything but politically correct. The Brooklyn-born Quinn, a former anchor on *Saturday Night Live*'s "Weekend Update" and a Fox News fan, can be Rumsfeldesque in his comic riffs, like this one deriding excessive worries about avoiding civilian casualties in Iraq: "This war is so polite," he grumbles. "We used to be *Semper Fi*. Next, we'll be dropping comment cards over Iraq saying 'How did you hear about us?' And 'Would you say that we're a country that goes to war sometimes, often, or never?'"

Then there's Dennis Miller, another *Saturday Night Live* alum, whose 2003 HBO stand-up comedy special *The Raw Feed* relentlessly derides liberal shibboleths. In his stream-of-consciousness rants, whose cumulative effect gets audiences roaring with laughter, Miller blasts the teachers' unions for opposing vouchers, complains about the sluggish work habits of government workers ("ironically, in our highly driven culture, it would appear the only people *not* interested in pushing the envelope are postal employees"), and attacks opponents of Alaskan oil-drilling for "playing the species card."

Miller, like Quinn, is unapologetically hawkish in the War on Terror. Dismissing the effectiveness of U.N. weapons inspectors in the run-up to the Iraq war, he says: "Watching the U.N. in action makes you want to give Ritalin to a glacier." On war opponents France and Germany, he's acid: "The French are always reticent to surrender to the wishes of their friends and always more than willing to surrender to the wishes of their enemies" and "Maybe Germany didn't want to get involved in this war because it wasn't on a grand enough scale." Lately, he's been campaigning with President Bush, crediting W. for making him "proud to be an American again" after the "wocka-wocka porn guitar of the Clinton administration." Fox has hired him to do weekly news commentary.

Why is cable and satellite TV less uniformly *Whoopi* or *West Wing* than ABC, CBS, and NBC? With long-pent-up market demand for entertainment that isn't knee-jerk liberal in its sensibilities, cable's multiplicity of channels has given writers and producers who don't fit the elite media mold the chance to meet that demand profitably.

Andrew Sullivan dubs the fans of all this cable-nurtured satire "South Park Republicans"—people who "believe we need a hard-ass foreign policy and are extremely skeptical of political correctness" but also are socially liberal on many issues, Sullivan explains. Such South Park Republicanism is a real trend among younger Americans, he observes: *South Park*'s typical viewer, for instance, is an advertiser-ideal 28.

Talk to right-leaning college students, and it's clear that Sullivan is onto something. Arizona State undergrad Eric Spratling says the definition fits him and his Republican pals perfectly. "The label is really about rejecting the image of conservatives as uptight squares—crusty old men or nerdy kids in blue blazers. We might have long hair, smoke cigarettes, get drunk on weekends, have sex before marriage, watch R-rated movies, cuss like sailors—and also happen to be conservative, or at least libertarian." Recent Stanford grad Craig Albrecht says most of his young Bush-supporter friends "absolutely cherish" *South Park*–style comedy "for its illumination of hypocrisy and stupidity in all spheres of life." It just so happens, he adds, "that most hypocrisy and stupidity take place within the liberal camp."

Further supporting Sullivan's contention, Gavin McInnes, co-founder of Vice—a "punk-rock-capitalist" entertainment corporation that publishes the hipster bible *Vice* magazine, produces CDs and films, runs clothing stores, and claims (plausibly) to have been "deep inside the heads of 18–30s for the past 10 years"—spots "a new trend of young people tired of being lied to for the sake of the 'greater good.'" Especially on military matters, McInnes believes, many twenty-somethings are disgusted with the Left. The knee-jerk Left's days "are numbered," McInnes tells *The American Conservative*. "They are slowly but surely being replaced with a new breed of kid that isn't afraid to embrace conservatism."

Polling data indicate that younger voters are indeed trending rightward—supporting the Iraq war by a wider majority than their elders, viewing school vouchers favorably, and accepting greater restrictions on abortion, such as parental-notification laws (though more accepting of homosexuality than older voters). Together with the Foxification of cable news, this new attitude among the young, reflected in the hippest cable comedy (and in cutting-edge cable dramas such as FX's *The Shield* and HBO's *The Sopranos* and *Six Feet Under*, which are unflinchingly honest about crime, race, sex, and faith, and avoid the saccharine liberal moralizing of much network entertainment), can only make Karl Rove happy.

What should make him positively giddy is the rise of the Internet, the second explosive change shaking liberal media dominance. It's hard to overstate the impact that news and opinion websites like the *Drudge Report*, *NewsMax*, and Dow Jones's *OpinionJournal* are having on politics and culture, as are current-event "blogs"—individual or group web diaries—like *AndrewSullivan*, *InstaPundit*, and "The Corner" department of *NationalReviewOnline* (NRO), where the editors and writers argue, joke around, and call attention to articles elsewhere on the web. This whole universe of web-based discussion has been dubbed the "blogosphere."

While there are several fine left-of-center sites, the blogosphere currently tilts right, albeit idiosyncratically, reflecting the hard-to-pigeonhole politics of some leading bloggers. Like talk radio and Fox News, the right-leaning sites fill a market void. "Many bloggers felt shut out by institutions that have adopted—explicitly or implicitly—a left-wing orthodoxy," says Erin O'Connor, whose blog, *Critical Mass*, exposes campus PC gobbledygook. The orthodox Left's blame-America-first response to September 11 has also helped tilt the blogosphere rightward. "There were damned few noble responses to that cursed day from the 'progressive' part of the political spectrum," avers Los Angeles–based blogger and journalist Matt Welch, "so untold thousands of people just started blogs, in anger," Welch among them. "I was pushed into blogging on September 16, 2001, in direct response to reading five days' worth of outrageous bullshit in the media from people like Noam Chomsky and Robert Jensen."

For a frustrated citizen like Welch, it's easy to get your ideas circulating on the Internet. Start-up costs for a blog are small, printing and mailing costs nonexistent. Few blogs make money, though, since advertisers are leery of the web and no one seems willing to pay to read anything on it.

The Internet's most powerful effect has been to expand vastly the range of opinion—especially conservative opinion—at everyone's fingertips. "The Internet helps break up the traditional cultural gatekeepers' power to determine a) what's important and b) the range of acceptable opinion," says former *Reason* editor and libertarian blogger Virginia Postrel. *InstaPundit*'s Glenn Reynolds, a law professor at the University of Tennessee, agrees: "The main role of the Internet and blogosphere is to call the judgment of elites about what is news into question."

The *Drudge Report* is a perfect case in point. Five years since Matt Drudge broke the Monica Lewinsky story, his news and gossip site has become an essential daily visit for political junkies, journalists, media types, and—with 1.4 *billion* hits in 2002—seemingly anyone with an Internet connection. The site features occasional newsworthy items investigated and written by Drudge, but mostly it's an editorial filter, linking to stories on other small and large news and opinion sites—a filter that crucially exhibits no bias against the Right. (Drudge, a registered Republican, calls himself "a pro-life conservative who doesn't want the government to tax me.") The constantly updated cornucopia of information, culled from a vast number of global sources and e-mailed tips from across the political spectrum, says critic Camille Paglia, a *Drudge* enthusiast, point up by contrast "the process of censorship that's going on, the filtering of the news by established news organizations." Other popular news-filter sites, including *FreeRepublic, Lucianne,* and *RealClearPolitics,* perform a similar function.

In a different register, *Arts & Letters Daily,* a site devoted to intellectual journalism, is similarly ecumenical in what it links to, posting articles from publications as diverse as *City Journal* on the Right to the *New Left Review.* When *Arts & Letters* ran into financial trouble last year, both neo-conservative elder Norman Podhoretz and *Na-*

tion columnist Eric Alterman rushed to its defense. Going from 300 page views a day in 1998 to more than 70,000 a day in 2003, and with many left-leaning readers (including a large number of academics), it has introduced a whole new audience to serious conservative thought.

Though not quite in *Drudge*'s league in readership, the top explicitly right-leaning sites, updated daily, have generated huge followings. Andrew Sullivan's blog, launched in the late 90s, attracted 400,000 visitors this July. *FrontPage*, vigorously lambasting political correctness, the antiwar campaign, and other "progressive" follies, draws as many as 1.7 million visitors in a month. More than 1.4 million visitors landed on *OpinionJournal* this past March, when the liberation of Iraq began, most to read editor James Taranto's "Best of the Web Today," an incisive guide to and commentary on the day's top Internet stories. *NRO*, featuring scores of new articles daily, averages slightly over 1 million a month—and over 2 million during the war. "More people read *NRO* than all the conservative magazines combined," the site's editor-at-large Jonah Goldberg marvels. The web's interconnectivity—the fact that bloggers and news and opinion sites readily link to one another and comment on one another's postings, forming a kind of twenty-first-century agora—amplifies and extends the influence of any site that catches the heavy hitters' attention.

It's not just the large numbers of readers that these sites attract that is so significant for the conservative cause; it's also *who* those readers are. Just as Fox News is pulling in a younger viewership, who will reshape the politics of the future, so these conservative sites are proving particularly popular with younger readers. "They think: 'If it's not on the web, it doesn't exist,'" says Goldberg. *FrontPage*'s web traffic shoots up dramatically during the school year, as lots of college students log on.

Equally important, these sites draw the attention of journalists. "Everyone who deals in media—and they're not all ideologues on the Left—is reading the Internet all the time," says *FrontPage* editor David Horowitz. "Michael," who co-authors the *2blowhards* culture-and-politics blog as an avocation while working full time for a major left-leaning national news organization (he uses a pseudonym because his bosses wouldn't like the blog's not-so-liberal opinions), reports: "I notice the younger people on staff in particular are aware of blogs—and that a lot of local newspapers seem to have people who stay on top of blogs, too." The Internet's power, observes Mickey Kaus, the former *New Republic* writer whose Kausfiles blog has become indispensable reading for anyone interested in politics, "is due primarily to its influence over professional journalists, who then influence the public." Judges Andrew Sullivan: "I think I have just as much ability to inject an idea or an argument into the national debate through my blog as I did through *The New Republic.*"

Almost daily, stories that originate on the web make their way into print or onto TV or radio. Fox and Rush Limbaugh, for instance, often pick up stories from *FrontPage* and *OpinionJournal*—especially those on the antiwar Left. Fox News's Sean Hannity surfs the net up to eight hours a day, searching sites like *Drudge* and the hard-right news site *WorldNetDaily* for stories to cover. Phrases introduced in the blogosphere now "percolate out into the real world with amazing rapidity," *InstaPundit*'s Glenn Reynolds recently noted. For example, the day after the humor blog *ScrappleFace* coined the term "Axis of Weasel" to satirize the antiwar alliance of Jacques Chirac and Gerhard Schröder, the *New York Post* used it as a headline, talk radio and CNN and Fox News repeated it, and it soon made its way into French and German media.

The speed with which Internet sites can post new material is one source of their influence. No sooner has the latest Paul Krugman *New York Times* column attacking the Bush administration appeared, for example, than the "Krugman Truth Squad"—a collective of conservative economic analysts—will post an article on NRO exposing the economist's myriad mistakes, distortions, and evasions. Earlier this year, the Truth Squad caught Krugman comparing the cost of Bush's tax cuts over *ten* years with the *one*-year wage boost associated with the new employment it would create, so as to make the tax reductions seem insanely large for the small benefit they'd bring—a laughably ignorant mistake or, more likely, a deliberate attempt to mislead in order to discredit Bush. The discomfiture web critics have caused Krugman has forced him to respond on his own website, offering various lame rationales for his errors, and denouncing the Truth Squad's Donald Luskin as his "stalker-in-chief."

The timeliness of web publication also means that right from the start a wealth of conservative opinion is circulating about any new development—often before the *New York Times* and the *Washington Post* get a chance to weigh in. A blog or opinion site "can have an influence on elite opinion before the conventional wisdom among elites congeals," notes Nick Schulz, editor of *Tech Central Station*, a site that covers technology and public policy. A case in point is the blogosphere "storm" (a ferocious burst of online argument, with site linking to site linking to site) that made a big issue out of the Democrats' unseemly transformation of Senator Paul Wellstone's funeral into a naked political rally, forcing the mainstream media to cover the story, which in turn created outrage that ultimately may have cost the Dems Wellstone's seat in the 2002 election. Blogosphere outrage over Republican senator Trent Lott's comments that seemed to praise segregation at onetime Dixiecrat Strom Thurmond's 100th birthday party, led by *NRO* and other conservative sites keen to liberate modern conservatism from any vestige of racism and to make the GOP a champion of black advancement, shaped the mainstream media's coverage of that controversy, too—helping to push Lott from his perch as majority leader.

Debunking liberal humbug is one of the web's most powerful political effects: bloggers call it the Internet's "bullshit-detector" role. The *New York Times* has been the Number One target of the B.S. detectors—especially during the reign of deposed executive editor and liberal ideologue Howell Raines. "Only, say, five years ago, the editors of the *New York Times* had much more power than they have today," Andrew Sullivan points out. "They could spin stories with gentle liberal bias, and only a few eyes would roll." If they made an egregious error, they could bury the correction later. The Internet makes such bias and evasion harder—maybe impossible—to pull off. It was the blogosphere that revealed Enron-bashing Krugman's former ties to Enron, showed how the paper twisted its polls to further a liberal agenda, exposed how it used its front page to place Henry Kissinger falsely in the anti–Iraq war camp, and then, as the war got under way, portrayed it as harshly as possible.

It's safe to say that the blogosphere cost Raines his job. When the story broke about *Times* reporter and Raines favorite Jayson Blair's outrageous fabrications in the paper's pages, Sullivan, Kaus, Drudge, blogger-reporter Seth Mnookin, and other web writers kept it alive, creating pressure for other media, including television, to cover it. When disgruntled *Times* staffers began to leak damning information about Raines's high-handed management style to Jim Romenesko's influential media-news site *Poynter*, the end was near. *Kausfiles*'s "Howell Raines-O-Meter," gauging the probability of the editor's downfall, was up barely a day or two when Raines stepped down. "The outcome would have been different without the Internet," Kaus rightly says. The *Times*'s new ombudsman acknowledged the point: "We're not happy that blogs became the forum for our dirty linen, but somebody had to wash it and it got washed."

But the Blair affair was more final straw than primary cause of Raines's fall. Unremitting Internet-led criticism and mockery of the editor's front-page partisanship had already severely tarnished the *Times*'s reputation. It may take the *Times* a while to restore readers' trust: a new Rasmussen poll shows that fewer than half of Americans believe that the paper reliably conveys the truth (while 72 percent find Fox News reliable); circulation is down 5 percent since March 2002.

Other liberal media giants have taken notice. In May, the *Los Angeles Times*'s top editor, John Carroll, fired an e-mail to his troops warning that the paper was suffering from "the perception and the occasional reality that the *Times* is a liberal, 'politically correct' newspaper." In the new era of heightened web scrutiny, Carroll was arguing, you can't just dismiss conservative views but must take them seriously. By the recent recall vote, though, the lesson had evaporated.

The third big change breaking the liberal media stranglehold is taking place in book publishing. Conservative authors long had trouble getting their books released, with only Regnery Books, the Free Press, and Basic Books regularly releasing conservative titles. But following editorial changes during the 1990s, Basic and the Free Press published far fewer conservative-leaning titles, leaving Regnery pretty much alone.

No more. Nowadays, publishers are falling over themselves to bring conservative books to a mainstream audience. "Between now and December," *Publishers Weekly* wrote in July, "scores of books on conservative topics will be published by houses large and small—the most ever produced in a single season. Already, 2003 has been a banner year for such books, with at least one and often two conservative titles hitting PW's best-seller list each week." Joining Regnery in releasing mass-market right-leaning books are two new imprints from superpower publishers, Random House's Crown Forum and an as-yet-untitled Penguin series.

These imprints will publish mostly Ann Coulter–style polemics—one of Crown Forum's current releases, for example, is James Hirsen's *The Left Coast*, a take-no-prisoners attack on Hollywood liberals. But higher-brow conservative books will pour forth over the next six months from Peter Collier's Encounter Books, Ivan R. Dee (publisher of *City Journal* books), the Intercollegiate Studies Institute (it's releasing Alexander Solzhenitsyn's *Russia in Collapse*, the Nobel Prize–winner's first book in English in nearly a decade), Yale University Press, Lexington Books, and Spence Books. Other top imprints—from HarperCollins to the University of Chicago Press—are also publishing books that flout liberal orthodoxy. And Bookspan, which runs the Book-of-the-Month Club, has announced a new conservative book club, headed by a former *National Review* literary editor.

It's no exaggeration to describe this surge of conservative publishing as a paradigm shift. "It would have been unthinkable ten years ago that mainstream publishers would embrace this trend," acknowledges Doubleday editor and author Adam Bellow, who got his start in editing in 1988 at the Free Press, where he and his boss, the late Erwin Glikes, encountered "a tremendous amount of marketplace and institutional resistance" in pushing conservative titles. "There was no conspiracy," avers Crown Forum publisher Steve Ross. "We were culturally isolated on this island of Manhattan, and people tend to publish to people of like mind."

Ross believes that September 11 shook up the publishing world and made it less reflexively liberal. And in fact, many new conservative titles concern the War on Terror. But what really overcame the big New York publishers' liberal prejudices is the oodles of money Washington-based Regnery was making. "We've had a string of best-sellers that is probably unmatched in publishing," Regnery president Marji Ross points out. "We publish 20 to 25 titles a year, and we've had 16 books on the *New York Times* best-seller list over the last four years—including Bernard Goldberg's *Bias*, which spent seven weeks at Number One." Adds Bernadette Malone, a former Regnery editor heading up Penguin's new conservative imprint: "The success of Regnery's books woke up the industry: 'Hello? There's 50 percent of the population

that we're underserving, even ignoring. We have an opportunity to talk to these people, figure out what interests them, and put out professional-quality books on topics that haven't been sufficiently explored.' " Bellow puts it more bluntly: "Business rationality has trumped ideological aversion. And that's capitalism."

There's another reason that conservative books are selling: the emergence of conservative talk radio, cable TV, and the Internet. This "right-wing media circuit," as *Publishers Weekly* describes it, reaches millions of potential readers and thus makes the traditional gatekeepers of ideas—above all, the *New York Times Book Review* and the *New York Review of Books*, publications that rarely deign to review conservative titles—increasingly irrelevant in winning an audience for a book.

Ask publisher Peter Collier. After only three years in business, his Encounter Books will sell $3 million worth of books this year, he says—not bad for an imprint specializing in serious works of history, culture, and political analysis aimed at both conservatives and open-minded liberals. Several Encounter titles have sold in the 35,000 range, and a Bill Kristol–edited volume laying out reasons for war in Iraq has sold over 60,000 copies. Instead of worrying about high-profile reviews in the media mainstream—"I've had God knows how many books published by now, and maybe three reviews in the *New York Times Book Review*," laughs Collier—Encounter sells books by getting its authors discussed on the Internet and interviewed on talk radio, Fox News, and C-Span's ideologically neutral *Book TV*. "A Q & A on *NRO* sells books very, very well," Collier explains. "It's comparable to a major newspaper review." A bold *Drudge Report* headline will move far more copies than even good newspaper reviews, claims Regnery's Marji Ross. A book discussed on *AndrewSullivan* will briefly blast up the Amazon.com best-seller list—even hitting the top five.

Amazon itself is another boon to conservatives, since the Internet giant betrays no ideological bias in selling books. Nor do big chain booksellers like Wal-Mart and Barnes & Noble, where Bill O'Reilly books pile up right next to Michael Moore's latest loony-left rant. "The rise of Amazon and the chain stores has been tremendously liberating for conservatives, because these stores are very much product-oriented businesses," observes David Horowitz. "The independent bookstores are all controlled by leftists, and they're totalitarians—they will not display conservative books, or if they do, they'll hide them in the back." Says Marji Ross: "We have experienced our books being buried or kept in the back room when a store manager or owner opposed their message." She's a big fan of Amazon and the chains.

Amazon's Reader Reviews feature—where readers can post their opinions on books they've read and rate them—has helped diminish the authority of elite cultural guardians, too, by creating a truly democratic marketplace of ideas. "I don't think there's ever been a similar review medium—a really broad-based consumers' guide for culture," says *2blowhards* blogger Michael. "I've read some stuff on Amazon that's been as good as anything I've read in the real press."

All these remarkable, brand-new transformations have sent the Left reeling. Fox News especially is driving liberals wild. Former vice president Al Gore likens Fox to an evil right-wing "fifth column," and he yearns to set up a left-wing competitor, as if a left-wing media didn't already exist. Comedian and activist Al Franken's new book *Lies and the Lying Liars Who Tell Them* is one long jeremiad against Fox. *Washington Post* media critic Tom Shales calls Fox a "propaganda mill." The Columbia Journalism School's Todd Gitlin worries that Fox "emboldens the right wing to feel justified and confident they can promote their policies." "There's room for conservative talk radio on television," allows CNN anchor Aaron Brown, the very embodiment of the elite journalist with, in Roger Ailes's salty phrase, "a pick up their ass." "But I don't think anyone ought to pretend it's the *New York Times* or CNN," Brown sniffs.

But it's not just Fox: liberals have been pooh-poohing all of these developments. Dennis Miller used to be the hippest joker around. Now, complains a critic in the liberal webzine *Salon*, he's "uncomfortably juvenile," exhibiting "the sort of simplistic, reactionary American stance that gives us a bad reputation around the world." The *Boston Globe*'s Alex Beam dismisses the blogosphere with typical liberal *hauteur*: "Welcome to Blogistan, the Internet-based journalistic medium where no thought goes unpublished, no long-out-of-print book goes unhawked, and no fellow 'blogger,' no matter how outré, goes unpraised." And those right-wing books are a danger to society, grouse liberals: their "bile-spewing" authors "have limited background expertise and a great flair for adding

fuel to hot issues," claims Norman Provizer, a *Rocky Mountain News* columnist. "The harm is if people start thinking these lightweights are providing heavyweight answers."

Well. The fair and balanced observer will hear in such hysterical complaint and angry foot stamping baffled frustration over the loss of a liberal monoculture, which has long protected the Left from debate—and from the realization that its unexamined ideas are sadly threadbare. "The Left has never before had its point of view challenged and its arguments made fun of and shot full of holes on the public stage," concludes social thinker Michael Novak, who has been around long enough to recognize how dramatically things are changing. Hoover Institute fellow Tod Lindberg agrees: "Liberals aren't prepared for real argument," he says. "Elite opinion is no longer univocal. It engages in real argument in real time." *New York Times* columnist David Brooks even sees the Left falling into despair over the new conservative media that have "cohered to form a dazzlingly efficient delivery system that swamps liberal efforts to get their ideas out."

Here's what's likely to happen in the years ahead. Think of the mainstream liberal media as one sphere and the conservative media as another. The liberal sphere, which less than a decade ago was still *the* media, is still much bigger than the non-liberal one. But the non-liberal sphere is expanding, encroaching into the liberal sphere, which is both shrinking and breaking up into much smaller sectarian spheres—one for blacks, one for Hispanics, one for feminists, and so on.

It's hard to imagine that this development won't result in a broader national debate—and a more conservative America.

From *City Journal*, Vol. 3, No. 4, Autumn 2003, pp. 14-30. Copyright © 2003 by the Manhattan Institute, Inc. Reprinted by permission of *City Journal*.

Spirit TV

The Small Screen Takes on Eternity

By Stephen Goode

No longer a "vast wasteland," television has become a window on a spiritual realm.

It's been nearly five decades since Federal Communications Commission Chairman Newton Minow labeled all of television a "vast wasteland." Television's many critics continue to level the same charge, and there's a lot of truth to it. All too often, TV shows have a predictable, lowest-common-denominator quality. Though meant to offend no one and appeal to everyone, they end up being bland and colorless.

But it's also a charge that's only partly right and certainly not very fair. It fails to take account of television's quality programming: Ken Burns' Civil War documentary on PBS, for example, or *CSI: Crime Scene Investigation*, CBS's popular whodunnit series featuring the work of a crack team of forensic scientists.

In fact, there is variety on TV, if you look for it. Some of that variety is surprisingly spiritual, for want of a better word, or at least otherworldly, in ways that most shows are not. It might be dubbed spirit TV, television that affirms the existence of a supernatural realm that we can know only indirectly. It has something to say about how we live our lives and what happens to us after death.

Amid daytime TV's aggressively materialistic game shows and intensely melodramatic soaps, one can find shows like CBS's widely watched *Crossing Over*. With a minimum of fanfare and folderol, its host, medium John Edward, makes contact with the dead loved ones of the people on his show. His admiring audience eats it up.

Late at night, when funnyguy cynics such as Dave Letterman and Jay Leno dominate the airwaves, there are programs like *It's a Miracle*, hosted by the now 50-year-old Richard Thomas. While playing John Boy on the tremendously popular *The Waltons* three decades ago, Thomas acquired the image of an honest, straightforward, and authentic kind of guy that he's really never lost.

It's an image that *It's a Miracle* takes advantage of. Each episode offers three or four segments based on true-life stories in which professional actors portray the characters. (In the Washington, D.C., viewing area, the show runs every weeknight at 11:00 on PAX-TV, the network that describes itself as "Feel Good TV.") Thomas unabashedly asks viewers to regard the stories as miracles, instances where the everyday course of events has been suspended and the divine has made its influence felt in worldly affairs.

Miracle Pets also offers stories based on real-life experiences, but in this case the heroes are animals—dogs large and small, cats, birds, beasts of all sorts—that do extraordinary things. They sometimes save human lives in the most self-sacrificing ways, always show exemplary courage under mind-numbing circumstances, and frequently communicate telepathically with their owners.

Some shows offer fictional accounts of inexplicable events, inspiring viewers to ponder the deep-down complexity of the world and the things that lie beyond our ken. One of them is CBS's *Touched by an Angel*, a series about three angels who intervene in the daily lives of people facing a moral or spiritual crisis. "God loves you," Monica, one of the angels, often tells them. Critics have called *Touched by an Angel* sentimental, even mawkish, but it's also been hard-hitting in ways TV often is not, dealing directly with such controversial subjects as abortion and present-day slavery.

Another fictional show is PAX-TV's *Mysterious Ways*, which takes an entirely different approach. Instead of supernatural beings, it features two human main characters: Declan Dunn, an anthropologist whose speciality is the investigation of events called miracles, and the skeptical psychiatrist Peggy Fowler. In each episode they examine an extraordinary event—a

stained-glass window in a slum neighborhood that weeps tears of blood, for example, or a woman who seems to bring good luck to everyone she touches. Dunn and Fowler then discuss whether it's a miracle or can be explained by science.

One series, *Beyond Belief*, presents segments based on real or made-up occurrences. At the end of program, viewers are asked to decide which ones actually happened. It's a clever though somewhat arbitrary way to suggest that fact is often stranger than fiction. Often, the stories that seem most outlandish are those that did indeed happen.

What's striking is how much all these shows owe to Rod Serling's *The Twilight Zone* and the police drama *Dragnet*, two black-and-white, half-hour television classics. Serling was a stark, lean, and tight writer whose bizarre and circuitous stories ultimately went for the jugular. In *Dragnet*, two laconic detectives caught bad guys; the bare-bones stories had few characters and no fluff at all. Both programs became icons of their times and have since developed cult followings.

The Twilight Zone introduced millions to "a fifth dimension, beyond that which is known to man." For its innumerable fans, nothing since has catered so well to their love of the uncanny, not the revived *Twilight Zone* of the 1980s—nor the one that premiered last fall (2002), whose generally lukewarm reviews called it a pale imitation of the original.

The Twilight Zone helped give TV audiences a taste for the mysterious that they've never lost. What *Dragnet* provided was a need for "just the facts, ma'am," the words spoken each episode by deadpan Sergeant Joe Friday as he tried to calm a hysterical witness. Friday's notion was that once the distress and emotion disappeared, the truth could be had. It's an approach that's favored by programs like *It's a Miracle*, where story lines are slim (too slim, some might say, to make things interesting) and characters sparse. Typically, just enough evidence is planted to convince viewers that something miraculous *might* have happened.

Are most viewers convinced? It's difficult to say. In the introduction to his 2002 book, *It's a Miracle*, a compilation of stories from the series, Thomas explains that the program is popular because "people LOVE good news." It's a claim that few would dispute, but it certainly underplays the life-changing role that miracles—such as the ones Christ performed—have traditionally played in religion. "I hope these stories will lift up our heart and give you faith in humanity," Thomas concludes. Not faith in God, he insists, but faith in humanity, something very different indeed.

In a typical episode from *It's a Miracle*, "Avalanche," two Methodist ministers plan to trek into the wilds of Northern California. On their last day in the wilderness, a Sunday, they take Communion together and begin their way back. It's been snowing hard, however, and one of them gets lost. His friend can't locate him. A rescue team can't, either. Everyone expects the lost man to be dead, but suddenly, five hours or more after his disappearance, he's found—much the worse for wear but alive.

The ministers both regard the event as miraculous. "Science would have had him dead and buried," one comments. "God touched us all in a very special way," says the other. "Well, that's our show," concludes Thomas. "It's our hope that when you need one, you'll find a miracle in your life."

It sounds well-meaning and very glib. As a nonbeliever will likely point out, everything that happened can be explained without bringing God into the equation. What's even more amazing is that the ministers do not mention the name of Jesus Christ, the founder of the faith they profess.

Similar ambiguities abound in another very popular spirit TV show, *Crossing Over*. John Edward, a thoughtful, personable man in his thirties, listens to the voices of those who have "crossed over" and reports their messages to relatives and friends in his audience. (He also offered private sessions until recently, when demands for his services became too large.) Edward—who dresses in dark colors, has dark hair, and looks like Eddie Munster, the kid on TV's *The Munsters* of three decades ago, all grown up—has made it big. *Crossing Over*, which started out on SciFi TV, a cable network, is now a CBS pro-

gram. Aired every weekday in many viewing areas, it runs for a whole hour.

Edward starts out vague. He'll say he has "a male figure coming through, a father figure." Or he'll say that he's hearing from the dead about a "family that's had a cancer scare." These are very general clues, but someone in the audience eventually latches on to what he's saying and decides that one of their loved ones is trying to get in touch. (*Crossing Over* takes several hours to shoot and then is edited down. Edward doesn't always make easy contact, nor are the loved ones being spoken to always identified immediately.)

Edward then zeroes in, offering less general remarks, often in the form of questions, from those crossed over. At times, he gets specific. "there's a pants connection. Did your grandmother wear pants?" he asked on a recent show. It turned out that the grandmother had been a very proper lady, and it was a family joke that she would never have worn pants. Impressively, on the same show, Edward said he was being told that the house the person he was talking to had died in wasn't the one she'd lived in most of her life. It was a statement the loved ones denied, until they remembered that the original house had burned down and been replaced by a new one.

Skeptics are unlikely to be convinced by Edward's claims, however specific or accurate they prove to be. What's truly striking is not their accuracy but how little connection the show has to traditional religion and its views on death.

The voices Edward says he hears don't speak of heaven or hell, the traditional abodes of the departed. If they do not seem distressed by their present situation, neither are they particularly blissful. Their conversation (as delivered by Edward) is matter-of-fact, mostly a means to let their relatives and loved ones know they're okay. That seems to be the ultimate goal of *Crossing Over*. During the show, Edward emphasizes the importance of meditation and prayer to a full life; the implication is that they're a kind of personal therapy, rather than arduous and demanding undertakings that religions of the past have made them out to be.

What do the loved ones get from the experience? The response may be the innocuous: "It was part of the closure I was looking for. As small as it seemed to be, it was huge," or "It's comforting to learn that people cross over and don't die." Though a lot of tears are shed on *Crossing Over*, the program's message is too relentlessly up-

beat to be convincing. It's life (and death) with the hard times absent.

If there's one exception to spirit TV's turning its back on the deeper concerns and teachings of traditional religion, it's *Touched by an Angel*. Not that *Touched* has an identifiable viewpoint. Its main character, the angel Monica, played by actress Roma Downey, speaks with a lovely Irish lilt but is never identified as Roman Catholic. The details of Monica's faith remain obscure.

What sets *Touched by an Angel* apart is its willingness to take up serious—and deeply controversial—ethical issues with an unusual degree of honesty. After September 11, *Touched* had a program about a high-school student coping with the death of a beloved teacher in the attack on the World Trade Center, for example. Another program condemned slavery in the Sudan. These were impressive subjects.

In one courageous episode, *Touched by an Angel* dealt with abortion, perhaps today's most controversial religious and political question. Betsy and Bud Baxter, a moderately successful couple, are about to lose the jobs they've had for decades. Years earlier, Betsy had an abortion because they felt the baby might interfere with their ambitions. Now their lives seem empty, and they regard that early decision as profoundly wrong. Betsy believes that she and Bud have been punished by God for that abortion. Maybe their unhappiness is "the price you pay," she says. But the angel Monica, who in her earthly form has joined Betsy and Bud in their despair, will have none of that. "No," she replies, "it's a consequence of a choice. But it's not a punishment from God. That's not the way He works," she says.

Monica's comments may differ from what the pope or other religious leaders might say to Betsy. Still, *Touched by an Angel* has shown that people can be profoundly disturbed by moral decisions they've made, and that religion can help them come to terms with those choices.

Like television generally, spirit TV often reduces its subjects to generic, jejune forms, leaving the spiritual world looking very thin indeed. But like TV, too, spirit TV can help us see ourselves more honestly, which is one of the things traditional religion does, when we allow it to do its job.

Stephen Goode is senior writer for *Insight* magazine.

THE TRIUMPH OF THE IMAGE

It has always had political power, but this time around, the image may finally trump substance—unless we find a way to make politics real

BY RICHARD C. WALD

Once, on a clear August night in East Berlin in 1961, when the cold war was at its most intense, I watched Soviet tanks rumble down Unter den Linden and turn into the bombed-out shell where the opera used to be. The tanks looked black. In the open hatch of each was a man in a dark, featureless hood. There were no commands. There were no voices in the street, no sounds other than the grinding of tank treads. Nothing gleamed in the moonlight, only the knowledge that behind this single file the Soviets had more tanks, NATO said, than America had troops in Germany. This was the real power behind the nominal East German control of this part of the city. This was the glove taken off. It was an image that radiated menace. For a moment, my *New York Herald Tribune* had a small scoop on what became the confrontation at Checkpoint Charlie, the first time armed Soviet and American tanks had faced each other since they met at the Elbe in friendship in 1945.

Recently, a television report about unsuccessful presidential candidates—in this case, Michael Dukakis, with his head and little round helmet sticking out of a tank—brought to mind that moment in East Berlin. Why was Dukakis comical and not powerful? We have more tanks than anyone in the world and more power than the founders ever dreamed, and he might have been the chief executive. But he looked funny and he lost. He got the image wrong.

The four decades of change since that first image have been fascinating. Then, there was a war against communism, in which the enemy had a defined geography, an articulated philosophy, vocabularies of reason and of power, and enormous resources. It had a face and a home and nuclear weapons. The confrontation fostered unity at home, us against them, at least for a while.

Now, in 2003, we have an amorphous war with a shadowy enemy who is everywhere and nowhere and we may not know for decades if we have won anything. We are together against terrorism, but that is not, in the advertising phrase of the sixties, "togetherness." You can see it in the ups and downs of the polls we take all the time. It's like a fever chart. We approve of the president, we don't approve of the president; we think the economy is on the right track, we don't think the economy is on the right track. Pick a topic—gun control, abortion, Medicare, Social Security, Iraq, Israel—and there are zealots on every side who want to define the world in terms of that one issue and will not listen. This is now our way.

And it goes with the changes in the way we see and hear each other. Consensus is less and voices are more. When the tanks rolled in Berlin the United States had more daily newspapers but fewer networks; no 24-hour radio or cable news; few broadcast commentators (and none promoting an insistent political agenda to a national audience). The Internet did not exist. Mail came and went on pieces of paper. Starting a magazine cost a fortune. There was no desktop publishing, just as there were no desktop computers. When Martin Luther King Jr. spoke in front of the Lincoln Memorial, the country watched the three television networks because they were there *and that's all the television pictures there were*. Then we were a manufacturing nation. Now we are a communicating nation. Or so it is said.

We are in the middle of the greatest explosion of self-expression that the country has known since the literate white male population debated the adoption of the Constitution. Everyone can find a place to speak.

But that comes with a problem. If everybody talks, who listens? The committed listen to each other. The believers find the niche reporting that bolsters belief. The single-issue people have single-issue Web sites and magazines.

There were always single-issue groups. But just think of how quickly the women's suffrage movement might have been able to accomplish its goals if it could have reached into more than two-thirds of the homes in America with an e-mail message, a Web site, blogs, a computer-published magazine, a few talk-show hosts, dedicated radio jocks, and TV coverage of their first march down Broadway. They would have scared the male establishment into fainting fits. Howard Dean moved to the front of the line of Democratic presidential hopefuls, not with TV but by using the Internet as no one has before. Dean bypassed the party, tying together people with a similar interest who would not have gotten his message forty years ago. Creating a constituency is incomparably easier now, and once he forged one, the press followed. Each "special interest" (my cause is the truth, yours is a special interest) has its own power of communication.

Yet each new mailing or magazine takes some of the nation's attention. There are still only twenty-four hours in a day, and just as the cable channels eat away at the hegemony of the broadcast networks, so the niche efforts chip away at mass-circulation media. The declining fortunes of mass media news organizations, in turn, help foster the breakup in consensus.

To pull in a mass audience, mass media tend to take the easy route, using the celebrities of the moment as a kind of totem to say, "This is what we are all interested in." Consider first the spectacular history of newsmagazines on television. *60 Minutes* once specialized in the serious and a lot of beating up on poor fools who did something stupid. Other newsmagazines followed suit. To this day, Wallace, Safer, Stahl, et al. decry the celebrity interview. But what has happened to *60 Minutes* is that the other magazines, to compete, and to compete in tougher time periods, brought on the singers, the murderers, the movie stars of the moment, and got ratings out of them. Everybody wants to see a movie star. So *60 Minutes* has to compete from time to time. There were *always* star interviews. Think back to the sainted Edward R. Murrow and *Person to Person*. But ten magazine hours a week? We would run out of celebrities if we didn't invent them so quickly.

Our time is a little like the Era of Wonderful Nonsense that followed World War I. It wasn't that the nation never had stars before that period; it was that we had never celebrated so many of them so often, so ubiquitously. To this mix, in our time, add the weight of new media, expanded media, cheap media. If you buy the TV set, all it costs is electricity to see the broadcast channels, and 70 percent of the country can afford cable, where a couple of hundred channels jostle for space. Another 10 percent get satellite TV. Each "personal" story gets repeated, recycled, regurgitated a thousand times before it wears out. We have infinitely more microphones and loudspeakers than they had in the twenties. We create the celebrities more quickly, and finish them off more certainly, than they ever could then. There is always a dizzying ride waiting for a Gary Condit, a Laci Peterson, an Elián González, a Kobe Bryant, because we need them to gather an audience.

It is not a tragedy to be interested in ourselves, in celebrity, in the moment. It is merely true and part of the sine curve of our lives. The Era of Wonderful Nonsense eroded with the Depression. Nothing has reached that depth in our time, at least not yet. It almost did, two years ago in New York and Washington, D.C. But all the talk of a more serious nation seems to have gone away. After the fighting in Iraq was declared over, we started to look a lot like we did before it began. We are the children of a cornucopia of plenty—shared poorly, perhaps, but abundant—and we relish our toys and our sensations.

Now we begin a presidential election year with a volume of communication never seen before. It is so large in quantity that it has changed the quality of discourse. There are lots of things reported on, but they are lost in the din of the flavor of the moment repeated endlessly. Any mild statement that is repeated just once—in every newspaper in America, in every Sunday supplement, on every Web site, in every chat room, in every printed magazine, on three all-news cable channels, on innumerable radio stations, on morning TV, local TV, evening TV, TV magazines, TV late-night comedy shows, radio call-in shows, all-news radio and the guy you spoke to at the water cooler—ceases to be a mild statement and becomes a roar.

We all live in this world. It is our culture. We think in its terms. But politicians will have to reach across all the individual outlets that constitute this avalanche of stuff to pull together a constituency and influence national discourse. How will they do it? They will reach for image.

Lesley Stahl tells the wonderful story of a night when she was sure she nailed a candidate with a hard-hitting report while he was on the campaign trail. To her surprise, she got a call from his campaign manager thanking her for the story. She saw smart reporting. He saw a candidate who looked great on TV. He was right.

To signal his role in the war, President Bush used an aircraft carrier and the image of Top Gun. What the banner behind him said may not have been dead on—mission has not been accomplished—but what he looked like was dead on. Senator John Kerry "officially" announced his candidacy in front of an aircraft carrier. He gave a snappy salute to fellow veterans. His record of military service with honor is unusual among the candidates, but all of them will use the imagery of red, white, and blue. The images speak to beliefs carried through generations, beliefs that really are The American Dream. They can mean different things to different people while still being positive signs. They take effort to arrange but need no effort by us to register. The unspoken language of politics is more powerful than any position paper. Arnold Schwarzenegger became an instant contender for governor of California not because he had policy ideas but because he *was* an idea—strength, command, heroism, celebrity.

Images have always been important in politics. Abraham Lincoln's campaign capitalized on the image of the log cabin and the backwoods railsplitter. George Washington cultivated the forms of a fellow citizen and would not take a third term because he thought it sent the wrong image.

Arnold Schwarzengger became an instant contender for governor of California not because he had policy ideas, but because he was an idea

What was different for them, in part, was a longer news cycle.

The address to Congress could register and reverberate. Speaker and audience expected serious attention. If there had been sound bites, they would have been very long. At Gettysburg, the address we think of was Lincoln's. He spoke poetry and ideas for two minutes. The address that made most of the reports was Edward Everett's, the Massachusetts politician and orator who preceded the president. He spoke prose for two hours and it was the entertainment of the day.

Now, speed is greater, context less. A serious person on the platform today must make an impression through a many-faceted press world with no time to spare. How to do it? Reach for a simple, graspable message.

Forty years ago Daniel Boorstin persuasively wrote about manipulated images and celebrities—people who are famous for being famous. Our improvement has been to find derivatives. The Russian tanks on Unter den Linden could have blown peace apart. Michael Dukakis's tank was a derivative of that menace. This is easier to understand than the Wall Street derivatives, but it works on the same principle: somewhere there is a reality. We use a bit of it to try to make our points.

If you doubt the potential power of this, think of the attack on 9/11. Putting the attack and the name of Saddam Hussein in the same sentence over and over again wound up convincing three-quarters of this country that they were causally connected.

All of this—the multiplicity of voices, the increasing volume of news, the limited attention span, the splintering of a mass audience and the attempts to rebuild it via the celebrification of the news—come to bear now in an election season.

Campaigns no longer take place on the stump, although it might look that way in front of well-gathered, well-prepped crowds. The coming well-spun contest will take place in the newspapers, the television screens, the radio reports, the Internet sites and chat rooms, the magazine spreads, the instant books, and insistent phone banks that are the life of a communications society. Lincoln and Douglas are not going to debate. They did that to attract and then persuade the crowds that were the voters. Those crowds now stay home. They watch a televised Q&A session between candidates and some reporters that we call a debate. Once, it was thought that the press was a mirror to reality, to our times. But there are so many outlets now, each with a small bit of the picture, that if they form a mirror it is one of those disco-ball faceted surfaces that reflect the lights well but don't give much of a picture. Politicians actually reach the voters via a million small, second-hand encounters. The audience in the room was tiny, but the real audience watching Bill Clinton in his famous MTV appearance was huge, because it was reported so often in other outlets. He told a lot of people about boxers and briefs. And the message of being in touch with youth, unspoken, was just one of the many little disparate touches that made the whole campaign.

So, how shall the 2004 campaign be reported? There are issues enough at stake. Each one has passionate advocates. But the general press, the mass media, tend to treat the real issues at arm's length, something like the way civics textbooks treat the three branches of government: descriptively, as though they occurred on Mars. It may be that the press has removed itself from the passion of our times. I don't think so. I think the truth is that we are just like everyone else and what interests us is essentially the gossip of the campaign trail. Or it may be that as reporters we are so fascinated by the machinery of politics that we forget the impact of politics.

The odd thing is that we continue to pay alms to the idea of the issues, but the juice in the reporting is about the horse race. We are so afraid of being biased, so wary of the single-issue people, that we withdraw. There are genuine excitements around us. Politics has a real effect on how we live. But we go at it with exactly balanced word counts that nobody pays any attention to, least of all us.

The do-good contingent says we must eschew the horse race and cover the issues. But the press faces an election, too, and it is far more constant than what the politicians face. We have to win a public vote of acceptance almost every day in order to stay viable commercially. And that means pleasing the public. We are caught in a dilemma that was a long time in the making: to win attention, we have sought celebrity and sensation; we won attention but competition raised the celebrity stakes and now we need all its trappings.

But we also need a way to be valuable and important to this democratic system. There is a peculiar arms-race feel to our problem. The politicians want to use our megaphone to slip past us and talk, unmediated, to that audience we have gathered. We want to use our megaphone to bring the entire political process to account. They move into image and sloganeering, and they define how the issues shall be framed and in what order; we thrash around for new ways to cover what they do and regain control of the flow of information.

If we want to come to grips with the way this election will be fought, we need to find a way to counter the image game. It is no longer good enough for a reporter to put in the stuff that tells the truth only to have a campaign manager say thank you for preserving the image. And it is uncomfortable to have *Newsweek* dismiss "the brutish simple-mindedness of the campaign press corps."

Can we use image or metaphor ourselves? Is there an Internet language that will deconstruct the spin to show what is really going on? (If anything is going on; there's always the chance that the candidate has no convictions or ideas.)

What we need now is a discussion about how to meet the world of images and bring it back to reality. When we put on the do-good hat and report on things we consciously think of as "serious," we are stuffy and unreadable; the rest of the time we create, exploit, and then abandon celebrities. We have bought derivatives.

Perhaps as a result, we and the politicians are being marginalized. Circulation is down; the vote is down. There is a hint that the public can do without us. Letterman and Leno are prime dispensers of what's happening in an election. Everyone seeks meaning but it doesn't seem to reside anywhere.

There is no point in exhorting the public to care. This is the only public we have and it will do what it wants. Our task is to point out—with the same persuasive power that images bring— that unreality is a bad thing and cheap manipulation will hurt everyone.

When *The New York Times* went through its travails with an errant reporter, newsrooms around the country sat down to worry if they should do something to protect themselves. This is more important. How do we bring home that what is decided a year from now will affect us all for decades to come?

Richard C. Wald, who has worked for *The New York Herald Tribune, The Washington Post*, Whitney communications, NBC News, Times-Mirror, and ABC News, is the Fred Friendly Professor at Columbia's Graduate School of Journalism.

UNIT 2
Covering News

Unit Selections

Key Points to Consider

- What is your take on media coverage of war and terrorism? What are your primary sources of information on these topics?

- Analyze an issue of a news magazine. Rate each page of editorial copy on a 1 (hard news) to 5 (soft news) scale. Note examples of editorial viewpoints and/or bias in the selection and presentation of article topics. If you were the editor, what would you do differently? Why?

- Watch newscasts on two different networks on the same evening (in many markets, you can find one network's early evening news airing on the half hour and another on the hour, or you can videotape one network while watching another). Record the stories covered, in the order in which they are reported, and the time devoted to each. Did you notice any patterns in the reporting? Were there any differences in the way stories on the same topic were presented? Did you note any instances in which editorial or entertainment values were reflected in story selection or coverage? What conclusions do you draw from your findings?

- To what extent do you agree with criticisms of news media? Is the American public's general disinterest in most hard news topics the media's fault? Explain. Should making news more interesting/appealing be a priority of news media? Why or why not?

 **Links: www.dushkin.com/online/**
These sites are annotated in the World Wide Web pages.

Cable News Network
http://www.cnn.com

Fairness and Accuracy in Reporting
http://www.fair.org

Organization of News Ombudsmen (ONO)
http://www.newsombudsmen.org

Television News Archive
http://tvnews.vanderbilt.edu

The reporting of news and information was not, in the beginning, considered an important function within broadcast media organizations. Television news was originally limited to 15-minute commercial-free broadcasts presented as a public service. Over the years, however, the news business has become big business. News operations are intensely competitive, locked in head-to-head popularity races in which the loss of one ratings point can translate into a loss of $10 million in network television advertising revenue, and in which local newspapers are aware that alienating a major advertiser can spell financial disaster.

News, by definition, is timely: It is "news," not "olds." Decisions regarding what stories to play and how to play them are made under tight deadlines. Media expert Wilbur Schramm has noted that "hardly anything about communication is so impressive as the enormous number of choices and discards and interpretations that have to be made between [an] actual news event and the symbols that later appear in the mind of a reporter, an editor, a reader, a listener, or a viewer. Therefore, even if everyone does his job perfectly, it is hard enough to get the report of an event straight and clear and true." Schramm's comments point to the tremendous impact of selectivity in crafting news messages. The process is called *gatekeeping*. Gatekeeping is necessary. News operations cannot logistically cover or report every event that happens in the world from one edition or broadcast to the next. The concerns associated with the reality of gatekeeping relate to whether or not the gatekeepers abuse the privilege of deciding what information or viewpoints the mass audience receives. Simply being selected for media coverage lends an issue, an event, or an individual a certain degree of celebrity—the "massier" the medium, the greater the effect.

In his novel *The Evening News*, Arthur Hailey observed: "People watch the news to find out the answers to three questions, Is the world safe? Are my home and family safe? and, Did anything happen today that was interesting?" Given cursory answers to those questions, viewers are satisfied that they are "keeping up," although the total amount of news delivered in a half-hour newscast would, if set in type, hardly fill the front page of a daily newspaper. Many adults report that they are too busy to follow the news, or are suspicious of the media, or find the news too depressing. In one recent study, 27 percent of television viewers described themselves as "stressed" while watching the evening news (51 percent reported feeling "stressed" while watching Martha Stewart).

News media are under enormous pressure to fill time and space with quality visuals and snappy stories. The competitive nature of the industry values gatekeeping choices influenced by profit motives. Some critics contend that there is a sensationalist bias in news coverage. Some note that tight deadlines deprive reporters and editors of time to adequately investigate, reflect, and evaluate before filing their stories. Some worry that media ownership megadeals pose a major challenge to providing objectivity and diversity in viewpoints.

Since 1990, both the combined circulation of the top 10 U.S. newspapers and the percentage of people reporting that they regularly watch a nightly network newscast have declined; the percentage of people who report they never watch a nightly news broadcast has more than doubled. ABC, CBS, and NBC evening news broadcasts together attract on average about 12 percent of the U.S. population, with another 1 percent watching CNN, Fox News, MSNBC, CNN Headline News, or CNBC during the 6-7 p.m. slot. A December 1999 poll of 822 randomly selected American adults found respondents nearly equally divided in their opinion of news media (45.5% favorable, 44.6% unfavorable, 10% don't know/declined). Sixty percent believed that the media make conditions in America seem worse than they actually are (60.1% worse, 18% better, 13.9% about right, 8% don't know/declined). Half reported getting most of their news from television (49.5% TV, 25.5% newspaper, 11% radio, 5% newsmagazine, 4.9% Internet, 2.9% friends/family, 1.2% don't know/declined). And, while 16% rated Tom Brokaw the most trusted television journalist (10% chose Peter Jennings, 9% Dan Rather, 3% Barbara Walters, 3% Walter Cronkite, 2% Ted Koppel, the rest local anchors), 14% of survey participants replied "none of them."

The articles in this section explore the changing landscape of contemporary news and information coverage. "The Pentagon Is Fighting—and Winning—the Public Relations War" starts with historical context of war reporting, from the mid 1800's through the Assistant Secretary of Defense for Public Affairs' decision to embed journalists with combat units in Iraq. "Baghdad Urban Legends" and "High Anxiety" explore pressures of an accelerated news cycle and demand for instant analysis on both governments and journalists. "Re-Thinking Objectivity," "Across the Great Divide: Class," and "Et Tu, 'Nightline'?" address gatekeeping in differing contexts. "Where TV Has Teeth" commends carefully crafted investigative journalism and its ability to trigger significant social change. "The Next Generation" summarizes the evolution of the nation's largest newspaper, USA Today.

News veteran Walter Cronkite has noted, "We've always known that you can gain circulation or viewers by cheapening the product, and now you're finding the bad driving out the good." Is the bad driving out the good in news media? It is arguable that news media have let a marketplace orientation get in the way of careful and credible coverage of important events and issues. It is equally arguable that they are simply, and rightfully, listening to public feedback and responding.

THE PENTAGON IS FIGHTING— AND WINNING— THE PUBLIC RELATIONS WAR

"Through the up-close-and-personal view of America's fighting men and women provided by embedded correspondents [in Iraq], the credibility of the individual soldier, sailor, airman, Marine, and Coast Guardsman has dramatically improved."

BY ROBERT S. PRITCHARD

AFTER YEARS OF FIGHTING with the media, the Pentagon can finally, and proudly, claim it has won the public relations war in Iraq. At least it has so far as its policy on how the media covers America's wars is concerned—for now.

Critics called it "the ultimate reality show," but what we witnessed was truly revolutionary coverage of armed conflict unprecedented in the annals of the military-media relationship. As Steve Bell, Ball State University telecommunications professor and veteran international news correspondent for ABC News, which included covering Vietnam, put it in April, 2003, "What we are living and watching is extraordinary. We have never fought wars like this."

Indeed, this news coverage was more closely akin to the way World War II was reported, although it was dramatically more radical a concept. Military censors were very much alive and well during World War II, and journalists' reports were still subjected to field press censorship. There was no censorship in Iraq. World War II correspondents were assigned to press camps, while the embedded journalists were assigned to individual units in Iraq. The manner of reporting on the individual soldier, sailor, airman, Marine, and Coast Guardsman in the Iraq war was similar to that of Ernie

Pyle, who became famous with his endearing and perceptive reports on the average American serviceman.

As Pyle wrote in one of his columns, "I love the infantry because they are the underdogs. They are the mud-rain-frost-and-wind boys. They have no comforts, and they even learn to live without the necessities. And in the end they are the guys that wars can't be won without." We saw these modern-day "underdogs" up-close-and-personal, beamed from the desert sands of Iraq, 24 hours a day, seven days a week. Some correspondents, like the late David Bloom, actually got close to Pyle's level of insight in his stories on soldiers and Marines. However, unlike World War II, we saw it all "live."

In another sense, there are similarities in the coverage of this conflict and how the Vietnam War was covered, except that reporters didn't just "hop a ride" to the war zone, cover the story, and head back to Saigon for a "cold one" at the end of the day. Film reports from Vietnam had to be flown out of the country before they could be shown a day or two later. Nonetheless, television brought the war into America's living room for the first time. Similarly, in the early days of the Iraqi conflict, we were glued to our TV screens, only now we were watching

endless hours of desert rolling passively by, waiting for that instant of "breaking news." As columnist John Fund put it in his article, "Attack in the Box: The Dangers of a Televised War," in early April, "An awful lot of people have become addicted to this kind of 'Live from Baghdad' reporting."

Much as the successful enforcement of family rules and policies can be judged by the intensity of complaints from the children upon whom they are inflicted, media criticism would provide further evidence that the Pentagon's policies succeeded. This criticism has covered the gambit from the ridiculous to the sublime. Evidence of the ridiculous is *Harper's* magazine publisher John MacArthur. In an interview quoted in a May 1 *Reuters* article, he said of arguably one of the most-lasting images of U.S. victory in the war—a U.S. soldier draping an American flag over the head of a statue of Iraqi leader Saddam Hussein in Baghdad—"It was absolutely a photo-op created for [Pres. George W.] Bush's re-election campaign commercials."

The sublime is evidenced in media commentary criticizing the performance of other journalists. Seemingly, it is fashionable now for journalists to dump on each other since, apparently, the Pentagon's policies have offered little to complain about. For example, as reported by Mary E. O'Leary, *New Haven* (Conn.) *Topics* editor, Michael Hirsh, a senior editor at *Newsweek*, told a Yale University audience that he was "fairly appalled" by television's coverage of the Iraqi war. "This has not been the media's finest hour," he said. Other naysayers maintain that the embedded reporters only churned out good news. Still others assert that they weren't allowed to say anything negative, so their stories are suspect.

As patently absurd as these claims might appear on their surface, they point out the very deep and entrenched adversarial relationship between the military and the media. This, by itself, illuminates just how difficult it has been for the Pentagon to achieve this victory. It also illustrates how fleeting that victory might be and how much work remains to be done.

To place the scope of the Pentagon's—and the public's—victory in the proper context, a brief synopsis of the military-media relationship is in order. The road has been a rocky one.

Prior to the Mexican-American War in 1846, the press operated freely as long as their views corresponded to local views. Information gathering was haphazard and usually based on other publications, letters, and government proclamations. There were no reporters in the field. Military leaders were concerned, however, that some news undermined the war effort, although they were powerless to control it.

By 1846, technology and newsgathering had improved to the point where reporters were competing daily for news. The telegraph and Pony Express offered quicker transmission of news, and correspondents routinely deployed with the military. George W. Kendall, founder of the *New Orleans Picayune*, was known to report from the front lines and spent time with generals. Newspaper accounts were still up to 10 days old, despite efforts like Kendall's and the arrival of the telegraph. "Camp newspapers" came into being to keep the troops informed (a prototype for later military public affairs efforts). Civilian newspapers were known to use these camp papers as a primary source.

Reporting on military conflict became quite problematic during the Civil War (1861–65). The telegraph made it possible for the first time to report military action in real time. Government and military leaders, both North and South, did all they could do to contain these reports. Pres. Abraham Lincoln, though, saw the press as a means to maintaining popular support and so did all he could to keep it unfettered. However, he, too, had to make difficult decisions with regard to press freedoms as he faced the venom of the Copperhead newspapers, which vehemently denounced the war and governmental and military leadership. "Must I shoot a simple-minded soldier boy who deserts, while I must not touch a hair of a wily agitator who induces him to desert… ?" he would write.

The Spanish-American War in 1898 was marked by two significant factors—substantial advances in technology and "yellow journalism." Printing presses were motorized; the transatlantic cable had been laid; and telegraph lines ran the width and breadth of the nation. Meanwhile, Joseph Pulitzer's *New York World* was locked in mortal combat with William Randolph Hearst's *New York Journal*. Some claim the war itself was the result of machinations the two enterprises engaged in simply to drum up sales and publicity for their papers. In any event, the atmosphere lent itself to severe government restrictions, with the banning of reporters in combat zones and the closing of cable offices. Nonetheless, information continued to be "leaked" to the public, making government retaliation largely ineffective.

20th-century wars

The most-restrictive period in the military-media relationship was World War I. Initially, this was not so. The Creel Committee created by Pres. Woodrow Wilson upon America's entry into the war in April, 1917, and headed by former newspaper editor George Creel, mounted an impressive program to mobilize public opinion in support of the war effort. Creel's agency was governed by a set of regulations drawn up by the State, War, and Navy departments that placed restrictions on publication of militarily sensitive information like troop movements, sailing schedules, anti-aircraft or harbor defenses, identification of units dispatched overseas, etc. The press voluntarily abided by these regulations.

Then Congress—prompted primarily by a national patriotic fervor reaching the level of wartime hysteria, and concern over internal hostile and disloyal activities as well as the effects of propaganda—enacted the most-onerous restrictions in history with passage of the Espionage Act in 1917 and the Sedition Act of 1918. The Espionage Act forbade publication of any information that might remotely be regarded as providing aid to the enemy. The Sedition Act prohibited any criticism of "the conductor actions of the United States government or its military forces, including disparaging remarks about the flag, military uniforms, [and] similar badges or symbols…" Reporters had to be credentialed as either accredited or visiting correspondents, swear an oath to write the truth, put up a $10,000 bond, and sign an agreement to submit all correspondence, except personal letters (which were censored elsewhere in the system), to the press officer or his assistant.

The high point in military-media relations—until the present—was World War II. This was probably due to the nature of the conflict and the fact that patriotism was the order of the day. The Office of War Information and the Office of Censorship were created by Pres. Franklin D. Roosevelt in 1941. The latter issued detailed guidelines for what could not be published. Included in the list of restrictions were location, identification, and movement of units, ships, and aircraft; war production and supplies; weather forecasts and temperatures in major cities; casualties; and even locations of art treasures and archives.

Accreditation was used by the military to control access to the battlefield. Correspondents received a press pass from the War Department and a passport from the State Department and, once deployed, were assigned to "press camps" that were attached to regular military forces. All administration, communication, and briefings were handled by the press camps. Typically, these consisted of about 50 correspondents, and each moved with a field army through Western Europe.

Accredited correspondents wore officer's uniforms without rank insignia. Visitors could wear civilian garb, but had to receive special permission to travel in the war zone, were accompanied by an escort officer, and had to stick to a fixed itinerary.

Most of the engagements in the Pacific theater of operations were maritime, and Naval Chief of Operations Ernest J. King placed severe restrictions on military correspondents, frequently holding unfavorable reports until they could be paired with favorable ones. It was also far easier to control the media because correspondents were obliged to travel aboard U.S. naval vessels and relied on the ship's communications equipment to transmit reports. Eventually, the Navy got better at the release of information, but it was only after journalists, editors, and publishers complained enough about the Navy's performance that the Office of War Information stepped in to force changes.

Gen. Douglas McArthur was even more restrictive with the correspondents traveling with him. He required multiple layers of censorship and frequently pressured reporters to change the tone of their stories to show the troops—and especially him—in a more-favorable light.

Initially during the Korean War (1950–52), there were no restrictions on either media access to the war zone or content. The media covering this "police action" adopted their own guidelines and voluntarily censored themselves. Predictably, this led to security leaks and confusion. Critics were quick to point out that the negative reporting was eroding public opinion in the U.S. The Overseas Press Club eventually petitioned the Defense Department to impose censorship so the media would know what its limits were.

Thus, a system similar to that existing in World War II was instituted, with censors reviewing each story. Reports on inferior U.S. equipment, corruption in the South Korean government, and/or food shortages and panics were forbidden. McArthur once again took things even further by disallowing stories that he (or his censors by proxy) considered would

be harmful to morale or cause embarrassment to the U.S., its allies, or the United Nations.

In Vietnam (1965–73), the media was free to move about the country, taking advantage of military transportation when it was available, and there was no censorship. Stories, photographs, and film were unimpeded by security review. For the media, this was the high-water mark in its relations with the military. Ultimately, though, a majority of military officers blamed the media for its "defeat" in that conflict, so Vietnam also provided the low-water mark in that relationship.

This opinion that the media lost the Vietnam War became deeply engrained in some of these officers and stayed with them as they rose through the ranks. The result was their ability to convince the Reagan Administration in 1983 to ban media access to operations in Grenada. The military was able to operate without regard to press scrutiny, which equated to success in the eyes of those senior commanders who distrusted the media. Criticism by the media was significant and vociferous, and rightly so. The good news is this tension drove both sides to find a better way to do things.

In 1984, Chairman of the Joint Chiefs of Staff John W. Vessey, Jr. appointed retired Major Gen. Winant Sidle to head a panel to study the issue. Vessey invited participation from the heads of major media organizations, such as the American Newspaper Publishers Association, American Society of Newspaper Editors, National Association of Broadcasters, and Radio-Television News Directors Association.

Their report, released in August, 1984, contained eight recommendations that were intended to ensure news media coverage of American military operations "to the maximum degree possible consistent with mission security and the safety of U.S. forces." One of the key recommendations of the Sidle Report, as it became known, endorsed media pools in combat zones when other methods of providing access were not feasible. A second notable recommendation was that access to military operations would be governed, as a basic tenet, by voluntary compliance with security guidelines or ground rules established by the De-

fense Department. Violation of them meant exclusion from further coverage of the operation.

The first test of these new roles was the invasion of Panama in 1989. Unfortunately for the media, the Pentagon's planning and response were poorly organized, much too slow, and did not involve the local military commanders upon whose support the public affairs effort was dependent. As a result, the media were notable to cover that operation until the key phases of the conflict were over.

Improving relations

After a very critical self-evaluation, the Pentagon went back to the drawing board and, under the able and energetic guidance of Assistant Secretary of Defense Pete Williams, completely revamped its Defense Department (DOD) National Media Pool procedures. Williams got former Associated Press Pentagon reporter Fred Hoffman involved in analyzing the media aspects of Panama. Chairman of the Joint Chiefs of Staff Colin Powell also emphasized to his commanders the importance of including public affairs planners as part of the overall operations preparation, and this emphasis dramatically improved attitudes about the media within the military.

Against that backdrop, the Pentagon and the media worked hard for the six months prior to the liberation of Kuwait in 1991 (Operation Desert Storm) to organize the influx of nearly 1,600 journalists into the combat zone and keep them fed with information. The coverage of the Gulf War was the most comprehensive to date, but was not without its difficulties. The media complained of their treatment, particularly with two aspects of the operation—the requirement that there be a public affairs escort with them wherever they went and the military's overreliance on pooling. Once again, representatives of media organizations and the Pentagon worked together to develop the *DOD Principles for News Media Coverage of DOD Operations*, which was published in 1992. This simply reiterated what had previously been published, but served to reinforce the importance of the military commanders' personal involvement in planning for media coverage of future conflicts.

During the operations in Somalia (1993–94) and Haiti (1995), the lessons learned were successfully applied. The level of cooperation between the military and the media was robust, and preparation for news coverage had the full attention of everyone in the planning process from the commander on down.

The relationship continued to improve as the military services sought to find innovative ways to accommodate the media. The Air Force went so far as to embark correspondents in B-52 bombers conducting combat missions during the air war in Yugoslavia. For the first time, media deployed with special operations forces while on sensitive missions in Afghanistan.

Yet, there were still shortcomings to this inventiveness. Too few correspondents could take advantage of these opportunities, the media complained. The solution often advanced by the news organizations was free and unfettered coverage of the war zone.

So, in a move as bold as any in the history of military-media relations, the Assistant Secretary of Defense for Public Affairs, Torie Clarke, and her staff prevailed on the Bush Administration, with the support of military commanders, to embed journalists with combat units, should it become necessary to take action in Iraq. They would be able to report "real time" without censorship or security review. A handful of prohibitions had to be agreed to, all common-sense, such as not providing specific locations and movements of troops, but reporters would be right in the thick of things, basically free and unfettered.

Preparation was intensive, and more than 600 journalists completed the required one-week course to familiarize them with military operations and equipment—a kind of miniboot camp. The media began to do some planning of its own, which contrasted greatly with their response to preparations for the first Gulf War.

When the first troops crossed the line of departure into Iraq, on their way to Baghdad, correspondents went with them. Some of the most-enduring images of those first hours and days were report-ers like Bloom reporting live from HUMVEEs as they rolled through the Iraqi desert. Reporters were getting shot at along with their units. It wasn't just American journalists who crossed over with the troops. Reporters from around the world traveled with them. Even *al-Jazerra* had embedded with correspondents. *Washington Post* columnist Howard Kurtz called it "old-fashioned war reporting, but with razzle-dazzle technology that brings it into our living rooms in real time."

Allowing this kind of war coverage was a huge risk for the Pentagon, but it has come with an equally large payoff. As independent observers, the media have corroborated the U.S. and Allied military's adherence to the Geneva Convention and the rules of war, as well as Saddam and his henchmen's lack thereof. If and when the smoking gun of evidence of chemical and biological weapons is found, the media will be there to convince the world the campaign was justified.

Perhaps the biggest payoff is what this has done for the military in terms of how it is now viewed by both the media and the public. Through the up-close-and-personal view of America's fighting men and women provided by embedded correspondents, the credibility of the individual soldier, sailor, airman, Marine, and Coast Guardsman has dramatically improved. We have been witness to the restraint they have exercised, sometimes with tragic consequences to themselves. We have seen the compassion and caring, as our troops have ignored their own comfort by giving away food and clothing and sometimes ignoring their own safety to pull an innocent victim out of the middle of the action.

Challenges

However, this news coverage significantly raises the ante as well as the challenges. Offered as evidence of the most-basic challenge this kind of coverage presents is the "poignant perspective" provided by Nancy Chamberlin, mother of Marine Jay Aubin, when she talked with NBC's Tom Brokaw about her son's death in a helicopter crash in the first week of the war.

"I truly admire what all of the network news and all the new technology is doing today to bring it into our homes," she said. "But for the mothers and the wives who are out there watching, it is murder. It's heartbreak. We can't leave the television. Every tank, every helicopter, 'Is that my son?' And I just need you to be aware that this technology is—it's great—but there are moms, there are dads, there are wives out there that are suffering because of this."

Brokaw's response was: "That is so eloquent, and it's so appropriate, and we will do whatever we can to reinforce that message repeatedly.... Behind those computer-generated graphics, there is a life at risk." Clearly, the media—and the public—need to stay focused on and be sensitive to the wideranging impacts this kind of coverage can have.

The real-time nature of embedded coverage and journalistic reports and images from the battlefield occasionally outpaced the Pentagon's reporting and confirmation process, especially with regard to next of kin in the event of a death or serious injury. Reporters in the thick of things and the attendant risk of someone being injured or killed "live" raise the stakes for both the media and the military. This has the potential for devastating consequences on families and loved ones and tends to erode the Pentagon's credibility.

On March 23, 2003, Secretary of Defense Donald H. Rumsfeld found himself face-to-face with this challenge as Bob Schieffer, host for CBS's "Face the Nation," decided to air breaking video made available by *al-Jazeera* showing American POWs as well as Iraqis displaying dead U.S. soldiers. In other cases, the military lagged behind the power curve in confirming incidents and answering questions based on those instant images. Clearly, we need to come to grips with what this immediacy means, especially in terms of impact on families of dead, injured, and captured U.S. soldiers. Further, both the military and the media need to analyze their respective reporting procedures and priorities more thoughtfully to find greater balance.

Inexperienced correspondents or those caught up in the emotion of the moment risk unwittingly divulging classified information. This is perhaps the most-serious challenge this new style of reporting creates for the media and the military. While the annals of the military-media relationship record a very small number of actual serious breaches of operational security, this risk is far too important to gloss over and must continue to be addressed.

Real-time reporting by embedded journalists risks presenting a false impression of the conflict. The ongoing phases of the war may be interpreted and presented by those without training in military strategy and planning as too lengthy, irrational, disjointed, or haphazard when, in fact, there is a clear military objective and plan for the sequencing and timing of actions.

Indeed, we only need look back at some of the early reporting to gather evidence of this concern. A *Wall Street Journal* editorial in March, 2003, pointed out that "the camera does lie, even unintentionally. The depressing weekend news—a firefight that caught our troops here, the American POWs there, the fragging of U.S. troops apparently by one of their own—are all real things that happened. But while the camera can record them accurately, the one thing it cannot do is provide the larger perspective. So a single ugly battle can mislead about the pace of the broader war."

Howard Kurtz commented in his March 27, 2003, online column *Media Notes* that, "If anything, the reports about individual units under attack may create the mistaken impression that the war effort is going to hell in a handbasket, rather than rolling inexorably toward Baghdad." On March 25, after just five days of conflict, the *Los Angeles Times* said, "The abrupt surge in bad news has given rise to questions: Has the U.S. battle plan come unraveled? Was it misconceived from the start?"

Columnist Charles Krauthammer put a fine edge on this point when he exclaimed, "Good grief. If there had been TV cameras not just at Normandy, but after Normandy, giving live coverage of firefights at every French village on the Allies' march to Berlin, the operation would have been judged a strategic miscalculation, if not a disaster."

The impact of embedded reporting on public opinion needs to be carefully studied. It has been said that images of Somalis dragging the bodies of dead American servicemen through the streets of Mogadishu hastened our departure from that country. ABC's Ted Koppel, in a report a few days before the Iraqi war, said, "What's totally unpredictable, of course, is the impact that all this coverage will have back at home and around the world." One pundit opined that this experiment in war coverage has the capacity to turn public opinion against the war, à la Vietnam, on "fast forward." This is more of a concern for the Pentagon and the Administration, however, for, as we've seen before, a flawed policy will not withstand much scrutiny, although it certainly demands further investigation.

A lesser, but equally destructive, consequence of this type of coverage is the potential for it to become an unintended distraction. Much of military training is based on habit patterns, and when they are broken, mistakes are made. Journalists represent potential, unintended "habit-breakers" unless they are quick to grasp the cultural imperatives of the military and its method of training.

Perhaps not a direct result of embedded correspondence as much as a shift in cultural expectations, another aspect of our national "fast forward" thinking is the concept of "victory on fast forward." The euphoria over the liberation of Baghdad lasted eight hours—literally a standard nine-to-five workday. Instant technology and instant reporting bring an expectation of instant gratification. This isn't just a problem for the Pentagon. The media have tended to largely ignore the phenomenon, claiming it is out of their hands. Now, it's time for them to be part of the solution.

Finally, a serious deficiency demonstrated in covering the Iraqi conflict with embedded journalists is the lack of "strategic" reporting that came out of the war.

Almost all of the reporting was tactical, which is not surprising since the embedded correspondents had only the local unit perspective to share. The media recognize this shortcoming. The *Philadelphia Inquirer* noted a week into the war that, "For the last week, we have had the unprecedented experience of watching a war unfold in real time. But analysts maintain that television's ride-along reporters are too close to the story they are covering. And the unfiltered torrent of images they are sending back—NBC anchor Tom Brokaw has likened it to 'drinking from a fire hydrant'—had been overwhelming, leaving viewers confused about the course of the conflict." This leaves an opportunity for the Pentagon to add value to embedded reports, but there needs to be a fundamental shift in thinking from providing perspective (some would say "spin") to providing strategic context and being aggressive from the outset in doing so. Rumsfeld was mostly reactive in his attempts to place military actions in context.

The experiment has been largely and historically successful. The Pentagon certainly should be proud of its achievements, but this isn't a time to gloat. Much needs to be done to refine the current concept of embedding journalists. The concept that accommodating the news media is vital still needs to be inculcated into *all* military leaders. We also have to resolve some thorny issues, and a sea change is necessary at the Pentagon in order to provide fewer "political messages" and more strategic context to reporting from the field. Yet, the rewards for continuing to allow media to report from the front lines, in real time, are huge and well worth the investment and risks.

Robert S. Pritchard, assistant professor of journalism, Ball State University, Muncie, Ind., served 27 years in the Navy, 23 of them as a public affairs specialist, concluding his military career as Director of Public Affairs for U.S. European Command.

From *USA Today* Magazine, July 2003, pp. 12–15. © 2003 by the Society for the Advancement of Education. Reprinted by permission.

BAGHDAD URBAN LEGENDS

By Lori Robertson

Armed with at least the opportunity to have learned much about the war in Iraq—what with the months-long buildup, the up-close-and-embedded coverage, the pages upon pages of newsprint and hours upon hours of airtime—and prodded with multiple-choice and yes-or-no answers, the American public still fared poorly on current events polls.

How come so many people think weapons of mass destruction have been found in Iraq, or that Saddam Hussein was personally involved in the September 11 attacks? Are the news media to blame?

The results from throughout this year suggest that a good portion of the public didn't do its homework. Polls have revealed people harbor a number of misconceptions or bits of false information about Iraq. For instance:

- In a January Knight Ridder poll, half of the respondents said that one or more of the 9/11 hijackers was an Iraqi
- Fifty-three percent of respondents in an April CBS/New York Times poll said Saddam Hussein was "personally involved" in the 9/11 attacks.
- In May, a poll for the Program on International Policy Attitudes at the University of Maryland revealed that 34 percent of those surveyed

believed weapons of mass destruction had been found in Iraq, and 22 percent said Iraq had used chemical or biological weapons in the recent war.

- The next month, a Washington Post/ABC News poll found a similar result: Twenty-four percent said Iraq had used such weapons against American soldiers. (Six percent said the U.S. had used those weapons against the Iraqis.)

We could cite these statistics as more evidence that the American public doesn't care about what happens outside U.S. borders or isn't paying attention to the news. The funny thing is, people *are* paying attention. Or at least they say they are.

In August, a time when most Americans have traditionally shunned news coverage in favor of serious beach time, 84 percent said they were either very closely or fairly closely following news about the situation in Iraq. That's according to the Pew Research Center for the People & the Press, which has been measuring the public's levels of interest in news since 1986. Other polls have found high levels of news consumption as well.

And consuming news usually—and logically—leads to greater understanding. Studies have shown that when the public is following a story and the press is covering a subject well, public knowledge increases. With the war in Iraq, it seems, this hasn't happened. Who is at fault? Did the news media fall down on the job? Could they have done something differently to better inform their audiences?

Or can we safely pass the blame to the clueless American people and their personal biases? What about the rhetoric of the Bush administration?

"What's curious is that [people] say that they're following it closely… and the news talks about it a lot, and somehow this is not getting through," says Steven Kull, director of the Program on International Policy Attitudes.

Kull and others say no matter the cause of mistaken notions, it's the media's responsibility to set the record straight. "If there are misperceptions emerging, if there are biases," he says, "if the goal is to end up with an informed citizenry or electorate, then one has to compensate for these tendencies."

Stephen Hess for one, is not losing sleep over the public's lack of political acumen. "I don't want it to sound like I think Americans are dumbbells," says Hess, senior fellow at the Brookings Institution and a one-time White House speechwriter. But the U.S. is "simply the most apolitical country in the world." Ask people what's on their mind, says Hess, and they'll answer family, health, job, religion. Anything but politics or foreign affairs.

"I don't want it to sound like I think Americans are dumbbells,"says Stephen Hess, senior fellow at the Brookings Institution and a one-time White House speechwriter. But the U.S. is "simply the most apolitical country in the world."

Most of those interviewed for this story agree that the public often is misinformed, particularly when it comes to international events. But some, like Michael Traugott, chair of the department of communication studies and professor of political science at the University of Michigan, say the current phenomenon is a little more disconcerting than similar findings in the past. The fact that weapons of mass destruction have not been used and yet people believe they have been is surprising, says Traugott. More surprising than, say, not being able to rattle off the names of foreign leaders.

Indeed, the last few decades are replete with examples of polls in which the public had plenty of opinions but was short on facts.

In March 1982, as a guerrilla war raged in El Salvador, a majority of those surveyed in a CBS News/New York Times poll said the U.S. should stay out of the conflict, though the poll showed many respondents would have had difficulty pinpointing the country on a map. "[H]alf the respondents said they believed that Soviet or Cuban troops were present in El Salvador, helping the insurgents, although there have been no news reports to that effect," wrote the Times.

In a 1988 Gallup Poll, half of those polled correctly identified Nicaragua as the country in which the Sandinistas and contras were fighting. The other half either didn't know or offered guesses ranging from Honduras to Iran to Lebanon.

But such foreign happenings didn't stir up massive public interest. According to the Pew Research Center news interest index, 13 percent of the public was "very closely" following the fighting in Nicaragua in November 1989; 37 percent said the same of U.S. troops being sent to Bosnia in January 1996; even the war in Afghanistan garnered 50 percent interest or less over the course of the conflict.

The war in Iraq and the 1991 Persian Gulf War, however, often scored 60 percent to 67 percent on the index. That level of interest suggests there might be something more at work than the "Americans don't test well" excuse.

Traugott, coauthor of "Election Polls, the News Media & Democracy," says the reasons for a lack of knowledge are usually a low level of education and partisanship. With questions about the war in Iraq, there is plenty of evidence that bias influences people's answers.

The Program on International Policy Attitudes asks factual questions in its monthly polls. Those believing that the U.S. has found weapons of mass destruction in Iraq had declined from 34 percent in May to 21 percent in July.

Among Republicans in the poll, says PIPA's Steven Kull, those who said they were closely following the news about Iraq were more apt to have these perceptions than those who weren't following the news closely. This "suggests that there's some kind of distorting process going on," he says. It's a distortion on two fronts: one being a personal bias that leads someone to reach conclusions that conform to that person's beliefs, and two, "some skewing in the way the information is being presented," he says.

Michael Traugott, coauthor of "Election Polls, the News Media & Democracy," criticizes the media for not providing much detail or explanation in their coverage of foreign policy and events in general. Also, he says, "there's an overwhelming tendency of the American media to adopt the government view."

PIPA further analyzed its data from this summer to see if there were relationships between people's beliefs and their main news sources. And it found some: Those who said they watched the Fox News Channel "very closely" were more likely to say evidence to WMD had been found or that people in the world favor the U.S. having gone to war with Iraq than those who watched Fox "not very closely" or "not closely at all." For CNN, the opposite was true—those watching the network very closely were less apt to have these misperceptions. There was little difference among the attention levels of NBC, ABC or CBS viewers.

When PIPA compared Republicans who supported the war, would vote for Bush in 2004 and listed Fox as their primary news source with Republicans who met the first two criteria but listed other news sources, it still found differences in beliefs. Loyal Fox viewers were more likely to have some misperceptions about Iraq.

It's debatable whether that means there's something in the way news is presented or in the way Fox fans choose to hear it.

Andrew Kohut, director of the Pew Research Center, says there is a purely emotional reaction that people have to Iraq—and one man in particular—that may have something to do with the poll results. On the public's assumption that Saddam Hussein was involved with 9/11, Kohut says, "A lot of that has to do with a perception that Saddam Hussein is a really bad guy who wants to do us harm, and he comes from a part of the world that is dangerous."

When a question like that is posed, he says, people make assumptions, even if they aren't absolutely certain of the facts. "They tell the pollster," says Kohut, " 'Yeah, I suspect that's true.' " It's a combination "of not having the facts, not studying the coverage and the willingness to think the worst of a bad guy."

Steven Kull, director of the Program on International Policy Attitudes, says the press needs to correct public misunderstanding. "If there are misperceptions emerging, if there are biases, if the goal is to end up with an informed citizenry or electorate, then one has to compensate for these tendencies."

We can't expect the public to know as much about the story as the press does. Unlike many journalists, most Americans don't follow day-to-day policy developments, says Karlyn Bowman, resident fellow at the American Enterprise Institute.

People are more likely to be guided by their values when answering these questions than by what's actually going on. "I think journalists assume that American opinions are based on facts, because most people in journalism are dealing with facts on a regular basis," says Bowman, who studies public opinion. "I'm not sure that's how the American people, being mostly inattentive, make decisions and form opinions." They are "more likely to consult their values."

Also, once the public establishes a basic level of trust in a president, "they do give their presidents latitude," she says, "and they just don't pay attention to the specifics of a debate."

And the specifics were confusing. It was "found mobile weapons labs" one day, and "that's not what they were used for" the next. Journalists would report what the Bush administration said about possible evidence and then follow with skeptical remarks from arms and intelligence officials. Can we blame the folks out there for being a tad confused?

Kathleen Hall Jamieson, director of the Annenberg Public Policy Center of the University of Pennsylvania, says we can't, and she isn't willing to say the public is wrong. One by one she ticks of valid reasons why people would answer these poll questions as they did.

On the hijackers-were-Iraqi response: "The Bush rhetoric and the rhetoric of the administration strongly implied that there was an association between Iraq and 9/11, so that the public thinks there is, when it has been told there is, isn't surprising," Jamieson says. "It's possible there's a link and we haven't found it yet."

On the WMD question: The administration still holds the position that the mobile labs could have been used to make weapons of mass destruction, she says. "So you can't say the public's wrong." What you can say is that there's a difference of opinion about what the labs were for.

On biological or chemical weapons used: It's not implausible for the public, knowing that gulf war illness may have been caused by some chemical interaction, to think such weapons may have been used in this war, Jamieson says.

Kathleen A. Frankovic, director of surveys at CBS News, agrees that conflicting information could have led to false beliefs. "There were certainly many reports about the finding of things that could be weapons of mass destruction at the end of the war," she says. "People could have generalized from that."

She sides with Kohut, as well, saying, "The opinion of Saddam Hussein is so negative and had been so negative for more than a decade… that it was very easy for people to believe the most horrendous acts" had been committed by the Iraqi leader.

On the public's assumption that Saddam Hussein had something to with 9/11, Pew Research Center Director Andrew Kohut says, "A lot of that has to do with a perception that Saddam Hussein is a really bad guy who wants to do us harm." It's a combination, he says, "of not having the facts, not studying the coverage and the willingness to think the worst of a bad guy."

That's not due to a failure on the part of the news media, Frankovic says, "but a deep-held feeling" about Hussein.

But can we let news organizations off the hook that easily? Jon Wolfsthal, deputy director of the Non-Proliferation Project at the Carnegie Endowment for International Peace, says he and his colleagues have been thinking about why the public is so misinformed. He says we need to realize the general public doesn't necessarily watch entire newscasts, read entire newspapers and consume the large quantities of reports that political types or those in Washington, D.C., might.

"If you're cooking dinner, and the lead story is the weapons of mass destruction search," Wolfsthal says as an example. "And then you start the blender." The next thing you hear is that a U.S. soldier has been killed in Iraq. It's likely, he says, that a person might associate American deaths with WMD.

The media, of course, can't make people listen.

But, Wolfsthal says, they *could* tone down the hype, especially when they're not completely sure what they're hyping. "In order to get viewers, [the media] feel they need to excite people's imagination," he says. They "tend to be more excited about events than warranted," which, he says, was true in the run-up to the war and when the U.S. revealed preliminary findings.

Journalists need to include more background in their stories, Wolfsthal adds, and "think about what goes above the fold as opposed to deep in the background."

A good percentage of the public might not make it to that "background" most of the time, but people do get the general message—if it's hammered home enough. In July, when the question "Where are the weapons?" was getting prominent play, the percentage of people who believed the weapons had already been found slipped in the PIPA poll. Kull says the press coverage certainly made a difference.

"I think the information keeps moving around and gradually it overrides" false beliefs, he says. "It's persistent enough so that it overrides people's resistance."

Editors and news directors can all breathe a small sigh of relief: Press coverage—at least eventually—does increase public knowledge. Media coverage matters.

"I think journalists assume that American opinions are based on facts, because most people in journalism are dealing with facts on a regular basis," says Karlyn Bowman, resident fellow at the American Enterprise Institute. "I'm not sure that's how the American people, being mostly inattentive, make decisions and form opinions."

"Accurate public knowledge goes up when the press is doing its job," says Jamieson. She saw the link in a year-long survey Annenberg conducted in 2000 on the presidential election. "When there were high levels of press coverage" and when candidates were talking about certain issues, public knowledge increased, she says. "When

one candidate was trying to confuse the public on where [he] stood, public knowledge went down."

But Jamieson doesn't know what more the press could have done in reporting news about the absence of proven links between Iraq and al Qaeda and the absence of evidence of weapons of mass destruction, subjects that elicited diverging viewpoints from the administration and outside experts. "What the press is not supposed to do is say, 'This side is right,' unless the press had some evidence to say that," she says.

Others don't have problems criticizing news outlets' performance, saying that they often failed to provide enough detail, were more likely to convey impressions than facts, and gave too much credence to administration claims.

On the WMD question: The Bush administration still holds the position that the mobile labs could have been used to make weapons of mass destruction, says Kathleen Hall Jamieson, director of the Annenberg Public Policy Center of the University of Pennsylvania. "So you can't say the public's wrong."

As for those elusive weapons of mass destruction, Kull says there were a series of headlines after the war that suggested a smoking gun had been found. The follow-up stories—saying many experts disagree—did not get such prominent play, he notes.

Traugott criticizes the media for not providing much detail or explanation in their coverage of foreign policy and events in general. Also, he says, "there's an overwhelming tendency of the American media to adopt the government view. And especially as the story develops… [the articles] turn into stories about conflicts within the administration, or about people taking sides in the Congress… and they focus on these aspects of conflict."

Danny Schechter, executive editor of MediaChannel.org, a Web site on media issues, and a frequent critic of the press, chastises journalists for being more concerned about presentation than information. The press, he says, "conveys and reinforces impressions, not facts; deals with ideology, not information." There's more emphasis on the tantalizing lead, he says, than on context and background.

Newspaper editors and others counter that the coverage of the war in Iraq was quite comprehensive, and they don't fault the media for any lingering public misperceptions. "I don't think this is a result of the press not doing its job," says Stephen Hess. "Look at the coverage of Iraq… Gee whiz, the amount of money and personnel spent to cover this war, I think, was quite outstanding."

Robert Ruby, foreign editor of the Baltimore Sun, says the poll results are an example "of how a lot of citizens divide the world into us versus them" and don't worry too much about the specifics. "I think all that newspapers can do is put the information out there. If people read it, that's great, and if they understand it, even better. And if they don't, there's not too much a newspaper can do," Ruby says. "We're not running a political campaign or information campaigns."

There is evidence that even if the media do provide details, the public doesn't pay close attention to them. Traugott mentions studies on the relationship between the number of U.S. troops killed in a conflict and American support for the fighting. "I think that the body count measure is just an indicator of the tone of the coverage," he says. "I don't think people are paying attention to how many people died.... But there's a relationship between a focus on a particular topic" and the tenor of the news.

The Annenberg 2000 study suggests that whether people caught snippets of election coverage or read a good portion of it, they walked away with similar levels of knowledge about the presidential candidates. "There was little difference between high, medium and low consumers of television news on knowledge of the candidates' issue positions," the report reads.

There were only small differences (5 percent to 10 percent) between the knowledge levels of those who had high exposure to newspapers or talk radio and those who said they had a low exposure.

So is it the coverage—or the public—that's fuzzy on the details?

Schechter describes a vicious cycle of news coverage: "Television helps in a sense limit the attention span of the audience," he says. "Now, it's creating programming geared to that phenomenon it's created."

Ed Jones, Associated Press Managing Editors president, says, "I think I was surprised—as were many newspaper editors—to find that rather than readership going up during wartime, it was either flat or down." That trend, he says, was "extremely unfortunate."

While he does say that "print is better," Schechter adds that newspapers are trying to look more like TV, with shorter stories and bigger pictures.

People do learn from the media, but they may not retain information for long. Hess says the relationship between news coverage and public knowledge is evident in the ratings of politicians—they move up at one event, and down at another. "The problem," he says, "is the degree to which people forget it. They just go on to something else."

The need for repetition is one lesson Peter Bhatia, executive editor of Portland's Oregonian, says the media can take from these poll results. "It's not so much correcting the public, it seems to me," he says on the question of whether the press has a responsibility to fix misperceptions, "it's more a matter of... understanding that people don't read every word of a newspaper every day, and especially on long-running stories like this one, we need to come back and revisit things over and over and over again," he says. "We need to keep telling people, taking the opportunity to tell people things in context that keep refreshing their knowledge of the story."

"Often," adds Bhatia, president of the American Society of Newspaper Editors, "we're guilty of moving on to the next thing."

He and Ed Jones, editor of the Free Lance-Star in Fredericksburg, Virginia, say the public wasn't following the news from Iraq all that closely, at least not in newspapers. "I think I was surprised—as were many newspaper editors—to find that rather than readership going up during wartime, it was either flat or down," says Jones, president of Associated Press Managing Editors.

"We need to keep telling people, taking the opportunity to tell people things in context that keep refreshing their knowledge of the story," says American Society of Newspaper Editors President Peter Bhatia. "Often, we're guilty of moving on to the next thing."

Jones says that trend was "extremely unfortunate," because while the public could see first-rate reporting in the broadcast media, people who didn't read the paper missed "more [of] the background and the context and the texture with all this.... I think they really missed an educational opportunity."

Jones and Bhatia understand the complaint that follow-up reports weren't always played prominently enough, but overall they say media coverage was solid and comprehensive.

But does the press need to correct public misunderstanding? Steven Kull says yes. "It's really the responsibility of the press to realize [what misperceptions exist] and make offsetting efforts to watch for things that they might say that contribute to it," he says.

The editors interviewed for this story agree the media have the responsibility, but say they can only do that through their reporting. "We couldn't do a scorecard every day," along the lines of, " 'We're smarter than you, so here, let me tell you,' " says Martin Kaiser, editor of the Milwaukee Journal Sentinel.

The larger question is whether knowledge alters opinions: If people held different beliefs—that weapons of mass destruction hadn't been found, for instance—would their views on the war change?

Kull says studies have shown the people's attitudes do change when they're given more information. In 2000, for instance, a PIPA poll found that 75 percent of respondents thought the U.S. spent too much on foreign aid. The median estimate, by those surveyed, was that 20 percent of the federal budget goes to foreign aid. When they were told that it was only 1 percent, Kull says, only 13 percent still thought that was too much.

Such studies do raise the question, says Kull, "if people had more complete information on the softness of the intelligence on weapons of mass destruction and links to al Qaeda, whether that would have influenced people's readiness for the war in Iraq."

But, then again, maybe the details don't much matter. Polls have indicated that a majority of the public feels the war was justified even if weapons of mass destruction are never found.

Kohut, of the Pew Research Center, says the purported linkage between Iraq and 9/11 was not an important element of support for the war. For the public, the more significant attitude was that the U.S. was vulnerable and Saddam Hussein was a threat.

"In the end, on the big question," Kohut says, "the public comes to judgments that are pretty rational, and it gets to know what it needs to know to make [decisions]—even though it might not have all the facts right."

Lori Robertson is AJR's managing editor.

From the *American Journalism Review,* October/November 2003, pp. 26-31. © 2003 by the Philip Merrill College of Journalism at the University of Maryland, College Park, MD 20742-7111. Reprinted by permission.

RE-THINKING
OBJECTIVITY

In a world of spin, our awkward embrace of an ideal can make us passive recipients of the news

BY BRENT CUNNINGHAM

In his March 6 press conference, in which he laid out his reasons for the coming war, President Bush mentioned al Qaeda or the attacks of September 11 fourteen times in fifty-two minutes. No one challenged him on it, despite the fact that the CIA had questioned the Iraq-al Qaeda connection, and that there has never been solid evidence marshaled to support the idea that Iraq was involved in the attacks of 9/11.

◆

When Bush proposed his $726 billion tax cut in January, his sales pitch on the plan's centerpiece—undoing the "double-taxation" on dividend earnings—was that "It's unfair to tax money twice." In the next two months, the tax plan was picked over in hundreds of articles and broadcasts, yet a Nexis database search turned up few news stories—notably, one by Donald Barlett and James Steele in *Time* on January 27, and another by Daniel Altman in the business section of *The New York Times* on January 21—that explained in detail what was misleading about the president's pitch: that in fact there is plenty of income that is doubly, triply, or even quadruply taxed, and that those other taxes affect many more people than the sliver who would benefit from the dividend tax cut.

◆

Before the fighting started in Iraq, in the dozens of articles and broadcasts that addressed the potential aftermath of a war, much was written and said about the maneuverings of the Iraqi exile community and the shape of a postwar government, about cost and duration and troop numbers. Important subjects all. But few of those stories, dating from late last summer, delved deeply into the numerous and plausible complications of the aftermath. That all changed on February 26, when President Bush spoke grandly of making Iraq a model for retooling the entire Middle East. After Bush's speech "aftermath" articles began to flow like the waters of the Tigris—including cover stories in *Time* and *The New York Times Magazine*—culminating in *The Wall Street Journal*'s page-one story on March 17, just days before the first cruise missiles rained down on Baghdad, that revealed how the administration planned to hand the multibillion-dollar job of rebuilding Iraq to U.S. corporations. It was as if the subject of the war's aftermath was more or less off the table until the president put it there himself.

◆

There is no single explanation for these holes in the coverage, but I would argue that our devotion to what we call "objectivity" played a role. It's true that the Bush administration is like a clenched fist with information, one that won't hesitate to hit back when pressed. And that reporting on the possible aftermath of a war before the war occurs, in particular, was a difficult and speculative story.

Yet these three examples—which happen to involve the current White House, although every White House spins stories—provide a window into a particular failure of the press: allowing the principle of objectivity to make us passive recipients of news, rather than aggressive analyzers and explainers of it. We all learned about objectivity in school or at our first job. Along with its twin sentries "fairness" and "balance," it defined journalistic standards.

Or did it? Ask ten journalists what objectivity means and you'll get ten different answers. Some, like the *Washington Post*'s editor, Leonard Downie, define it so strictly that they refuse to vote lest they be forced to take sides. My favorite definition was from Michael Bugeja, who teaches journalism at Iowa State: "Objectivity is seeing the world as it is, not how you wish it were." In 1996 the Society of Professional Journalists acknowledged this dilemma and dropped "objectivity" from its ethics code. It also changed "the truth" to simply "truth."

TRIPPING TOWARD THE TRUTH

As E.J. Dionne wrote in his 1996 book, *They Only Look Dead*, the press operates under a number of conflicting diktats: be neutral yet investigative; be disengaged but have an impact; be fair-minded but have an edge. Therein lies the nut of our tortured relationship with objectivity. Few would argue that complete objectivity is possible, yet we bristle when someone suggests we aren't being objective—or fair, or balanced—as if everyone agrees on what they all mean.

Over the last dozen years a cottage industry of bias police has sprung up to exploit this fissure in the journalistic psyche, with talk radio leading the way followed by Shout TV and books like Ann Coulter's *Slander* and Bernard Goldberg's *Bias*. Now the left has begun firing back, with Eric Alterman's book *What Liberal Media?* (CJR, March/April) and a group of wealthy Democrats' plans for a liberal radio network. James Carey, a journalism scholar at Columbia, points out that we are entering a new age of partisanship. One result is a hypersensitivity among the press to charges of bias, and it shows up everywhere: In October 2001, with the war in Afghanistan under way, then CNN chairman Walter Isaacson sent a memo to his foreign correspondents telling them to "balance" re-

ports of Afghan "casualties or hardship" with reminders to viewers that this was, after all, in response to the terrorist attacks of September 11. More recently, a CJR intern, calling newspaper letters-page editors to learn whether reader letters were running for or against the looming war in Iraq, was told by the letters editor at *The Tennessean* that letters were running 70 percent against the war, but that the editors were trying to run as many prowar letters as possible lest they be accused of bias.

Objectivity has persisted for some valid reasons, the most important being that nothing better has replaced it. And plenty of good journalists believe in it, at least as a necessary goal. Objectivity, or the pursuit of it, separates us from the unbridled partisanship found in much of the European press. It helps us make decisions quickly—we are disinterested observers after all—and it protects us from the consequences of what we write. We'd like to think it buoys our embattled credibility, though the deafening silence of many victims of Jayson Blair's fabrications would argue otherwise. And as we descend into this new age of partisanship, our readers need, more than ever, reliable reporting that tells them what is true when that is knowable, and pushes as close to truth as possible when it is not.

But our pursuit of objectivity can trip us up on the way to "truth." Objectivity excuses lazy reporting. If you're on deadline and all you have is "both sides of the story," that's often good enough. It's not that such stories laying out the parameters of a debate have no value for readers, but too often, in our obsession with, as *The Washington Post*'s Bob Woodward puts it, "the latest," we fail to push the story, incrementally, toward a deeper understanding of what is true and what is false. Steven R. Weisman, the chief diplomatic correspondent for *The New York Times* and a believer in the goal of objectivity ("even though we fall short of the ideal every day"), con-

cedes that he felt obliged to dig more when he was an editorial writer, and did not have to be objective. "If you have to decide who is right, then you must do more reporting," he says. "I pressed the reporting further because I didn't have the luxury of saying X says this and Y says this and you, dear reader, can decide who is right."

It exacerbates our tendency to rely on official sources, which is the easiest, quickest way to get both the "he said" and the "she said," and, thus, "balance." According to numbers from the media analyst Andrew Tyndall, of the 414 stories on Iraq broadcast on NBC, ABC, and CBS from last September to February, all but thirty-four originated at the White House, Pentagon, and State Department. So we end up with too much of the "official" truth.

More important, objectivity makes us wary of seeming to argue with the president—or the governor, or the CEO—and risk losing our access. Jonathan Weisman, an economics reporter for *The Washington Post*, says this about the fear of losing access: "If you are perceived as having a political bias, or a slant, you're screwed."

Finally, objectivity makes reporters hesitant to inject issues into the news that aren't already out there. "News is driven by the zeitgeist," says Jonathan Weisman, "and if an issue isn't part of the current zeitgeist then it will be a tough sell to editors." But who drives the zeitgeist, in Washington at least? The administration. In short, the press's awkward embrace of an impossible ideal limits its ability to help set the agenda.

This is not a call to scrap objectivity, but rather a search for a better way of thinking about it, a way that is less restrictive and more grounded in reality. As Eric Black, a reporter at the *Minneapolis Star Tribune*, says, "We need a way to both do our job and defend it."

AN IDEAL'S TROUBLED PAST

American journalism's honeymoon with objectivity has been brief. The press began to embrace objectivity in the middle of the nineteenth century, as society turned away from religion and toward science and empiricism to explain the world. But in his 1998 book, *Just the Facts*, a history of the origins of objectivity in U.S. journalism, David Mindich argues that by the turn of the twentieth century, the flaws of objective journalism were beginning to show. Mindich shows how "objective" coverage of lynching in the 1890s by *The New York Times* and other papers created a false balance on the issue and failed "to recognize a truth, that African-Americans were being terrorized across the nation."

After World War I, the rise of public relations and the legacy of wartime propaganda—in which journalists such as Walter Lippman had played key roles—began to undermine reporters' faith in facts. The war, the Depression, and Roosevelt's New Deal raised complex issues that defied journalism's attempt to distill them into simple truths. As a result, the use of bylines increased (an early nod to the fact that news is touched by human frailty), the political columnist crawled from the primordial soup, and the idea of "interpretive reporting" emerged. Still, as Michael Schudson argued in his 1978 book *Discovering the News*, journalism clung to objectivity as the faithful cling to religion, for guidance in an uncertain world. He wrote: "From the beginning, then, criticism of the 'myth' of objectivity has accompanied its enunciation ... Journalists came to believe in objectivity, to the extent that they did, because they wanted to, needed to, were forced by ordinary human aspiration to seek escape from their own deep convictions of doubt and drift."

By the 1960s, objectivity was again under fire, this time to more fundamental and lasting effect. Straight, "objective" coverage of McCarthyism a decade earlier had failed the public, leading Alan Barth, an editorial writer at *The Washington Post*, to tell a 1952 gathering of the Association for Educa-

tion in Journalism: "There can be little doubt that the way [Senator Joseph McCarthy's charges] have been reported in most papers serves Senator McCarthy's partisan political purposes much more than it serves the purposes of the press, the interest of truth." Government lies about the U2 spy flights, the Cuban missile crisis, and the Vietnam War all cast doubt on the ability of "objective" journalism to get at anything close to the truth. The New Journalism of Tom Wolfe and Norman Mailer was in part a reaction to what many saw as the failings of mainstream reporting. In Vietnam, many of the beat reporters who arrived believing in objectivity eventually realized, if they stayed long enough, that such an approach wasn't sufficient. Says John Laurence, a former CBS News correspondent, about his years covering Vietnam: "Because the war went on for so long and so much evidence accumulated to suggest it was a losing cause, and that in the process we were destroying the Vietnamese and ourselves, I felt I had a moral obligation to report my views as much as the facts."

Objectivity makes reporters hesitant to inject issues into the news that aren't already out there.

As a result of all these things, American journalism changed. "Vietnam and Watergate destroyed what I think was a genuine sense that our officials knew more than we did and acted in good faith," says Anthony Lewis, the former *New York Times* reporter and columnist. We became more sophisticated in our understanding of the limits of objectivity. And indeed, the parameters of modern journalistic objectivity allow reporters quite a bit of leeway to analyze, explain, and put news in context, thereby helping guide readers and viewers through the flood of information.

Still, nothing replaced objectivity as journalism's dominant professional norm. Some 75 percent of journalists and news executives in a 1999 Pew Research Center survey said it was possible to obtain a true, accurate, and widely agreed-upon account of an event. More than two-thirds thought it feasible to develop "a systematic method to cover events in a disinterested and fair way." The survey also offered another glimpse of the objectivity fissure: more than two-thirds of the print press in the Pew survey also said that "providing an interpretation of the news is a core principle," while less than half of those in television news agreed with that.

THE MORE THINGS CHANGE

If objectivity's philosophical hold on journalism has eased a bit since the 1960s, a number of other developments have bound us more tightly to the objective ideal and simultaneously exacerbated its shortcomings. Not only are journalists operating under conflicting orders, as E.J. Dionne argued, but their corporate owners don't exactly trumpet the need to rankle the status quo. It is perhaps important to note that one of the original forces behind the shift to objectivity in the nineteenth century was economic. To appeal to as broad an audience as possible, first the penny press and later the new wire services gradually stripped news of "partisan" context. Today's owners have squeezed the newshole, leaving less space for context and analysis.

If space is a problem, time is an even greater one. The nonstop news cycle leaves reporters less time to dig, and encourages reliance on official sources who can provide the information quickly and succinctly. "We are slaves to the incremental daily development," says one White House correspondent, "but you are perceived as having a bias if you don't cover it." This lack of time makes a simpleminded and lazy version of objectivity all the more tempting. In *The American Prospect* of November 6, 2000, Chris Mooney wrote about how "e-spin," a relentless diet of canned attacks and counterattacks e-mailed from the Bush and Gore campaigns to reporters, was winding up, virtually unedited, in news stories. "Lazy reporters may be seduced by the ease of readily provided research," Mooney wrote. "That's not a new problem, except that the prevalence of electronic communication has made it easier to be lazy."

Meanwhile, the Internet and cable news's Shout TV, which drive the nonstop news cycle, have also elevated the appeal of "attitude" in the news, making the balanced, measured report seem anachronistic. In the January/February issue of CJR, young journalists asked to create their dream newspaper wanted more point-of-view writing in news columns. They got a heavy dose of it during the second gulf war, with news "anchors" like Fox's Neil Cavuto saying of those who opposed the war, "You were sickening then; you are sickening now."

Perhaps most ominous of all, public relations, whose birth early in the twentieth century rattled the world of objective journalism, has matured into a spin monster so ubiquitous that nearly every word a reporter hears from an official source has been shaped and polished to proper effect. Consider the memo from the Republican strategist Frank Luntz, as described in a March 2 *New York Times* story, that urged the party— and President Bush—to soften their language on the environment to appeal to suburban voters. "Climate change" instead of "global warming," "conservationist" rather than "environmentalist." To the extent that the threat of being accused of bias inhibits reporters from cutting through this kind of manipulation, challenging it, and telling readers about it, then journalism's dominant professional norm needs a new set of instructions.

Joan Didion got at this problem while taking Bob Woodward to task

in a 1996 piece in *The New York Review of Books* for writing books that she argued were too credulous, that failed to counter the possibility that his sources were spinning him. She wrote:

> The genuflection toward "fairness" is a familiar newsroom piety, in practice the excuse for a good deal of autopilot reporting and lazy thinking but in theory a benign ideal. In Washington, however, a community in which the management of news has become the single overriding preoccupation of the core industry, what "fairness" has often come to mean is a scrupulous passivity, an agreement to cover the story not as it is occurring but as it is presented, which is to say as it is manufactured.

Asked about such criticism, Woodward says that for his books he has the time and the space and the sources to actually uncover what really happened, not some manufactured version of it. "The best testimony to that," he says, "is that the critics never suggest how any of it is manufactured, that any of it is wrong." Then, objectivity rears its head. "What they seem to be saying," Woodward says of his critics, "is that I refuse to use the information I have to make a political argument, and they are right, I won't." Yet some of Woodward's critics do suggest how his material is manufactured. Christopher Hitchens, reviewing Woodward's latest book, *Bush at War*, in the June issue of *The Atlantic Monthly*, argues that, while reporting on a significant foreign-policy debate, Woodward fully presents the point of view of his cooperative sources, but fails to report deeply on the other sides of the argument. Thus he presents an incomplete picture. "Pseudo-objectivity in the nation's capital," Hitchens writes, "is now overripe for regime change."

TO FILL THE VOID

Jason Riley is a young reporter at the *Louisville Courier-Journal*. Along with a fellow reporter, R.G. Dunlop, he

won a Polk award this year for a series on dysfunction in the county courts, in which hundreds of felony cases dating back to 1983 were lost and never resolved. Riley and Dunlop's series was a classic example of enterprise reporting: poking around the courthouse, Riley came across one felony case that had been open for several years. That led to more cases, then to a drawer full of open cases. No one was complaining, at least publicly, about this problem. In a first draft, Riley wrote that the system was flawed because it let cases fall off the docket and just disappear for years. "I didn't think it needed attribution because it was the conclusion I had drawn after six months of investigation," he writes in an e-mail. But his editor sent it back with a note: "Says who?"

In a follow-up profile of the county's lead prosecutor, a man Riley has covered for three years, many sources would not criticize the prosecutor on the record. He "knew what people thought of him, knew what his strengths and weaknesses were," Riley says. "Since no one was openly discussing issues surrounding him, I raised many in my profile without attribution." Again his editors hesitated. There were discussions about the need to remain objective. "Some of my conclusions and questions were left out because no one else brought them up on the record," he says.

Riley discovered a problem on his own, reported the hell out of it, developed an understanding of the situation, and reached some conclusions based on that. No official sources were speaking out about it, so he felt obliged to fill that void. Is that bias? Good reporters do it, or attempt to do it, all the time. The strictures of objectivity can make it difficult. "I think most journalists will admit to feeding sources the information we want to hear, for quotes or attribution, just so we can make the crucial point we are not allowed to make ourselves," Riley says. "But why not? As society's watchdogs, I think we should be asking questions, we should be bringing up problems, possible solutions ... writing what we know to be true."

Last fall, when America and the world were debating whether to go to war in Iraq, no one in the Washington establishment wanted to talk much about the aftermath of such a war. For the Bush administration, attempting to rally support for a pre-emptive war, messy discussions about all that could go wrong in the aftermath were unhelpful. Anything is better than Saddam, the argument went. The Democrats, already wary of being labeled unpatriotic, spoke their piece in October when they voted to authorize the use of force in Iraq, essentially putting the country on a war footing. Without the force of a "she said" on the aftermath story, it was largely driven by the administration, which is to say stories were typically framed by what the administration said it planned to do: work with other nations to build democracy. Strike a blow to terrorists. Stay as long as we need to and not a minute longer. Pay for it all with Iraqi oil revenue. There were some notable exceptions—a piece by Anthony Shadid in the October 20 *Boston Globe*, for instance, and another on September 22 by James Dao in *The New York Times*, pushed beyond the administration's broad assumptions about what would happen when Saddam was gone—but most of the coverage included only boilerplate reminders that Iraq is a fractious country and bloody reprisals are likely, that tension between the Kurds and Turks might be a problem, and that Iran has designs on the Shiite region of southern Iraq.

David House, the reader advocate for the *Fort Worth Star-Telegram*, wrote a piece on March 23 that got at the press's limitations in setting the agenda. "Curiously, for all the technology the news media have, for all the gifted minds that make it all work ... it's a simple thing to stop the media cold. Say nothing, hide documents."

In November, James Fallows wrote a cover story for *The Atlantic*

Monthly entitled "The Fifty-First State? The Inevitable Aftermath of Victory in Iraq." In it, with the help of regional experts, historians, and retired military officers, he gamed out just how difficult the aftermath could be. Among the scenarios he explored: the financial and logistical complications caused by the destruction of Baghdad's infrastructure; the possibility that Saddam Hussein would escape and join Osama bin Laden on the Most Wanted list; how the dearth of Arabic speakers in the U.S. government would hinder peacekeeping and other aftermath operations; how the need for the U.S., as the occupying power, to secure Iraq's borders would bring it face to face with Iran, another spoke in the "axis of evil"; the complications of working with the United Nations after it refused to support the war; what to do about the Iraqi debt from, among other things, UN-imposed reparations after the first gulf war, which some estimates put as high as $400 billion.

Much of this speculation has since come to pass and is bedeviling the U.S.'s attempt to stabilize—let alone democratize—Iraq. So are some other post-war realities that were either too speculative or too hypothetical to be given much air in the prewar debate. Looting, for instance, and general lawlessness. The fruitless (thus far) search for weapons of mass destruction. The inability to quickly restore power and clean water. A decimated health-care system. The difficulty of establishing an interim Iraqi government, and the confusion over who exactly should run things in the meantime. The understandably shallow reservoir of patience among the long-suffering Iraqis. The hidden clause in Halliburton's contract to repair Iraq's oil wells that also, by the way, granted it control of production and distribution, despite the administration's assurances that the Iraqis would run their own oil industry.

In the rush to war, how many Americans even heard about some of these possibilities? Of the 574 stories about Iraq that aired on NBC, ABC, and CBS evening news broadcasts between September 12 (when Bush addressed the UN) and March 7 (a week and a half before the war began), only twelve dealt primarily with the potential aftermath, according to Andrew Tyndall's numbers.

The Republicans were saying only what was convenient, thus the "he said." The Democratic leadership was saying little, so there was no "she said." "Journalists are never going to fill the vacuum left by a weak political opposition," says *The New York Times*'s Steven R. Weisman. But why not? If something important is being ignored, doesn't the press have an obligation to force our elected officials to address it? We have the ability, even on considerably less important matters than war and nation-building. Think of the dozens of articles *The New York Times* published between July 10, 2002 and March 31 about the Augusta National Country Club's exclusion of women members, including the one from November 25 that carried the headline CBS STAYING SILENT IN DEBATE ON WOMEN JOINING AUGUSTA. Why couldn't there have been headlines last fall that read: BUSH STILL MUM ON AFTERMATH, or BEYOND SADDAM: WHAT COULD GO RIGHT, AND WHAT COULD GO WRONG? And while you're at it, consider the criticism the *Times*'s mini-crusade on Augusta engendered in the media world, as though an editor's passion for an issue never drives coverage.

If something important is being ignored, doesn't the press have an obligation to force our elected officials to address it?

This is not inconsequential nit-picking. *The New Yorker*'s editor, David Remnick, who has written in support of going to war with Iraq, wrote of the aftermath in the March 31 issue: "An American presence in Baghdad will carry with it risks and responsibilities that will shape the future of the United States in the world." The press not only could have prepared the nation and its leadership for the aftermath we are now witnessing, but should have.

THE REAL BIAS

In the early 1990s, I was a statehouse reporter for the *Charleston Daily Mail* in West Virginia. Every time a bill was introduced in the House to restrict access to abortion, the speaker, who was solidly pro-choice, sent the bill to the health committee, which was chaired by a woman who was also pro-choice. Of course, the bills never emerged from that committee. I was green and, yes, pro-choice, so it took a couple of years of witnessing this before it sunk in that—as the antiabortion activists had been telling me from day one—the committee was stacked with pro-choice votes and that this was how "liberal" leadership killed the abortion bills every year while appearing to let the legislative process run its course. Once I understood, I eagerly wrote that story, not only because I knew it would get me on page one, but also because such political maneuverings offended my reporter's sense of fairness. The bias, ultimately, was toward the story.

Reporters are biased, but not in the oversimplified, left-right way that Ann Coulter and the rest of the bias cops would have everyone believe. As Nicholas Confessore argued in *The American Prospect*, most of the loudest bias-spotters were not reared in a newsroom. They come from politics, where everything is driven by ideology. Voting Democratic and not going to church—two bits of demography often trotted out to show how liberal the press is—certainly have some bearing on one's interpretation of events. But to leap to the conclusion that reporters use their precious column inches to push a left-wing agenda is specious rea-

soning at its worst. We all have our biases, and they can be particularly pernicious when they are unconscious. Arguably the most damaging bias is rarely discussed—the bias born of class. A number of people interviewed for this story said that the lack of socioeconomic diversity in the newsroom is one of American journalism's biggest blind spots. Most newsroom diversity efforts, though, focus on ethnic, racial, and gender minorities, which can often mean people with different skin color but largely the same middle-class background and aspirations. At a March 13 panel on media bias at Columbia's journalism school, John Leo, a columnist for *U.S. News & World Report*, said, "It used to be that anybody could be a reporter by walking in the door. It's a little harder to do that now, and you don't get the working-class Irish poor like Hamill or Breslin or me. What you get is people from Ivy League colleges with upper-class credentials, what you get is people who more and more tend to be and act alike." That, he says, makes it hard for a newsroom to spot its own biases.

Still, most reporters' real biases are not what political ideologues tend to think. "Politically I'm a reporter," says Eric Nalder, an investigative reporter at the *San Jose Mercury News*. Reporters are biased toward conflict because it is more interesting than stories without conflict; we are biased toward sticking with the pack because it is safe; we are biased toward event-driven coverage because it is easier; we are biased toward existing narratives because they are safe and easy. Consider the story—written by reporters around the country—of how Kenneth L. Lay, the former CEO of Enron, encouraged employees to buy company stock as he was secretly dumping his. It was a conveniently damning narrative, and easy to believe. Only it turned out, some two years later, to be untrue, leading *The New York Times*'s Kurt Eichenwald to

write a story correcting the record on February 9.

Mostly, though, we are biased in favor of getting the story, regardless of whose ox is being gored. Listen to Daniel Bice, an investigative columnist at the *Milwaukee Journal-Sentinel*, summarize his reporting philosophy: "Try not to be boring, be a reliable source of information, cut through the political, corporate, and bureaucratic bullshit, avoid partisanship, and hold politicians' feet to the fire." It would be tough to find a reporter who disagrees with any of that.

In his 1979 book *Deciding What's News*, the Columbia sociologist Herbert Gans defined what he called the journalist's "paraideology," which, he says, unconsciously forms and strengthens much of what we think of as news judgment. This consists largely of a number of "enduring values"—such as "altruistic democracy" and "responsible capitalism"—that are reformist, not partisan. "In reality," Gans writes, "the news is not so much conservative or liberal as it is reformist; indeed, the enduring values are very much like the values of the Progressive movement of the early twentieth century." My abortion story, then, came from my sense that what was happening violated my understanding of "altruistic democracy." John Laurence distills Gans's paraideology into simpler terms: "We are for honesty, fairness, courage, humility. We are against corruption, exploitation, cruelty, criminal behavior, violence, discrimination, torture, abuse of power, and many other things." Clifford Levy, a reporter for *The New York Times* whose series on abuse in New York's homes for the mentally ill won a Pulitzer this year, says, "Of all the praise I got for the series, the most meaningful was from other reporters at the paper who said it made them proud to work there because it was a classic case of looking out for those who can't look out for themselves."

This "paraideology," James Carey explains, can lead to charges of liberal bias. "There is a bit of the reformer in anyone who enters journalism," he says. "And reformers are always going to make conservatives uncomfortable to an extent because conservatives, by and large, want to preserve the status quo."

Gans, though, notes a key flaw in the journalist's paraideology. "Journalists cannot exercise news judgment," he writes, "without a composite of nation, society, and national and social institutions in their collective heads, and this picture is an aggregate of reality judgments … In doing so, they cannot leave room for the reality judgments that, for example, poor people have about America; nor do they ask, or even think of asking, the kinds of questions about the country that radicals, ultraconservatives, the religiously orthodox, or social scientists ask as a result of their reality judgments."

This understanding of "the other" has always been—and will always be—a central challenge of journalism. No individual embodies all the perspectives of a society. But we are not served in this effort by a paralyzing fear of being accused of bias. In their recent book *The Press Effect*, Kathleen Hall Jamieson and Paul Waldman make a strong case that this fear was a major factor in the coverage of the Florida recount of the 2000 presidential election, and its influence on journalists was borne out in my reporting for this piece. "Our paper is under constant criticism by people alleging various forms of bias," says the *Star-Tribune*'s Eric Black. "And there is a daily effort to perform in ways that will make it harder to criticize. Some are reasonable, but there is a line you can cross after which you are avoiding your duties to truth-telling." In a March 10 piece critical of the press's performance at Bush's prewar press conference, *USA Today*'s Peter Johnson quoted Sam Donaldson as saying that it is difficult for the media—especially during war—"to press very hard when they know that a large segment of the population doesn't want to see a president

whom they have anointed having to squirm." If we're about to go to war—especially one that is controversial—shouldn't the president squirm?

It is important, always, for reporters to understand their biases, to understand what the accepted narratives are, and to work against them as much as possible. This might be less of a problem if our newsrooms were more diverse—intellectually and socioeconomically as well as in gender, race, and ethnicity—but it would still be a struggle. There is too much easy opinion passing for journalism these days, and this is in no way an attempt to justify that. Quite the opposite. We need deep reporting and real understanding, but we also need reporters to acknowledge all that they don't know, and not try to mask that shortcoming behind a gloss of attitude, or drown it in a roar of oversimplified assertions.

TOWARD A BETTER DEFINITION OF OBJECTIVITY

In the last two years, Archbishop Desmond Tutu has been mentioned in more than 3,000 articles on the Nexis database, and at least 388 (11 percent) included in the same breath the fact that he was a Nobel Peace Prize winner. The same search criteria found that Yasser Arafat turned up in almost 96,000 articles, but only 177 (less than .2 percent) mentioned that he won the Nobel prize. When we move beyond stenography, reporters make a million choices, each one subjective. When, for example, is it relevant to point out, in a story about Iraq's weapons of mass destruction, that the U.S. may have helped Saddam Hussein build those weapons in the 1980s? Every time? Never?

The rules of objectivity don't help us answer such questions. But there are some steps we can take to clarify what we do and help us move forward with confidence. A couple of modest proposals:

Journalists (and journalism) must acknowledge, humbly and publicly,

that what we do is far more subjective and far less detached than the aura of objectivity implies—and the public wants to believe. If we stop claiming to be mere objective observers, it will not end the charges of bias but will allow us to defend what we do from a more realistic, less hypocritical position.

Secondly, we need to free (and encourage) reporters to develop expertise and to use it to sort through competing claims, identify and explain the underlying assumptions of those claims, and make judgments about what readers and viewers need to know to understand what is happening. In short, we need them to be more willing to "adjudicate factual disputes," as Kathleen Hall Jamieson and Paul Waldman argue in *The Press Effect*. Bill Marimow, the editor of the Baltimore *Sun*, talks of reporters "mastering" their beats. "We want our reporters to be analysts," he told a class at Columbia in March. "Becoming an expert, and mastering the whole range of truth about issues will give you the ability to make independent judgments."

Timothy Noah, writing in *The Washington Monthly* for a 1999 symposium on objectivity, put it this way: "A good reporter who is well-steeped in his subject matter and who isn't out to prove his cleverness, but rather is sweating out a detailed understanding of a topic worth exploring, will probably develop intelligent opinions that will inform and perhaps be expressed in his journalism." This happens every day in ways large and small, but it still happens too rarely. In a March 18 piece headlined BUSH CLINGS TO DUBIOUS ALLEGATIONS ABOUT IRAQ, *The Washington Post*'s Walter Pincus and Dana Milbank laid out all of Bush's "allegations" about Saddam Hussein "that have been challenged—and in some cases disproved—by the United Nations, European governments, and even U.S. intelligence." It was noteworthy for its bluntness, and for its lack of an "analysis" tag. In commenting on that story, Steven Weisman of *The New York Times* illustrates how conflicted journalism is over whether such a piece belongs in the news columns: "It's a very good piece, but it is very tendentious," he says. "It's interesting that the editors didn't put it on page one, because it would look like they are calling Bush a liar. Maybe we should do more pieces like it, but you must be careful not to be argumentative."

Some reporters work hard to get these same "argumentative" ideas into their stories in more subtle ways. Think of Jason Riley's comment about "feeding information" to sources. Steven Weisman calls it making it part of the "tissue" of the story. For example, in a March 17 report on the diplomatic failures of the Bush administration, Weisman worked in the idea that the CIA was questioning the Iraq-al Qaeda connection by attributing it to European officials as one explanation for why the U.S. *casus belli* never took hold in the UN.

The test, though, should not be whether it is tendentious, but whether it is true.

There are those who will argue that if you start fooling around with the standard of objectivity you open the door to partisanship. But mainstream reporters by and large are not ideological warriors. They are imperfect people performing a difficult job that is crucial to society. Letting them write what they know and encouraging them to dig toward some deeper understanding of things is not biased, it is essential. Reporters should feel free, as Daniel Bice says, to "call it as we see it, but not be committed to one side or the other." Their professional values make them, Herbert Gans argues, akin to reformers, and they should embrace that aspect of what they do, not hide it for fear of being slapped with a bias charge. And when actual bias seeps in—as it surely will—the self-policing in the newsroom must be vigorous. Witness the memo John Carroll, editor of the *Los Angeles Times*, wrote last month to his staff after a front-page piece on a new Texas abortion law veered left of center: "I want everyone to understand how serious I am about purging all political bias from our coverage."

Journalists have more tools today than ever to help them "adjudicate factual disputes." In 1993, before the computer-age version of "precision journalism" had taken root in the newsroom, Steve Doig helped *The Miami Herald* win a Pulitzer with his computer-assisted stories that traced damage done by Hurricane Andrew to shoddy home construction and failed governmental oversight of builders. "Precision journalism is arguably activist, but it helps us approach the unobtainable goal of objectivity more than traditional reporting strategies," says Doig, who now teaches computer-assisted reporting at Arizona State University. "It allows you to measure a problem, gives you facts that are less controvertible. Without the computer power, our Hurricane Andrew stories would have essentially been finger-pointing stories, balanced with builders saying there is no way any structure could have withstood such winds."

On April 1, Ron Martz, a reporter from the *Atlanta Journal-Constitution* embedded with the Army in Iraq, delivered a "war diary" entry on National Public Radio in which he defended his battlefield decision to drop his reporter's detachment and take a soldier's place holding an intravenous drip bag and comforting a wounded Iraqi civilian. The "ethicists," Martz said on NPR, tell us this is murky territory. That Martz, an accomplished reporter, should worry at all that his reputation could suffer from something like this says much about journalism's relationship with objectivity. Martz concluded that he is a human being first and a reporter second, and was comfortable with that. Despite all our important and necessary attempts to minimize our humanity, it can't be any other way.

ACROSS THE GREAT DIVIDE
CLASS

Today's Journalists Are More Isolated than Ever from the Lives of Poor and Working-Class Americans.

So What?

BY BRENT CUNNINGHAM

In the January 19 issue of *The New Yorker*, Karl Rove told the writer Ken Auletta that President Bush thinks the press is "elitist," that "the social and economic backgrounds of most reporters have nothing in common with those of most Americans." For decades now, the political Right has made considerable hay out of the liberal elite bogeyman, and such a sentiment from Bush might be dismissed as mere culture-war blather. But class, which is what the president really means, *will* play a role in the coming election: tax cuts, unemployment, corporate greed, health care, the echo of John Edwards's "two Americas."

And Bush is right. Sort of. The class divide between journalists and the poor and working-class Americans many of us claim to write for and about is real, though it has little to do with political ideology and is more complicated than the faux populists of the Right would have us believe. Russell Baker, the former *New York Times* columnist, got closer to the mark in the December 18 issue of *The New York Review of Books*. "Today's top-drawer Washington news-people … belong to the culture for which the American political system works exceedingly well," he wrote. "The capacity for outrage had been bred out of them."

So much for comforting the afflicted and afflicting the comfortable. As Baker points out, we are the comfortable. The demographics confirm it. We are part of the professional class, reasonably affluent and well educated. By 1996, for example, the last time the American Society of Newspaper Editors conducted a broad survey of the U.S. newsroom, 89 percent of journalists had finished college. Meanwhile, only 27 percent of all Americans have four or more years of college, according to the latest census.

Yet numbers alone can't explain the uneven and often subtle contours of this story. The press has the power to shape how people think about what's important, in effect to shape reality. But whose reality is being depicted? This is how the class divide between journalists and a large swath of the populace comes into play. Just one example: Andrew Tyndall, a media analyst who began measuring the evening newscasts of ABC, CBS, and NBC in 1987, finds that since then coverage of economic issues has steadily skewed away from stories of poverty and toward stories concerning wealth. Thus, the poor have become increasingly invisible. The Catholic Campaign for Human Development, the social justice arm of the U.S. Conference of Catholic Bishops, reported in 2002 that its annual survey of American attitudes toward poverty showed that "the general public substantially underestimates the dimensions of poverty in the United States." Most respondents, it said, "maintained that poverty affects some one million people in this country." The real number is thirty-five million.

This divide, this inability of one America to see and understand the other Americas, has something to do with the collective howl from the mainstream press over the "offshoring" of white-collar jobs — turning Lou Dobbs into a protectionist — after years of writing off blue-collar job losses as the price of progress. And with why the Democratic candidates' anti-poverty policies were all but ignored, despite the fact that both John Edwards and John Kerry had extensive "urban America" proposals on their Web sites. And with why Philip Hersh, a *Chicago Tribune* sportswriter, wrote in January that the disgraced skater Tonya Harding "grew up in an environment that … reeked of white trash," and when called on it by a reader and the *Tribune*'s public editor, replied that he had "thought long and hard before using it. The term fit Tonya Harding perfectly." The divide helps explain why Frank Gilliam, a political scientist at UCLA who studies issues of race and local TV news, was told by residents in both a poor black neighborhood and a poor white neighborhood in Indianapolis that the press "only focused on the bad stuff, that they had no access to the media, and were not treated with respect by the media." It also helps explain the growth of ethnic newspapers. And it has something to do with why Abby Scher, who runs the New York Office of the Independent Press Association, got the following response from a magazine editor in Chicago when she told him, after graduating from college in the eighties, that she couldn't afford to take a job for $8,500 a year: "Can't your parents help you out?"

We in the press have a responsibility to engage everyone, not just those readers and viewers with whom we share cultural and economic touchstones. The good news is that the best reporters and serious news outlets find ways to bridge this divide. The bad news is that we don't do it often enough, and our reluctance to talk about class — in the newsroom and elsewhere — makes it hard to change the equation. There are consequences to the fact that millions of people in this country see little of themselves and their lives in the media, unless they are connected somehow to a problem. It may have something to do with why the press is so disliked and distrusted; or why daily newspaper circulation has been in decline for twenty years. Every reporter has his blind spots. But when we all share many of the same blind spots, it makes it difficult to see the forty-four million people who lack health insurance in this country, for example, as anything but the face of failed social policies — important but abstract.

IN SEARCH OF THE WORKING CLASS

Anthony DePalma, who has been a national correspondent and a foreign correspondent for *The New York Times*, and now covers environmental issues, says that for years he felt as though he had "snuck my way into the paper." DePalma grew up the son of a longshoreman in Hoboken, New Jersey. He recalls seeing his father sitting at the kitchen table at the end of a workday, in T-shirt and reading glasses, paging through the *Jersey Journal*. "I never saw my dad read anything else, but he would spend forty-five minutes with the *Journal* every day," DePalma says. "It sent a semiconscious message about a newspaper's ability to reach a wide audience."

DePalma graduated from Seton Hall in 1975 (the first in his family to go to college), married, and went to work unloading trucks for UPS on the overnight shift. During the day, he freelanced. In 1986, after doing quite a bit of work for the *Times* over the years, he was hired as a reporter in the real estate section. "The lowest rung, the backdoor, whatever you want to call it," he says. Inside, DePalma felt the divide. "The Pulitzers, the Ivy Leagues. I felt it very strongly," he says. "You have to understand, the *Times* never crossed the threshold at our house, growing up."

The very idea of class makes Americans, including journalists, uncomfortable. It grates against the myth, so firmly ingrained in our national psyche, that ours is a society of self-made men, with bootstraps. This idea persists even though upward mobility, in any broad sense, is becoming a myth. It adds a moral tinge to discussions of poverty, a notion that the poor must shoulder much of the blame for their plight, and the corollary, that the wealthy should be credited for their success.

Class is also difficult to discuss because it has become so connected to the polarizing issue of race. When Alexis Patterson, a black seven-year-old from Milwaukee, and Elizabeth Smart, a fourteen-year-old white girl from Salt Lake City, vanished within a month of each other in 2002, the press turned Smart into a national crusade while few people outside of Milwaukee ever heard of Patterson. Race had something to do with why, as did the circumstances of each case; Elizabeth's abduction from her bed, which was witnessed by her terrified little sister, arguably made for a better story than Alexis, who vanished on her way to school. But class played a role, too. Patterson came from a poor neighborhood, and her stepfather had done time on a drug charge. Smart's father is a real-estate broker, and her uncle a photographer with the local newspaper.

Class is problematic, too, because we don't agree on how to define it. Is it about education? Income? Where do the swelling ranks of the working poor fit in? Under the headline WHAT IS RICH? a *Houston Chronicle* article last year illustrated how "in one of the world's most affluent countries, few seem to see themselves as rich, even if they're in the upper-income brackets." Michael Zweig, an economist at the State University of New York at Stony Brook who directs the Center for Study of Working Class Life, defines class based on power. Using data from the census bureau and the Bureau of Labor Statistics, he designated occupations as working class, middle class, or capitalist class by the relative power each job affords. A truck driver is working class, for example, but a truck driver who owns his own rig is an independent contractor and is therefore middle class. By this measure, Zweig says, 62 percent of the country's workforce is actually working class. "That's eighty-five million people, hardly a special interest group," he says.

Zweig's formula resonated with Paul Solman, an economics reporter on *The NewsHour with Jim Lehrer*, on PBS. In the spring of 2003, Solman was doing a series of reports on the jobless recovery, and he interviewed Zweig. With the camera rolling, Solman said to Zweig, "By your measure, I am middle class, right?" Zweig agreed, then nodded to the cameraman behind Solman, "And he is working class." Solman looked over his shoulder at his well-paid cameraman, "Is that true, Kevin?" Kevin thought for a minute and said that it was. "Why?" Solman asked. Kevin answered, "Because I can't say 'cut.'"

Says Solman: "I was struck by that because it suggested that the variable wasn't income, but power, and to a lesser extent security."

Yet in our national discourse, we are a middle-class country, period. In polls people tend to identify as middle class, regardless of what they do or how much money they make. (Zweig notes that poll respondents are rarely given the choice of "working class," but when they are more choose that than "middle class.") From a journalistic standpoint, the working class has historically been linked to organized labor. As labor's numbers, and thus its political power, declined, so did our coverage of it. With its most important public countenance fading, the working-class perspective largely disappeared, too.

DePalma recently got a taste of just how difficult it can be to recapture that perspective in any consistent way. When the *Times* began its "Portraits of Grief" project on those killed in the World Trade Center, DePalma volunteered. "They were people

The press has the power to shape how people think about what's important, to shape reality. But whose reality is depicted?

I knew," he says, "and I realized that this is a world I had been running away from all these years." DePalma wrote a portrait of someone who had gone to his high school. He wrote six portraits of fellow Seton Hall graduates. Afterward, he discussed his experience writing portraits with Jonathan Landman, then the paper's Metro editor. "Jon said there are all these people out there who we never write about," DePalma recalls. "People who basically play by the rules, don't make huge demands on public services. We ignore them except when they die in a tower." Together they decided that DePalma would take on a new beat that sought to fill this gap in the coverage, a working-class beat.

From June 2002 to August 2003, only two of DePalma's stories from this mini-beat — he was still a general assignment reporter — made page one. The centerpiece was a series about a block in Ozone Park, Queens. DePalma wrote about Rosemere and Danny Messina, who were struggling to save ten dollars a week to celebrate their son's first Holy Communion; about Joseph Raia, retired on permanent disability, who agonized over whether to raise the rent on his long-time tenants — a couple with two young children whom Raia is close to — in the face of the city's property tax increase; about Antoinette Francisco's frustrating effort to care for a neglected tree, which the city eventually cut down.

In September of last year, DePalma got a fellowship at Notre Dame, and handed the beat off to a fellow reporter to tend in her spare time until he got back. When he returned in January, no stories had been done, Landman had been promoted, and interest in the working-class beat seemed lacking. "It had tremendous support from the Metro desk, but it is hard to see how that support was carried out more broadly in the paper," DePalma says. "I always took that to mean there was a discomfort with terms like 'working class', and attempts to define class in meaningful ways." DePalma chose to move on.

Landman, now an assistant managing editor, disputes the notion that the beat had little support beyond Metro. "I never heard anybody express or signal discomfort with the idea of reporting on class," he said via e-mail, noting that "support in Metro is what you need to succeed in Metro," anyway. As for why the beat was dropped, Landman says that DePalma asked for the environmental beat when he returned from Notre Dame.

For his part, DePalma doesn't hide his disappointment.

"The idea was to expose our readers to a world we normally ignore, the same way we would with villagers in, say, Suriname," he says. "It is fairly pitiful to compare the working class in this country to villagers in Suriname, but they are almost equally unknown."

'A SECURE LODGMENT'

Contrary to the comforting notion of the press standing firmly behind the little guy, there was never a Golden Age when American journalism consistently sided with the powerless against the powerful. By 1927, H.L. Mencken was already lashing the press for what he saw as its upwardly mobile ambitions. "A good reporter," he wrote, "used to make as much as a bartender or a police sergeant; he now makes as much as the average doctor or lawyer, and probably a great deal more. His view of the world he lives in has thus changed. He is no longer a free-

lance in human society, thumbing his nose at its dignitaries; he has got a secure lodgment in a definite stratum, and his wife, if he has one, maybe has social ambitions."

There was once, though, a prominent strain of American journalism that was much more organically connected to the poor and the working class. In the first two decades of the twentieth century, for instance, *Appeal to Reason*, a socialist weekly out of Kansas, drew hundreds of thousands of readers with its scathing indictments of the inequities of unfettered capitalism by the likes of Upton Sinclair and Eugene Debs. In the 1940s, the short-lived New York paper, *PM*, was a more mainstream incarnation of this same spirit. Its motto: "*PM* is against people who push other people around." In the years before Rupert Murdoch bought it in 1976, the *New York Post* made something of a last stab at bottom-up journalism. By the 1960s, though, TV was on its way to becoming the dominant journalistic force, the newspaper business began hitching its star to Wall Street, and the age of corporate media was under way. The path to a journalism job led, increasingly, through journalism school, and thus began a new round of professionalization in the business.

Meanwhile, in the late 1960s the Republican Party began recasting itself as the party of the hardhats, those angry white men (mostly) — real Americans — who resented the decade's emphasis on the struggles of blacks, the poor, and the spoiled hippies who were against the Vietnam war. Part of this strategy was to portray the press as members of a liberal elite, the New Class, that was out of touch with these real Americans. This charge, remarkably, has kept the press more or less on its heels ever since. The soul-searching on display in a column Joseph Kraft wrote in the wake of the 1968 Democratic National Convention — "Most of us in what is called the communications field are not rooted in the great mass of ordinary Americans …" — echoes today in the press's paralyzing fear of being accused of liberal bias. By the time Ronald Reagan was elected and began vilifying the poor, the press — increasingly corporate and cowed — was in no position to resist.

In the 1980s, the gap between the haves and the have-nots widened — and journalists were increasingly among the haves. The middle class split, as blue-collar manufacturing jobs disappeared and were replaced by a tide of low-paying, insecure service sector jobs and an expansion of the professional class. Under Reagan, the country sprinted into the ample arms of a shiny new money culture, offering salvation through free markets (and later through technology). Media deregulation launched a leap-frogging series of media mergers that culminated — for the time being — in the ill-fated AOL purchase of Time Warner in 2001. So as journalists joined a broader professional elite, the companies they worked for swelled into corporate behemoths.

In the 1990s, the Internet economy and its overnight millionaires sharpened the wage envy of the new generation of journalists for their professional-class counterparts. David Denby's new book, *American Sucker*, about his own sad money chase, lays bare this phenomenon of irrational exuberance. So many journalists either bolted for the Internet ether or threatened to that some newspapers began offering stock options to hang on to their talent. The divide got a little wider. "A world where money is a marker and all comparisons are directed upward makes it hard to understand people for whom a million dollars would be a fortune, or those for whom

$10,000 would be the difference between affording college or not, not to mention those for whom $246 is a full week's earnings, before tax, at the minimum wage," wrote James Fallows in an essay called "The Invisible Poor," published in the March 19, 2000 issue of *The New York Times Magazine*. Later in that same piece, he wrote, "Compared with the software elite, the professional-class American finds it easier to imagine financial ruin … . But there is a great similarity between the view from the top and the view from the next few tiers: the increasing haziness and 'Oh, yes, now that you remind me' nature of the view of the poor."

The evolution of journalism as a profession — with its higher ethical standards and emphasis on expertise, good writing, and analysis — was crucial for the press to keep pace with the world. But it came at a cost. When the barriers to entry into journalism were lower, newsrooms were open to people who brought a wider range of life experiences to their reporting and editing than we have today. To be sure, that era had its problems. It was inhabited almost exclusively by white men, for one. But an interesting thing about that ASNE survey, mentioned earlier, is how so many attitudes cut across age, race, gender, or ethnic lines. What diversity there is, it seems, is only skin deep.

EMPATHY AND IMAGINATION

The opening scene in Alex Kotlowitz's 1991 book, *There Are No Children Here*, offers a hint as to how we might begin to bridge this divide. It starts with a group of boys from a Chicago public housing project hunting for garter snakes in the weeds beside some train tracks. Even for someone who didn't grow up in public housing, this is a familiar scene. And that, says Kotlowitz, is the point. "The obvious place to open it is with a scene of violence, because there is violence all through the book," he says. "But instead I began with this benign moment, to show that even kids whose lives are so precarious find refuge in some of the same things we all did."

Kotlowitz's subjects were poor, not working class, and in some ways the press does a better job of covering poor people and their issues. The poor have agencies and policies and activists to create pegs for stories. We have a public discourse about poverty in a way we don't about the working class. Still, that discourse is too often one-dimensional: the poor are a problem, victims and perpetrators, the face of failed social policies. Such stories need to be done, of course; news is often about problems, things that are broken. Yet for those of us who are lucky enough to have health care, plenty to eat, a home, and a job that gives us discretionary income, the news has a lot to offer besides problems. We see our lives reflected in the real estate section, the travel section, the food section, the business section. When was the last time you read a story about how to buy a good used car for less than a thousand dollars?

The press has difficulty seeing, as Kotlowitz puts it, what is familiar about the poor. "There are so few reporters who spend time in these communities, that when they are there it seems exotic and foreign," he says. "We are so appalled by what we see

that we are only looking for what is unfamiliar." This makes it hard to empathize.

Fear, too, makes it difficult to see what is familiar about the poor. Most people working in journalism today grew up in a society that taught us that housing projects were only dangerous places to be avoided. As Jamie Kalven, a Chicago-based writer and public housing activist, put it in *Slate* in 2002, fear "blocks our capacity for perception, for learning. When mediated by fear, ignorance can coexist with knowledge, blindness with vision. As a result, decent people find it possible to support indecent policies." In an interview, Kalven amplifies the point. Fear, he says, makes us hostage to a "one-dimensional moral geography" composed of good places and bad places, and "somehow people who are decent and morally sensitive are able to read *The New York Times* and listen to NPR every day and still hold this notion."

This flattened coverage is evident in the press's treatment of Chicago's massive "transformation plan," which began in 1996 and involves razing all of the city's public housing highrises and replacing them with mixed-income developments. The plan represents a fundamental shift in the way the city houses its poor, and a number of cities around the country are following Chicago's lead. There has been a fair amount of coverage over the last seven years, both local and national, and some of it has been important and thoughtful. For example, a series by the *Chicago Tribune* in 1998 showed how, contrary to the goals of the plan, many displaced public housing residents were ending up in neighborhoods that were just as solidly poor and racially monochrome as the ones they left.

But much of the coverage is top-down, focused on the problems and the process, and heavy with official sources. It is full of middle-class assumptions and fears, including this from a November 10, 1999, *USA Today* piece on the new mixed-income developments: "The wealthier families bring a greater work ethic and sense of community pride to once-desolate neighborhoods, officials say."

Against this backdrop, Mary Schmich's columns in the *Tribune* on Cabrini-Green, one of Chicago's most famous projects, stand out. Since May 2000, Schmich, a Metro columnist, has written two dozen columns on various characters tied to the closing of Cabrini. Those characters — from three black girls saying goodbye to their old school and hello to a new one, to a young white couple who bought into the new, mixed-income Cabrini community — spring from the page fully formed. As one of the schoolgirls, referring to her anxieties about going to school with white kids for the first time, said to Schmich, "We the same kind of people inside." It was impossible not to feel a connection to these people, partly because Schmich refused to romanticize their situations. But she also showed us their insecurities, their prejudices, their joy. "Too often reporters who want to write about public housing have very fixed ideas of how to write these stories," she says. "They have the characters in their heads, because they watch too much *Law & Order*."

Schmich, who has been at the *Tribune* since 1985, says three things allowed her to feel as if she weren't writing about "someplace else" when doing the Cabrini columns. For starters,

When was the last time you read a story about how to buy a good used car for less than a thousand dollars?

she lives in an affluent neighborhood that abuts Cabrini, and has been "hanging out" around Cabrini for ten years. She also grew up in Georgia near people who were poor and black, and her own father had, as Schmich says, "numerous jobs and we were often broke. The differences between me and the people in Cabrini is that there were patches in my childhood when I wasn't so poor, my parents were educated, and I was white, people helped me out," she says. "When I did these columns it wasn't anthropology, but rather from a sense that these were my neighbors."

Her main criticism of how her paper covers the poor in Chicago is really a criticism of journalism broadly. "I think this paper has a very deep commitment to covering the whole range of people and issues in Chicago," Schmich says. "But it is a question of how we do it. We bite off a huge project every few years, and that has the effect of reducing the poor to a problem. Then they disappear largely until the next big project."

'WHAT IF'

There are consequences to covering the poor in this one-dimensional way, consequences that the more affluent subjects of news stories can avoid. "You're dealing with a population that has extremely limited resources for self-representation," says Jamie Kalven. "They have no mechanism for holding folks accountable." In a *Newsweek* article on the Chicago transformation plan from May 15, 2000, for instance, Mayor Richard M. Daley is quoted as saying, "What people want is education, jobs and job training." But in a survey that Kalven's organization did in 2000 that asked residents of the Stateway Gardens housing project what they most wanted for their neighborhood, three of the top five answers were related to better health care, but the other two were "more activities for children" and "more cultural activities," like theater and music. Says Kalven: "These people were asserting their dignity as human beings. Our entire discourse defines them as problems, and they quietly resist it, but no one is listening."

All this would seem to suggest that if we want more nuanced coverage of the poor and the working class, then we should hire more reporters and editors who come from poor and working class backgrounds. But, as many good reporters continue to prove, you don't have to be a coal miner's daughter to write well about Appalachia. Kotlowitz, for example, grew up comfortably middle class on New York's Upper West Side. In fact, being an insider can bring some unexpected problems. Wil Cruz, a *Newsday* reporter who was born and raised in the LaGuardia Houses, a public housing project on New York's Lower East Side, knows something of this. "If you and I were to go cover a story in the south Bronx, they would see you as official and treat you with some respect," he says. "They would be more comfortable with me, but I'm not sure that works to my advantage. They might see me as showing off my success."

Reporters do, however, need to be motivated to get beyond our assumptions. To do that it helps, as the *St. Paul Pioneer Press*'s Maja Beckstrom says, to be able to imagine "What if?" An interesting thing emerged as I interviewed reporters for this piece: a large number of them were raised by single mothers, including Beckstrom, the author David Shipler, *The Washington Post*'s Anne Hull, and *The Guardian*'s Gary Younge. All said

something similar, that experiencing the fragility of a broken family — no matter how quickly or comfortably things settled — allowed them to imagine how close they are to those in society whose lives seem, from the outside, to be nothing but problems. Hull, a national features writer at the *Post*, isn't sure just how her background shaped her as a reporter, but says this: "I'm much more comfortable around these people than I am being at, say, the courthouse, or places where everyone wears a suit. Maybe I'm intimidated by power. I don't know."

"These people" Hull refers to include the young immigrants and children of immigrants in Atlanta whom she wrote about in a four-part series in late 2002. The original idea, not surprisingly, was a piece on the growth of Latino gangs in Atlanta — a problem. But Hull came back with a richer story about kids who were caught between their desire to escape the world of their parents and an American society that often failed them, either in the classroom or on the streets. "A lot of writing about immigrants today is really precious, and reduces them to a single dimension: hard-working," Hull says. "But they're real people, with flaws. They make bad decisions."

It takes time for outsiders to write these stories; Hull spent sixteen months on her Atlanta series. That may be an extreme, but to do these stories right requires that such coverage be a newsroom priority.

OBSTACLES

Spurred by its 1998 project on poverty, the *Pioneer Press* created a poverty beat and gave it to Maja Beckstrom. In 2002 she went on maternity leave and the beat died, a victim, she says, of the paper's "effort to rethink priorities of coverage given a tight budget." Once back at work, she was given the choice of a twenty-something lifestyle beat or one on parenting and families. Beckstrom chose the latter.

Even if reporters are attuned to the complexities of life for the poor and the working class, they face a number of obstacles to getting those stories in the paper or on the air. The profit expectations of newspapers and television news operations have had a dramatic and well-known effect on the quality of journalism: shorter stories, fewer reporters, and a focus on those readers who appeal to advertisers. "There aren't too many publishers who come striding into the newsroom demanding more coverage of the ghetto," says Walker Lundy, a former editor of the *Pioneer Press* and *The Philadelphia Inquirer*, who is now retired. "You can't sell many ads when your readers don't have credit cards, and thus some readers are worth more than others."

The priorities of corporate media aside, the very ways we define and deliver news today works against the kind of coverage Hull, Schmich, and the others are after. Our devotion to the ideal of objectivity produces too many stories that are so concerned with "balance" that they end up saying very little. The pace of the news cycle, as well as the shrinking newshole, foster a way of thinking about the news that doesn't lend itself to nuance and complexity. We are trained to find the quick hit, not to connect the various dots and reach conclusions. For example, a new study of how New York City's daily newspapers covered the city's post-9/11 budget crisis, commissioned by the nonprofit Drum Major Institute for Public Policy, found that the coverage failed "to clarify the stakes of policy decisions on various socioeconomic classes." The coverage, the study concluded, suggested that "everyone's interests are identical." Not surprisingly, the sources used to delineate and explain those interests were mostly politicians and government officials.

For David Shipler, the former *New York Times* correspondent whose latest book is about the working poor, it took a newsroom strike to free him of the confines of daily journalism. "I was in Moscow with the *Times* when we went on strike in 1978," he says. "For three months I didn't have to write for the paper, and I stopped thinking in terms of the seven-hundred-word story. I began to notice things that I hadn't stopped to consider, to see patterns and connections. That's why I was able to write a book. I got a different lens. When your antennae are highly tuned for the 'good story,' these things go by you. Unless a paper is willing to give reporters the freedom to not write every day, then it will be hard for them to find a new lens."

Dale Maharidge, who won a Pulitzer for his 1989 book *And Their Children After Them*, about rural poverty, never found it difficult to see the world from the bottom up. Since taking his first journalism job at *The Gazette of Medina* in Cleveland, his hometown, in 1977, Maharidge has been referred to by editors, somewhat derisively, he says, as the "bum writer." He was the son of a steelworker who had a side business at home, grinding cutting tools for industrial use. "I literally grew up breathing steel dust," says Maharidge. His new book, *Homeland*, due out July 4, is about an undercurrent of working-class — really working-poor — anger that Maharidge says predates 9/11. The book highlights the kinds of stories the press misses because of this "lens" problem Shipler talks about.

Among the people Maharidge introduces us to are a mother and son who live together in Bridgeview, a blue-collar neighborhood in Chicago, where, following the terrorist attacks on New York and Washington, a white mob marched on a local mosque, threatening to burn it down. In 2002, on the first anniversary of the attacks, there was another march in Bridgeview, and Maharidge was there for it. He saw the mother and son, carrying an American flag, being chased off by the police, and he followed them and got their names and address. A few days later he went to their house. Two hours later he had a deeper understanding of the anger on display in that march, and it wasn't as much about anti-Muslim bigotry as press accounts surmised. The son, who was in his mid-thirties, couldn't work because of a heart condition. He showed Maharidge a grocery bag full of medical bills — $200,000 worth, the son said — that he had no way to pay. The mother, who needed knee-replacement surgery that she couldn't afford, lifted her shirt to show him a pain patch on her back. She worked for seven dollars an hour at J.C. Penney, but had no insurance. "Would they have still been racists if they had jobs and insurance?" Maharidge says. "Sure. But would they have been out there marching? Maybe not."

OUTRAGE

There are things that we could do to address this class divide and get a news report that is, as the Columbia sociologist Herbert Gans put it, "multiperspectival." The most obvious is to broaden our diversity recruitment programs to include a specific focus on class. Efforts to bring racial and ethnic diversity to the newsroom have struggled, and this one wouldn't be any easier. But Tim Rutten, a columnist for the *Los Angeles Times*, cautions against fatalism on the question of building socioeconomic diversity. "I worked with the first black in the *L.A. Times* newsroom, the first Latino, the first woman editor, and the first woman on the masthead," he says. "All those things are commonplace now in journalism, but there was a time when each seemed an impossible social barrier."

Editors might do more to encourage reporters like *Newsday*'s Wil Cruz as he struggles to figure out how to use his background — he dropped out of high school before eventually getting a degree from New York's City College — to inform his reporting on his new beat, education. "I don't know if it gives me power," he says of his atypical path to journalism. "If it does, I haven't been able to channel that advantage into my stories. But I need to, because I see it as a responsibility to do it right."

Newspapers need to play to their strengths, and stop trying to compete with the electronic media on every breaking story. The ability of even the sharpest journalism to effect real change is incremental at best, but the stories that have a shot — the scoops that matter — are those that go deep and tell us important things about the world, that challenge the way we think about something. David Barstow and Lowell Bergman's Pulitzer-winning articles last year in *The New York Times* said something important about worker safety in this country, but they took seventeen months to complete and involved a dozen reporters, researchers, producers, and editors. As important as those stories were, though, they are indicative of how the press approaches the poor and the working class. As Mary Schmich says, we embrace the big project, then ignore them until time for the next big project. Day to day, their perspectives and concerns are missing from the media.

A bit of outrage would help, too. Russell Baker says that outrage has been "bred" out of us, that we come from a class for whom the system has largely worked, and he's right. The working class has all but disappeared from our pages and no one seems to notice. We report on the poor, but do little to empower the poor. That's what makes the recent crusade by the *New York Daily News* to raise the state's minimum wage so noteworthy. Not only did the paper have a reporter dogging the issue from the field, but its editorial page hammered away at it for months.

Anthony DePalma says that the outrage is still with us, but that it takes a crisis — a pair of kids starving to death in Newark, an innocent man being shot forty-one times by the police in the Bronx — to draw it to the surface. Well, how about this for a crisis: We are the richest country in the history of the world, and we tolerate thirty-five million of our fellow Americans living in poverty; we tolerate forty-four million without health insurance. Meanwhile, Gannett pays Larry Miller, its outgoing CFO, $600,000 a year for an open-ended "consulting" contract, in addition to a car and golf club membership.

Brent Cunningham (wbc7@columbia.edu) is CJR's *managing editor.*

HIGH
ANXIETY

Americans made a panic-fueled run on duct tape and plastic sheeting in the wake of government terrorism warnings. Sure, the media were merely the messengers, but many news organizations could have reported this story with more context and less hype.

BY LORI ROBERTSON

In one of the surreal moments amid coverage of the February orange terror alert—and in an age of color-coded levels of threat, there were a number of surreal moments—the MSNBC show "Buchanan and Press" sought to explore whether the media were hyping the alert stories. It was February 13, and MSNBC had that little "Terror Alert: High" label affixed to the bottom corner of its screen. But the network wasn't shy in discussing that target of much lambasting and ridicule. Bill Press introduced Washington Post Metro columnist Marc Fisher, asking, "Do you really think that the media would, for the sake of ratings, fan the flames about an orange terror alert?"

Fisher's response: "Sure."

"Would we stoop that low?" asked Press.

"Yes, absolutely."

You can't say that the media weren't concerned about how they were covering this confusing, scary and, most of the time, shadowy story—from the raising of the terror alert on February 7; to the water, batteries, duct tape and plastic sheeting advice on February 10; to all those reaction stories on fear and indifference, to tape or not to tape. Most news executives say they continually have conversations about how to cover alarming stories, how to inform people without inciting fear. They don't take these things lightly.

But many say that this time around, they did a poor job of it. The critics came out in force.

"We seem to have only one volume these days: very loud," says Washington Post media writer Howard Kurtz. "I think it's entirely possible to write about potential terror attacks and suggested precautions without in effect yelling from the rooftops, and yet that's something that modem media or today's media seem to have great difficulty with."

Likewise, Martin Kaplan, associate dean of the University of Southern California Annenberg School for Communication, seems almost resigned to the belief that the media don't always take seriously their responsibility to think about how stories will affect people. "That's such a quaint notion," says Kaplan. Especially on television, with its dramatic "Showdown Iraq" and "Countdown Iraq" branding, he says, "everything gets turned into a soap opera.... Yes, they have a responsibility not to scare the wits out of us, and no, they don't live up to that responsibility. But that long ago has gone away.... The notion that the press should be responsible probably existed in our gauzy memory.

" Living in this massive-amount-of-media culture, one does have the feeling that the are-you-afraid? coverage was too flamboyant. But hysteria was hardly universal: Some news organizations either held back on or underplayed their stories, depending on your viewpoint. The Boston Globe, for instance, ran the February 11 story on how to prepare for a terrorist attack on A5; the Chicago Tribune put it on A12; and the New York Times shoved it back to A16. The Los Angeles Times didn't run it at all. CBS' and NBC's evening newscasts talked about "duct tape and plastic sheeting" in larger pieces, sure, but they weren't alarmist. A day or two later, though, the networks, like everyone else, were chasing after the fear-factor phenomenon.

Endless discussions about duct tape dominated cable news shows. Reports surfaced that a man in Connecticut had wrapped his house in plastic. A whole new genre of jokes was born. "Anxiety" made the cover of Newsweek and Time, the latter taking a comic look at the frenzy by picturing an eyeball peeking out from crisscross swaths of silver-gray tape.

The government's recommendations for preparing for a terrorist attack didn't seem like big news until people started panicking, says the Los Angeles Times' Scott Kraft.

"The truth is really... we didn't think it was much of a story until it created this panic," says Los Angeles Times National Editor Scott Kraft, who adds that people on the West Coast were not nearly as concerned about being the target of an attack.

It seemed no matter how softly some news organizations had initially whispered "duct tape and plastic sheeting," the words provoked quite a reaction. And the disparate play this story received suggests the media were in just as much disagreement as the public about what to do with this information.

Some news organizations played both the terror alert and the government advice stories prominently. The Washington Post and USA Today, Cleveland's Plain Dealer and the Miami Herald, Pennsylvania's Lancaster New Era and Allentown Morning Call ran stories on government advice on page one. Editors had no doubt that this was big news, and they don't buy charges that they were scaring the public.

"Washington is increasingly being singled out as a potential target," says Washington Post Executive Editor Leonard Downie Jr. "And so our readers are really nervous even if we didn't put anything in the paper."

Some people, he continues, feel the media shouldn't be talking about these things—that it makes people afraid. "I don't feel that's right," he says. "We now know information before the September 11 attacks didn't get disseminated." The possibility that valuable information about an attack wouldn't be released is "a great fear of mine."

What the coverage lacked, say critics, was context, perspective and, initially, critical examination of government advice. The public was made aware of different types of possible attacks—chemical, biological and radiological—with not much explanation of what is more likely to occur (and what is extremely unlikely to occur) or what the scope of the damage could be. Reading the early media coverage gave one the impression that a nuclear holocaust could occur tomorrow. Despite the volume of news stories, say critics, the media raised more questions than they answered. It really wasn't clear how all of that duct tape and plastic sheeting was to be deployed, and under what circumstances it would help.

Stories on the alerts and related precautions "have to be couched and put into proper perspective," says Calvin Sims, a former visiting fellow at the Council on Foreign Relations who recently taught a course on the media and terrorism at Princeton. Perhaps the public reaction would have been muted, he says, had someone explained that you have to be skilled to effectively seal a room with duct tape, or that it's unlikely there would be an attack on such a large scale that you would need to use the tape.

"I think the coverage so far falls into a couple of categories," says Karen Brown Dunlap, dean/president-designate of the Poynter Institute. "Media have done a good job at just providing the information, and that's basically saying what the government is saying.... They're not quite doing as good a job in analyzing what the government is saying.... You sense a certain reserve in challenging the government too much."

The vagueness of the coverage wasn't a comfort to anyone. "The sort of questions I wanted to have answered weren't answered," says Sims, now a New York Times reporter. "In the event of an attack, what kind of a response can we expect?... Why do we need to stock water for three days?"

When the government raised the terror alert level to orange, or "high," on February 7, most news organizations led with that story. (The New York Times played it on A8, though an A1 story about France and China opposing war on Iraq mentioned the high alert.) There were signs early on that some journalists were doing their best to ferret out why and if the orange designation was warranted.

The Washington Post, for example, included this interesting paragraph in its story: "However, others with access to the intelligence upon which the alert was based said it was largely an effort to make sure government officials could not be blamed for not warning Americans, as they were after the Sept. 11, 2001, attacks. 'That's what this whole process is about,' said one well-placed intelligence source."

While public anxiety probably increased somewhat, it was nothing compared with what would soon take place. Everything changed after the duct tape.

When the government raised the alert, Tom Ridge, secretary of the Department of Homeland Security, urged people to talk to their families and be prepared for a potential terrorist attack. Some news organizations referred their viewers or readers to Web sites for more information on what they could do.

But on February 10, Department of Homeland Security officials held what one reporter calls "a poorly organized press conference to put out an extremely complicated message."

Nine days later, officials would launch the "Ready" campaign that was much clearer and more detailed in terms of explaining which items were more important to have in the event of an attack. But once the alert was raised to orange February 7, officials decided to hold a briefing, led by U.S. Fire Administrator David Paulison and department spokesman Gordon Johndroe, to get some advice out to the public in a hurry.

The reporter quoted earlier feels some journalists didn't take the briefing as seriously as they should have, commenting as they left that this information had been on Web sites months ago. That's true, says this reporter, but "what percentage of people had actually heard of this?... It was not news because anybody in government had ever said it before in some remote Web site. It was news because... they were worried it was going to happen. It was connected to a real fear."

USA Today's Mimi Hall says journalists have to take government officials at their word on terror more than on other subjects because so much information is off-limits.

That fear quickly went public. The next day, after reading and seeing news reports, people ran out to buy duct tape and plastic sheeting. The reporter at the briefing "totally" expected the public reaction. "Were they overreacting to media hype? Hell no.... The government people who really get this aren't saying that it's an overreaction for people to say they need to have water and food in their home... and even have plastic sheeting and duct tape.... This represents the most sophisticated thinking in civil preparedness in this country."

Mimi Hall, homeland security reporter for USA Today, says officials took some steps to curb potential panic: Cameras were not allowed at the briefing, which was conducted by Johndroe, not Tom Ridge. It would have been much more dramatic, Hall says, to have the homeland security chief on camera telling Americans to assemble their survival kits. Despite that, Hall says she thought most reporters at the briefing thought it was "a pretty big deal."

"It was significant that you had representatives of the federal government telling all Americans to take steps like this." She says editors and reporters at USA Today debated how the story should be played and how it should be written, and they felt it was "significant

enough to put on page one. We certainly felt we were being really responsible with it."

The media reports were chilling. "Terror Attack Steps Urged" was the off-lead on the Washington Post's front page February 11. The Post noted that "officials suggested privately that they do not want the gravity of the threat overlooked."

Downie says he didn't think that putting the story on the front page would unduly frighten readers. "People thinking the media are scaring people have a rather low opinion of the American public," he says, adding that those in the Washington area were already concerned about a possible attack. "Whether we put a story on the front page does not raise or lower that concern."

Downie may be underestimating the influence of an off-lead in a paper of the Post's stature. Even the Post's Marc Fisher remarked on MSNBC: "It was my own newspaper that got people to head out to Home Depot and start buying duct tape and plastic sheeting by putting a story on the front page."

Looking at the coverage that day, some news outlets certainly deemed the story to be more urgent than others.

The New York Times' front page featured a photo of increased security in Times Square, with the following refer: "The Bush administration issued guidelines on how to prepare for a terrorist attack. Page A16." That story twice stressed that officials were not issuing advice because of an impending strike. The fourth paragraph: "'There is no specific, credible intelligence that says an attack using chemical or biological weapons is imminent,' said Gordon Johndroe."

A Times spokeswoman said that editors at the paper would not discuss their handling of this story, saying they don't want to be put in a position of defending their coverage or comparing it with what other news organizations did. The reporter who wrote the February 11 story, Philip Shenon, did not return phone calls. But apparently the Times wanted to be doubly sure officials didn't know more than they were revealing. The story later included this: "Mr. Johndroe said in telephone interview that the administration had long been planning to organize a public education campaign about disaster preparedness, and that today's news conference was not meant to signal an imminent threat."

The Wall Street Journal's story, which ran on D1, included a similar line: "[T]he government restated that it had no specific information that a particular attack was imminent." USA Today included this quote from Johndroe: "We don't have any specific intelligence that says everyone should rush out to the grocery store." (But in a mixed message all too typical of the episode, later in the same story law enforcement officials said "an attack against Jewish-owned businesses or other high-profile targets is 'imminent.'")

The nature of the government's advice had to suggest to many readers that officials must know something more. Should such qualifiers (that there was no evidence of an impending attack) have been included in all stories? And did their absence—from articles in the Post and other news outlets—make stories sound too alarming? Says Downie: "I'm just not as concerned about that tone.... Our responsibility is to tell [readers] as much as we can about... realistic possibilities of the threat."

The Washington Times did not share the Post's zeal. The paper's A3 story, "Higher alert level spurs tighter aviation security," focused on airspace restrictions and relegated scant information on the need for public precautions to the last three paragraphs. Homeland security reporter Audrey Hudson says her paper played the story "absolutely" where it should have. Hudson monitored the February 10 briefing from the office and called the Federal Emergency Management Agency to confirm her sense that this was old news. She says a spokeswoman told her, "Yeah, we did that last year, and we mailed it to the media and nobody paid attention to it." For Hudson, "It was more newsy that there were restrictions on air that had gone into effect," she says.

Other papers had a more difficult time: They had to judge how important this was from wire stories. Joycelyn Winnecke, associate managing editor for national news at the Chicago Tribune, expresses frustration that her paper wasn't included in that February 10 government briefing. "The reason we were so upset to be excluded... was that we didn't feel like we had the information necessary to judge what [the Department of Homeland Security was] trying to do.... We felt like we were in the dark, and we were hearing from people we were interviewing that they were in the dark, too."

The frenzied run on duct tape and plastic sheeting led to cover stories on national anxiety in Time and Newsweek.

The briefing, says Winnecke, was geared to East Coast newspapers (officials said they were particularly concerned about threats against New York and Washington). But that left others without the information they needed to evaluate the recommendations. For that reason, and the fact that the story came over the wires late in the day, the Tribune ran it on page 12.

Winnecke says Tribune editors have tried to avoid panicking readers with their terrorism coverage. "Our managing editor [James O'Shea] specifically raised the point that we need to be careful with our stories," she says. For instance, in articles about people rushing out to buy duct tape, reporters need to "capture what's really going on" and make sure they don't "fuel something that shouldn't be fueled."

The first AI story the Tribune ran on the subject was on February 13, headlined, "Critics unglued by government's advice to buy duct tape." Many said such precau-

tions wouldn't offer much protection and compared the advice to the "duck and cover" guidelines during the Cold War—which now seem quite silly.

The Post's Downie acknowledges he would have liked to have included such duct-tape questioning on day one. The paper, he says, initially did not consult enough "outside-the-government experts" on whether this advice was solid. The Post ran such a piece two days later.

Critics, and some journalists, agree the questioning should have come sooner.

Marcy McGinnis, CBS' senior vice president for news coverage, says perhaps the media were late to go beneath the surface. When there's a press conference, the initial reaction "is to take the information and spit it back out again.... One important thing is saying, 'Wait a second, what exactly are you telling us to do?'"But there's not always two-way communication. "There's not always an opportunity to say, 'What's this all about?'"

The Department of Homeland Security launched an advertising campaign to make people aware of steps they could take to protect themselves in the event of a terrorist attack.

CBS News, not unlike ABC, NBC, cable news and a number of papers far removed from Washington and New York, stepped up its coverage when it became apparent some people were freaking out. "It picked up steam as the days went on, I guess as people said, 'Oh my God, I better get survival kits,'" says McGinnis. "The more that started to happen, the more [the media were] writing about it."

Downie likewise emphasizes that the Post "is reflecting the concern of our community instead of driving the concern."

But did the reaction to the concern simply fuel greater concern?

Many newspapers ran boxes that explained what chemical, biological and radiological attacks were and how you could best protect yourself in the event of one. They ran Q&A columns that tried to provide simple answers to public concerns. And they detailed what constitutes a survival kit with bulleted items.

But critics say such lists weren't helping. "Newspapers and television love lists, and that's part of our sort of self-help and news-you-can-use mentality," says Bob Giles, curator of the Nieman Foundation for Journalism at Harvard University. "But I think under these circumstances, there needs to be a very careful vetting of the suggestions by the government as soon as possible so people can read these lists in as accurate a context as possible."

Giles says the overreaction of the public wasn't unusual; many people horde supplies when a hurricane is approaching. "The government and the press both need to recognize that this is a natural impulse when these kinds of alarms are raised," he says. "Instead of simply reporting… the lists of what would go into a safety locker, there should be some interrogation of public officials as to why would you put this in there, when would you use it…. Maybe there could have been some stronger reporting at the very beginning that might have prevented this."

Journalists say it's tough to raise questions immediately, and with this story there was an additional hurdle: Homeland security is brand-new territory. "We are inventing coverage of an area where very few if any reporters have spent time working on these issues before," says Doyle McManus, the Los Angeles Times Washington bureau chief. "I think you are beginning to see those stories sifting though all the different kinds of emergencies and various possible responses. But it's taking longer than I think most readers wanted, and I think they were right to want the information right away. I went searching through the papers myself."

Before January, Audrey Hudson was covering Congress for the Washington Times. Then she got the new homeland security beat. The halls of the Capitol, this is not. "It is very challenging," she says. "You're sort of isolated…. Your sources are limited and the information is limited."

USA Today has tried to answer readers' questions. The paper ran a Q&A on February 11, and a more comprehensive one the next day that addressed different types of threats. The paper also referred people to the FEMA Web site. Says Hall: "We tried to do what we could to provide the information, but you're right, it does raise questions, and these things are extremely complicated." For example, with chemical attacks, she says, there are different steps people should take depending on the various kinds of chemicals that could be employed.

The charge that people just weren't given enough—or the right—information is prevalent. Some go so far as to say that the media have been timid in criticizing the government for fear that an attack might occur. "I think there is abject fear about that. I absolutely do," says Hub Brown, a former local TV news reporter and documentary producer who teaches broadcast journalism at the S.I. Newhouse School of Public Communications at Syracuse University. The media are "afraid that if we question it too much and something does happen… [it] makes us sound like we're bashing the system and makes us sound unpatriotic."

The Post's Kurtz says, "There's a certain reluctance, except perhaps on the part of late-night comics, to criticize government warnings, just in case something big does happen. But that doesn't mean that journalists have to act as if doomsday is just around the corner."

Certainly the press, like the government, wouldn't want to be in a position of failing to warn the public of an attack. But some journalists don't buy the "timid" charge. CNN's Keith McAllister, executive vice president for national newsgathering, says, "I think my view of patrio-

tism is if I'm doing my job well…. My job is to report the news and to ask tough questions" and to find the truth.

Reporters would love to have more information from officials, says Hall, but they're only going to get so much. "We all feel somewhat helpless in the face of terrorist threats both as reporters and as citizens, I think," she says. "You want to convey as much information as possible to an anxious public, but there's only so much you can do…. We have to take government officials sort of at their word on this more than we might otherwise" because so much of the information is classified or exempted from the Freedom of Information Act.

The Washington Post has been the most aggressive paper on this story, at least in terms of the sheer amount of coverage. It's a local story for the paper, says Downie, and his philosophy is the more information, the better.

On February 12, the Post ran a photo of a woman shopping for duct tape and plastic sheeting on the front page, with a refer to the survival-frenzy story on the Metro front. Many critics say these reaction stories are important because they give the press and government officials an idea of how people are responding. The scare in Washington lasted more than one day, however, and the Post carried two more stories on whether people were afraid or not.

Kurtz says the reaction stories—not just in his paper; everyone carried something on the duct-tape panic— were too much. It's a legitimate story, he says. "I just think they should have been scaled way back…. [T]o pound away at this on the front page day after day was the newsprint equivalent of saturation cable coverage. It's a very easy story to do and it tells you almost nothing other than that some people out there are starting to get nervous."

The news media did a good job reporting what the government was saying about the threat, but seemed leery of challenging officials, says Karen Brown Dunlap, president-designate of the Poynter Institute.

Slowly, perspective trickled into some media reports. On March 16, the Post published a special section on emergency preparedness that had a decidedly different tone: calm. The lead piece reminded readers of the incredibly low probability of dying from terrorism (less than the 1-in-4.5 million chance of death by lightning) and talked about the great number of people who escape attacks unharmed. The Post spelled out the unknowns—saying it couldn't predict how likely an attack is or what kind might occur. A story on respirators laid out the pros and cons of each type and cautioned that incorrectly using a gas mask could result in death. A massive evacuation is very unlikely, the Post reported, and smallpox is considered a "low-probability, high-impact risk."

You get a sense from talking with both media critics and people in Washington that they needed this type of information to cling to—something that gives the public an idea of how fearful they should really be, and of what, something that puts the risks in context. (Some experts and columnists did make comments about the small statistical chance of being the victim of a terrorist attack, but these were lost in the din.) And by discussing multiple terrorism possibilities and trotting out experts to talk about gas masks and hazmat suits, say critics, the media provided lots of information, sure, but left the public wondering what to make of it all.

CBS' Marcy McGinnis says coverage of the terrorism scare picked up steam when people started saying, "'Oh my God, I better get survival kits.'"

Syracuse's Hub Brown says more sober discussions were needed. "It's up to the news organizations to put this into perspective." When you combine the government precautions story with news of another Osama bin Laden audiotape, released on February 11, and more talk of a potential war with Iraq, how can someone who's watching this not be afraid? he asks.

But it is difficult to tell people what to do in a nonfrightening way against a background of intelligence "chatter" that doesn't provide the time, location or method of an attack.

Some critics are willing to cut the media, and the government, some slack. Everybody's new at this, says Philip Meyer, a journalism professor at the University of North Carolina at Chapel Hill. "You can't blame us on being confused on how to... establish warning systems in the first place and how to react to them in the second place," Meyer says. "You can't expect the government or the media to get it right" the first time out.

From the Onion's February 26 issue: "Orange Alert Sirens To Blow 24 Hours A Day In Major Cities." It was the perfect comic commentary on the government's mixed messages. The satirical story included this fake quote from Tom Ridge: "These 130-decibel sirens, which, beginning Friday, will scream all day and night in the nation's 50 largest metro areas, will serve as a helpful reminder to citizens to stay on the lookout for suspicious activity.... Please note, though, that this is merely a precautionary measure, so go about your lives as normal."

Indeed, some say officials deserve the blame for spreading fear and confusion, not the press. "I don't see the problem with the media," says Meyer. "I see it with the administration not making up its mind on how it wants people to behave."

Says Barbara Cochran, president of the Radio-Television News Directors Association: "It's so important for the government to provide as much information as possible.... Rather than causing panic, information can help dispel panic." She says the problems that have arisen are

more because of the government's message than the media's relaying of that information. On February 11, she says, we "get a warning that everyone should go and buy duct tape and plastic sheeting.... Three or four days later, the message is... well, we didn't really mean everybody."

Two days after the Department of Homeland Security included duct tape and plastic sheeting in its list of recommendations, U.S. officials emphasized that constructing a safe room wasn't the priority. Stockpiling food and water was more important. Two days later Ridge and President Bush were trying to institute some calm. "I want to make something very very clear at this point," Ridge said. "We do not want individuals or families to start sealing their doors or windows."

And there were other signs that public relations wasn't the new department's strong point. According to Time magazine, Ridge told senators at a private meeting that there was a "50 percent or greater" chance of an attack against the U.S. in the following weeks. But the secretary's spokesman denied he said that. On February 7 on ABC's "Nightline," Ridge put the threat of a major attack happening in the next few weeks at an eight on a scale of 10. He later told PBS' Jim Lehrer: Ted Koppel is "a very good journalist and he got me to do something that initially I started to say I'm not going to do.... But I gave him a number and rue the day, obviously."

The media are afraid that if they raise questions about the terror warning and then an attack occurs, it will seem as if they are unpatriotic, says Syracuse University's Hub Brown.

Officials seemed to be struggling with what they should say and how they should say it. For journalists, this reinforced the frustrating nature of the story.

Scott Kraft, national editor at the Los Angeles Times, says part of the discussion editors have about where to play terror alerts includes an evaluation of the strength of the government's information. Kraft says the paper needs to be careful about overplaying such news if officials aren't forthcoming about what their actions are based upon. The L.A. Times did run the news of the terror alert going up and then down on the front page.

But, in the end, there still wasn't a clear idea of why the alert had changed, he says. "I feel like the reporting [by all media] on the reasons for the alert level having gone up, on what it was based upon, has been kind of all over the map," Kraft says. "A few people have suggested that maybe the White House was hoping to gain some support for the potential war in Iraq." On the other hand, others say the raising of the alert was legitimate, he says. "I don't as a reader sit here and feel I know the answer.... We understand why the government is stingy in sharing some of this…. There is a sense from Washington that the American people should just trust us on this."

Neither the government nor the news media are exactly sure how to handle the terrorist threat, says CNN's Keith McAllister. "[T]hey're learning as they go."

The paper isn't giving up, mind you. "We're always trying to find out what the extent of the threat is," he says. "That's a reporting track that we have several people on."

On March 17, when President Bush issued an ultimatum to Saddam Hussein to go into exile or face a military attack, the alert jumped back up to orange. This time, the reasoning was clear: A war against Iraq could spark terrorist strikes.

The duct tape story didn't get any easier as the doubting experts came forward; it just got more confusing.

The February 11 edition of ABC's "World News Tonight with Peter Jennings" quickly raised questions about the effectiveness of duct tape in the face of a terror attack. "The recommendation to use duct tape and plastic is going to cause more fear and will have virtually no effect on any protection," said Dr. Peter Katona of UCLA's medical school.

But the next day, the network's "Good Morning America" aired a segment on how to properly pick and seal a safe room, with the show's home improvement editor helping a family in Connecticut tape up their laundry room. "USE DUCT TAPE AND PLASTIC SHEETING 46MM THICK," read a graphic.

A case of media confusion?

"I don't think there was confusion on how to report the story," says Jeffrey W. Schneider, ABC News vice president. "I think the whole country was trying to understand… what the advice was that they were giving." It was clear, he says, "that different people had different opinions about how to interpret that information…. On the one hand, you could be a little skeptical about duct tape and plastic sheeting, and on the other hand, there appeared to be some efficacy of using those materials."

A variation on the above example could be given for any number of news organizations. One day on CBS' "Early Show," Harvey Kushner, owner of the personal security store Safer America, showed a somewhat skeptical Hannah Storm what kind of gas masks and hazmat suits people could buy That night, CBS News questioned whether duct tape could offer any real protection. If people are concerned about their security and health, said one expert, what they should really do is "stop smoking, wear their seatbelt and not drink and drive."

CBS' McGinnis says the network received a lot of e-mails from people asking what types of protection are available. "It's not us saying what you should do," she says of segments like the one with Kushner. "It's telling people what there is." The network gives people informa-

TONE IT DOWN

These may not slow down the run on duct tape, but they're easy fixes. AIR offers three suggestions for improved terror alert coverage.

• Lose the terror alert labels. It's a rare media critic who isn't willing to give his two-cents' worth on why the cable news networks went too far when they added "Terror Alert: High" labels to their screens shortly after February 7. CNN discontinued use of the graphic relatively early, on February 12. Fox News Channel kept it up until the 21st; MSNBC didn't drop the label until early the next week. And the cable news networks aren't offering any apologies. Sharri Berg, vice president of news operations for Fox News Channel, emphasizes that the terror alert doesn't change with the wind. It's "so infrequently upgraded," she says, that "it's important to keep it up on the screen to get [the information] out there." MSNBC's Mark Effron says it's "ascribing too much power to cable television… by saying that a little bug on the bottom of the screen is going to scare people." AJR isn't ready to charge that this was a ratings ploy, but we will say it was a bad idea. Critics who said a label was like an alarm going off, or that it was meaningless without context or explanation, were right. Put it in the crawl, if you must, but lose the label.

• Look up "imminent" in the dictionary. Politicians and the press could use a reminder of what "imminent" means. According to Merriam-Webster's: "ready to take place; esp: hanging threateningly over one's head"—as in, in imminent danger of being run over. Code red is supposed to signify that an attack is "imminent" or under way. ABC News, and others, reported that the government insisted "the threat of an attack is real and imminent." That must not have been what officials meant. The same day, the New York Times was cautioning readers that officials weren't signaling a threat is imminent. Throughout the coverage, other journalists and politicians said an attack "could be imminent." Most things could. When you're talking to a jittery nation about a terrorist attack, word choice is important.

• Don't remind us. The words "duct tape" or "code orange" popped up in stories about books and fashion and theater. It's a common journalistic technique: "If you're tired of worrying about duct tape…" CNN aired a segment on escaping from anxiety by going to the movies, which included this helpful advice: "Well, escapists, be 'careful' which movie you choose. 'The Hours,' also nominated for best picture, is about depression and suicide. 'The Pianist,' another nominee, is about being a Jew under Hitler. Get too caught up in one of those and you may use the duct tape to hang yourself." Does every story have to be linked somehow to terrorism? Answer: No.

—Lori Robertson

tion and allows them to make their own decisions, she says.

There was also a range of messages coming from experts and health officials. So viewers could see terrorism expert Brian Jenkins offering this bit of reassurance on CNBC: "We can't overreact to this. Even the heightened probability of a terrorist attack does not automatically translate into great danger to the individual citizen." And the same day, CNN's Mike Brooks, cautioning, "We can't also forget some of the small towns. Some people say, 'I live in Smalltown, USA, nothing's going to happen here.' I think we were proved wrong when we looked at Oklahoma City and the bombing of the Murrah federal building there.... So no matter where you are, from a small town to a large town, here in the United States, you have to remain vigilant."

More mixed messages to add to the stew.

It's also possible that stories about terror alerts and intelligence and what to do about it all will never be clear. After September 11, news reports revealed information that suggested the attacks could have been prevented. John Miller and Michael Stone pinpointed the warning signs in their book "The Cell: Inside the 9/11 Plot, And Why the FBI and CIA Failed to Stop It." Yet, in the March 10 New Yorker, Malcolm Gladwell makes a convincing argument that it would not have been that easy. Gladwell uses a number of examples to show that evaluating intelligence before—instead of after—an attack is complicated, mired by much false information and bogus tips.

The public is going to depend on the press to serve as a guide through whatever confusing messages we're sure to receive in the future. But public attention fades faster than news coverage. And skepticism, it seems, is destined to rise.

On February 28, the day after the country's threat level went back down to code yellow, the Los Angeles Times carried the story on the front page. But National Editor Kraft wondered how many times the alert could fluctuate before it was no longer news. "If it had happened five or six times, [the story] probably wouldn't be as strong," unless more powerful evidence was produced, he says.

The Boston Globe didn't put the lowering of the alert on page one. Editor Martin Baron says the news came "well after the period of greatest apparent concern had passed." It had been two weeks, he points out, since the end of the hajj, the annual Muslim pilgrimage to Mecca during which officials had said an attack might come. The day before, National Editor Kenneth Cooper said he mentioned the alert change in the morning meeting, and "there were a few chuckles." He doubted the news would make the front page. It ran on A13.

Even journalists' attention can fade before a change in the terror alert.

Unfortunately, the media are at the beginning of the learning curve with this story. "To some degree, the learning experience of the U.S. government is similar to that of journalists in this country," says CNN's Keith McAllister. "They're not exactly sure how to handle it either, and they're learning as they go."

There are no rule books to consult, says Mark Effron, MSNBC's vice president, live news programming. The media aren't quite making it up as they go along, Effron says, but they're constantly thinking about what's appropriate. "It's as much instinct as anything else."

Lori Robertson is AJR's managing editor. Editorial assistants Michael Duck and Sofia Kosmetatos contributed to this story.

Journalism **Without** Profit Margins

In an era of **concentration, conglomeration** and **commercialization** of news, a small band of news outlets takes a **radically different** approach. The journalists at these noncommercial outposts definitely seem **happier. But is the journalism better?**

By Carl Sessions Stepp

Senior producer Michael Mosettig is running through his lineup for tonight's "The NewsHour with Jim Lehrer" when a colleague darts into his office and exclaims, "They've just beheaded a hostage."

Mosettig doesn't lunge for the phone to deploy reporters or scramble crews for sensational reaction shots. Instead, he thinks a moment and then asks, "What can we say about that?"

Five hours later, Mosettig will watch approvingly from the back of the control room as "The NewsHour" devotes more than six minutes to analyzing the story (three times the amount of coverage of the "NBC Nightly News with Tom Brokaw," by comparison), forgoing the shots of the hostage's weeping relatives that run on the commercial networks.

It is a typical response at "The News-Hour," which prizes depth and analysis over pizazz. And it illustrates a theme found repeatedly in an AJR examination of an array of noncommercial news outlets. In an era of concentration, conglomeration and commercialization of news, a few holdouts steer their own eccentric courses, typically more civic-minded and serious, and they take pride above all else in working toward ideals that are mostly their own, not prescribed by corporate bosses, focus groups or advertisers.

Says "NewsHour" senior correspondent Gwen Ifill, who has experience at NBC, the New York Times and the Washington Post: "We don't have to break things up for ads. We don't have to have people fighting with each other. We just cover the news."

Whether they work at large, visible operations (such as "The NewsHour" on PBS or the St. Petersburg Times) or in smaller niches (Pacifica Radio or the Day in New London, Connecticut), whether they have abundant resources (NPR, recent recipient of a $225 million bequest) or almost none (Ms. Magazine, once a glossy commercial monthly, now a quarterly on a shoestring), whether they're supported by foundations, listeners or complex trusts, Ifill and others at less-commercial media savor their liberation from a marketplace mentality.

They shy away from criticizing their commercial counterparts, where most of them began, and they acknowledge that such news organizations often do outstanding reporting. But they treasure the opportunity to present journalism to their standards, albeit with often limited resources and firepower.

Beyond journalists' feelings lies the more vital matter of the public interest. What, if any, special content or services does the public gain from the relatively few noncommercial news operations? What advantages do these media have over their for-profit cousins?

The broadest answer seems to be that readers and viewers gain streams of information vetted by journalists more attuned to public service than to circulation, ratings or the bottom line. Less-commercial media can think more in terms of social responsibility, with less oppression from short-term profit demands.

In content, that often leads to more coverage of foreign affairs, the economy and government, to less fluff and celebrity stalking, and to extra tolerance for controversy and alternative views. The journalism may or may not be superior to that produced elsewhere, but it comes from newspeople who are aiming high and relishing their independence.

Bill Marimow became one of NPR's two managing editors in May after 34 years working for newspapers, most recently as editor of the Baltimore Sun. "At NPR," Marimow says, "what I've seen is a real attempt to cover national and foreign news in a way that is illuminating, that serves the public, and that represents a long-term commitment to the public-service mandate."

Only a handful of mainstream newspapers follow the relatively noncommercial model, but two that do, the St. Petersburg Times and New London's Day, seem to have larger newsholes (perhaps in the area of 10 percent) than papers of similar size, more local news and art, greater insulation from economic downturns, and stronger focus on long-term goals.

"Here, our staffing levels and overall newshole ... didn't suffer nearly as much during the recent newspaper recession as those with higher profit pressures," says Neil Brown, St. Petersburg's executive editor.

Outside the mainstream, other types of media can follow their own less-conventional avenues. It isn't so much that

their journalism is better than the commercial brand. But it is theirs to choose and present, whether it is the feminist voice of foundation-owned Ms., the conservative tilt of the Unification Church-affiliated Washington Times, the "bless all mankind" spirit of the Christian Science Monitor or the "progressive" agenda of listener-supported Pacifica Radio.

"We're in no way beholden to anybody," boasts Patrick Burke, news editor of Pacifica station KPFK in Los Angeles. "We have the liberty to be cutting edge with style and language—to test the boundaries of news. If you've got your facts right, you can go after any company. There's no limit on who to talk trash about."

That feeling of independence resounds.

Joe Smyth's company carries the concept into its name: Independent Newspapers Inc. For more than a decade, its papers (mostly weeklies but including the daily Delaware State News in Dover) have been owned by a nonprofit holding company.

"Our purpose is journalistic service, pure and simple," says Smyth, the CEO. "We don't have any owners to whom dividends must be paid or who could profit by selling us to the highest bidder."

But independence has its downsides: often fewer resources compared with income-generating media; the temptation of complacency or self-indulgence; the loss of competitive edge; potential aloofness from readers and viewers.

But the less-commercial path clearly appeals to those who travel it, and it seems to energize a devotion to what Lance Johnson, managing editor of the Day in New London, calls "pure journalism."

"I know what our playing field is like," says "NewsHour" anchor and Executive Editor Jim Lehrer, "and it is unencumbered by any outside pressures. Anybody who cannot say that doesn't have it as good as I do."

It was a murder that upset even hard-boiled police. As desperate officers pounded on a locked apartment door one morning, a 10-year-old girl was being stabbed to death on the other side, her

screams audible, her assailant inches away but unreachable.

For the Day, a 42,000-circulation daily, it was the kind of hard local news the paper thrives on. Six reporters provided blanket first- and second-day coverage. Stripped across page one the third day was a banner story quoting anonymous sources on a shocking angle: The fire department had refused to give police a master key that would have opened the apartment door.

Inside the newsroom, Managing Editor Johnson kept pressing for answers and details, for what he calls "concentrated immediate coverage of high quality when people want to read it." Editors and reporters huddled frequently in Johnson's cramped office, debating when to depend on anonymous sources and whether to allow an after-the-fact off-the-record claim. Late one night, editors joined a battery of reporters feverishly working the phones to locate a key source.

Tim Cotter, assistant managing editor for local news, unhesitatingly assigned one reporter after another to the story. If other small papers did that, he says, "they wouldn't have enough reporters to get the rest of the paper out." But the Day "generally has enough bodies to get the job done."

To police reporter Andrew Ryan, a 28-year-old with two years on the job, it was a typical sprint. "They have become more and more willing to throw resources at a big story when it happens," Ryan says proudly of his editors. "For a paper our size, we have a large staff and better resources and more money to do things."

The resources exist thanks to the Day's unusual ownership model. Under a plan conceived in the 1930s, the paper is owned by a charitable trust. The newspaper company has just a few minor stockholders to pay (the trust owns 99.9 percent of the stock), and it can't be sold unless it loses money for two consecutive years. Profits are either reinvested in the paper or distributed through the trust, at the rate of several hundred thousand dollars a year, to social and civic organizations in the coverage area.

"It is a Knight and Day difference," quips Editor and Publisher Gary Farrugia, who came to the Day three years ago

"If you've got your facts right, you can go after any company. There's no limit on who to talk trash about."

after 18 years with Knight Ridder's Philadelphia newspapers. "We are not driven by an ever-growing profit margin directive. There are neither Wall Street corporate shareholders directing us nor family members. All the decisions the paper makes are to benefit itself and the community."

The paper accepts what Johnson calls "single-digit profits" and Farrugia labels "a fraction—less than half, often a third—of what newspapers owned by corporations are getting."

The result seems to be more resources than are typical for a 42,000-circulation paper: about 70 news and editorial-page staffers, for example, compared with a national average of about 57 for similar-size papers, according to Inland Press Association research. Then there are starting salaries in the mid- $30,000 range and a payroll Johnson labels "probably at least 40 percent higher than the average paper our size," as well as a generous newshole. One staff member tells of leaving a supervisory position at a comparable paper to take a line job in New London, still enjoying a pay increase from $43,000 to $48,000.

But the Day's managers also concede they don't live in paradise. The paper must make a profit to stay independent, and economic woes have hit Connecticut hard. The Day lived without a local business writer for most of the past two years, lost a handful of positions through an early retirement program, cut the newshole by 5 percent and, in an especially unpopular move, began charging for obituaries beyond the basic information. "We had to make some decisions," Johnson says. "Do we want to get several hundred thousands of income, or do we want to cut positions?"

Even so, says Farrugia, when the paper missed its budget "pretty severely" last year, the governing board "gave us profit forgiveness" rather than forcing further cuts.

Another tricky area involves covering community groups that receive tens of thousands of dollars from the paper's trust. The paper's managers say the bal-

ance is workable. "On our end there are no sacred cows," says Johnson.

But staff members acknowledge the awkwardness. "The readership has a tremendous sense of ownership of this paper," says Features Editor Elissa Bass, "sometimes to the point it's a real pain. Because of the trust, the Day has a strong financial stake in some nonprofit organizations around here. We have an obligation to cover that stuff. We review a ton of stuff [performances by groups that receive money from the trust], and if it stinks, we say it stinks. But we're expected to cover it."

Reporters say they feel free to tackle tough stories. Writer Kate Moran remembers attending a crowded funeral for a prominent city figure at which one staffer whispered to a colleague that at some time or other "we've offended everyone in this room."

"The best part," stresses AME Cotter, "is that all the decisions are made in this building, and if I disagree with the decision, I can talk to the person who made it. If we were chain-owned, that person might be in New Jersey or somewhere."

This refrain reverberates through the newsroom, a pride in journalistic independence combined with a conviction that it gives readers a better paper.

Cotter ticks off places he has sent reporters—South Carolina, Washington, even to Normandy with a returning veteran. This spring the paper sent two reporters, a columnist and a photographer to cover the University of Connecticut's men's and women's basketball champions in New Orleans and San Antonio.

In a significant commitment, military reporter Bob Hamilton was embedded on the USS Providence for three weeks last year. "The attitude was, 'Let's go for it,'" says Hamilton, a longtimer like many at the paper. "My sense is that nothing is off-limits, and whatever we need to do, we'll do it."

Several staffers who came to New London from elsewhere make stark com-

parisons with their previous papers. "It seems that the outside influences on the news decisions are very, very rare here," says designer Jill Blanchette, who joined the paper two years ago after working at a chain-owned paper. "The ad director, the publisher are not in the room very often. Those people practically had desks [in the newsroom] at my old paper."

Reporter Claire Bessette also arrived from a chain paper, where she had experienced "a lot of corporate direction—mostly bad. Here it's just news. That's the big difference."

In many tangible ways, the Day feels like any other newspaper. It certainly doesn't throw away its money on plush surroundings. Johnson presides from a small cluttered office looking out onto roof exhaust fans. There's a football in the corner, a Calvin and Hobbes panel on the wall.

A half-dozen editors crowd into the office each morning to brainstorm the next day's paper and deal with the usual newsroom emergencies. One morning, for instance, a reporter has had an accident headed for work on I-95 (it turns out to be minor), and with one photographer on vacation and another calling in sick, there's a bit of a crisis getting the assignments covered.

Afternoon budget conferences take place at pushed-together tables in the paper's snack room, where editors must almost shout to be heard over the rumble of vending machines. As the ritual blend of irreverence and serious talk takes place, you get the impression that newspeople behave pretty much the same whether they work at a chain giant or a trust-owned independent. "Journalists are sort of an odd bunch, and you find that no matter where you go," agrees Johnson. "Newsrooms have a lot of similarities, the type of people they attract, the general training they receive, the way we go about our jobs."

But he maintains that the Day is nonetheless distinct. "When a paper has to think twice about how it plays the news because of its bottom line, that's when

"When a paper has to think twice about how it plays the news because of its bottom line, that's when you get in trouble. And we don't do that."

you get in trouble. And we don't do that," says Johnson, who has been managing editor since 1986. "Everybody knows they are here at a special place. It's one of those jobs where you never really feel like you're coming to work."

Rosalie Stemer, a newsroom coach with experience at the San Francisco Chronicle and New York Times, has visited the Day on and off since 1999. "I've coached at papers with circulation as low as 12,000 and as large as the Boston Globe, and the Day stands out," she says. "The Day is really unique in how it relates to the community. People there are very proud of what they do.... There seems to be a shared ethic and enthusiasm among everybody on the staff to make their copy as good as it can be."

For better or worse, there are not many places with similar ownership structures. Besides the Day and the Delaware State News, they include Manchester, New Hampshire's Union Leader, owned by the Nackey S. Loeb School of Communications; the Champaign, Illinois, News-Gazette, controlled by a local foundation; and Alabama's Anniston Star, working its way toward foundation ownership.

Don't expect the roster to grow dramatically. Veteran newspaper analyst and AJR columnist John Morton explains that, while noncommercialism has its appeal, "I don't think this is going to sweep through the newspaper industry. The lure of getting a high price for your property is going to make that unlikely."

Probably the best known such operation is the St. Petersburg Times, which since owner Nelson Poynter's 1978 death has been owned by the nonprofit Poynter Institute.

Executive Editor Neil Brown, who came to St. Petersburg after eight-and-a-half years at Knight Ridder's Miami Herald, uses almost the same words as Lance Johnson to describe the difference. "There is a sense that you have landed someplace special," Brown says.

Brown says the paper can hire even when it has no openings ("I'm 12 people over right now and I still have my job") or "put diversity at the top of the agenda without worrying whether it fits into some corporate strategy in some other town." The 335,000-circulation paper has an editorial staff of 390, which is high for a paper of its size.

During one downturn, Brown says, the Times "did pinch newshole like everybody else, but not as much. We actually used the phrase, 'We'll take less profit.' We make a profit. We wish we made more. But it doesn't become the defining point around here."

Philip Gailey, the paper's editorial page editor and a member of its board, says it isn't unheard of for the Times to "drop our profit margin down to the single digits if we think we need to invest more money in printing technology or new bureaus. We've done it. It's not a hypothetical."

What do readers get? Gailey, Brown and others mention increased local news coverage, a larger newshole, more investigative projects and enterprise, a greater willingness to take on advertisers or special interests. I worked at the paper briefly in the 1970s and have visited its newsroom many times, and there's little question journalists there exude a special sense of purpose.

Anne Hull, a St. Petersburg Times writer for 15 years before joining the Washington Post four years ago, remembers the paper as "less of a bureaucracy, more of a journalistic enterprise."

"Every top editor there has ink on his hands," Hull says. "There's no corporate power a plane ride away. It's a place people scratch and claw to get to. You know that every quarter there are not going to be [profit] figures released and the anxiety that results from all that."

Across Tampa Bay sits Times competitor Gil Thelen, publisher and president of the Tampa Tribune, both envious and appreciative.

Competing with St. Petersburg, says Thelen, is "extremely challenging because they can relentlessly execute their plan no matter what the economic climate is." But competition has its advantages. Two years ago, Thelen says, the Media General-owned paper took "a profit stepback" in order to invest in eight new staffers and two pages of newshole to cover a county contested by both the St. Petersburg and Tampa papers.

"Another huge advantage for them is the image-making machine of the Poynter Institute. They have been very, very effective at telling a purer-than-driven-snow story about themselves. It gives them a very large recruiting edge," Thelen says. The edge is magnified, he adds, because St. Petersburg can offer about 10 percent more money than Tampa for prime job candidates.

"They are a formidable competitor doing a lot of things very well," Thelen concludes. "We welcome their challenge. They make us better."

You don't necessarily associate Ms. magazine with the tony boutiques and salons surrounding it, but here the magazine sits, in its stately South Beverly Drive home that once housed the Beverly Hills Bridge Club.

Staff members appreciate the Beverly Hills irony ("we're not of it but we enjoy it," says one editor) but they also know why the magazine moved here from New York three years ago: money and survival. Now owned by the Feminist Majority Foundation, whose offices it thriftily shares, Ms. is a trimmed-down quarterly published by a skeleton staff of four full-time editors and lots of part-timers and contributors.

It may be a long way from its zenith as the revolutionary iconic voice of an insurgent women's movement, edited by Gloria Steinem and prominent on every newsstand. But it lives on, liberated by its newest owners to press forward with its mission. "We're editorially free," says Managing Editor Michel Cicero. "We can publish things other people can't."

Editorial freedom is the watchword for specialized media such as Ms., one of numerous magazines and a few broadcast outlets that, under noncommercial owners, follow the bliss of their own creative spirits. It's hard to make direct comparisons to other media, since niche outlets are by definition specialized. But because they don't seek to serve entire communities, as newspapers such as St. Petersburg or New London must, they can be iconoclastic and irreverent, off-center and opinionated, without kowtowing to advertisers or marketplace fads.

"The lines are blurring at many publications," says Cicero. "But when we put something on our cover, it's what we want to be on the cover." Adds Senior Editor Michele Kort, "We choose the advertisers rather than the advertisers choosing us. We're not trying to write anything that draws in the ads."

Since its founding in 1971, Ms. has lived through almost every ownership model, from the for-profit, ad-supported mainstream to totally ad-free noncommercialism. Today, with a circulation of just over 100,000, it accepts ads again, although selectively, mostly for issues and activities consistent with its feminist vision. Staff members hope the magazine will grow and eventually return to bimonthly frequency.

And while appreciating their relative independence, they are fiercely practical about what it costs. Asked how her magazine differs most from more commercial publications, for instance, Cicero replies quickly, "They have more money than we have."

The magazine works with fewer perks and a lower budget than it had in New York, where there were more than 20 staffers. Cicero laughs as she recalls how shocked some cover story subjects are when they learn Ms. can't pay for hair stylists or other expected amenities.

Appearing only four times a year has its costs. Early this spring, editors were considering devoting a cover photo to Judy Dean, wife of then Democratic frontrunner Howard Dean. By the time

the issue appeared in the summer, they were glad to have chosen otherwise.

Then there's the foundation connection. For one thing, it means the magazine can't make election endorsements or even appear to. One idea that Ms. spiked, for instance, was a look at prominent female candidates; lawyers thought it might "make us a target," Kort says. Editors also deal with what she calls "constraints within the organization," sometimes traveling across the hall to check out themes with the owning foundation.

Still, Ms. editors say they accept such tradeoffs for the satisfaction of pursuing a vital mission and offering coverage hard to find elsewhere. Cicero points, for instance, to an article critical of drug advertising that ran last year, something a magazine dependent on ads might avoid.

And Ms. has a stature that attracts eminent writers regardless of pay or perks. For example, the Associated Press' Martha Mendoza, who shared the 2000 Pulitzer for investigative reporting, came to the magazine with her riveting personal account of abortion. "I love feeling not constrained by anything other than your own good taste," says Kort.

Ms. Research Director Camille Hahn freelances for commercial magazines that are "all about the ads and selling that to the readers." But at Ms., "we all feel really strongly about this magazine. I freelanced for the silly local magazine, but I don't care about it. I care about this."

A few miles across town, in a decidedly less glamorous setting at a listener-supported Pacifica radio station, KPFK News Editor Patrick Burke makes the same point about doing news his own way.

"I don't think I would want to do news radio if I didn't have the freedom to do what I do now," Burke says. "I believe in the cause. I don't think it would be worth it to trade a higher salary for advertising and commercial pressures."

KPFK operates out of a low-slung building in a strip of dry cleaners, bike shops and neighborhood cafés just off Ventura Boulevard in North Hollywood. Burke, one full-time reporter, a half-timer and a stable of volunteers produce a half-hour newscast at 12:30 p.m. and an hour-long show at 6 p.m. each weekday.

Like the editors at Ms., he admits "we could use a little bit more money." On the day I visit, Burke is trying to figure out who will anchor the next day's news and coping with the fact that his only reporter is at the dentist.

But the 6 p.m. newscast he produces that night is substantive as well as different. Featuring staff reports as well as those from the Pacifica affiliate Free Speech Radio News, the ad-free program opens with a 30-minute block of international news. The lead looks at how Brazil and China are challenging major nations' trade policies. Stories follow on unrest in rural Peru, economic recovery in Argentina and flooding in Haiti. While the Los Angeles ABC affiliate is broadcasting a segment on a local shooting, KPFK is examining mistreatment of refugees in Thailand and Africa.

At 6:30, KPFK turns to its business and labor report, featuring union concerns about the sale of Boeing plants in the Midwest and criticism of Wal-Mart's use of government subsidies.

Local news comes next. Burke himself covers a rally by janitors at local hospitals who are seeking higher salaries and better health benefits. Another segment spotlights a new center for homeless teenagers and tells listeners how to volunteer.

The broadcast clearly reflects what Burke calls Pacifica's "commitment to represent voices that aren't otherwise heard—implicitly progressive-agenda type stories."

So his station pays priority attention to Iraq-related rallies ("Pacifica is a reference to peace, so it's inherently an antiwar-type operation"), labor concerns and issues such as homelessness and immigration.

Burke says he aims for a generally straight approach but doesn't mind an editorial jab or two. When the Abu Ghraib prison scandal broke, for instance, he decided to term it a "humiliation, torture, homicide and possible rape scandal."

"That seemed more accurate than calling it an abuse scandal," Burke says slyly. "I try not to have too much commentary within the news items. But we definitely have our context."

"They're going to get a lot of international news and economic news and stuff that is our stock in trade. And they're not going to get any showboating."

Overall, he believes, the station can often ignore the news everyone else is covering and offer listeners something entirely different.

"If I see something is getting massive exposure elsewhere, I'll push it down on the agenda or maybe leave it out," Burke says. "I don't want to be redundant."

On the air live, "The NewsHour with Jim Lehrer" is proceeding in its customary oh-so-serious way, but in the control room things are getting a little snarky.

Moans break out when a segment on competitive colleges shows a kid being rejected because his grades slipped one semester in 10th grade. When an admissions officer is asked what will get an applicant in, a control room technician snorts, "His dad's gotta build them a new gym."

But the loudest whoops erupt when an on-air guest refers to a State Department report as "squirrelly."

"Squirrelly" is about as wild as it gets at the Arlington, Virginia-based "News-Hour."

It is a serious news program produced by serious newspeople who generally feel insulated from ratings and marketing strains (see "No Frills. No Bells. No Whistles," October 2001). But even they worry about attracting viewers and fending off the dreaded B-for-boring label. "There's no point in doing this if nobody is watching," says senior producer Kathleen McCleery. "There are those of us who do want to pep up the show."

"We want as large an audience as possible, and we want this program to be as interesting as possible," agrees Executive Producer Lester Crystal, a 21-year "NewsHour" veteran who once headed NBC News. "But our income is not dependent on the ratings as much as the commercial operations are."

Terence Smith, "The NewsHour's" media correspondent, joined the show after 13 years at CBS. He says ratings and resource issues dominated meetings at his former network. "The editorial meetings weren't editorial at all. They never had time to talk about how to cover the news. From the day I came here, the talk was about the news, what's in the news, what ought to be on the show."

Smith's producer Anne Davenport, with her own experience at CBS and ABC, says the PBS show, unlike commercial networks, can ignore "the appeasement factor" and think instead of audience needs.

Perhaps the firmest of all is the boss himself, Lehrer, who has been with the program since it premiered as a half-hour newscast in 1975 (it expanded to an hour in 1983). "Somebody might call us old-fashioned, and that's fine. I'm not the least bit concerned about that," Lehrer says. "Our mission is to tell the folks what is happening that we think is important, and take two or three of those things and flesh them out. They aren't going to get the sports results, the weather, the O.J. Simpson-type stories. They're going to get a lot of international news and economic news and stuff that is our stock in trade. And they're not going to get any showboating."

Evidence suggests "The NewsHour" has a relatively small but loyal following. A survey this spring by the Pew Research Center for the People & the Press found that 5 percent of the public watched regularly, compared with 16 to 17 percent for each of the three network evening news shows. The program attracts just under 3 million viewers a night.

"The NewsHour" audience skews older (6 percent to 8 percent of people over 50 watch regularly compared with 2 percent of those under 30), well educated and well off. It got higher marks than any other outlet for international news coverage and second highest, behind C-SPAN, for Washington news. It also showed greater reach among moderate viewers (44 percent of its audience) than any other medium.

The program can seem cautious, even overly deferential to those in power, but Lehrer professes no worries that public television will one day decide the program needs a jump start, in the way that NPR dumped longtime "Morning Edition" host Bob Edwards earlier this year. "It may be blind stupidity on my part, but I don't feel that happening," he says. "The people out in the country really understand what we are doing."

What they are doing, Executive Producer Crystal says, "is depth and balance. People come to us for explanation and understanding."

In fact, the show could be called "The AnalysisHour." It doesn't chase breaking news and depends on clients and vendors for much of its video. "The NewsHour" generally opens with a six-to-eight-minute news summary, then switches to three or four "focus segments," each exploring a single story through interviews, panels, commentaries or news-documentary packages.

"The NewsHour" unapologetically zeroes in on government and public affairs, matters that senior correspondent Ray Suarez calls "as vital as oxygen to a functioning democracy." Suarez warms to the point like a keynote speaker: "You can't shy away from budget wrangles that involve the chairman of the Ways and Means Committee, the formulas that underlie Medicare reform, block grants to the states. These are the building blocks, the beams and floorboards of our common life. Somebody has to explain it. Just because it is visually lousy doesn't mean you don't explain Medicare cards to senior citizens.... You gotta do it. The you-gotta-do-it philosophy underlies a lot around here."

What "The NewsHour" doesn't do, Suarez acknowledges, is "pull out all the stops and spend money like crazy." Senior producer McCleery, for instance, remembers a time when she worked for NBC and producers weren't happy with a setup shot of a doctor walking into his office. So a crew flew from Washington to Florida to reshoot one scene, about seven seconds' worth. "That won't happen at 'The NewsHour,'" she laughs.

"We are in effect trading resources for time," Crystal explains. "We have more time to do the story, but fewer resources on the ground."

Like colleagues at other noncommercial operations, "NewsHour" staff members constantly mention their autonomy. "I could be making more money working elsewhere," Suarez says, "but I wouldn't be a happy guy, and I wouldn't work out of the conviction that I would be allowed to do the best work I am capable of."

What matters most in the end, according to senior correspondent Gwen Ifill, is that programs such as "The NewsHour" give viewers extra choices. "They don't have to like it. They may think it is too long. But it gives them the option, and it is not what commercial broadcasting can do."

A similar feeling prevails across the Potomac in Washington, D.C., at National Public Radio, where autonomy is also prized—and journalists enjoy even more resources. (See "Quicker *and* Deeper?" June/July.)

After receiving an estimated $225 million in bequests from the late philanthropist Joan Kroc, NPR in June announced a three-year, $15 million plan to add 45 reporters, editors and producers and open new bureaus at home and overseas.

Managing Editor Bill Marimow says the gift allows NPR "to really put its money where its ideals are." Here, Marimow says, "the editors can make decisions based solely on what they think is interesting, important or relevant," reflecting a long-term commitment "that is not as subject to economic vicissitudes as a for-profit corporation is."

Scott Simon, host of NPR's "Weekend Edition Saturday," jokes that Kroc is "a perfect underwriter—somebody prosperous, generous and who can't pick up the phone." But Simon also maintains that he has always felt independent at NPR. "I've never had an underwriter pick up the phone and apply any pressure, and I can confidently say it would have no effect if it happened," he says.

"We do have some conventional pressures that others would recognize," he adds. "Some of the material is influenced by the tastes of the audience. We want to keep the audience expanding. We want to keep as many people as possible listening."

My own observation, based on years of working in, visiting and studying news operations, is that noncommercial journalists have no monopoly on commitment or quality. Large media corporations have the resources and clout for in-depth coverage, investigations and enterprise. No matter who pays their salaries, journalists tend by tribal habit to be aggressive, competitive and mindful of public service.

Yet in visiting less-commercial newsrooms and interviewing their journalists, I was struck by the palpable sense of relief and liberation, the exhilaration of professional autonomy.

When journalists feel in control, audiences gain something extra and special: news, analysis and opinion tailored to community and civic needs by professionals who care deeply.

Bob Steele, a media ethics specialist at the Poynter Institute, says less-commercial newsrooms often breed "a culture that allows decisions to go a different way." Editors at papers like St. Petersburg, Steele says, "often have more independence in making decisions at the local level, in terms of executing a mission, commitment of resources, and values balancing. It doesn't guarantee it, but when you answer to people in the same building as you are, you have a different tabletop from which to make decisions, and that can be a positive force."

As the "The NewsHour's" Michael Mosettig puts it, "We don't have the ax of the ratings hanging over us, so we can go where the news leads."

That is a professional's delight, and most of the journalists I spoke to cherish it.

"I am a blessed person," Jim Lehrer said at the end of our interview. "And, more importantly, I know it."

Senior Editor Carl Sessions Stepp teaches at the Philip Merrill College of Journalism at the University of Maryland. He wrote about newspapers' efforts to increase readership in AJR's December 2003/January 2004 issue.

Et Tu, "Nightline"?

The Kobe Bryant and Michael Jackson sagas are the latest manifestations of the media's infatuation with celebrity—even Ted Koppel ditched President Bush for the erstwhile King of Pop. But is that so wrong? In an era with so many sources of news, is celebrity overkill a major threat to the republic?

BY JILL ROSEN

"If you don't want it printed, don't let it happen."

That's the blunt, somewhat plucky motto of the Aspen Daily News, a small Colorado newspaper that in October made a blunt and somewhat plucky move. The paper, its editors decided, would no longer print news of arguably the area's biggest happening in ages: the rape trial of basketball superstar Kobe Bryant. It happened and, news judgment of the rest of the world be damned, they weren't printing it.

The ski mecca of Aspen is about a 70-mile snowy drive from the county seat of Eagle, a serene mountain town until this summer, when a resort worker from there accused Bryant of raping her. For months the Daily News had willingly fed its 12,000 or so readers steady offerings about the essentially local case, wire stuff usually but occasionally one of the paper's two staff reporters would wander up the road to send back a dispatch from the fray. But on October 9, as most media outlets from the area and the nation were revving their engines for the opening of the preliminary hearing and the release of what could be the first solid details of what happened between Bryant and the woman in the hotel room halfway between Eagle and Vail, the Daily News called it quits. In an editorial that day headlined "Kobe Who?" the paper promised readers that it was done covering the case until the verdict, done publishing minute and irrelevant tidbits surrounding it and, above all else, done running with the media pack.

"We just felt like enough is enough," Editor Rick Carroll said in December, a

couple months into the no-Kobe diet and not feeling particularly deprived. Carroll, a thoughtful sounding guy, comes off equal parts proud of his decision and flustered by the attention it has brought. The media, naturally, with their insatiable need to devour all things Kobe, couldn't miss covering the paper that decided not to cover Kobe. So Carroll ended up hearing from hundreds of people, many of whom jadedly accused him of trying to make a statement, which, of course, he most certainly was.

And the statement was the Aspen Daily News' version of the evergreen parental refrain: If all the kids were jumping off a bridge . . . Or, just because every Tom, Dan and Peter was covering this or any story doesn't mean everyone has to. "We wanted to make a statement to show we don't have to do that dance of the mainstream media," Carroll explains. "We felt like the coverage was just going way beyond what it was worth."

Anymore, too much is just the way things feel. Overblown is par for the course and eye-rollingly expected when it comes to stories of a certain ilk. With Kobe, with Laci and Scott, with Michael. With Paris and O.J. and Chandra. With sharks and the flu and Britney's kiss. Whether it needs it or not, America gets this stuff like its fries: supersized.

And is that bad? Is there such a thing as too much? Depends whom you ask.

Stephen Bell logged 20 high-profile years as a correspondent for ABC News beginning in the late 1960s. It was a time, he says, when overkill was all but nonexistent.

Back then only a handful of news organizations anointed the stories of the day. These alpha dogs, which Bell calls "gatekeepers," all sung more or less the same tune, serious and sedate. The news people were seeing on ABC or NBC or CBS was what they were reading in the three news-weeklies or in the major newspapers.

Moreover, on TV, there was only 15 minutes to tell it all, then eventually 30. Even if a network did want to include a piece on, say, a famous basketball player's alleged sexual transgressions, it would all be said in about 30 seconds, hardly enough room to even begin anything resembling overkill.

Bell still remembers the day in 1977 when Elvis died and one of the big three networks led with it. "The other networks were aghast," recalls Bell, who now teaches broadcast journalism at Ball State University in Indiana.

Walter Podrazik, a media contributor for Chicago Public Radio who has just co-authored a book called "Watching TV: Six Decades of American Television," says the contrast between the way so-called big news is treated today and the way it was historically is best evidenced by looking at the coverage following the assassination of John F. Kennedy.

The president had just been killed yet, at the end of the day, each of the three major networks signed off. Yes, they pre-empted scheduled entertainment shows to broadcast live aspects of the tragedy—and that at the time was rather revolutionary. But when they ran out of new things to say, they said goodnight. They said, " 'Nothing is happening now so we're not going to be on the air,'" Podrazik says. "'We'll come back tomorrow morning.'"

Ironically, Podrazik says it was the tasteful and appropriate coverage of the assassination that opened the door to the wall-to-wall excesses that define modern news. For one thing, it showed that sometimes the public appreciates seeing everything—the world fixated on each plodding step in the funeral procession, breathed in every tearful detail at the burial. And it all demonstrated the power and the drama of going live. Until then, "live" was a rare treat for viewers, extended only to the occasional presidential address or other scheduled events of state. But cameras—rolling live as the arrested shooter, Lee Harvey Oswald, was led out of a Texas jail en route to another—captured his death as Jack Ruby fired on him from the watching crowd.

Now viewers expect no less for much less. These days it hardly takes an assassination. And if Elvis died in 2004 it would lead every newscast and make every front page in a heartbeat, the proverbial news meeting no-brainer.

What's changed? Everything really. First off, there's no such thing as a gatekeeper. There are bazillions of media outlets, and any one of them at any time can catapult a story into national play. A then-unheard-of guy with a Web site named Drudge broke the story about Bill and Monica—when the traditional "gatekeeper" Newsweek wasn't ready to go with it. And during the trial of O.J. Simpson, the established and respected journalists chased stories published by the not-exactly-lofty National Enquirer. "Now you have even chat rooms putting stories into play," Bell says, adding that anyone will chase the slightest whiff of news reported by anyone else, for fear of being the only one without it. "For competitive reasons alone you can't afford to be left out."

And add to the ever-increasing list of places to get news a seemingly ever-intensifying celebrity-centric culture. A Newsweek with Tom Cruise on the cover is as likely as one featuring Saddam. Entire cable networks are seemingly devoted to finding out the brand of Jennifer Aniston's shoes. And if somehow legitimate news intersects with fame, just throw up your hands, then stand back for the unstoppable force. If someone is arrested for rape, it may or may not make the local news. If Kobe Bryant is arrested for rape, the na-

tional media won't only trip over themselves to report the courtroom details, they'll tell you the cut, color and carat of the "oops-I'm-sorry" diamond ring he gave his wife afterward.

The thing is, say Bell and others, anyone who realizes the status celebrities have in today's world can hardly deny their place in a newscast or above the fold or in any legitimate news position. Elvis' death, Bell says, *should* have led the newscast.

"Why not?" he asks. "No matter how much people claim not to be interested or are quite tired of Monica or whatever, back we come with extreme interest. Ratings tell how much people really do fixate on this. People love to deny being obsessed with these things, but ratings tell otherwise."

That they do.

When Leroy Sievers, executive producer of one of network news' most esteemed programs, ABC's "Nightline," sent out an e-mail memo on November 19 telling the show's newsletter subscribers that the staff was bumping coverage of President Bush's visit to London for news about pop star Michael Jackson's arrest on multiple counts of child molestation, well, you would have thought he'd just said Ted Koppel would be broadcasting live from MTV's spring-break beach house—in a Speedo. The memo was quickly posted on media news sites with commentary dripping with surprise and thick disdain.

"Even 'Nightline'?" Sievers squeaks, mimicking the general sentiment that was aimed at him. Is nothing sacred? We'd expect this from the likes of "Dateline," but "Nightline"? Et tu, Ted?

Sievers says he sent the memo after a late-morning meeting with the entire staff, a meeting that featured a rather intense back and forth about what to do—it was anything but a given that a presidential diplomatic visit was of more gravity than a freaky pop star's supposed sexual misadventures. They went around and around about it, about half the staff believing that Bush was the way to go. Michael Jackson, they felt, was "lurid and meaningless," a scandalous pouf of a story that really didn't warrant the Ted Koppel treatment. But others adamantly felt that here is one of the best-known figures on the planet, involved in something sordid, but something he could possibly buy his way out of. Plus, they argued, the president could still be fresh the next day.

"We agonized over this one," Sievers says. In the end, after a show of hands,

Michael won. "It was pretty obvious that was the way to go . . . It's a big story."

Big and popular. The report was "Nightline's" top-rated show of the year, handily besting Koppel's reportage from the war in Iraq. Though the Jackson piece was no dispatch from the front, its ratings are deserved and its subject matter is nothing to be ashamed of, Sievers says. He says "Nightline" reported this story like it would any other, thoughtfully and with a hard-news mentality. "We treated it as a serious story," he says.

As other news reporters swarmed outside Jackson's amusement park-like Neverland ranch, aiming cameras at helicopters that may or may not have been ferrying the star, or trying to wrench scoops from "Jackson family friends," this is how Ted Koppel opened his report: "The word voyeurism was created for a day like this. Whatever it is that makes us slow down and crane our necks as we pass a traffic accident, whatever causes us to linger at the checkout counter as we scan the headlines on the Star and the National Enquirer, whatever relish we derive from the misadventures of the rich, powerful and famous, you could not ask for a more blatant self-destructive target than Michael Jackson. And today, he has descended into the deepest valley of a trouble-plagued career."

Sievers knows that plenty of media outlets blew the November 19 Jackson news out of all logical proportion. But, he insists, there was a story there, a significant one, crying out for the right kind of treatment. "Was there excess?" he asks. "You bet. But the issue for us was, are there broader issues? Illuminate this."

The "Even—gasp— 'Nightline'!" cries of disappointment perfectly demonstrate something of a cottage industry in journalism that's sprung up in the shadow of saturation coverage. It's shame. It's self-loathing. It's the whole idea that by covering a Michael Jackson or a Kobe Bryant, the media are falling down on the job, somehow abdicating their responsibilities to be eternally highbrow, their noses buried in stacks of government documents. And that if they do stoop so low as to join the "circus" or the "feeding frenzy" or the "spectacle," they need to somehow distance themselves from the others elbowing one another in the morass, to find a way to say, as they're standing, palms sweating, in front of Neverland's gate, that "yeah, I'm here, but it's not what you think."

This is one of Bill Powers' favorite topics, one he's written about in his "On the Media" column in National Journal. In December, in the context of Michael Jackson's arrest, he served up these words with a healthy side of sarcasm: "If you're a respectable media outlet doing a Jackson story, there's a kind of purification rite you have to perform, in which you demonstrate that although you're technically part of the feeding frenzy, you yourself are actually very much above it."

The Boston Globe reported from Santa Barbara the day Jackson was arrested, Santa Barbara where all the reporters were, that "the world's media jostled for the money shot of the pop superstar in handcuffs." MSNBC's Chris Matthews asked Sam Donaldson this, as if Matthews hadn't heard about Jackson on his own network: "Sam, this Michael Jackson story, it's been all over your radio show on ABC this week. What's the big story here?" And how many journalists informed readers and viewers that this Michael Jackson thing, it's going to be the biggest media frenzy, the most crazed media circus since O.J.?

Inevitably, everyone excessively covering whatever the story of the day is pauses for a second to ask a media expert how much is too much. Invariably, said media expert will all but scream, "This! This is too much!" At which point the reporter will type up his story, slugged "frenzy," or turn to the camera saying, "Back to you, Gary, in Neverland."

Bob Thompson, director of the Center for the Study of Popular Television at Syracuse University, gets these calls all the time. In fact, he jokes, it's almost at the point where he's fearing an overkill of stories about overkill. He says it used to be the case that a story would need to spin for a few weeks before reporters, concerned about whether the media were overdoing it, would start calling him. Now, he says, it only takes a day or two.

Thompson says that the discussion about the coverage can be thought-provoking and certainly worthwhile after a stakeout at an airport to see if Michael Jackson's plane *might* land there. However, he says, as often as the media sincerely ask whether or not things have gone overboard, they're just looking for another reason to talk about Michael, Kobe or whomever. "It's our mea culpa," he says. "It's the media slapping its own hand while also keeping these things alive."

It's the televised reports, Thompson says, more than anything else, that contribute to the feelings of absurdity and the sense that things are out of control. That's because instead of the traditional style of reporting a story after assembling the facts, on TV reporters feel their way as they go along, speculating about probable causes and possible outcomes on air with experts. "You don't report it and get the facts," he says. "It's happening as part of the programming, while you're figuring it out . . . You're talking to people like me about whether or not you should be talking about it."

The story of Michael Jackson, though frighteningly overdone, is "damn interesting," Thompson says. He's tuned in to it not as a television sociologist but as a guy who's fascinated. "I'd be watching it if I were an electrician," he says.

And with that, he's just like much of the rest of the country. As Fox's Eric Burns pointed out in a column, when the Jackson story broke, his network's daytime ratings jumped 25 percent, CNN's leaped 44 percent and MSNBC's were up 51 percent. People wanted to know what was up and expected the 24-hour news channels to tell them.

Of course some of those very same people turned around later and said that the coverage was disgusting them, that they couldn't believe it was Jackson, Jackson, Jackson, him and his demented, powdery mug shot, all over the dial. It happens every time, Thompson says. "There were people complaining about the O.J. coverage. With Tonya Harding, the thing wasn't out four days before people were complaining about the backlash of that," he says. "But the big paradox is at the very same time they are complaining about how they're so sick of all this Michael Jackson coverage, if I see the mug shot one more time I'll throw up, they're flipping through the dial looking for more."

Columnist Bob Kravitz of the Indianapolis Star, writing about everyone's "secret" fascination with the Kobe Bryant trial, put it like this: "In a sexual assault case, no means no. In the case of the consuming public and the media, no means, 'OK, I'll watch the Stone Phillips exclusive with the alleged victim's camp counselor, but that's where I draw the line.' "

The people are transfixed and the media—people, too, despite themselves—are as well. "We're all drawn to these things and hate ourselves for it," Powers says, adding that it's almost puritanical, the conventional media wisdom that if something is popular, journalists shouldn't dwell on it. It's not "important" enough. He calls it "institutional snobbery." "There's only a certain kind of story that concerns important issues that we can care about," he says. "All we're supposed to really care about is policy. We're not supposed to care about anything about entertainment or celebrities, but they're the most powerful people in a society like ours."

Thompson agrees. "I don't think news must constantly be about a civic duty, civic duty, civic duty," he says. "I don't think that's journalism's charge."

Powers remembers that when media types were criticizing then-New York Times Executive Editor Howell Raines, they'd point accusingly to the time he put a story about pop vixen Britney Spears on the front page. "It was mentioned as a low point in Howell Raines' tenure," Powers says. "In my opinion, that was a good sign—he knew enough about the cultural mind-set to know this will hit people where they live."

If anyone is taking the brunt of the blame for exacerbating the media's inability to know when to say when, it's the 24-hour news operations. When the subject is breathless reporting, everyone knows that those voted most likely to pant are over on cable.

So it could seem ironic to some that Anderson Cooper, host of CNN's "Anderson Cooper 360," takes a few moments most weeks on his program to feature something in the news that he thinks has "been done to death." The segment's apt name? Overkill. So far they've cast a bored eye on such over-discussed topics as Christmas, Jessica Lynch and Paris Hilton. Oddly, no Jackson or Kobe, but the irreverent Cooper is more likely than most anchor types to crack the occasional joke at his profession's expense.

"On the first day of Michael Jackson, at the end of my program, after everyone had done the story to the nth degree, I joked there should be an obit for all the stories no longer being told because of Michael Jackson," Cooper says. "We try to keep it in perspective as much as you can. But this will probably be in the overkill hall of fame."

Joking aside, as of December, Cooper wasn't overly concerned that the Jackson soap opera was getting disproportionate play. The day that Jackson was officially charged, Cooper led his show with John Lee Malvo being found guilty in the 2002 sniper shootings. Next up was an update in the case of a U.S. citizen held as an "enemy combatant." Only then came the Jackson. But earlier, after the pop star's arrest, Cooper unabashedly showed, for 15 minutes, shots of Jackson's motorcade inching through the streets of Las Vegas.

"One of the biggest entertainers ever is about to be arrested and shown in handcuffs. I don't think it's crazy that people would want to see that. I see no reason to apologize for that," Cooper says. "I thought it was fascinating. People were mobbing his car, the window would roll down and this little pale hand would pop out and wave. There are live moments that happen to be fascinating whether or not it's earth-shattering."

Nor does Cooper think much of the decision by some of his fellow journalists to take a pass on some of the more sensational stories. Like Powers, Cooper sees snobbery in that attitude. "There's an elitist part of that that is unattractive," he says. "I think it's a mistake."

Joe Howry, managing editor of California's Ventura County Star, probably wouldn't mind terribly if someone labeled him elitist for his refusal to go gaga over Michael Jackson's arrest. He's watched the cable coverage, and if it's elitist to not want to be a part of it, then count him in. He's not though. He's merely sickened by the idea that a child might have been molested, and he can barely see that point being made through all the klieg light glare shining on Jackson, his glamorous motorcade, whether or not that's his plane landing—right now!—at the Santa Barbara airport.

"They were live watching a plane come in. It was like the president was landing, or some great dignitary. But three ordinary businessmen get out of the plane," Howry says. "It makes you just ill to watch that. It's not why I got into journalism."

Howry's paper did give Jackson's arrest A1 play, with a story that they took great care to make sure included the singer's denial of the crime. And the infamous mug shot was out there too—in color. In retrospect, however, Howry still wonders about running that mug shot. Who's to say if that's a fair portrayal of the way the guy really looks and not just a frightful image the police specifically

chose to release because it helped their case? All of it troubles Howry. "There are just so many things," he says, "that really bother me . . .

"A celebrity story is a media happening," he continues. "In the great scheme of things, do you really stop to think about how you're coming across to readers? Are you following the pack, part of the horde, as caught up in the curiosity of celebrity as everyone else? What are we really saying to our readers?"

What we seem to be saying and showing, with the breaking news updates, the extensive live footage and the extreme interest in the size of Kobe Bryant's wife's diamond, is that these things are of huge, huge national concern. The intensity of the media coverage, Stephen Bell says, ends up distorting the significance of events or of people.

"I think we have distortion by magnification," Bell says. "There are so many bright lights being focused on the same little thing. The systematic reaction is an overreaction; it assumes an unnatural importance. The people themselves become so magnified by the intensity, their importance to the societal order becomes totally distorted. They become bigger than life."

Journalists aren't doing this on purpose, Bell adds. But they're doing it. The question becomes, what harm is it causing?

None, National Journal's Bill Powers would argue. He says that when big Michael Jackson or Kobe Bryant news breaks, it certainly seems like that was all anyone heard on that particular day. "You get the impression that's all they saw that day," he says, "but they didn't see the piece about Medicare right next to it."

"It would be troubling if we only had three networks and a handful of papers, but there are so many places to go for your news," Powers insists. "I just don't see anything that this is blotting out. It doesn't take up your whole front page, it's just one story." And, he adds, "Everyone has a clicker."

And there are a few places to aim those clickers if you're one of the Americans who truly mean it when they say they're fed up with the curiosity du jour. A tiny

band of contrarians like Joe Howry are just saying no, knowing they can because their peers are saying yes, yes, yes. Howry's trying to confine Jackson to the inside pages. CNN's Lou Dobbs told viewers, on the very night of Jackson's arrest no less, that "pop star Michael Jackson has been arrested in California. The cable news networks have devoted hours of programming to the story. We have just reported ours." CBS' Bob Schieffer announced in his weekly commentary that the very fact that the rest of the world's lens was aimed at Jackson meant he could point his elsewhere.

And there's the Aspen Daily News, standing firm in its decision to be Kobe-free, most days a little proud, others a little sheepish. Editor Rick Carroll laughed when someone told him he ought to be nominated for an ethics award. He'd rather, he says, get the accolades for doing something than for the mere act of doing nothing, weirdly heroic as doing nothing is in this day and age.

Still, many readers and even a few journalists have complimented the Aspen Daily News' stand, calling the move "refreshing," "uplifting" and courageous. But others, many of them journalists, call it "appalling," a cop-out, and "a cowardly disservice to your readers." Carroll is the first to admit, sighing, that the naysayers make good points.

Yes, there are worthy stories about Kobe Bryant's case to be done. And yes, while the paper has nixed Kobe, it's all right with Michael Jackson—and what's really the difference there? But they were making a point, Carroll says, trying to anyway. "You have to take risks in the business," he says, "and with this risk, we created a really good discussion about the media's role."

And if any of his 12,000 readers need to know whether Kobe wore a tie to court, they know where to go. "There are plenty of options out there aside from the Aspen Daily News," Carroll says. "It's out there. You can't avoid it."

Assistant Managing Editor Jill Rosen wrote about the Denver Post in AJR's December/January issue.

The Next Generation

USA Today *shed its lightweight "McPaper" persona in the 1990s, becoming a serious national paper and luring topflight talent from places like the Washington Post. Its next challenge is to step up its enterprise reporting and achieve the consistency of the nation's best papers. But does it have the commitment, resources and newsroom culture to pull it off?*

BY RACHEL SMOLKIN

Three G. It's a phrase as snappy as the newspaper it describes.

Born to derision in 1982, USA Today saucily called itself "The Nation's Newspaper" and shocked journalists with its bold color, its big weather map, its late sports scores. And, oh, those stories. So short, so fluffy. "USA is eating its vegetables," declared one chipper front-page headline. Another proved the paper's perspicacity: "MEN, WOMEN: We're still different."

The mocking media, no slouches at cleverness themselves, dubbed the upstart "McPaper" and its product "junk-food journalism."

So went the first generation.

Then the jokes began to fade. After hemorrhaging nearly $1 billion by early 1993, the paper turned its first profit that year and reached the 2 million mark in circulation. Tom Curley, president and publisher from 1991 to 2003, and David Mazzarella, editor from late 1994 to 1999, pushed for more serious journalism and more enterprise. Stories got a bit longer. Editors recruited respected reporters from prestigious publications. (See "USA Today Grows Up," September 1997.)

By the end of the second generation, USA Today had shed its reputation as a journalistic punch line.

The nation's largest newspaper is now 21 and a half. In human years, it's barely old enough to drink legally. And as the young adult learns to compete journalistically with its more decorated elders, its leaders want the paper to remain committed to its reader-friendly roots. Hence the third generation, or, as Editor Karen Jurgensen calls it, "3G," a concept that aims to combine the first generation's emphasis on accessible news and visual elements with the second generation's focus on enterprise and sophistication.

"You want an absolutely consistent, authoritative newspaper that is enterprising and breaks stories every day," says Jurgensen, who has been at USA Today since its launch and became editor in 1999. "We put a great deal of emphasis on graphics, on photos, on the way pages are designed, as well as on the quality of the stories and the quality of the scoops and the expertise of our reporters."

The third generation also will test USA Today's journalistic ambition and leadership. Over the next few years, the paper will answer questions about whether it can keep the reporters and editors it has worked hard to recruit, how well it uses their talents and how effectively it melds their skills with the paper's distinctive mission. As an investigation led by three respected editors continues to probe the work of former star reporter Jack Kelley and the paper's culture, the coming months also will challenge USA Today's ability to learn from its first major embarrassment. (See "Who Knows Jack?".)

Interviews with more than 40 current and former staffers portray a paper that earnestly wants to improve and has matured greatly since its inception. Journalists speak of the paper and its reader-oriented mission with nearly universal affection. But many lament that the lean staff and limited space for news and enterprise place them at a competitive disadvantage. Some say a heavy-handed, corporate approach to personnel matters makes staff jittery. Journalists describe pressures to produce splashy stories and, somewhat paradoxically, an "institutional insecurity" that can suppress aggressive, authoritative reporting.

Although it long ago bucked its McPaper image, the challenges USA Today faces bear some resemblance to those of the fast-food giant. Like McDonald's, USA Today is a known product, beloved and purchased by millions of Americans.

And like the Big Mac, it must sell itself every day. The paper circulates to 2.15 million people Monday through Thursday, and 2.6 million readers buy its weekend edition, published each Friday. But less than 15 percent of those sales are home subscriptions.

USA Today is a traveler's newspaper, purchased at newsstands, convenience stores, hotels and airports. Far more than its competitors, it must grab readers with its front-page appeal inside a coin box. "We have to have something that's going to catch someone's eye at 7-Eleven or at the newsstand," says cover story editor Linda Mathews. Because the front page must sell the newspaper, "we work harder, argue more about leads, about headlines and about photos." The decisions are particularly crucial because USA Today puts three or four stories out front each day, compared with seven or eight on the front pages of other major papers.

Mathews plans the feature that will be in the coveted cover spot—the one that jumps inside the paper. She looks for enterprise, trends, profiles and variety: a piece about Janet Jackson's flash dance at the Super Bowl; a profile of the police chief in Fallujah, Iraq; an examination of hip-hopper Snoop Dogg's efforts to go mainstream.

Executive Editor Brian Gallagher quotes a former editor, John C. Quinn, in describing USA Today as a "readers' paper," where the editing is tight and the pace fast, entrepreneurial and intensely detail-oriented. "Context, impact and uniqueness" are 3G tenets, and staff members have attended mandatory workshops that reinforced the 3G philosophy. "This is a place people come to work to invent the future," Gallagher says. "The third generation is evolutionary. It resolves the conflicts of the first two generations."

But each generation brings its own conflicts, and the current one has been marked in part by administrative and personnel upheaval. Staffers talk of a "corporate mentality," and some describe fears in the news department of being "targeted" or "forced out."

In 2001, USA Today relocated to a suburban 25-acre complex in Northern Virginia's Tysons Corner. The move eased cramped conditions at its former home in Rosslyn, Virginia, just across the Potomac River from Washington, D.C., where the burgeoning staff had worked since USA Today's birth, and it gave reporters a bit more privacy. The glass structure housing USA Today and owner Gannett's headquarters is both impressive and vaguely Orwellian. I was escorted to and from each interview. (I was permitted to eat lunch by myself in the shiny cafeteria after I promised not to wander off.) A sculpture on red panels in the marble lobby reads, "WORDS IN THEIR BEST ORDER." The campus is designed to give staffers everything they need without having to leave, including a softball field, tennis courts and a fitness center.

Because the new building is not near a subway stop and is isolated from downtown Washington, reporters who focus on federal agencies now work in a D.C. bureau. Three-quarters of the paper's 429 editorial staffers are at Tysons; the rest are based in Washington, New York and other offices.

Richard Curtis, managing editor for graphics and photography, served as the newsroom liaison with the architects and says the new quarters are "uplifting. It contributes to creativity. It contributes to the community. The staff is proud. It was built for them."

But some staffers are less enthusiastic. Patrick O'Driscoll, a reporter in the Denver bureau, says it feels like a "cold, soulless, white, glassed-in fish bowl." Other descriptions included a "morgue" and a "death star," with one longtime staffer saying, "there's a certain deadliness to the place. There's no energy"— the staffer even suggested it may have "bad karma."

Boosters of the bad-karma theory could have perceived supporting evidence soon after the move. On December 3, 2001, sports staffers Karen Allen, Denise Tom and Cheryl Phillips were fired for writing in the dusty coating of a blue ball sculpture outside the office of Gannett Chairman and CEO Douglas H. McCorkindale (see Bylines, January/February 2002). Security cameras captured their actions. Although the women apologized and offered to pay for the damage, they were fired without severance pay.

The firings upset many journalists inside and outside USA Today. Several staffers interviewed for this article spoke of their shock at the "blue ball" episode and their fears that the company's response signals even longtime staffers can't expect loyalty.

"It was a really sad time for us, and I think it still has a place in people's hearts," says Sports Managing Editor Monte Lorell, who, citing personnel reasons, declined to discuss specifics. (Phillips has said Lorell initially told the women that their actions were "dumb" but he didn't think it was a "firing offense," then fired them four days later.)

Several staffers said unexplained departures by other respected journalists—who left without other jobs—also stirred anxieties about their own security. Projects Editor Doug Pardue, recruited in 2000 from a similar role at the Tampa Tribune, departed in July 2003. White House reporter Larry McQuillan, the senior White House correspondent at Reuters before his recruitment to USA Today in 1999, left last fall.

"There is some fear because of the way they handle personnel matters, which is in a very corporate, secret way," says Justice Department reporter Toni Locy, a veteran of the Washington Post and U.S. News & World Report who came to USA Today in 2000. After McQuillan and Pardue left, "there was no announcement from management," Locy says. "It was like they disappeared."

"You want an absolutely consistent, authoritative newspaper that is enterprising and breaks stories every day," says Editor Karen Jurgensen, who has been at USA Today since its launch.

Locy notes all reporters are "drama queens, and everything gets blown completely out of proportion." But she adds, "when management doesn't say anything, that scares folks. I do rightly or wrongly attribute it to the corporate culture."

Another unsettling personnel change at USA Today was the departure of President and Publisher Curley, who is widely credited with bringing more substance to the paper and was one of USA Today founder Allen H. Neuharth's four "whiz kids" who helped figure out how to create the paper.

Curley left last May to become president and CEO of the Associated Press, and Gannett named Craig Moon, executive vice president of its newspaper division, as his replacement (see By-lines, June/July 2003). Moon, 54, rose in the industry's business side, joining Gannett as a vice president of advertising for the Cincinnati Enquirer in 1985. He later served as president and publisher of the News-Press in Fort Myers, Florida, the now-defunct Arkansas Gazette and the Tennessean in Nashville.

Curley is still deeply missed at the paper, and Moon remains a somewhat unknown figure. Moon says he does not get involved with daily news decisions and describes his role as to "really build the brand" of USA Today. But Moon notes he is an experienced publisher and says the only difference between his current and former roles is that USA Today is "just a hell of a lot bigger."

The "nation's newspaper" has made recruiting a hallmark in recent years, concentrating on reporters in the mid-1990s and then focusing increasingly on editors in the late 1990s. One of its star recruits, former Newsday White House reporter Susan Page, is now Washington bureau chief. Cover story editor Mathews is a veteran foreign and national editor from the New York Times, the Los Angeles Times and ABC's "World News Tonight."

But unlike the Tribune Co.-owned L.A. Times, where many top editors were hired directly from other prestigious papers, nearly all USA Today's leaders are longtime staffers and Gannett employees. Jurgensen was most recently editorial page editor before taking over as editor. Gallagher, her deputy and successor on the editorial page, became executive editor in June 2002.

"The Gannett culture rewards folks on results," Moon says. "They are going to be first in line for jobs." Gannett only would look outside, he adds, "if we weren't producing results within the company, and that isn't going to happen."

Jurgensen, 55, characterizes her style as collaborative. She and Gallagher launched a series of task forces to improve the paper, including a page-one task force and groups on accuracy, hiring practices and staff evaluations. "I don't have all the answers," she says. "No single editor could have all the answers. And I think you get much better results when you work with a group of people and have them come up with answers."

Jurgensen is well liked, and staffers frequently describe her as personable and as caring deeply about the paper. Several complimented her for occasionally inviting journalists to her office to drink tea and chat. But some say she is not widely perceived as a strong leader and does not frequently mingle in the newsroom.

That perception may exist in part because Jurgensen, at least early in her tenure, tried to approach the paper as a reader and leave the daily news direction to Gallagher. After years of expending "every drop of energy" on putting the paper out

every day, she says, she wanted to step back and "take care of some of these larger issues that ultimately improve the daily journalism."

Gallagher, 55, is often described as reserved, even shy, and has frustrated some staffers with what they perceived as unnecessarily late intervention in stories. Gallagher says that has happened infrequently, adding that he needs to make sure stories are "up to standards" before they appear in the paper.

Each section has its own managing editor, and Hal Ritter, the ME for news, is a controversial figure. Ritter is responsible for hiring many of the paper's most respected journalists. He is an exacting editor, a stickler for proper grammar and punctuation and for banning jargon. But many characterize his manner as brusque and bruising, and say reporters and editors often are reluctant to question or contradict him because they fear retaliation. Ritter denies he would retaliate against a staffer for crossing him and says, "My door's always open. I love when people come in and yell at me."

The leadership team faced its most public personnel challenge earlier this year when foreign reporter Jack Kelley, one of two Pulitzer finalists in the paper's history, resigned after he misled editors during an investigation into the accuracy of his work. As the story unfolded in rival publications, USA Today foundered. Jurgensen initially told outside reporters and her own journalists that she could not discuss the details of what she termed a "personnel matter," infuriating many on her staff. She said the paper had no plans to retract or correct any of Kelley's stories or to continue the probe.

But as outside reporting intensified and the staff continued to raise questions, the paper's leaders changed their approach. Jurgensen released a lengthy statement describing the events that led Kelley to resign under threat of dismissal. On January 29, Moon announced that an independent panel of three veteran editors would oversee a review of Kelley's stories over his 21-year tenure and any related matters the committee chose to explore. The committee includes John Seigenthaler, the paper's founding editorial director and former editor and publisher of the Tennessean; Bill Kovach, chairman of the Committee of Concerned Journalists and former editor of the Atlanta Journal-Constitution; and William Hilliard, former editor of the Oregonian in Portland.

The probe's findings were devastating. On March 19, the paper reported that its investigation had unearthed "strong evidence that Kelley fabricated substantial portions of at least eight major stories, lifted nearly two dozen quotes or other material from competing publications, lied in speeches he gave for the newspaper and conspired to mislead those investigating his work." The paper said USA Today reporters examined 720 of Kelley's stories between 1993 and 2003. They conducted interviews, reviewed Kelley's expense records and traveled to Cuba and the Middle East. Their investigation is continuing.

Cover story editor Mathews, a former national editor at the New York Times, says she believes the Kelley flap hurts USA Today more than the Times was damaged by the furor over Jayson Blair, who fabricated or plagiarized parts of more than three dozen articles during his tenure there (see "All About the Retrospect," June/July 2003). "We're starting from a lower place on the ladder," Mathews says. And Kelley "wasn't some one-year wonder. He was one of the founders of the paper. . . . It feels like this is a cloud that's going to hang over us longer."

As USA Today positions itself in the big leagues, it is still battling some cultural and journalistic tensions. Founder Neuharth, who didn't return calls or e-mail requests for comment for this story, and others launched a national paper that needed less than two decades to assert itself as a major player. He did so with a small, scrappy staff that included dozens of "loaners" from other Gannett papers—reporters who were prepared to return home if Neuharth's experiment failed.

"It was uncharted territory for a company and a lot of journalists who had young and midcareer lives working for community and small and midsize papers and not really playing with the national powerhouses," says Denver correspondent O'Driscoll.

O'Driscoll came from the Reno Evening Gazette and Nevada State Journal (now the Reno Gazette-Journal) in January 1983. "It was both heady and a little daunting," he says of the early days. "There was a combination of the small-town 'gee-whiz' and a bit of a fear factor, a 'What am *I* doing going up against big national papers?'" He left for the Denver Post in 1989 and returned to USA Today in 1997 when it opened its Denver bureau. "The paper has mostly overcome that mind-set," O'Driscoll says, "but it clearly was there when I was first there, and there are some vestiges today."

A common complaint among reporters who have joined the paper in the last five to 10 years is that the paper needs to attract more editors who have experience overseas or at big metropolitan dailies. Some describe a lack of sophistication in editing, while others characterize the problem as too little trust among editors in reporters' instincts.

In August 2003, Jurgensen met with reporters and editors in the Washington bureau for more than an hour. The reporters who work there decried the "endless second-guessing" of their stories, saying too many editors were involved, according to notes of the meeting obtained by AJR.

They said "institutional insecurity" at the paper means no one feels empowered to make decisions and that line editors are unwilling to say a story is good before hearing that their superiors agree. They said their ideas have to be validated by "six other news organizations before there's consensus that they're worth pursuing," which makes the paper late on some stories it could have had first.

Reporters described their frustration at the difficulty of getting good work into the paper. They said everybody spends too much time guessing how Gallagher will react and that the process has made the paper slow to respond to breaking stories, including the Washington-area sniper killings. Journalists also complained about a shift away from reporters driving coverage, saying the assignment editors who oversee reporters don't fight for their work and "often seem compelled to talk reporters out of pursuing stories, rather than encouraging them to go after stories."

Some reporters shared concerns about "forced" trend stories and pressures to try to create trends where none exists. Others warned of a "whomp-up factor" in which a desire for impact sometimes causes an editor to add sentences or paragraphs that can be wrong or distort the story. These concerns, reporters said, were contributing to a "degradation of the camaraderie in the newsroom and a budding us vs. them environment," compounded by a "harsh" review process for evaluating reporters' work.

The notes state Jurgensen "seemed taken aback" and said if there is a "cultural issue," she wants to address it. She responded that if the impression exists that ideas are coming solely from the top down, "that's a horrible indictment." She said she wants newsrooms with devoted, upbeat people and doesn't like hearing that the situation is the opposite—a sentiment she reiterated when I interviewed her in her office in mid-February.

"I'm always concerned when staffers think there are things that need to be addressed," Jurgensen told me. "I want an organization where people feel empowered." She said the concerns raised in the Washington bureau represented a "small part" of the paper and its four sections—News, Life, Money and Sports.

Bureau staffers say the late intervention in stories declined slightly after the meeting, but the top-down approach and institutional anxiety over decision-making remain.

"Everyone at USA Today, from reporters to top management, is under a lot of pressure," says Kathy Kiely, a congressional reporter who has been at the paper for five years. "Our mission is to out-think, out-report and out-write competitors who have far more resources in terms of personnel and newshole than we do. The pressure can be exhilarating when it pushes you to go beyond what you thought you could do. But it can be demoralizing when we go after each other for falling short of goals that are very hard to meet."

Bob Davis, a reporter in the Life section, wrote an acclaimed three-day series about the performance of emergency medical services in the nation's 50 largest cities. The paper nominated his series, published last summer, for the Pulitzer, and top editors speak of his work with pride. But Davis once experienced the downside of editors' high expectations.

In the mid-1990s, after Ritter left the Money section and became ME for news, "I was one of the victims of the concerted effort to reinvent the newsroom and get more experienced, seasoned national reporters in there," Davis says. "Many of us who came as loaners from small Gannett papers were pushed out. I was covering aviation safety at the time and was, I thought, pretty successful, but they [Ritter and his deputies] didn't think my work was up to their standards."

During his nine months on probation, Davis covered the 1996 TWA 800 crash and the subsequent investigation. The New York Times was reporting that a criminal act, such as a bomb, might have caused the crash, but Davis' sources were telling him it appeared to be a mechanical problem. The results of the investigation later vindicated his work, but he felt he never regained his editors' trust. Near the end of Davis' probationary period, his immediate editor told him to start looking for another job.

Davis managed to stay at USA Today, moving to the Life section with the help of senior editors at the paper. While he says he disagreed with Ritter's assessment of his work, a grateful Davis says he's "very pleased with the way the paper treated me" and describes Life as a "healthier" part of the paper. (After Davis moved to Life, he received a letter from his former editors terminating him from News.)

A former paramedic, Davis started working on his EMS series while on a fellowship in 2001. His editors then freed him up for another eight months to continue on the story—no small commitment at a paper with such a thin staff.

He and many others describe the paper's operation as lean. Its editorial staff size is down slightly from the peak monthly average of 456 in 2001, but it avoided layoffs that hit many publications during the economic downturn.

"We don't have a lot of depth, in the foreign editing range in particular," cover story editor Mathews says. The lack of depth is an issue of both bodies and experience. During Mathews' years at the Los Angeles Times, a copy desk composed largely of former foreign correspondents handled world news. When she served as the paper's first Beijing correspondent, one of the copy editors was a former reporter in Hong Kong and spoke Chinese. He could help with story ideas or problems and catch mistakes. Another copy editor had spent 25 years in Latin America and knew all the generals in Argentina.

At USA Today, two editors are primarily responsible for world news, and the same group of copy editors handles all news (the Money, Life and Sports sections each have their own copy desks). "We have very good copy editors," Mathews says. "But they're young, very young. The L.A. Times, the New York Times, the Wall Street Journal are all privileged in that way, but those are our competitors."

Five years into its third generation, USA Today remains a fundamentally national newspaper. The paper had no foreign bureaus until 1995, when Editor Mazzarella opened one in Hong Kong. It has added bureaus in London, Beijing and Brussels (the London reporter is currently on assignment in Rome). Its approach to the Middle East has been inconsistent, although editors say they plan to establish a bureau there during the next few months. The Mexico City bureau closed in 2002. There is talk of assigning a reporter in Miami to focus on Latin America, but no timetable has been set.

Lacking an extensive overseas presence, the paper dispatches reporters to parachute into hot spots during major events, as Kelley built his daredevil reputation doing. He and other roving reporters often have faced the daunting task of matching competitors based in Moscow, Jerusalem or Baghdad.

For years, Kelley satisfied his editors' desire for the paper to be different and exciting. As one reporter says, "Jack was giving them the gee-whiz, holy-shit stuff that they really want."

Jonathan Weisman, who spent nine of his 18 months at USA Today as an economic policy reporter before leaving for the Washington Post, felt editors tended to value what he terms "scooplets"—exclusive but often inconsequential developments.

"I felt the only way to get stories on the front page was not to be particularly analytical or thoughtful but just to find some teeny, tiny nuggets that other papers wouldn't have," Weisman says. "It got to be a little tedious." As an example, he cites a story he wrote about the Pentagon sending a team to India to consider evacuating Americans during the 2002 nuclear flare-up between India and Pakistan. Although the Pentagon was a long way from making any such decision, "it was a scoop, so we had this big, blaring headline."

But Weisman praised the paper's wide reach, cited by many staffers as central to its allure. When he was considering leaving the Baltimore Sun for USA Today in 2000, he went to Wisconsin during the presidential campaign and stopped at a McDonald's in downtown Green Bay. "It was an early-morning swing shift, and there were these working-class guys, all reading USA Today," Weisman says. "In 99 percent of this country, USA Today is a better newspaper than the paper being thrown onto people's doorsteps."

Other journalists also take pride in the paper's impact and approach. Tom Kenworthy, a former Washington Post reporter in USA Today's Denver bureau, says readers perceive it as "straight down the middle." USA Today reinforces its even-handed approach through its editorial pages, which publish an opposing view to the main editorial each day and refrain from endorsing presidential candidates.

When reporter Locy travels around the country, readers tell her they love the paper. "So USA Today has touched something and filled a need out there," she says. "That's not to be dismissed."

During USA Today's second generation, Editor Jurgensen says it lost some of its distinctive edge and began to look more like other papers. Making matters more difficult, other papers had begun to look a lot more like USA Today, copying its weather page and shorter stories and improving their color, graphics and sports coverage.

John Morton, a leading media analyst, AJR columnist and early skeptic about USA Today, describes the paper as "doing very well" from a business perspective and as publishing some "very serious" journalism. "They're right up there with the Washington Post and Philadelphia Inquirer and others in terms of standing in the political community and halls of power," Morton says.

But he adds that it has not achieved the status of national "institutions" such as the New York Times and the Wall Street Journal and may never attain it. "They still have an awful lot of the McPaper-type stuff," Morton says, "a lot of light stuff that you won't find in papers like the Times and the Journal unless they're trying to be funny."

Tom Rosenstiel, who covered the paper's early years as a media writer for the Los Angeles Times, says USA Today is "now a profitable business and a recognizable brand. But their business has become harder because it probably depends more on producing a quality product and less on occupying a unique niche than it did 20 years ago."

Rosenstiel, now director of the Project for Excellence in Journalism, notes USA Today's early advantages included its late deadlines, late ball scores and hometown coverage away from home—the "Across the USA" news blurbs on every state. "Those mean much less in the age of the Internet, where you could sit in an airport waiting area, go online and get all that instantly," he says.

With those competitive pressures in mind, Jurgensen and her team have focused on presentation of information. They have emphasized sophisticated graphics and photos, and sections have added new features.

Life now provides regular DVD features. Inside the section, pages about "A Better Life" offer stories on health, education and science. Life's front page often showcases celebrities, movies and television.

Some new features attempt to give readers more than the stock prices and sports scores they can readily access online. The Money section added a "Market Trends" feature each Monday that offers a three-dimensional view of the stock market. Green poles show which industry groups rose for the week, red poles show which fell.

The Sports section, which faces an explosion of competition from the Internet, ESPN and other outlets, compiles lists of players' salaries and bonuses, and readers can sift through the information on the paper's Web site. Thanks to database reporting, fans can see how golfers' strengths and weaknesses might affect their chances at particular tournament sites.

Perhaps the paper's biggest challenge, however, remains news. Tom Squitieri, a national correspondent who started at the paper in 1989, says the paper's other sections more easily defined themselves. "They busted out early and got respect as must-reads," he says. The news section gradually moved to more substantive journalism, but "we're still not a consistent newspaper."

Managing Editor Ritter rates his staff as "terrific" on big breaking stories but says the challenge is to produce excellent enterprise coverage on slower news days.

USA Today has produced some distinguished investigative work but does not publish such pieces with the regularity of other top papers. It was not conceived as a showcase for the long, multipart series that are standard investigative fare. Space in the news section is tight (largely because of restrictions imposed by the presses and the placement of advertising). The paper has made its reputation as a smart digest on the day's news, which is where its reporters tend to concentrate their efforts.

Jurgensen disbanded the enterprise department that Mazzarella created. Of four full-time reporters assigned there, only one, Peter Eisler, remains. The senior investigative reporter, Ed Pound, left in 2001 to join U.S. News & World Report.

USA Today has not yet added a Pulitzer to its pedigree. Former Editor John Quinn used to joke that if the paper ever won the prize, it would be for "best investigative paragraph."

Jurgensen says the best projects grow from beat reporting, and she wants to see projects developed from each of the paper's sections. She and other editors laud Davis' EMS series for its importance to readers, and Life Managing Editor Susan

Weiss calls it "the most ambitious project to come out of my section and, frankly, pretty ambitious for the paper."

Editors also praised two 9/11-related projects. One examined who survived the collapse of the World Trade Center towers and why. Another traced the Federal Aviation Administration's unprecedented order grounding every plane during the attacks. The narrative style of that two-part series was a creative departure for USA Today.

The paper has placed less emphasis on projects about the poor, the homeless and the mentally ill—the types of investigations that expose heartbreaking social conditions, force changes and win Pulitzer Prizes. The New York Times won a 2003 Pulitzer for investigative reporting on the abuse of mentally ill adults in state-regulated homes; the Washington Post won the year before for a series that prompted District of Columbia officials to overhaul the city's child welfare system.

USA Today has not yet added a Pulitzer to its pedigree. Former Editor Quinn used to joke that if the paper ever won the prize, it would be for "best investigative paragraph." Alex S. Jones, director of Harvard University's Joan Shorenstein Center on the Press, Politics and Public Policy, admires the paper and says it has steadily attained stature but has a hard time competing in prestige in elite journalism circles without that gold standard. He notes other papers, particularly the Philadelphia Inquirer under the leadership of Gene Roberts, enhanced their journalistic reputations with a succession of Pulitzers.

USA Today's editors say not all enterprise stories must be based on long investigations. They value "conceptual scoops" that show context and impact, such as a prescient story by reporter Jill Lawrence last November about the perceived temper problem of then-presidential hopeful Howard Dean—published more than two months before his fateful Iowa scream.

Recently recruited reporters are learning how to live within the framework of USA Today's limited space and mission. Reporter Kenworthy says he rarely attempts the quirky stories he sometimes wrote for the Washington Post, such as a front-page piece about a doctor in Oregon who shot his neighbor's cows after they persistently wandered onto his property.

Some reporters feel "we sometimes shortchange ourselves by overanalyzing what's going to have broad appeal to readers," Kenworthy says. "Some of us would like the paper to be somewhat more adventurous in its story selection."

Joan Biskupic, a former Supreme Court reporter for the Post who now covers that beat for USA Today, has found that editors' appetite and the paper's space for day-to-day court business is smaller than at other publications where she has worked. Successful policy coverage in Washington often requires sustained reporting and gradually putting information before the public, but USA Today picks its shots.

"You've got to keep thinking about how to fit in with their mission—about the journalism you want to do and the mission USA Today has," Biskupic says. "It's a challenge to find the space for stories that don't have a strong time element but are important to the overall coverage of the beat." Biskupic has sought outlets outside the paper to supplement her desire for more detailed coverage of the court. She is currently on leave writing a book about Justice Sandra Day O'Connor.

The challenge in USA Today's third generation will be finding the right fit—between substantive journalism and fun visuals, between new recruits who can make the paper more like its competitors and its long-standing desire for distinctiveness, between tightly formatted and edited stories and respect for reporters' expertise and instincts.

USA Today fills a newspaper niche that its current leaders, by stressing a return to the paper's roots, clearly hope to sustain.

Given those aspirations, and questions about the newsroom culture and a lack of institutional confidence, it seems unlikely that USA Today will become a national paper of record or attain the aura of prestige and influence that surrounds the New York Times or the Wall Street Journal. But so far, the young paper has made a habit of proving skeptics wrong.

From the *American Journalism Review*, April/May 2004, pp. 20, 22-28. Copyright © 2004 by the Philip Merrill College of Journalism at the University of Maryland, College Park, MD 20742-7111. Reprinted by permission.

UNIT 3
Players and Guides

Unit Selections

Key Points to Consider

- What are the arguments for deregulation of media ownership? Against deregulation? Which do you see as stronger? Why?

- What is your view on the quality of media marketed to children? On why you do or don't choose educational programming more frequently than other television channels? If ratings and sales figures indicate that the public is attracted to lowbrow content, should media owners give media consumers what they want? Why or why not?

- How would you define the rules of "ethical practice"? Who, besides the subject of a news story, is affected by such judgments?

 **Links: www.dushkin.com/online/**
These sites are annotated in the World Wide Web pages.

The Electronic Journalist
 http://spj.org
Federal Communications Commission (FCC)
 http://www.fcc.gov
Index on Censorship
 http://www.indexonline.org
International Television Association
 http://www.itva.org
Internet Law Library
 http://www.phillylawyer.com
Michigan Press Photographers Association (MPPA)
 http://www.mppa.org
Poynter Online: Research Center
 http://www.poynter.org
World Intellectual Property Organization (WIPO)
 http://www.wipo.org

The freedoms of speech and of the press are regarded as fundamental American rights, protected under the U.S. Constitution. These freedoms, however, are not without some restrictions; the media are held accountable to legal and regulatory authorities, whose involvement reflects a belief that the public sometimes requires protection.

Regulatory agencies, such as the Federal Communications Commission (FCC), exert influence over media access and content through their power to grant, regulate, and revoke licenses to operate. They are primarily concerned with electronic media because of the historically limited number of broadcast bands available in any community (called spectrum scarcity). The courts exert influence over media practice through hearing cases of alleged violation of legal principles such as the protection from libel and the right to privacy. Shield laws grant reporters the right to promise informants confidentiality. Copyright law is the basis for the Recording Industry Association of America's September, 2003 lawsuits against 261 defendants for alleged illegal downloading of music from the Internet. The Federal Trade Commission and U.S. Food and Drug Administration have regulatory controls that affect advertising.

There is, however, a wide grey zone between an actionable offense and an error in judgment. For example, while legal precedence makes it particularly difficult for public figures to prevail in either libel or invasion-of-privacy cases, it is not necessarily right to print information that might be hurtful to them. Nor is it necessarily wrong to do so. Sometimes being "truthful" is insen-

sitive. Sometimes being "interesting" means being exploitive. Media sources are constantly aware that their reporting of an event has the potential to affect the lives of those involved in it.

The first articles in this section, "Behind the Mergers: Q&A" and "Tripping Up Big Media," examine regulatory rules, focusing on proposed relaxation of FCC code governing how many media voices in a single market can be owned by one company. In 1996 the FCC eliminated many of its radio consolidation rules. Since then, the number of radio station owners has declined by 30%, and one company, Clear Channel, has grown from running 43 radio and 16 TV stations to owning more than 1,200 stations. FCC chair Michael Powell has been an outspoken advocate of expanding deregulation, believing that spectrum scarcity arguments limiting collective "reach" of a single media company are no longer relevant. "Media Money: How Corporate Spending Blocked Political Ad Reform & Other Stories of Influence" criticizes the influence of powerful broadcast corporations on FCC policy. After reading these articles, try drafting an argument for the opposing viewpoint, that corporate mergers may in fact bolster rather than erode content diversity. For example, a 1999 article by veteran media writer Paul Farhi (*Annual Editions: Mass Media 2001/02*) contends that larger companies are more apt to have their gatekeeping decisions scrutinized and can better afford production and distribution of niche media that serve minority interests.

The next article, "Children, Entertainment, and Marketing" looks at self-regulation of decency in media content. Federal law also addresses sexual content, restricting radio stations and over-the-air (not cable and satellite) television channels from reference to sexual and excretory functions between 6 a.m. and 10 p.m., when children are likely to be tuning in. Pressure to enforce this rule escalated following exposure of Janet Jackson's breast during the 2004 Super Bowl halftime show. The FCC received over 500,000 complaints following the Jackson incident. About a month later, the House and Senate passed similar bills to increase maximum indecency fines to $500,000. In May 2004, Clear Channel was fined $495,000 for Howard Stern's broadcasts.

The remaining articles in this unit raise questions of ethical practice. Some media organizations seem to have a greater concern for ethical policy than do others; however, even with the best intentions, drawing the line is not always simple. For example, journalists are frequently criticized for insensitivity in covering tragedy. Yet, results of a poll reported in the March 2000 issue of *Brill's Content* found that although 78 percent of respondents said that a television station should not broadcast a live hostage situation where the victim is held at gunpoint, 59 percent said they would tune in and keep watching. "Weighing the Costs of a Scoop" presents ethical dilemmas encountered in covering police investigations. "Ethically Challenged" and "Who Knows Jack?" look at recent cases of plagiarism and fabrication in news reporting, exploring why reporters cross the line, fact-checking policies, and potential consequences of cut-and-paste journalism. "The Information Squeeze" presents tensions between protection of privacy and regulatory policy as defined by the Freedom of Information Act.

What rules of practice should be applied in balancing the public's right to know against potential effects on individuals and society at large? Which great photograph shouldn't run? Which facts shouldn't be printed? What is the ethical response if the subject of a story threatens to kill him- or herself if the story runs? Is it ethical for journalists to cover stories on issues about which they have strong personal views, or does such practice compromise objectivity? Is it fair to become a "friend" to win trust, then write a story that is not flattering or does not support the source's views or actions? Should the paparazzi be held legally responsible for causing harm to those they stalk, or should that responsibility be borne by consumers who buy their products? And what of the well-intentioned story that attempts to right a social wrong but hurts people in the process?

These are not easy questions, and they do not have easy answers. The practice of journalism in the United States is grounded in a legacy of fiercely protected First Amendment rights and shaped by a code of conducting business with a strong sense of moral obligation to society. But no laws or codes of conduct can prescribe behavior in every possible situation. When people tell us something in face-to-face communication we are often quick to "consider the source" in evaluating the message. Media-literate consumers do the same in evaluating media messages.

do media monsters devour diversity?

Politicians and critics have long lamented that the rise of huge media conglomerates means the death of diversity in newspapers and on the airwaves. But research suggests that media conglomeration, however distasteful, does not necessarily reduce diversity.

joshua gameson and pearl latteier

Something odd is going on when Ted Turner, Trent Lott, Al Franken, the National Rifle Association, Jesse Jackson and Walter Cronkite agree. Opposition to media consolidation has turned these adversaries on most issues into bedfellows. When the Federal Communications Commission (FCC) prepared to further loosen restrictions on media ownership—a move approved by the FCC in June 2003 and then blocked by a circuit court three months later—the decision was met with a motley chorus of criticism. FCC commissioner Jonathan Adelstein called the problem "the McDonaldization of American media." Former Senator Carol Moseley-Braun stated that "we have to ensure that there is a diversity of ownership, a diversity of voice." And Cronkite, the veteran and widely-respected news anchor, declared concentration "an impediment to a free and independent press." The new rules would "stifle debate, inhibit new ideas, and shut out smaller businesses trying to compete," said Turner, whose vast holdings include CNN, TBS, and Hanna-Barbera cartoons, and who is a major shareholder in parent company Time Warner AOL. "There are really five companies that control 90 percent of what we read, see and hear. It's not healthy," Turner added.

Critics and policymakers have long been troubled by consolidation among America's mainstream media. Opponents of the Communications Act of 1934—which established the FCC and allocated the majority of the airwaves to commercial broadcasters—warned that commercial, network-dominated radio would squelch, as the ACLU director then put it, the few small stations that "voice critical or radical views." And in 1978, the Supreme Court ruled "it is unrealistic to expect true diversity from a commonly owned station-newspaper combination." Nonetheless, during the past two decades—and with a big boost from the Telecommunications Act of 1996—media ownership has become increasingly concentrated in fewer and fewer hands. Time and Warner Brothers merged into the world's biggest media company in 1989. A decade

later, Viacom and CBS set a new record for the largest corporate merger ever. And the 2000 AOL-TimeWarner merger was several times bigger than that.

The critics' logic is this: Citizens need access to diverse sources of news and opinions to make well-informed decisions about how to vote and live. Also, media should address the needs and interests of America's diverse population, and not just those of its elite. When a small group of "gatekeepers" controls how information circulates, the spectrum of available ideas, images and opinions narrows. Big media companies prefer programming and voices that conform to their own financial interests, and they make it nearly impossible for smaller, independent companies to offer alternatives.

This frightening vision is intuitively reasonable. But a close look at decades of scholarship on the relationship between media ownership and content diversity uncovers a surprising story—one much more complicated than the vision of media monsters gobbling up diversity. Scholars have zeroed in on three broadly defined types of diversity in media: format diversity, demographic diversity and idea diversity. The research suggests that when it comes to "diversity," media-consolidation critics are, if not barking up the wrong tree, at least in need of a more nuanced, sharper, more carefully directed bark. Indeed, effective opposition to media ownership consolidation may require, ironically, acknowledging the ways media giants sometimes promote diverse content.

format diversity

Suppose you turn on your TV after dinner, and every single channel is broadcasting either an *American Idol* spin-off or a makeover show. That would mean the after-dinner time slot in your area lacks "format diversity"—or variety in programming—turning everything into, as FCC commissioner Adelstein describes it, "Big Mac, fries and a Coke." In particular, observers worry that consolidation undercuts local content. Most experts agree that this has happened to radio since the late 1990s, as Clear Channel Communications has gobbled up stations throughout the country. Programming that was once determined locally is now overseen by Clear Channel programmers headquartered elsewhere, and local disc jockeys have been replaced by a single show that plays simultaneously in multiple markets. Consolidation of radio ownership encourages this centralized, cost-cutting format. The same logic would be expected in newspapers and television; running wire service copy is cheaper than employing staff reporters, and standardized production is less expensive than hiring a team of local broadcasters.

Of course, because different audiences are attracted to different content and format types, it also makes business sense for a conglomerate to maintain different sorts of programming—including locally produced content—just as General Motors produces lines of cars for different types of customers. This can actually promote format diversity. In a market with three competing stations, argues communications law expert Edwin Baker, each station will try to attract the largest possible audience by providing fare that the majority prefers. The stations will wind up sounding pretty similar. In contrast, if all three stations are owned by the same company, ownership has no incentive to compete against itself, and will try to make the stations dissimilar in order to attract different audiences. Similarly, it makes sense for entertainment conglomerates to make their various holdings more rather than less distinct in format, and to build a "diverse portfolio" of media properties. Viacom does not want its UPN (" America's Top Model," "The Parkers," "WWE Smackdown") to be like its CBS "CSI," "Judging Amy," "Late Show with David Letterman"), its Sundance Channel (documentaries on HIV/AIDS, the films of Patrice Chereau) to air the same kind of material as its Spike TV ("Sports Illustrated's 40th Anniversary Swimsuit Special"), or its Downtown Press ("chick-lit" like Alexandra Potter's *Calling Romeo*) to publish what its Atria Press does ("academic" titles like bell hooks' *The Will to Change*). This multiple-brand logic promotes rather than reduces format diversity.

Research suggests that media consolidation does not simply increase or decrease format diversity. Some studies compare the fate of local or public-affairs programming in independent versus conglomerated companies. Others look for shifts in content after a publication is bought by a bigger company. The results are tellingly mixed. Some find big differences between the offerings of independent and corporate-owned outlets, but ambiguous effects on format diversity. Others find little or no difference at all. For example, a 1995 study found that two years after Gannett—owner of *USA-Today*, among many other papers—bought the *Louisville Courier-Journal*, the paper devoted almost 30 percent more space to news than it had before, and 7 percent less space to advertising. On the other hand, the average story became shorter, the percentage of hard-news stories smaller, and wire stories came to outnumber staff-written ones. Within the expanded news reporting, the

proportions of local, national, and international news changed little. The paper became more like *USA Today*, but simultaneously the "news hole"—the amount of content consisting of news reporting—increased from when it was independently owned. Other studies of Gannett-bought papers—in Arkansas and Florida—found that international and national news decreased after the company took over. Local news, often in the form of crime or disaster stories, actually increased after consolidation.

A recent large-scale, five-year study by the Project for Excellence in Journalism also found mixed results. The researchers asked who produces "higher quality" local television news, which they defined as news that "covers the whole community," is "significant and informative," demonstrates "enterprise and courage," and is "fair, balanced, and accurate," "authoritative" and "highly local." Although they did not isolate "format diversity" in their study, they nonetheless offer some clues about the relationship between ownership and formats. On the one hand, just as anti-consolidation critics would predict, of 172 newscasts and 23,000 stories, researchers found the "best" programs overall tended to come from smaller station groups or from stations affiliated with but not owned by networks. On the other hand, they also found that "local ownership offered little protection against newscasts being very poor." As an evening's cursory viewing might confirm, local news is weak regardless of whether or not it is part of a conglomerate. Even more to the point, the researchers found that stations whose parent companies owned a newspaper in the same market—exactly the kind of "cross-ownership" that consolidation critics worry about—produced" higher-quality" newscasts, including more locally relevant content. They ran more stories on "important community issues" and fewer celebrity and human-interest stories. Cross-ownership shifted the types of programming provided, but in the direction most critics of cross-ownership seem to favor. Moreover, being owned by a small company, while an advantage when it came to "quality," was certainly no guarantee of a diverse mix of local and non-local content.

For a glimpse of how big media corporations—aided by government deregulation—sometimes do reduce format diversity, look at the current state of commercial radio. In a series of scathing articles for *Salon*, Eric Boehlert exposed Clear Channel as "radio's big bully," known for "allowing animals to be killed live on the air, severing long-standing ties with community and charity events, laying off thousands of workers, homogenizing playlists, and a corporate culture in which dirty tricks are a way of life." Concentrated, conglomerate ownership is certainly a prerequisite for being a big bully, and Clear Channel has used its power to undercut local programming and standardize rather than diversify both music and talk on radio. But radio's striking homogeneity is not just the result of concentrated ownership. As Boehlert wrote in 2001, radio "sucks" (similar-sounding songs, cookie-cutter stars) because record companies, through independent promoters, pay radio stations huge amounts to get their songs on playlists. With or without Clear Channel, material without money behind it—alternative styles of music, music by artists who do not fit the standard celebrity model, innovative and therefore risky formats—does not get airplay. It is not that ownership has no effect on format diversity, only that the impact is neither uniform nor inevitable. It is instead influenced by particular corporate strategies and the inner-workings of particular media industries.

demographic diversity

In everyday conversations, diversity usually refers to demographics: whether a workplace employs or a school enrolls people of various racial, ethnic, gender and economic categories. How the media represents and addresses the interests of America's diverse populations—who gets seen and heard—is, appropriately, often in question. Studies routinely find that the individuals appearing in mass media are disproportionately white, middle-class men between the ages of 20 and 60. But they have not figured out how, if at all, concentrated corporate ownership affects representation. This should not be surprising. A gap between the diversity of the population and media images of that population existed long before the rise of the media giants. And it clearly cuts across commercial and non-commercial media: studies of public broadcasting's guests show little demographic diversity, while daytime talk shows produced by for-profit conglomerates—however tawdry—offer some of the greatest demographic diversity on television.

Both government agencies and scholars have assumed that the key to ensuring demographically diverse content is demographically diverse ownership. Until recently, the FCC and the courts attempted to promote this kind of diversity by giving licensing preferences to minority-owned (and sometimes female-owned) broadcast stations. The FCC halted the licensing preferences in 1995, and the rapid consolidation of deregulated media companies makes it even less likely that companies and stations will be minority-owned today. Although it might seem reasonable to think that fewer minority-owned companies will mean less demographically diverse content—in surveys, minority owners do report being more likely to produce "minority" programming—studies of content do not back up such claims. Two studies comparing minority-owned (African American and Latino) radio stations to white-owned stations in the 1980s found that owners' ethnic backgrounds did not significantly affect demographic representation in their programming. There are many good reasons to pursue affirmative action in media ownership and employment, but ensuring diversity in media content is not one of them.

If anything has promoted demographic diversity in media content, it is the rise of niche-marketing and narrow-casting, which target previously excluded demographic groups with images of themselves. Although minority owners often typically start that process—gay marketers tapping the gay niche, Latino publishers targeting Latino readers—it proceeds regardless of whether they remain owners. Indeed, niche marketing has become a media-giant staple: Time Warner AOL started the highly successful *People en Espanol* in 1996, NBC-owned Bravo produced the summer 2003 hit "Queer Eye for the Straight Guy," Robert Johnson became the first African American billionaire when he sold Black Entertainment Television to Viacom in 2002, and the largest shareholder of radio's Hispanic Broadcasting Corporation is Clear Channel. Multicultural content and oligopoly media ownership are clearly not incompatible.

idea diversity

Almost everyone pays lip service to the notion that citizenship thrives when people are exposed to a variety of contending viewpoints. As the number of owners decreases, critics of media conglomeration argue, so does the number of voices contributing to the "marketplace of ideas." Media conglomerates with holdings in all kinds of other media and nonmedia industries have the power to censor the news in accordance with their interests. There is plenty of anecdotal evidence that consolidation tips content against ideas critical of the corporate owners. The *Los Angeles Times*, for example, failed in 1980 to cover a taxpayer-funded $2 billion water project that stood to benefit the Times-Mirror Company. Likewise, NBC remained silent on the 1990 boycott of their owner GE. And CBS's *America Tonight* show had a pro-tobacco bias in the mid-1990s, when the Loews Corporation, owner of Lorillard Tobacco, held a controlling interest in CBS. Disney-owned ABC News even cancelled an investigative report about sloppy background checks at Disneyworld. A recent study also found a "synergy bias" among media giants, in which media companies slip unannounced promotions of their other products and services into newscasts—as when ABC devoted two hours of *Good Morning America* to Disneyworld's 25th Anniversary. In short, media corporations act in their own special interests, promote ideas that suit those interests, and sometimes "spike" stories through self-censorship.

Beyond these forms of direct self-interest, though, the connection between ownership concentration and idea diversity is harder to discern. Generally speaking, one might observe that the American media environment has been an inhospitable place for radical, dissenting voices before, during and after the rise of media giants. More specifically, scholars have found that viewpoint diversity does not line up neatly with particular ownership structures. For example, the recent Project for Excellence in Journalism study of local television measured how many sources were cited in a story and how many points of view were represented in stories involving a dispute or controversy. Locally owned stations presented no more viewpoint diversity than non-locally owned ones, and small companies no more than big ones. Network-owned-and-operated stations did better than smaller, less well-funded affiliates. The weak connection between viewpoint diversity and monopoly ownership is actually old news. In a classic 1985 study, Robert Entman examined the first page and editorial section of 91 newspapers in three types of markets: competitive local markets with multiple, separately owned papers; monopolistic markets with only one local newspaper; and "quasi-monopolies," where joint-owned or joint-operated papers share a market. He measured diversity as the number of people or organizations mentioned in each story, and the number of stories that presented conflicting opinions. The study found that on no measure did independent papers present more diversity than papers in monopoly or quasi-monopoly situations. In all of the papers, more than half the stories involved fewer than two actors, and less than one-tenth presented conflicting opinions. In other words, regardless of who owned them or how competitive their markets were, the papers were not exactly brimming with lively debate and diverse ideas.

the challenge for media reformers

The radical concentration of global media ownership has spawned at least one excellent, rebellious child: a vibrant, smart, broad-based media reform movement. Groups like Fairness & Accuracy in Reporting, the Media Alliance, the Center for Digital Democracy, Independent Media Centers, the People's Communication Charter, and many others, are growing in strength, alliance and effectiveness. There are many reasons to object to media oligopolies that research on diversity does not speak to: the concentration of private power over a public resource in a democracy is wrong in principle; standardized media are part of a distasteful, branded, chainstore life of Barnes and Noble, Starbucks, and Disney; corporate, multinational media are increasingly unaccountable to the public; and a corporate press is probably a less adversarial press. But the research on media concentration should challenge this reform movement to relinquish at least one sacrosanct belief. If our goal is vibrant, diverse media content—what the People's Communication Charter, an international activist group, refers to as the "plurality of opinions and the diversity of cultural expressions and languages necessary for democracy" then research suggests that concentrated ownership is not equivalent to reduced diversity. Sometimes corporate media giants homogenize, and sometimes they do not. Sometimes they shut people up and stifle dissent, and sometimes they open up extra space for new people to be visible and vocal. That they do so not because they are committed to the public good but because diversity sometimes serves their interests does not negate the outcome. And, romantic notions notwithstanding, independently owned and noncommercial media hardly guarantee diverse content.

Just as there are different kinds of diversity, there are also different kinds of ownership concentration. A single corporation might own all the major outlets in a single market, or a chain of newspapers, or a film production company and a theater chain, or music, television and book companies. These different kinds of concentration promote and inhibit different kinds of content diversity. Researchers, activists, and policymakers must identify the conditions under which concentrated, conglomerated media ownership facilitates diverse media formats, opinions and demographic representations. A genuine commitment to diverse media content may require an unsettling task: encouraging those conditions even while opposing the corporate domination of media, feeding the giants while trying to topple them.

recommended resources

Bagdikian, Ben H. *The Media Monopoly* (6th ed.). Boston: Beacon Press, 2000. In this new edition of a now classic book, Bagdikian presents an impassioned argument against media concentration.

Baker, C. Edwin. *Media, Markets, and Democracy*. Cambridge, MA: Cambridge University Press, 2002. Baker demonstrates that media products are not like other commodities, and he argues that market competition alone fails to give media audiences what they want.

Columbia Journalism Review. "Who Owns What?" Online. `http://www.cjr.org/tools/owners`. This informative website lists the holdings of approximately 50 major media companies.

Croteau, David, and William Hoynes. *The Business of Media: Corporate Media and the Public Interest*. Thousand Oaks, CA: Pine Forge Press, 2001. This book contrasts two different views of media conglomeration: the market model, which regards people as consumers, and the public-interest model, which regards people as citizens.

Compaine, Benjamin M., and Douglas Gomery. *Who Owns the Media? Competition and Concentration in the Mass Media Industry*. Mahwah, NJ: Lawrence Erlbaum Associates, 2000. This book provides a detailed look at the current media industry and challenges common assumptions about the dangers of ownership concentration.

Entman, Robert M. "Newspaper Competition and First Amendment Ideals: Does Monopoly Matter?" *Journal of Communication* 35, 2 (1985): 147–65. This study of newspapers in competitive and noncompetitive markets concludes that market competition does not guarantee content diversity.

Horwitz, Robert. "On Media Concentration and the Diversity Question," Department of Communication, University of California, San Diego, 2003. Online. `http://communication.ucsd.edu/people/ConcentrationpaperICA.htm`. This is a careful discussion of the media ownership debate, empirical research and the virtues of a "mixed media system."

Napoli, Philip M. "Deconstructing the Diversity Principle." *Journal of Communication* 49, 4 (1999): 7–34. Napoli argues that the FCC policies on media ownership have long been based on unproven assumptions about the relationship between ownership diversity and content diversity.

TRIPPING UP BIG MEDIA

*One of the strangest Left-Right coalitions in recent memory
has challenged a free-market FCC. What's the glue that holds it together?*

BY GAL BECKERMAN

The angels of the public interest, with large pink wings and glittering halos, descended on Michael Powell this fall, five years after he had, somewhat sarcastically, first invoked them.

That was back in April 1998, when Powell was speaking to a Las Vegas gathering of lawyers. Only a few months had passed since his appointment to one of the five spots on the Federal Communications Commission, and the new commissioner had been invited to speak about a longstanding and contentious issue: Was it the FCC's responsibility to keep the media working toward the public good?

Powell made clear that he placed his faith in the invisible hand of the market: the business of the FCC, he said, was to resolve "matters that predominantly involve the competing interests of industry" and not some vague "public interest." The FCC had no role in deciding whether to give free airtime to presidential candidates, for example, or in forcing television channels to carry educational or children's programming. "Even if what is portrayed on television encourages or perpetuates some societal problem, we must be careful in invoking our regulatory powers," Powell insisted.

To highlight the point, Powell used biblical imagery. "The night after I was sworn in, I waited for a visit from the angel of the public interest," Powell said. "I waited all night but she did not come. And, in fact, five months into this job, I still have had no divine awakening."

This September 4 the angels finally arrived.

Fifteen women dressed entirely in fluorescent pink and spreading frilly wings emblazoned with the words "Free Speech" stood on the sidewalk outside the large glass doors of the FCC. They banged on bongos and shouted chants, unfurling a large pink scroll containing

their demands: full repeal of the new rules that Michael Powell had just shepherded into existence.

By this time, Powell had become FCC chairman and had overseen the biggest relaxation of media ownership rules in over thirty years. But the day before, a federal appeals court in Philadelphia had granted an emergency stay barring the FCC from putting his new rules into effect. The court gave as one of its reasons "the magnitude of this matter and the public's interest in reaching the proper resolution." So the angels were celebrating, and they were not alone.

The massive public response to the rule changes, in fact, had been unprecedented. For months before and after the new rules were announced on June 2, opposition had been loud, passionate, and active. Hundreds of thousands of comments were sent to the FCC, almost all in opposition. It was the heaviest outpouring of public sentiment the commission had ever experienced.

Even more striking was the makeup of this opposition, what *The New York Times* called "an unusual alliance of liberal and conservative organizations." Together in the mix, along with Code Pink, the activists in angel wings, were the National Rifle Association, the National Organization for Women, the Parents Television Council (a conservative group focused on indecency in television), every major journalism association, labor groups like the Writers and Screen Actors Guilds, and a collection of liberal nonprofit organizations that had been focused on media issues for decades.

It is not every day that the ideological lines get redrawn over an issue, let alone an issue that had been destined to remain obscure and complex for all but telecommunications experts to debate. What's the glue that has held this unlikely coalition together?

Victoria Cunningham is the twenty-four-year-old national coordinator of Code Pink, a grass-roots women's organization that engages in wacky direct action. Code Pink has sung Christmas carols outside Donald Rumsfeld's home and arrived at Hillary Clinton's Senate office wearing underwear over their clothing to deliver her a "pink slip" of disapproval for her early support of the war in Iraq. I met with her a month after her group's boisterous visit to the FCC. Code Pink's office is little more than a broom closet on the fifth floor of a building a few blocks from the White House. Pink beads and rainbow flags cram the walls. Cunningham was wearing—what else?—a very pink shirt.

Why were her members, who number in the thousands, so interested in this issue? "Our people are informed enough that they understand what happens when there are only one or three or four companies that are controlling the information we get," Cunningham said. "A lot of our people would love to turn on the evening news and see a variety of opinions coming out."

Like everyone I talked to who was involved in the opposition to the FCC rules, Cunningham spoke of the intuitive understanding most people had of an issue that seems complex on the surface. Over and over, as I attempted to understand what it was that was holding together this diverse coalition, I heard the same phrase: "People just get it." And I heard this from groups both left and right. The oddest invitation Cunningham said she had received in the last few months was to appear on Oliver North's conservative radio talk show to debate the FCC issue. "And when we talked about that," she said, "we just couldn't say anything bad to each other."

Next, I made my way to a rather different scene, the headquarters of the United States Conference of Catholic Bishops, to talk with Monsignor Francis J. Maniscalco, its director of communications. No broom closet, the conference's home is in a giant modern Washington building behind a large sculpture of Jesus pointing to the sky.

Monsignor Maniscalco, a clerical collar under his soft, round face, spoke like a weathered telecommunications professional about his opposition to the FCC's new rules. The bishops are concerned about the loss of religious shows, like Catholic mass on television—but also the loss of a time when, he says, in order for broadcasters to keep their licenses they had to "prove they were being responsive to the local community." The further consolidation of the media that would be spurred by the new FCC rules, he said, would only increase the lack of responsiveness to community needs. "We see the media as being very formational of people, formational of a culture, formational of people's attitudes," he said, "and if certain strains of community life are not on television they are, by that very reason, considered less important, less vital to society."

Even though he and the conference had always opposed media consolidation, Maniscalco said, until recently they felt they were working in a vacuum. When the monsignor began talking about the current effort, though, he visibly brightened. His eyebrows, which are red, lifted, and he rolled forward in his chair. "The consumption of media is a passive consumption, it is a passive act in itself," he said. "And it is a passive audience that has said, 'We just have to take what they give us.' But interestingly enough, this seems to be something that has finally caught people's imagination, that they could make a difference in terms of turning back these rules and saying no, we don't see that as being very helpful to our situation."

Media industry insiders were taken by surprise at how fast these groups managed to come together and exercise political influence. In addition to the emergency stay issued by the Philadelphia federal appeals court on the day before Powell's six new rules were to go into effect, Congress has responded with zeal to their demands. Consider: on July 23, only a month after the rules were approved, the House of Representatives voted 400 to 21 to roll back the ownership cap to 35 percent. Then, on September 16, the coalition had an even greater success. The Senate used a parliamentary procedure, called a resolution of disapproval—used only once before in history—to pass a bill repealing *all* the new regulations. It passed 55 to 40, and was supported by twelve Republicans, and cosponsored, astonishingly, by none other than Trent Lott. Such quick legislative action has generated excitement, but it is unlikely that the coalition will find such easy victory in the future. The Senate bill must now face House Republican leaders who have vowed to prevent the measure from going to a vote, partly to keep this political hot potato away from the president during an election year. The court case that has put the new rules on hold, meanwhile, promises a complicated legal contest when it takes place next year.

But these challenges don't take away from what has been achieved. Such ideologically disparate groups rarely find common cause. As Powell himself has pointed out, the reasons behind most of these groups' opposition are parochial and narrow. The unions are worried that more consolidation will lead to fewer jobs; the left-leaning groups are still shivering from what they saw as nationalistic coverage of the war; groups like the Parents Television Council want less *Buffy the Vampire Slayer* and more *Little House on the Prairie*. Yet there they were, at countless public hearings over the last half-year, the bishop sitting next to the gun lobbyist sitting next to a woman from NOW, all united around some common denominator.

To get a better idea of what that common denominator might be, I went to visit Andrew Schwartzman, the fifty-seven-year-old president of the Media Access Project, a small public-interest law firm that has been fighting big media and the FCC for more than three decades. Schwartzman was the lead lawyer in the case that led to the September 4 emergency stay.

A week after that triumph, he looked exhausted, his bloodshot eyes contrasting with his white hair and bushy moustache. He looked a little like Mark Twain—a very tired Mark Twain. He spoke slowly and deliberately. "Michael Powell has significantly misunderstood what this is about, to his detriment," Schwartzman said. "He repeatedly says, somewhat disdainfully, that all the disparate organizations are unhappy about what they see on the air. The right-wingers think the media is liberal and the left-wingers think the media is a corporate conspiracy, and they all can't be right. This is a way of dismissing and trivializing their position. For me, what these groups have in common is that they represent people who are within the relatively small group of Americans who choose to be active participants in the political process, the people who exercise their First Amendment rights aggressively. And even where their principal areas of interest may be the Second Amendment or other things, they understand the importance of the electronic mass media in the democratic process. And Michael Powell hasn't understood that."

What unites these groups, he told me, is that they all generally believe that the media are limited, and that this limitation comes from the fact that there is too much control in too few hands. This leads to a lack of diversity of voices, to programming that is out of touch with local concerns, to increasingly commercial and homogenized news and entertainment. And this is what has triggered people's passions. It is not the fear that their own voice won't echo loud enough, he said, but that further consolidation will produce media in which only the powerful few will be heard at all.

But why *now*? Neither Schwartzman nor anyone else I talked to could explain why, coming from so many different directions, all these groups landed in the same place at the same time. After all, this is not the first time that free-market enthusiasts have smashed up against the defenders of the public interest.

The 1980s saw a major crack in the idea that the public interest was the top priority for the FCC. President Reagan's FCC chairman, Mark Fowler, presided over the death of the Fairness Doctrine, which required broadcast stations to provide airtime for opposing voices in controversial matters of public importance. Then in 1996 Congress passed, and President Clinton signed, a major overhaul of U.S. telecommunications law, permitting greater media concentration. Radio was significantly deregulated, leading to the growth of companies such as Clear Channel, which now operates more than 1,200 stations in more than 300 markets. It was in that period that the national ownership cap for television stations went from 25 percent to 35 percent.

Such developments happened away from the public eye, in a place where only members of Congress and lobbyists roam. According to Celia Wexler, director and researcher for Common Cause, the nonpartisan citizens' lobby, those past fights were "very much inside the Belt-

way. It was very complicated, and there were no groups able to tell the story in a way that really made people understand what was at stake. There were media reformers who understood, who wanted a discussion of the public-interest obligations of broadcasters. But it didn't really catch fire."

At a morning session on media issues at a Common Cause conference, I saw how dramatically the situation had changed. Seats to the event were in hot demand. Next to me an elderly couple sat clutching newspaper clippings, one of which was headlined NEW FCC RULES SAP DIVERSITY IN MEDIA OWNERS.

Wexler, a small woman with the air of a librarian, was sitting on stage in a panel that included Gloria Tristani, a former FCC commissioner, who said of Michael Powell at one point: "I think he has lost touch with people or maybe never had touch with people in this country." The star of the morning, though, was John Nichols, a *Nation* Washington correspondent, who, together with Robert McChesney, another media reformer, this year started an organization called Free Press. Nichols has a professorial air, but he started his talk so dramatically that the couple next to me started nodding furiously.

He contended that, in the wake of September 11 and in the buildup to the war in Iraq, Americans had come to realize how shallow and narrow were their media. "People said maybe I support this war, maybe I oppose it, but I would like to know a little more about who we're going to bomb," Nichols said. "And I would like to know more about what came before and how this works—not just cheerleading. And all of that churned, combined, to have a profound impact."

This was an explanation I had heard from other liberal groups involved in the media movement. But it still didn't explain why conservatives had chosen this particular moment to join this coalition. As with the liberals, there have always been conservative groups that have opposed media deregulation, most notably the Catholic Church, but the message never resonated widely.

That, too, has changed. Take, for example, the Parents Television Council, an organization with 800,000 members that monitors indecency. The group regularly sends letters to the FCC when a show contains what they call "foul language" or racy subject matter. In August, L. Brent Bozell, the council's president, joined Gene Kimmelman of Consumers Union, a longtime advocate of media reform, in an editorial that was published in the *New York Daily News*, writing that in spite of their ideological differences they "agree that by opening the door to more media and newspaper consolidation, the FCC has endangered something that reaches far beyond traditional politics: It has undermined the community-oriented communications critical to our democracy."

Conservatives see a link between the growth of big media and the amount of blood and skin they see on television. The smaller and more local that media are, the argument goes, the more attuned to community standards of decency. If local stations could preempt what was being fed from New York and Los Angeles, then programming could be more reflective of family values. Here again, the sense is that media have become too large and all-encompassing and lost touch with their audience.

Melissa Caldwell, director of research at the council, points out that the new ownership rules were a way for big media companies to buy up even more local stations. This is worrisome, she explained, because locally owned broadcast affiliates tend to be more responsive to community standards of decency. The council's surveys, Caldwell says, show that network-owned stations almost never preempt network shows, "whereas locally owned and operated stations were more likely to do so. We don't want to see the networks become even less responsive to community concerns than they already are."

By the end of September, with his rules in deep freeze, Powell, speaking to *The New York Times*, expressed exasperation with the effectiveness of the opposition. "Basically, people ran an outside political campaign against the commission," Powell was quoted as saying. "I've never seen that in six years."

"We don't want to see the networks become even less responsive to community concerns"

At the core of this "campaign" were four groups— Consumers Union, led by Kimmelman, and the Consumer's Federation of America, represented by Mark Cooper, as well as Andrew Schwartzman's Media Access Project and the Center for Digital Democracy, run by Jeffrey Chester. The four men (who often referred to themselves as the "four Jewish horsemen of the apocalypse") played the central role in translating the growing anger and frustration of the Left and the Right into a cohesive movement.

Early on, these groups realized that to fight the FCC they would need more political power than their dependable but small progressive base could offer. One of their first steps, in addition to beginning a conversation with conservative groups like Parents Television Council, was to call on labor organizations like the Writers Guild and AFTRA, which could provide the resources and the manpower to get the message out.

By the beginning of 2003, a loose coalition was in place. And at that point, Powell's personality, of all things, began to play a galvanizing role. In pronouncement after pronouncement, he trumpeted the importance of these new rules—highlighted by his decision to vote on all of them in one shot. He insisted that their rewriting would be based purely on a scientific examination of the current broadcasting world.

It was true, as Powell claimed, that reexamining the rules was not his idea. The District of Columbia Court of Appeals, interpreting the 1996 Telecommunications Act, had ordered him to conduct a biennial assessment. But Powell had many chances to include the public in this review, and he did not. No public hearings were necessary, he said; the facts would do the talking, and would point to the rightness of his free-market convictions. "Michael Powell deserves a public-interest medal because he practically single-handedly created this enormous opposition," said Jeffrey Chester.

In December, Powell announced a single public hearing, to be held in what one opponent jokingly referred to as "the media capital" of Richmond, Virginia. Soon, groups who had been only peripherally involved in the loose coalition became increasingly angered by Powell's intransigence. One story often invoked to illustrate the unifying power of Powell's stubbornness involves a meeting that took place between members of the Hollywood creative community and labor groups, including producers and writers, and Kenneth Ferree, the chief of the media bureau at the FCC. According to several people present at the gathering, when a request for public hearings was made, Ferree was dismissive and rude, saying he was only interested in "facts," not "footstomping." "The sense of helplessness and anger that he generated by that meeting was enormous," said Mona Mangan, executive director of Writers Guild East.

If Powell's refusal to hold public hearings galvanized the opposition in one direction, the desire of another commissioner, Michael J. Copps, to engage with the public on this issue also played a key role. Copps, one of the two Democrats on the FCC, was unhappy with Powell's insistence on keeping the issue within the Beltway. When Powell finally announced that the number of public hearings would be limited to one, Copps issued a statement that read like the complaints of the growing grass-roots opposition. "At stake in this proceeding are our core values of localism, diversity, competition, and maintaining the multiplicity of voices and choices that undergird our marketplace of ideas and that sustain American democracy," he said.

"The idea that you are changing the basic framework for media ownership and you don't really want to make this a public debate was a reflection of Powell's own sort of arrogant, narrow mind-set," said Chester. "He didn't understand that this is about journalism, this is about media. No matter what the outcome, you have to go the extra mile to encourage a serious national debate."

Through the winter and early spring, Copps organized *unofficial* hearings around the country in collaboration with groups like the Writers Guild, earning the nickname Paul Revere in some quarters. As media reform groups searched for a wide range of witnesses to speak at these hearings, the coalition grew to include groups like the National Rifle Association and the National Organization for Woman. Out of the meetings came the first sense that this issue could resonate.

In the spring, after Powell refused to delay the June vote for further discussion, the FCC was flooded with calls and letters. Petitions were signed with hundreds of thousands of names and comments. Something was happening. Despite the scant press coverage, citizens were responding. The Internet helped to make this response immediate and numerous, mostly through an Internet-based public interest group called MoveOn.org, which had been an organizing force against the Iraq war, capable of turning out thousands upon thousands of signatures and donations in a matter of days. Now it turned its attention to media reform, and the result surprised even its organizers.

"We thought it was just kind of a weird issue because it's this wonky regulatory thing, it's not a typical MoveOn issue like stopping the drilling in the Arctic," said Eli Pariser, MoveOn's young national campaigns director. "After we heard from a critical mass of people we decided to pursue it and see what happened. And when we went out with our petition we got this amazing response."

A few days before the September 16 Senate vote on the resolution of disapproval, I accompanied lobbyists from Consumers Union and Free Press as they delivered a huge MoveOn petition. Lining one of the halls in the Hart Senate Office Building were stacks upon stacks of paper, 340,000 names in all. It was the quickest and largest turnover MoveOn had ever experienced, including its antiwar effort.

As the activists, young and in rumpled, ill-fitting suits, delivered these petitions to Senate aides, everyone was struck by the fact that they were more than just names printed on paper, more than a rubber-stamp petition drive. Many of the statements seemed heartfelt. Sometimes they were only a line, "I want more diversity and freedom of speech," and sometimes long letters, taking up whole pages. People expressed their personal dissatisfaction with what they saw when they turned on the TV. But mostly, they expressed passion. It popped off the page. People in Batesville, Arkansas, and Tekamah, Nebraska, were angry. Media had become a political issue, as deeply felt as the economy, health care, or education. Senate Republicans and Democrats alike understood this. A few days later, they voted to repeal all the new regulations.

When I asked the coalition partners how long their alliance could last beyond the battle over the ownership rules, their answers were uniform: not long. If the Parents Television Council and the Writers Guild ever sat down and tried to figure out rules for TV, the decency monitors would demand stricter limits on sex and violence, and the screenwriters who make up the guild would recoil in horror, shouting about the First Amendment.

But on the question of what these groups' larger and long-term objectives were for the media, I did get some kind of consensus. At the most fundamental level, there is a demand for a forum, for a place where diverse ideas can be heard and contrasted. The ideal seemed to be media that better reflect America, with its diversity, its ideological contentiousness, its multitude of values and standards.

When I asked Monsignor Maniscalco how he would want broadcasters to act in an ideal world, I assumed he would posit some narrow vision of an all-Catholic twenty-four-hour news channel, but he didn't.

"We would like them to take a chance on things that are noncommercial, that are simply not on television," the monsignor said. "Not for the sake of how much money they can make, but because they represent significant aspects of the community. We would really like to see the concept of broadcasting in the public interest be recognized by these people as a legitimate aspect of their work."

When I posed the problem of whether he could eventually agree to share airtime with all the groups in this coalition, groups like NOW with which he had fundamental and deep disagreements, Monsignor Maniscalco had a simple answer: "You could say that the goal is for the media to give us access so we can finally have a space to argue amongst ourselves."

Gal Beckerman is an assistant editor at CJR.

CAMPAIGN 2000

MEDIA MONEY

How Corporate Spending Blocked Political Ad Reform & Other Stories of Influence

BY CHARLES LEWIS

In his January 1998 State of the Union address, after decrying the campaign fundraising "arms race," President Bill Clinton proposed a major new policy that would address a big part of the problem—the high cost of campaign commercials. "I will formally request that the Federal Communications Commission act to provide free or reduced-cost television time for candidates," the president said. "The airwaves are a public trust, and broadcasters also have to help us in this effort to strengthen our democracy." Within twenty-four hours, Federal Communications Commission chairman William Kennard announced that the FCC would develop new rules governing political ads.

But days later, the powerful broadcast corporations and their Capitol Hill allies managed to halt this historic initiative. In the Senate, Senator John McCain of Arizona, the Commerce Committee chairman, and Conrad Burns, a Republican from Montana and the chairman of that panel's communications subcommittee, announced that they would legislatively block the FCC's free-air-time initiative. "The FCC is clearly overstepping its authority here," McCain said. In the House of Representatives, seventeen Republicans—including Majority Whip Tom DeLay, Appropriations chairman Bob Livingston, future House Speaker Dennis Hastert, and Billy

Tauzin, chairman of the House Commerce Committee's telecommunications subcommittee—sent a blunt letter to Kennard: "Only Congress has the authority to write the laws of our nation, and only Congress has the authority to delegate to the Commission programming obligations by broadcasters." John Dingell, the Michigan Democrat and ranking House Commerce Committee member, also sent an opposing letter to Kennard. Faced with the very real threat that his agency's budget would be cut, Kennard had no choice but to retreat from the proposed rule making.

It was a humiliating and metaphorical moment for the FCC. The threat of a shrunken budget and a congressional backlash—"the likes of which would not be pleasant to the Federal Communications Commission under any circumstances" is the way Livingston described it—was too much for the FCC. Many politicians in power tend to fear free air time for the leg up it would give to challengers. More than that, free air time for political candidates would directly affect the bottom line of a very important industry and Washington player—the media industry. It would cost broadcasters millions of dollars in lost advertising revenue, and they were not about to allow a direct affront to their financial self-interest become law. Free air time quickly went from the fast track to the back

burner. In a very public way, the agency and the White House had been "rolled like a pancake," recalls former FCC chairman Reed Hundt, Kennard's immediate predecessor.

Indeed, the media's success in handling the threat of free air time for candidates is but one of a stack of pancakes that media companies have rolled in Congress and the White House in recent years. Which is why the media industry is widely regarded as perhaps the most powerful special interest today in Washington.

How do media corporations win friends and influence people in our nation's capital? The old-fashioned way, by using the time-honored techniques with which business interests routinely reap billions of dollars worth of subsidies, tax breaks, contracts, and other favors. They lobby vigorously. They give large donations to political campaigns. They take politicians and their staffs on junkets.

LOBBYING An investigation by CJR and the Center for Public Integrity found that since 1996, the fifty largest media companies (defined as companies that derive half or more of their revenues from broadcasting, cable operations, publishing, online media, and their content providers) and four of their trade associations have spent $111.3 million to lobby Congress and the executive branch of the government. The number of registered, media-related lobbyists has

MEDIA DONATIONS

THE TOP RECIPIENTS, 1993-2000

PRESIDENTIAL	CANDIDATES	AMOUNT
Al Gore, D	Dem nominee	$1,163,490
George W. Bush, R	Rep nominee	1,070,728
Bill Bradley, D	Primary challenger	1,034,004
Bill Clinton, D	42nd President	634,456
Bob Dole, R	'96 Rep nominee	294,095

SENATORS	COMMITTEE	AMOUNT
John McCain, R	Chair, Commerce	685,929*
Edward Kennedy, D	Judiciary	529,970
John Kerry, D	Commerce	470,944
Charles Schumer, D	Judiciary	435,550**
Barbara Boxer, D	Foreign Relations	417,249

REPRESENTATIVES	COMMITTEE	AMOUNT
Howard Berman, D	Judiciary	315,598
Richard Gephardt, D	Minority Leader	252,997
Edward Markey, D	Ranking, Commerce	250,350
John Dingell, D	Commerce	193,136
Mark Green, R	Science	157,340

Through 6/30/00.
Source: Analysis of data provided by the Center for Responsive Politics
*–Includes contributions to Presidential campaign.
**–Includes contributions to House campaigns.

TOP TEN DONORS, 1993-2000

COMPANY	AMOUNT
Time Warner, Inc.*	$4,605,209
Walt Disney Co., Inc.*	4,086,195
National Cable Television Ass.	1,992,090
National Assn. of Broadcasters	1,932,057
Tele-Communications, Inc.	1,861,935
Viacom International*	1,851,310
DreamWorks SKG	1,754,150
Joseph E. Seagram & Sons	1,484,333
News Corp*	1,477,905
Universal Studios, Inc.	1,396,274

Through 6/30/00.
Source: Analysis of data provided by the Center for Responsive Politics
*– Includes subsidiaries.

THE MONEY

CYCLE	INDIVIDUAL (WITH SOFT)	PAC	TOTAL
93-94	$9,334,507	2,402,569	11,737,076
95-96	20,293,975	2,902,250	23,196,225
Subtotal			**34,933,301**
97-98	16,051,540	2,885,909	18,937,449
99-00*	19,584,564	1,695,560	21,280,124
Subtotal			**40,217,573**
TOTAL			**$75,150,874**

*– Through 6/30/00.

Source: Analysis of data provided by the Center for Responsive Politics

---

increased from 234 in 1996, the year the historic Telecommunication Act became law, to 284 in 1999. And last year, the amount of money spent on lobbyists was $31,408,965, up 26.4 percent from the $24,835,961 spent in 1996.

By way of comparison, in 1998, when media firms spent $28.5 million for lobbying, securities and investment firms spent $28 million, labor unions spent $23.7 million, and lawyers spent $19.1 million. Media companies weren't the biggest lobbying interests (airlines spent $38.6 million, defense contractors $48.7 million, and electric utilities $63.7 million). But no other sector of the economy has the perceived power to shape coverage in the news, a factor that greatly increases the media companies' lobbying weight.

No media corporation lavishes more on lobbyists or politicians than Time Warner

CAMPAIGN CONTRIBUTIONS Since 1993 through June 30th of this year, media corporations have given $75 million in campaign contributions to candidates for federal office and to the two major political parties, according to data provided by the Center for Responsive Politics. The next president of the United States will have gotten to 1600 Pennsylvania Avenue with more than a million dollars in political donations from media interests; Vice President Al Gore has taken in $1.16 million, Governor George W. Bush has received $1.07

million. The sitting member of Congress with the biggest haul in media money—including his presidential campaign—is Senate Commerce Committee chairman McCain, who has collected $685,929. Over all, the amount of campaign cash from the media industry is skyrocketing every election cycle, which is typical of political giving in general. For example, media corporations gave $18,937,449 in 1997–1998, a 61 percent increase over the previous, 1993–1994 mid-term election cycle.

No media corporation lavishes more money on lobbyists or political campaigns than Time Warner, Inc. The media giant spent nearly $4.1 million for lobbying last year, and since 1993 has contributed $4.6 million to congressional and presidential candidates and the two political parties. The second-heaviest media spender in Washington is the Walt Disney Co., Inc., which paid $3.3 million for lobbying and just under $4.1 million in political donations during the same period of time. This is not a subject either company appears anxious to discuss. Calls to Gerald Levin, chairman of Time Warner, and to Michael Eisner, chairman of Disney, were not returned. Nor would the c.e.o.s of the other big media political spenders answer our questions: AT&T/ Liberty Media (formerly Tele-Communications, Inc.) chairman John Malone; Viacom's Sumner Redstone; Seagram's Edgar Bronfman; Ralph Roberts, chairman of the board of Comcast; DreamWorks' part-owner David Geffen; and News Corporation's chairman Rupert Murdoch.

JUNKETS Since 1997, media companies have taken 118 members of Congress and their senior staff on 315 trips to meet with lobbyists and c.e.o.s to discuss legislation and the policy preferences of the industry. Lawmakers and their staffs have traveled near and far, to events as close as Alexandria, Virginia, and as far away as Taiwan. They've spoken at anniversaries of news organizations, gone fact-finding in Capetown, South Africa, and toured movie studios. Blaine Merritt, chief counsel to the courts and intellectual property subcommittee, wrote that the purpose of his trip to Burbank, paid for by Walt Disney, was to "learn about Disney production facilities and review relevant legislative issues which affect the company's operations."

The cumulative cost of these 315 trips was $455,867. The top three sponsors of the all-expense-paid jaunts were News Corporation, the National Association of Broadcasters, and the National Cable Television Association.

No member of Congress traveled more frequently on the media industry's nickel than Congressman Billy Tauzin, the Louisiana Republican. He and his senior staff have been taken on forty-two trips—one out of eight junkets the industry has lavished on Congress. In December 1999 Tauzin left with his wife Cecile on a six-day, $18,910 trip to Paris, sponsored by Time Warner and Instinet, ostensibly for a conference there on e-commerce. Another member at-

tending the same meeting, Rep. John E. Sweeney, a New York Republican, reported half the costs incurred by Tauzin, $7,445. Tauzin's wife and his son Michael have accompanied him on several industry-sponsored trips to New York, New Orleans, and Palm Springs, California.

The FCC, Justice, and Congress have allowed media companies to mate like rabbits

---

Despite calls to his office and home, Tauzin declined to be interviewed. Andrew Schwartzman, a public interest lawyer and the director of the Media Access Project, who has been watching Tauzin for years, says he is not the least bit surprised about Tauzin's trips. "Billy Tauzin is an active, knowledgeable, and involved member of Congress who spends a great deal of time on telecommunications issues," he says. "But unlike some other members, he is not the least bit embarrassed about accepting large quantities of their generosity. This is the Eddy Edwards, Huey Long kind of streak in these guys of 'wink, wink, I'm a rogue'... Billy just kind of revels in it."

The second most frequent flier in Congress courtesy of the media has been Thomas J. Bliley, the Republican who chairs the House Commerce Committee. Bliley and his staff have logged nineteen junkets over the last three years.

At the GOP convention in Philadelphia, Tauzin, who hopes to succeed chairman Bliley, hosted a Mardi Gras-style celebration, complete with floats from Louisiana. The affair, attended by lobbyists and pols and reportedly costing $400,000, was underwritten by, among others, SBC Communications, which owns cable properties; BellSouth Corp.; and Comsat Corp. Not to be outdone, Tauzin's rival for the top job on Commerce, Michael Oxley, threw an American Bandstand-themed bash, complete with the show's host, Dick Clark, the day before. Oxley's dance party was paid for by contributions of up to $75,000 a pop, according to *Legal Times*,

from the likes of COMSAT Corporation, Satellite SuperSkyway Alliance, and SBC Telecommunications; the total cost was estimated in the $300,000-to-$400,000 range.

The largess extended by the media industry is not limited merely to Congress. We also found that Federal Communications Commission employees were taken on 1,460 all-expenses-paid trips sponsored by media corporations and associations since 1995, costing a total of $1.5 million. A group called the Institute for International Research paid for sixty-two trips at a cost of more than $95,000. The innocuous sounding IIR is a privately held, global conference organization group, designed to allow corporate clients "an excellent opportunity to showcase your products in front of key decision makers... and to ensure maximum networking opportunities." The FCC's Office of Policy Planning chief, Bob Pepper, tops IIR's list of favorite regulators, with eight trips totaling more than $23,500.

THE BIG PLAYERS

The intermeshing of public and private sectors has, of course, been an endemic problem in Washington for years, and the social and professional interaction between the media business and the government that regulates it is, not surprisingly, quite extensive. For example, Podesta & Associates, now known as Podesta.com, is the outside lobbying firm representing the widest array of media behemoths. Since 1996, the company has received $1.62 million as the Washington representative for Viacom, Time Warner, and NBC. It is headed by Tony Podesta, whose brother John happens to be the White House chief of staff. Twenty-three members of its staff of thirty-three formerly worked on Capitol Hill for one party or the other. One of them, Kimberley Fritts, is the daughter of the president of the National Association of Broadcasters, NAB.

No media organization spends more money lobbying or has more people covering Washington than the NAB, which has spent $19.42 million to persuade government officials since 1996. NAB president Eddie Fritts was a college classmate and is

LOBBYING

WHAT THE MEDIA WANT: TOP TEN LOBBYIST ISSUES SINCE 1996

1 Intellectual property: 556 lobby registrations*
2 Violent programming restrictions: 469
3 Satellite systems: 287
4 Tax issues: 272
5 Telecommunications: 272

6 Political ads/campaign finance: 220
7 Cable issues: 192
8 Tobacco/alcohol advertising: 178
9 Antitrust/ownership issues: 170
10 Broadband/spectrum issues: 105

LOBBYING FEES PAID BY MEDIA COMPANIES SINCE 1996

1996	$24,835,961
1997	26,600,229
1998	28,493,371
1999	31,408,965
TOTAL	**$111,338,526**

THEN AND NOW: MEDIA LOBBYISTS IN 1996 AND 1999

YEAR	LOBBYISTS REGISTERED	FEES COLLECTED
1996	234 lobbyists	$24,835,961
1999	284 lobbyists	$31,408,965

[Rate of increase: 26.4%]

TOP TEN MEDIA LOBBYING SPENDERS IN 1996 AND 1999

1996		1999	
National Assoc. of Broadcasters	$5,280,000	National Assoc. of Broadcasters	$5,320,000
Time Warner	4,530,000	National Cable Television Assoc.	4,130,000
National Cable TV Assoc.	3,463,054	Time Warner	4,060,000
Newspaper Assoc. of America	2,110,631	Disney World Services	3,300,000
Cox	1,800,000	Comcast	3,240,000
Disney	1,680,000	Assn. of American Publishers	1,600,000
CBS	1,592,837	Newspaper Assoc. of America	1,556,000
News Corp	1,079,632	News Corp	1,510,000
ABC	570,000	Viacom	1,380,000
Gannett	520,000	CBS	1,300,000
TOTAL	**$22,626,154**	**TOTAL**	**$27,396,000**

TOP TEN MEDIA ORGANIZATIONS BY LOBBYING COSTS SINCE 1996**

1 National Assoc. Of Broadcasters, $16.92 million
2 Time Warner Turner, $15.77 million
3 National Cable Television Assoc., $13.68 million
4 Walt Disney, $11 million
5 Viacom/CBS, $9.29 million

6 News Corp./Fox/AskyB, $7.48 million
7 Newspaper Assoc. Of America, $6.51 million
8 Cox Enterprises, $4.61 million
9 Comcast Corp., $4.12 million
10 Assoc. Of American Publishers, $3.12 million

* —Lobbyists register with the Clerk of the House of Representatives, and must list specific bills that they are paid to try to influence
** —Includes in-house lobbying operations and trade groups

a close friend of Senate Majority Leader Trent Lott, and on occasion this relationship has been immensely helpful to the broadcasters. There are twenty registered lobbyists at the NAB, seven of whom came from congressional staffs, the FCC, and the Federal Trade Commission. Until recently, their ranks included Kimberly Tauzin, daughter of Billy Tauzin.

The Newspaper Association of America has spent $6.5 million on lobbying since 1996, using four in-house lobbyists and four outside firms, most notably Wiley, Rein & Fielding, whose founding partner, Richard Wiley, once served as chairman of the FCC. They've lobbied on everything from the Freedom of Information Act—certainly an understandable concern for journalists—to postal reform bills and amendments to the Fair Labor Standards Act that could change the rules governing independent contractors. They've also sought to overturn FCC rules that limit the number of stations any broadcaster—including newspapers—can own.

Media corporations have spared no expense in Washington, hiring all of the "usual suspects" kind of big-name lobbyists. They include former Republican party chairman Haley Barbour (CBS); Tommy Boggs, son of the long-deceased House Majority Leader Hale Boggs and U.S. Ambassador to the Vatican Lindy Boggs, and brother of ABC News correspondent Cokie Roberts (National Cable Television Association; Maga-

JUNKETS

No Congressman traveled more frequently on the media industry's nickel than Louisiana's Billy Tauzin

1997-2000 SPONSORS OF TRIPS	
SPONSOR	**TOTAL COST OF TRIPS**
1 News Corp	$68,175
2 National Assn. of Broadcasters	56,212
3 National Cable Television Assn.	48,168
4 Media One	41,159
5 Walt Disney	33,868
6 NBC	26,929
7 World College of Journalism & Communication	18,700
8 Assn. of Local Television Stations	18,490
9 Instinet	15,260
10 Discovery Channel Foundation	13,900

1997-2000 CONGRESSMEN AND STAFF TRIPS	
1 W.J. "Billy" Tauzin (42)	$77,389
2 Thomas J. Bliley (19)	18,110
3 Elizabeth Furse (3)	14,710
4 Orrin G. Hatch (12)	12,846
5 John Conyers Jr. (12)	12,616
6 Michael G. Oxley (7)	12,488
7 John F. Kerry (3)	11,340
8 J. Dennis Hastert (6)	10,540
9 Henry J. Hyde (9)	10,134
10 John M. Shimkus (6)	9,332

zine Publishers of America); a former Reagan White House chief of staff, Ken Duberstein (Comcast, National Cable TV Association, Time Warner); a former Nixon White House aide, Tom Korologos (Cox Communications); a former Carter White House aide, Anne Wexler (Comcast, Univision); and former FCC chairman Richard Wiley (CBS). After all, from copyright issues to broadband access to media ownership rules, billions of dollars are at stake in the changing media industry.

Corporate executives are often directly involved in the lobbying process, and media moguls are no different. In his recent memoir, *You Say You Want A Revolution* (Yale University Press), former FCC chairman Hundt recounts important conversations he had with Turner Broadcasting System, Inc., chairman and president (at the time) Ted Turner; QVC Network, Inc., chairman Barry Diller; TCI chairman John Malone; DreamWorks executive Steven Spielberg; and Disney vice president (at the time) Michael Ovitz.

Hundt candidly describes the atmosphere of influence-peddling at his agency: "I learned quickly that the volume of lobbying defined the major issues before the agency.... A single company might send soldiers from its regiments to the commission as many as 100 times, visit or phone the chairman on a dozen occasions, call some member of the chairman's staff perhaps daily. Congressional staffers made tens of thousands of telephone calls to the commission staff. Congressmen wrote letters on behalf of different parties, up to 5,000 or more a year. Sometimes, when the members wanted a particular result they phoned the commissioners to solicit votes as they might call each other on the Hill. Smart and well-financed lobbyists also ran media strategies to persuade the commission to write rules in their favor. Industries might spend millions of dollars on television advertising to influence a handful of commissioners."

The nature of the media's political power remains fascinating to Hundt. "The media industry does not mobilize great numbers of voters and it actually is not comprised of America's largest, economically most important companies...." The media's significance and political clout, he argues, come "from its near ubiquitous, pervasive power to completely alter the beliefs of every American." Members of Congress and presidential candidates, he believes, are afraid to take on the news media directly for fear that they will simply "disappear" from the TV or radio airwaves and print news columns.

THE BIG ISSUES

These have been spectacular times for media corporations, and the task of their Washington lobbyists is to keep the party going for as long as possible. The past decade has seen stunning annual revenues and unprecedented corporate concentration. No reasonable person would accuse the FCC of overzealous enforcement of the antitrust laws. In 1992, for the first time in twenty-two years, the FCC allowed network-cable TV cross ownership, allowing a single company to own such outlets in the same market. (TV and newspaper ownership in the same market is a violation of cross-ownership rules.)

And the FCC, the Justice Department and the Congress generally have allowed media companies to mate and merge like rabbits. To name just a few, we have watched Time Warner merge with Turner

Broadcasting, and Disney merge with Capital Cities/ABC, and News Corporation acquire Heritage Media, and AT&T merge with TCI, and CBS buy King World, and Viacom buy CBS, and Tribune Co. buy Times Mirror, and Time Warner and America Online announce the mother of all mergers—a $350 billion deal to create the "world's first fully integrated media and communications company."

Today, 98 percent of Americans live in communities with only one local newspaper. The same percentage of citizens is served by a single cable provider. Some fifty cable channels are available in at least 40 million American homes, and three companies—Disney, Time Warner, and Viacom— own all or part of twenty-eight of them. Not far behind is General Electric, which owns NBC, CNBC, and shares joint ownership of MSNBC, A&E, the History Channel, and PAX-TV, a family-oriented cable channel.

In this marketplace milieu, media corporations press for further advantage in Washington. In the current Congress, more than sixty bills aimed at the broadcasters, networks, cable operators, and satellite operators—as well as at the FCC that regulates them—were proposed in the House and Senate. And that number doesn't include the tax, trade, labor, and non-binding resolutions that draw the industry's attention.

Below are some of the industry's legislative concerns:

INTELLECTUAL PROPERTY Media companies spend tens of billions of dollars each year securing the right to content—whether it's paying reporters' salary while they get the story or buying the rights to a free-lance magazine piece, or the rights to air a *Seinfeld* episode or *Jurassic Park*. They spend millions more on lobbyists who seek legislation designed to protect their investment in such properties, a major concern to media firms, especially as the Internet grows in sophistication.

VIOLENCE Lobbyists for the media industry have consistently raised First Amendment freedoms as a carte blanche protection against any regulation of violent content broadcast over the airwaves. The current system that rates violence in programs was agreed to voluntarily by broadcasters only after Senator McCain threatened to have the FCC block station license renewals for those broadcasters who refused to participate.

THE SATELLITE HOME VIEWER IMPROVEMENT ACT Signed into law by President Clinton last November, this permits satellite broadcasters to offer local signals to subscribers. Cable companies, who railed against the "must carry" provisions that require them to provide customers with all local broadcast channels, were only too happy to see their satellite competitors saddled with the same burden.

MEDIA OWNERSHIP Under current FCC rules, a single company is permitted to reach only 35 percent of the national audience through the stations it directly owns, preventing a handful of companies from owning all of the television stations in the country. With the CBS deal, Viacom went over the cap. To meet regulatory muster, Viacom will have to sell off some of its stations by May 2001. Within a week of the merger's announcement, Senate Commerce chairman McCain introduced a bill that would help Viacom skirt that requirement, raising the audience cap to 50 percent of the national audience. As noted in the Center for Public Integrity's book, *The Buying of the President 2000*, Viacom was McCain's fourth most generous "career patron."

NBC would also benefit from McCain's bill to lift the ownership cap. NBC acquired a 32 percent stake in Paxson Communications, the Florida-based broadcaster (whose interests McCain has promoted, in a letter to the FCC demanding action on one of the company's pending license requests. The letter was written just a day after the senator flew on the company's corporate jet). NBC has an option to purchase a controlling interest in Paxson by February 1, 2002, "if FCC rules then permit," the company's parent, GE, announced in documents filed with the SEC. Should McCain's bill pass, NBC won't face any FCC hurdles exercising its option.

REPEAL OF ESTATE TAXES Last July, the Senate joined the House in passing legislation to repeal estate taxes. The measure was strongly supported by some well-known family-owned publishers. Copley Newspapers, Cox Enterprises, and Morris Communications have paid a lobbyist $950,000 since 1996 to fight for the end of the "death tax." In June the *San Diego Union-Tribune*, a Copley newspaper, published an editorial entitled, "The Death Tax: Repeal the Most Unfair of All Federal Levies": "House Republicans and Democrats were right to pass legislation that phases out the death tax not only on family farms, but on all family-owned businesses and other assets." Not mentioned was the direct financial interest of the Copley family in the legislation, and attendant lobbying efforts in that regard. "We are contributors to a fund that is trying to eliminate the estate tax," Hal Fuson, Copley's chief counsel, told us. "There was nothing particularly surreptitious about it."

CAMPAIGN FINANCE REFORM

Still, no single recent media issue more poignantly portrays the clash between public and private interest than the debate over free air-time for political candidates. In early 1998, before the president and FCC chairman made their rule-making move, the broadcast networks, ABC, CBS, and NBC, were already targets of criticism. They were excoriated for reaping, potentially, billions of dollars in 1997 when Congress gave them—free—the government-owned digital spectrum, to use for the next generation of technology. There was a rising public clamor around the question, Do broadcasters have public-interest obligations anymore?

Against this backdrop, television stations and networks separately have been making a financial killing from political advertising. According to data collected by a firm called Competitive Media Reporting, local and national TV political advertising will earn broadcasters $600 million this year. In fact, income from political ads has been steadily rising for twenty years—from $90,570,000 in 1980 to $498,890,600 in 1998. In the first four months of this year, TV stations in the top seventy-five media markets took in $114 million for 151,000 commercials from the candidates alone.

At the same time, around the nation, news coverage of political candidates is getting minuscule. For example, the Annenberg School of Communication at the University of Southern California discovered that in the final three months of the 1998 California governor's race, local TV news on the subject comprised less than one-third of one percent of possible news time. In 1974, the amount of gubernatorial coverage in California was ten times greater. Another USC Annenberg finding: sixteen of the nineteen top-rated TV stations in the top eleven markets broadcast, on average, only thirty-nine seconds a night (from 5 p.m. to 11:30 p.m.) about political campaigns. Top stations in Philadelphia and Tampa averaged six seconds a night.

As Robert McChesney, a University of Illinois professor, wrote in *Rich Media, Poor Democracy*, "Broadcasters have little incentive to cover candidates, because it is in their interest to force them to purchase time to publicize their campaigns."

Recent research seems to bear this out. For example, in the New Jersey Senate primary, in which Jon Corzine spent more of his own money than any Senate candidate in U.S. history, local television stations in New York and Philadelphia made $21 million from political ads. In the last two weeks of the campaign, citizens watching top Philadelphia and New York TV stations were ten times more likely to see a campaign ad than a campaign news story.

Broadcasters, says Paul Taylor, founder and executive director of Alliance for Better Campaigns, "are profiteering from democracy." Since 1998, his group, co-chaired by former

presidents Jimmy Carter and Gerald Ford and the former CBS News anchor, Walter Cronkite, has been calling for the networks and 1,600 TV stations to give at least five minutes of political news coverage a day during the last month before the 2000 election. So far, only two percent of the broadcasters have agreed.

The free air-time reform idea is not altogether dead. The FCC still seems to hold some interest, as do a few members of Congress, who have included proposals requiring broadcasters to provide free air time to political candidates in campaign-finance reform measures in the current congress. But industry lobbyists do not give an inch on any of them. In formal comments before the agency in March, the NAB said it "respectfully submits that there is no lack of political news and information available for persons who have any interest in obtaining such information. Thus, a voluntary or mandatory requirement for broadcasters to offer additional free time for political candidates is unnecessary." The Radio and Television News Directors Association (RTNDA) stated, "Proponents of mandatory air time for political candidates would prefer that the FCC ignore altogether the First Amendment rights of broadcasters. They would have the commission turn its back on political coverage decisions made by experienced, professional journalists."

Meanwhile, some newspaper editorials about the free-air-time proposal have been curiously consistent with the extent of their ownership of broadcasting properties. The *Los Angeles Times*, with no TV stations, wrote supportively of the initiative. The *Chicago Tribune*, owned by the Tribune Co., which recently purchased the *Los Angeles Times* and Times Mirror and also contributes to political candidates and parties and owns nineteen TV stations, saw the issue differently. It wrote in 1998, "It might be good if candidates didn't have to raise and spend so much money to finance broadcast ads. In that case, let Congress provide public

funds to subsidize campaigns. If the public stands to gain from improved candidate access to the airwaves, the public ought to bear the cost." In other words, let the citizens pay for the ads they increasingly must watch.

The dirty little secret is that from 1996 through 1998, the NAB and five media outlets—ABC, CBS, A.H. Belo, Meredith Corp., and Cox Enterprises —cumulatively spent nearly $11 million to defeat a dozen campaign finance bills mandating free air time for political candidates. One company lobbyist willing to talk to us was Jerry Hadenfeldt, who represents the Meredith Corporation, owner of a dozen TV stations and twenty magazines, and publisher of more than 300 books. "Free political ads are basically picking the pockets of a select group, namely television broadcasters," he says. "They [candidates] already get the lowest available rates, and that's the way we believe it should stay."

One of the free-air-time bills he opposed was introduced by Congresswoman Louise Slaughter, a New York Democrat. She apparently did not realize the extent of the industry maneuverings against her. Told that $11 million had been spent lobbying against her bill and others like it, she was taken aback. "Oh, good Lord," she said. "It seems excessive to me. I am absolutely astonished. They paid $11 million to kill it? Well, it sure worked, didn't it?"

Charles Lewis, a former producer for 60 Minutes, *is the executive director of the Center for Public Integrity in Washington. Bill Allison, Erin Gallavan, Shannon Rebholz, Helen Sanderson, and Derrick Wetherell of the Center contributed to this article. The Joyce Foundation and the Town Creek Foundation provided project support.*

The Center's complete investigative report on media lobbying can be found at www.publicintegrity.org.

How to rate the ratings

Children, Entertainment, and Marketing

Rhoda Rabkin

Most American parents want to restrict children's access to entertainment glamorizing violence, sex, drug use, or vulgar language. Ideally, purveyors of "mature" entertainment would voluntarily adhere to a code of advertising ethics. Self-regulation would obviate the need for burdensome government regulation. In practice, threats of legal restriction have always played an important role in persuading "morally hazardous" industries to observe codes of conduct and to avoid aggressive marketing to young people. Specifically, self-regulation on the part of makers of entertainment products (for example, movies and comic books) has allowed Americans to shield children and adolescents from "mature" content with minimal recourse to government censorship.

This tradition may, however, be about to change. In April 2001, Sen. Joseph Lieberman (D-Conn.) introduced the Media Marketing Accountability Act (MMAA)—a bill to prohibit the marketing of "adult-rated media," i.e., movies, music, and computer games containing violent or sexual material, to young people under the age of 17. The MMAA would empower the Federal Trade Commission to regulate the advertising of entertainment products to young people. The proposed legislation, if enacted, would inject a federal agency into decisions about the marketing of movies, music, and electronic games—and thereby potentially into decisions about what sorts of movies, music, and games are produced. Lieberman's hearings, well publicized at the time, provided a valuable forum for exposing entertainment-industry practices to public scrutiny. Even so, the expansion of the federal government's regulatory powers in the area of entertainment and culture is undesirable compared to the traditional, and still-workable, system of industry self-censorship. It is worth noting that the FTC itself, in its testimony before the House Commerce Subcommittee on Telecommunications in July 2001, did not seek regulatory authority over the marketing of entertainment products, and in fact argued, in view of the First Amendment protections enjoyed by these products, that industry self-regulation was the best approach.

Why Voluntary Ratings? Even in the 1930s, when America was a much more conservative country (at least in terms of popular culture) than it is today, public outrage over the emphasis on sex and crime in the movies led not to censorship by the federal government but to a system wherein Hollywood regulated itself. The movie moguls created their own Production Code Administration (PCA) in 1930, supervised first by William Hays and later, in 1934, with more seriousness, by Joseph Breen.

The so-called Hays Code presumed that movies were far more influential than books and that standards of cinematic morality consequently needed to be much stricter than those governing novels and other literature. The code forbade any mention at all of certain controversial topics, such as "illegal drug traffic," "sex perversion," "white slavery," and "miscegenation." The code did allow for the depiction of some crime and some immorality (such as adultery), but stipulated that no presentation should encourage sympathy for illegal or immoral acts.

The American film industry has a long history of self-censorship for the simple reason that offending audiences has never been in its self-interest. Business concern for the bottom line, not moral sensitivity, dictated the willingness of the film industry to regulate itself. For example, during the 1920s and 1930s, Hollywood seldom produced mass market movies with dignified portrayals of black Americans. Scenes of racial mixing on terms of social equality were avoided because they were known to offend white Southern audiences. By the 1940s, however, tentative efforts at more dignified portrayals could be seen, and soon the industry was censoring itself to avoid offending black Americans. The National Association for the Advancement of Colored People's threat of a boycott caused Walt Disney to withdraw *Son of the South* (1946), a partly animated musical based on the Uncle Remus stories. The NAACP found the film's depiction of happy slaves demeaning. For a long time, this feature was available only on a Japanese laserdisc, and even today one can obtain a video version only from Britain or Germany.

The Hays Code assumed that adults and children would and should share the same entertainment at the movie theater. But the code applied only to American-made films, and in the 1950s and '60s, Hollywood found itself losing box office share to "sophisticated" European imports. In 1968, the movie industry abandoned its code of conduct approach and replaced it with a system of age-based ratings devised by Jack Valenti, then (as now) president of the Motion Picture Association of America.

The history of the comic book industry also illustrates the effectiveness of industry self-regulation in shielding the young from "mature" content. Public concern about crime and horror comics in the 1950s led to congressional hearings sponsored by Sen. Estes Kefauver (D-Tenn.) The hearings did not come close to proving that lurid comics caused juvenile delinquency, but in the face of negative publicity, an embarrassed comic book industry opted for self-regulation. The system was voluntary, but the fact that most retailers chose not to display or sell comics without the industry seal of approval meant that objectionable comics soon languished, unable to reach their intended market.

Television greatly reduced the popularity of comic books among children, but the comic book medium did not die. Instead, a new reading audience for "adult" comics came into being.

Television greatly reduced the popularity of comic books among children, but the comic book medium did not die. Instead, a new reading audience for "adult" comics came into being. In the 1970s and '80s, as graphic violence became more acceptable in movies and on television, the industry rewrote its code to be more permissive. In September 2001, the largest comic book company, Marvel, released several new lines (Fury, Alias, and U.S. War Machine) completely without code approval. The new titles, which allowed for profanity, sexual situations, and violence, were big sellers. But they are not sold at newsstands, airports, or convenience stores; they are distributed through specialized comic book stores which tend to be patronized by older purchasers (average age: 25).

An age-based classification system has also been employed since 1994 by the video and computer games industry, which has an Entertainment Software Rating Board. The board classifies products as EC (everyone including young children), E (everyone), T (teen), M (mature—may not be suitable for persons under 17), and AO (adults only).

The Oppositional Music Industry. Of all branches of entertainment, the music recording industry has been least responsive to parental concerns and most resistant to self-regulation. The best explanation is that "oppositional" teenage music, although far from the whole of youth-oriented recordings, accounts for a significant proportion of sales. Many music performers who cater to the adolescent audience view themselves as anti-establishment rebels, and this self-image is inseparable from their marketing strategies. Irreverence and defiance seem grown-up and sophisticated to many teenagers.

What comic books were to young people in the 1930s and '40s, popular music is to today's generation of adolescents. Many adults focus on television as a baleful influence on the younger generation, but this is just a sign of how out of touch with teenagers they are. Survey evidence indicates that, in terms of both hours logged and overall meaningfulness, music listening has an importance in the lives of many adolescents far beyond what most parents understand. Parents can easily monitor what their children watch on television, but most adults find it impossible to listen to teenage "noise" on the radio or CD, let alone distinguish among the many varieties, such as album rock, alternative, grunge, world beat, progressive rock, salsa, house, technopop, etc. Yet involvement in a particular sub-genre of music is often an important aspect of adolescent social identity. Conversance with popular culture seems to enhance a teenager's social contacts and status, and contrariwise, the young person who remains aloof from pop music is likely to be excluded from many teen peer groups.

One should not assume that music with lyrics featuring profanity, violence, casual sex, drug use, and so on is itself the cause of negative behaviors. Adolescence is a time of life when young people must adjust to startling discoveries about sex, violence, and other potentially troubling aspects of the real world. Just as many adults enjoy watching movies about gangsters, with no inclination toward becoming gangsters themselves, many teenagers find in their music a safe way to satisfy curiosity about the darker aspects of life. The key to understanding this segment of the entertainment industry is that "mature" content actually signifies the opposite, a puerile interest in everything so taboo that parents will not discuss it with their children. The good news is that the teenager who does not die first (or become pregnant or addicted to drugs) almost always grows out of it. On the other hand, undoubtedly some troubled teenagers focus on music with morbid, aggressive, profane, or vulgar lyrics because it seems to legitimize their impulses—in which case the music may indeed reinforce their predispositions. Many different forms of music are popular with teenagers, so preoccupation with "oppositional" music should draw parental attention—which does not mean that underlying problems are addressed by simply prohibiting a form of music.

Movies were controversial from their inception. Comic books were born innocent, but aroused parental concern when they began to exploit themes of violence and sex. Scantily clad women and heads dripping blood came as a shock to adults who had thought comics were about funny talking animals. Similarly, coarse, violent, misogynistic lyrics (to say nothing of offensive references to race, religion, and sexual orientation) prevalent in some youth-oriented music came as a shock to many parents raised on the "outrageous" music of their day, 1950s rock and roll.

Back in 1985, when Tipper Gore, together with several other Washington wives of politicians, founded the Parents Music Resource Center (PMRC), their new organization successfully drew public attention to the problematic content of rock lyrics, particularly those of heavy metal groups with names like Twisted Sister, Black Sabbath, Judas Priest, etc. In the view of the PMRC, it was a straightforward issue of consumers' rights that parents know about references to sex, drugs, alcohol, suicide, violence, and the occult in their children's music. The PMRC proposed that music companies affix warning labels to their products to alert parents about questionable content (for example, V for violence, X for sexually explicit lyrics, O for occult).

Defenders of the music industry predictably accused the PMRC of advocating censorship. The charge was unfair, but the music industry was right that there were real problems with the PMRC approach, which viewed any reference to a topic, regardless of how the topic was treated, as cause for a warning label. Thus, an anti-drug song would call for a warning sticker the same as a song that promoted drug use. This was one of the problems with the Hays Code and the comics code as well. For years, movie executives shied away from *The Man with the Golden Arm,* until Otto Preminger made this powerful anti-drug drama and successfully released it without PCA approval. In 1970, after receiving a letter from the Department of Health, Education, and Welfare, Marvel Comics incorporated an anti-drug story into its popular Spider-Man series, but had to release the titles without code office approval.

Another difficulty that arises with attempts at age-classification of music lyrics is the problem of double meanings, which have a long tradition in songwriting. John Denver testified to good effect at the 1985 hearings that his song "Rocky Mountain High" about the beauty of nature had been unfairly banned by some radio stations out of misplaced zeal against drug references. But those responsible for age-ratings will have to face such issues as what Marilyn Manson means when he sings about someone who "powders his nose." Most parents will not have a problem with children hearing Bessie Smith sing: "Nobody in town can bake a sweet jelly-roll like mine"—but of course she meant something by that, too. The enterprise of routing out double-entendres can quickly turn ridiculous, seeming to prove the truth of Lenny Bruce's observation: "There are no dirty words; there are just dirty minds."

In response to the 1985 Commerce Committee hearings, and because of a wave of local prosecutions (utilizing charges of obscenity) against retailers, in 1990, the Recording Industry Association of America (RIAA) announced that it had designed a "Parental Advisory/Explicit Lyrics" label, with a distinctive logo. But whereas the movie industry's trade association, the MPAA, rates individual movies, the RIAA created no guidelines or recommendations and left the use of the labels to the discretion of the individual recording companies. "This consistent reference to parents is offensive. We are all parents," said RIAA president Hilary Rosen. "I don't want to tell parents whether Chuck Berry is singing about his ding-a-ling."

The PMRC was disturbed by the lyrics of heavy metal rock groups, but many parents soon would be concerned by the violence and sexual vulgarity in a new form of teenage music: hip-hop, or as it is sometimes (though not accurately) called, rap music. And with this new form of music, the question of morality in music became entwined in questions about racism and double standards.

Sen. Lieberman did not invite Russell Simmons, a longtime hip-hop entrepreneur and chairman of the Hip-Hop Summit Action Network, to testify at his hearings. But Simmons attended anyway and managed to speak. Simmons complained that Lieberman had unfairly targeted hip-hop as objectionable. In the *New York Times,* he wrote: "hip-hop is an important art form, really the first new genre of music to emerge since rock and roll. … To deny its power and artistic merit in an attempt to silence it is downright dangerous." Criticism of violent, profane, and vulgar music lyrics, Simmons implied, betrays unconscious racism because black performers are the main creators of "gangsta rap" and hip-hop.

Many parents upset by hip-hop would not be similarly disturbed by traditional songs, such as "Whiskey in the Jar," which celebrates drinking or "Tom Dooley," about a murder.

Simmons was wrong to equate Lieberman's proposed legislation with censorship but still had a point worth considering: Many parents upset by hip-hop would not be similarly disturbed by traditional songs, such as "Whiskey in the Jar," an Irish song that celebrates drinking or "Tom Dooley," a Civil War-era song (which became a popular hit for the Kingston Trio in the early 1960s) that recounts a murder. Of course, some parents would be equally disturbed by these songs (just as some are offended by the "occult" in a children's classic such as *The Wizard of Oz*). Many parents believe that evil has enormous inherent attractiveness, so that any depiction of wicked conduct is morally dangerous. But should the law require the makers of all such recordings and videos to affix a warning sticker and submit their advertising plans to federal supervision?

There is some basis for optimism that the value of voluntary labeling has become apparent even to the music industry. A hip-hop summit held in July 2001 brought recording company executives together with established black organizations, such as the NAACP. The three-day conference (at which Minister Louis Farrakhan spoke and urged the musicians to display more "responsibility") led to considerable reflection within the hip-hop community. Industry representatives at the summit agreed on a uniform standard for the "Parental Advisory" label, which should be one size, plainly displayed, and not removable, on the cover art of the recordings and visible on all advertising as well. The RIAA continues to insist, however (as noted critically in the FTC's December 2001 report), on its right to market labeled music aggressively to young people.

The Tobacco Model. As it turns out, the music industry was right to argue that any concession to parental interest in labeling would stimulate additional demands for regulation of entertainment. One of the most well-respected citizen groups concerned with media, the National Institute on Media and the Family (NIMF), has paid considerable attention to media ratings and is dissatisfied with the current system. The NIMF, along with other children's health advocates, has argued for an independent ratings oversight committee and a unified media ratings system to cover movies, television programs, music, and games.

Some politicians and children's "advocates" seem entranced by the prospect of identifying the entertainment industry in the public mind as the successor to Big Tobacco as a threat to the health of young people. In the late 1990s, Sen. Sam Brownback (R-Kan.) helped persuade the American Medical Association to assert a causal connection between violent entertainment and individual acts of aggressiveness and violence. In fact, an impressive list of highly respectable organizations, such as the National Institute of Mental Health, the National Academy of Sciences, the American Psychological Association, and the American Academy of Pediatrics, are on record agreeing that exposure to media violence presents a risk of harmful effects on children. These claims in turn help support litigation that seeks tort damages from the producers of violent entertainment. For example, families of victims of the Paducah, Ky. school shooting filed lawsuits against entertainment companies on the grounds that their products created a mindset that led to murder. Thus far, lawsuits of this nature have been dismissed in court, but then, so were tobacco suits—until they weren't.

Many essentially moral concerns tend to be packaged and presented in terms of concern for danger to "children's health." And there is no shortage of experts whose research alleges that violence (and sometimes sex) in entertainment presents proven health hazards analogous to cigarette smoking. According to Harvard researcher, Dr. Michael Rich: "The findings of hundreds of studies, analyzed as a whole, showed that the strength of the relationship between television exposure and aggressive behavior is greater than that of calcium intake and bone mass, lead ingestion and lower IQ, condom nonuse and sexually acquired HIV, or environmental tobacco smoke and lung cancer, all associations that clinicians accept and on which preventive medicine is based." Of course, some experts have come to the opposite conclusion about the effects of media on behavior. The September 2000 FTC report acknowledged that there are abundant studies on both sides of the issue.

It is possible that, even if passed, the Media Marketing Accountability Act would be found unconstitutional in the first federal court to hear a challenge to it. In one recent case, *Lorillard v. Reilly* (2001), which involved efforts by Massachusetts to restrict the advertising of tobacco products, the Supreme Court stated that retailers and manufacturers have a strong First Amendment interest in "conveying truthful information about their products to adults." Supreme Court decisions in recent years have tended to expand protection for commercial speech, even when the advertising in question is for products recognized as presenting moral hazards.

"Marketing to children" is not a clear, unambiguous concept. Many adults watch children's programming, such as "The Wonderful World of Disney," and more than two-thirds of the audience for MTV consists of viewers aged 18 or older. The FTC objected to the industry practice of showing movie trailers for R-rated movies before G- and PG-rated movies. But as Valenti testified, "the R rating does not mean 'Adult-Rated'—that is the province of the NC-17 rating. Children are admitted to R-rated movies if accompanied by a parent or adult guardian. The rating system believes that only parents can make final decisions about what they want their children to see or not to see." A Pennsylvania statute banning the practice of showing previews for R-rated features at G- and PG-rated movies was ruled unconstitutional by a federal court. Some industry executives responded to complaints about movie trailers for R-rated movies by asking where the regulation of advertising would stop: Should R-rated movies be removed from newspaper ads? But Jack Valenti eventually responded to congressional criticism by promulgating new MPAA guidelines, including: "Each company will request theater owners not to show trailers advertising films rated R for violence in connection with the exhibition of its G-rated films. In addition, each company will not attach trailers for films rated R for violence on G-rated movies on videocassettes or DVDs containing G-rated movies." This suggests that parent groups have enough clout to persuade the entertainment industry that it should voluntarily refrain from advertising R-rated movies in certain venues.

Valenti, representing the movie industry at the Senate hearings on the Media Marketing Accountability Act, argued convincingly that the proposed legislation would likely jeopardize the voluntary ratings system on which the FTC regulatory regime is supposed to be based. As Valenti noted, "the bill immunizes those producers who do not rate their films." "Why," he asked, "would sane producers continue to submit their films for voluntary ratings when they could be subjected to fines of $11,000 per day per violation?" A good question. What seems likely is that Lieberman's approach requires the creation of a different, compulsory ratings system staffed not by unaccountable, anonymous industry insiders but by "members of the entertainment industry, child development and public health professionals, social scientists and parents," as one witness recommended.

If children's "health" is the primary concern, there is no reason to expect such an independent board to stop with rating entertainment for violent content when there are so many other "threats" to the health of young people and so many pressure groups concerned with such health. What would certainly follow would be calls for adding a ratings category to restrict the depiction of tobacco and alcohol products. There would also be pressure to address other social problems as well, such as eating disorders among teenage girls allegedly promoted by un-realistically slender actresses. Health-oriented raters might consider "safe sex" scenes with condoms more youth-appropriate than sexual depictions without them. Racial, religious, and sexual stereotyping also present a threat to the health of children, to be dealt with accordingly.

In Britain and Canada, where age rating has legal force, all kinds of issues, such as cruelty to animals, racial slurs, and even "presentation of controversial lifestyles" can be grounds for restriction. At least in those countries, local authorities have the final say, an important check on the system lacking in Lieberman's plan to give the FTC regulatory authority.

The Bull in the (Video) Shop. Representatives of the entertainment industry have deployed two serious arguments against the MMAA: first, that violence in entertainment does not cause young people to behave violently; and second, that the proposed legislation excessively empowers government to control speech and art through control over the marketing of entertainment.

Entertainment executives are right that media messages have a complex, indirect relationship to behavior. Consequently, our society wisely vests control over the entertainment choices of young people in their parents using common sense, not in a clumsy, heavy-handed government bureaucracy relying on the latest, and soon to be controverted, social science research. A sense of proportion is needed if we are to reinforce parental authority without attempting to supplant it. Self-regulation is a system in which all citizens assume civic responsibility. The MMAA, by contrast, assumes that young people are helpless victims of the advertising and media to which they are exposed. Much of the rhetoric supporting the legislation is uncomfortably reminiscent of the campaigns directed at tobacco products,

junk foods, and guns. One collateral result is likely to be encouragement for lawyers to sue entertainment companies.

What cannot be achieved by the heavy hand of the law can be achieved by industry self-regulation—but this requires the cooperation of the regulated. Lieberman's bill does not seem well thought out. It would punish companies that rate their material, but no law can compel the companies to rate their material satisfactorily in the first place. What is involved here obviously calls for much more complex judgments than, for example, listing the alcohol content of a beverage or the nicotine content of a cigarette. If the music or movie industry resists rating because it leads to punitive fines, the next step would have to be rating by quasi-official "independent" boards whose judgments would then be utilized by FTC regulators. Self-censorship would give way to federal regulation. Congress will have performed its usual sorry trick—enact a vague regulatory regime and then settle back as lobbying interest groups funnel money to Washington politicians in hope of gaining favorable treatment.

The MMAA empowers the FTC only to regulate advertising to young people, so the legislation would not truly establish a system of federal censorship over entertainment. But it would bring us much closer to such a system than we have ever come in our history. Averting this outcome is in everyone's interest, but the entertainment industries themselves have the greatest responsibility to do so—through voluntary observance of codes of conduct acceptable to American parents.

Ms. Rabkin is an adjunct scholar at the American Enterprise Institute for Public Policy Research. This article is excerpted from Policy Review, *February & March 2002.*

The Information Squeeze

Openness in government is under assault throughout the United States—at every level. Can the news media, reluctant combatants thus far, mount a successful counterattack?

By Charles Layton

RONALD REAGAN MOVED INTO THE WHITE HOUSE IN 1981. The American hostages came home from Iran that year. And IBM introduced its first personal computer, with a $6,000 price tag and an operating system by a company most people had never heard of: Microsoft.

In 1981, reporter Seth Rosenfeld requested FBI documents under the Freedom of Information Act. He finally got them—starting in 1996. His article on questionable FBI tactics in dealing with liberals and radicals at the University of California at Berkeley at last appeared in the San Francisco Chronicle in June.

That was also the year Seth Rosenfeld mailed off a request to the FBI for records under the Freedom of Information Act. Rosenfeld was a journalism major at the University of California at Berkeley and a writer for the campus paper, the Daily Californian. He wanted to find out about the FBI's history of political skulduggery at Berkeley and hoped the records he requested would shed new light on it.

"So," Rosenfeld remembers, "I thought, I'll just submit this FOIA request and I'll get these records and I'll write a story. And I'll be done in a year or so."

It took a good deal longer—more than 17 years—during which time the FBI did everything possible to keep the records secret: stalling, evading, appealing court rulings. Only after orders from five different federal judges did the FBI begin to surrender information in earnest.

Once it did, Rosenfeld was amazed at how much stuff the agency had been hiding. From 1996 through 1998, dozens of boxes arrived at the offices of his pro bono attorney. "We had to get a pickup truck," says the reporter.

The documents—more than 200,000 pages—occupied two rooms of his six-room flat. It took him several years to sort through them all, do the follow-up reporting and write his story, which explained how the FBI had conspired, sometimes unlawfully, with then-Gov. Reagan to discredit campus liberals and radicals.

The story ran in the San Francisco Chronicle, where Rosenfeld now works, on June 9 of this year.

AS ROSENFELD DISCOVERED, GOVERNMENT OFFICIALS ARE loath to part with their secrets. But lately, the problem has grown worse. Openness in government is under broad attack throughout the United States—at every level. Using the threat of terrorism as a rationale, the Bush administration has been moving fast to erect new barriers. But state governments also play the terrorism card.

In New Jersey, Gov. James McGreevey tried to seal more than 500 categories of public records this summer by executive order. Under press and public pressure, McGreevey eventually reopened most of them. He had based his actions on national security, although many of the records had nothing to do with security.

A greater threat, in the long run, comes from well-intentioned advocates of personal privacy who fear that, in the computer age, more public access means less security for individuals. The privacy movement has been under way for more than a decade, gathering public support and scoring some notable legislative successes. Driver's license information—a fundamental public record if ever there was one—has been restricted in many states. And basic medical news—such as the condition of a hospitalized crime or accident victim—may soon become unattainable.

The personal privacy issue makes the case for open government much trickier now than ever before. In an age when the most intimate, embarrassing details of a couple's divorce may end up on the Internet, for all their neighbors to read, the standard arguments for openness grow less persuasive. Ken Paulson of the Freedom Forum's First Amendment Center writes that the public is "willing to handcuff the news media if that's the price to be paid for shoring up personal privacy."

Last February, fresh from a discouraging legal fight over autopsy records in Florida, the editor of the Orlando Sentinel, Tim Franklin, told an Investigative Reporters and Editors workshop: "We are confronted with a broad move toward secrecy and restricted public access that could reshape how Americans do business and monitor their government for decades."

Faced with such a challenge, most of the journalism community has not risen to the occasion. It has not marshaled the money, time, legal commitment or sense of conviction necessary to fight back.

Writing in the IRE Journal this spring, Charles Davis, executive director of the Freedom of Information Center at the Missouri School of Journalism, describes "the docile reaction from reporters and newspaper editorial boards, who seem reluctant to enter the fray."

The head of the American Society of Newspaper Editors' freedom of information committee says that when it comes to challenging government secrecy, he finds "a lack of real passion all across editorland." Douglas C. Clifton, editor of Cleveland's Plain Dealer, says many newsrooms place so little emphasis on freedom of information "that reporters accept as a given that they are going to be shut out of open records."

"Reporters are more than willing to go to court," Harry Hammitt, the editor of Access Reports, a Virginia-based government watchdog publication, has observed, "but editors and publishers have decided they don't really want to spend the money."

THE LOCKDOWN ON PUBLIC INFORMATION HARDLY BEGAN with George W. Bush. Seth Rosenfeld can attest to that. So can Max Jennings, former editor of the Dayton Daily News, which in the mid-1990s published an award-winning series on military courts-martial. The paper's struggle to get information under FOIA was so frustrat-ing and time-consuming that it led Jennings to declare, in a 1996 interview with Quill, "The FOIA simply doesn't work most of the time for journalists. There are few news organizations and reporters who have the patience, money and determination to work through what seems an inevitable series of appeals, requests and other road-blocks."

But Jennings was describing the good old days, under President Clinton's relatively information-friendly attorney general, Janet Reno. In October of last year, Reno's successor, John Ashcroft, issued a memorandum to all federal agencies announcing a stricter policy. Henceforth, he wrote, agencies could refuse FOIA requests whenever they could find any legal basis for doing so. He promised that the Justice Department would stand behind them.

At an IRE conference in San Francisco in June, Seth Rosenfeld said he had seen "a real big change in the government's response" since the Ashcroft memo. Rosenfeld is still waiting for the FBI to release records. But now, he said, "They don't return calls. They don't answer letters. We have new requests that are pending, which are just languishing. And records that were supposed to be released have just become even slower."

I have a source who has witnessed blatant defiance of FOIA within the Department of the Interior, the Environmental Protection Agency, the Department of Labor and other agencies. "There was a dramatic, clearly visible change throughout these agencies after Bush came in," the source says. "Sometimes the Clinton people would be reluctant but they would go ahead and obey the law. These guys have meetings and try to figure ways to have FOIA requests delayed...."

Watergate figure John Dean has called the Bush administration "startlingly Nixonian" in its passion for secrecy. Says National Journal's William Powers, "This administration keeps secrets like nobody in Washington has kept secrets for a long time—maybe ever."

"Normally, before Bush, we just played it by the book. But I'm saying within weeks of the Bush administration coming into power, we noticed that when FOIA requests were made, they were deliberately delayed."

One case dealt with a technical report sought by journalists and labor union officials, which my source described as "a critical report that would have helped the public be more aware of hazards to their health and safety." The government delayed releasing the report and related documents for many months. "I knew that the FOIA request had been made, and I knew the data was there. The attorney [for the agency] told me the agency was violating every FOIA law known to man by not releasing these documents, by deliberately stalling, by even hiding some things."

The documents finally were released, but only after the information had been leaked through other channels and published. Had it not been for that, my source believes, the government might never have complied with the FOIA request, because the information was damaging to business interests friendly to the administration.

WATERGATE FIGURE JOHN DEAN HAS CALLED THE BUSH administration "startlingly Nixonian" in its passion for secrecy. William Powers of National Journal writes: "This administration keeps secrets like nobody in Washington has kept secrets for a long time—maybe ever." Journalist Bill Moyers said recently: "Not only has George W. Bush eviscerated the Presidential Records Act and FOIA, he has clamped a lid on public access across the board."

The White House failed to respond to repeated requests for comment for this article.

Some of the administration's most widely reported actions are the Ashcroft memo on freedom of information, the secret imprisonment of more than 1,200 foreigners on American soil, the closing of once-public deportation hearings, the proposal for secret prosecutions by military tribunals, Vice President Dick Cheney's refusal to release the names of those who advised his energy task force, and efforts by the Pentagon to shield the conflict in Afghanistan from the eyes of reporters.

Less widely reported is the administration's effort to exempt its proposed new Department of Homeland Security from both whistleblower protection and, in part, from the FOIA.

When I asked Paul McMasters, the Freedom Forum's First Amendment ombudsman, for his assessment of the proposed FOIA exemption, he said it "would blow a gaping hole in the Freedom of Information Act. It is very troubling."

(FOIA establishes every citizen's right to federal records. It declares all such records public except for specific exemptions, and it allows anyone to sue if the government fails to produce requested records in a timely manner.)

In what was, perhaps, the administration's boldest move, Bush on November 1 issued an executive order declaring that presidents are not required to follow the Presidential Records Act.

This act was passed in 1978 in reaction to the Watergate scandals and to President Nixon's failed attempt, after resigning, to take possession of the records of his presidency. The law requires the unsealing of papers of a former president 12 years after he leaves office. This gives the ex-president exclusive access for a long enough time to write his memoirs. After that, the papers revert to the public and to posterity.

Bush countermanded that requirement late last year, just as records of the Reagan administration—in which Bush's father and many top members of his present administration served—were about to enter the public domain. Because of Bush's executive order, more than 68,000 documents remain sealed.

There has been remarkably little complaint about this maneuver in the media.

BAD AS THINGS ARE IN WASHINGTON, THEY MAY BE WORSE at the state and local levels, where the problem gets less attention.

During the 1970s and 1980s, using the federal FOIA as a model, all 50 states either passed new laws or strengthened their old laws on open records and open meetings. These "sunshine laws" have been invaluable in keeping government honest. However, almost as soon as a sunshine law is enacted, its enemies set out to weaken it.

In 1998, a legislative task force in California reported that the state's Public Records Act had been "interpreted, reinterpreted and fiddled with to the point that it has become of little appreciable value to the public." In an analysis published last spring, the California First Amendment Coalition agreed with that assessment. It cited rulings by state courts allowing police to keep certain records secret even after investigations are closed; allowing city council members to withhold phone records that might reveal who was influencing their official actions; and allowing officials to hide documents showing how they reached decisions.

After the sheriff of Edwards County, Illinois, balked at releasing a document in 1999, a reporter took out a copy of the state's open records law and showed it to him. The sheriff wadded it up, threw it away and said, "I don't have to tell you nothing."

Even when the laws are clear, officials tend not to honor them. In Indiana, says Larry Lough, editor of Muncie's Star Press, "There's no criminal penalty for not giving a record, but if you give a record that you're not supposed to, it's a misdemeanor for which you can be charged. So the safest thing to do in Indiana is, don't give it to them."

Another problem, Lough and others say, is that most public officials don't receive enough training on how to handle requests for public information. Many are totally ignorant of their states' sunshine laws.

Here are some examples of how local officials have responded to requests for supposedly open records:

- Last year, when Jay Young of Pennsylvania's Altoona Mirror asked a clerk in Cresson Township for a public record, the clerk called the police. According to Young, the police chief told him he'd have to make his request in writing. After he wrote out the request, Young says, "the police chief said it might as well be ripped up, since there was no good reason for the request."
- In East Cocalico Township, Pennsylvania, Linda Weiner Seligson of the York Daily Record was ushered into a windowless room in 1998 and questioned by the police chief after she requested the log of police calls, a document supposedly available to anyone. "When I told him I thought I was allowed by law to see these records," Seligson says, "he replied: 'You are not.'"
- After the sheriff of Edwards County, Illinois, balked at releasing a document in 1999, a reporter took out a copy of the state's open records law and showed it to him. The sheriff wadded it up, threw it away and said, "I don't have to tell you nothing."
- Two years ago, when John McCormick of the Des Moines Register asked to see gun permit records in Knoxville, Iowa, a sheriff's deputy told him, "None of the sheriff's department records are public." When reporter Thomas O'Donnell made the same request in Decatur County, the sheriff there threatened to arrest him if he did not leave the courthouse. The sheriff also asked to see O'Donnell's driver's license, and the information on the license was included in an advisory to other sheriffs warning that O'Donnell was asking to see public records.

These are not rare, hard-to-find cases. In the last five years, hundreds of cases of open defiance have been documented by reporters conducting organized tests of their states' sunshine laws. These tests, sometimes called "freedom of information audits," are the most objective evidence we have of how often officials ignore state open records laws. During the audits, reporters for a consortium of newspapers fan out across a chosen area, usually an entire state, asking for records that the law says are open to any citizen—the minutes of a council meeting, the arrest records at a local jail, perhaps the employment contract of the school superintendent. The participating newspapers then tabulate their findings and write stories.

I have read summaries of 32 of these audits in 25 states, and almost without exception they document massive violations of the law. A California audit reported that officials turned down legitimate requests for information 77 percent of the time. A Connecticut audit found only a 22 percent rate of compliance. In Massachusetts the compliance rate was 25 percent. An audit of 200 state offices in Missouri reported that "44 percent of

the offices violated the Sunshine Law, either by not responding to requests in a timely fashion, denying requests or ignoring requests altogether." (A list of these audits can be found at the Freedom of Information Center's Web site: foi.missouri.edu.)

In a story describing an FOI audit in Illinois, Christopher Wills, an Associated Press reporter in Springfield, wrote this summation: "Ask for public documents in Illinois and you may get hostile questions, bureaucratic delays, even threats from a sheriff or two. What you won't get, in many cases, is the information you wanted."

In 1989 A YOUNG MAN NAMED ROBERT JOHN BARDO DEALT a serious blow to the cause of open government—although that isn't what he set out to do. What he set out to do was murder an actress named Rebecca Schaeffer.

Bardo, 19, a fast-food worker from Tucson, developed a fixation on Schaeffer, 21, who had appeared in the television sitcom "My Sister Sam" and was embarking on a movie career. According to press reports, Bardo built a shrine composed of Schaeffer's media photos and videotapes. When he saw the actress in a bedroom scene in a movie, he reportedly decided she had to be punished.

Bardo hired a detective to find out where Schaeffer lived. It wasn't hard to find out; the detective went straight to the California Department of Motor Vehicles and looked up her driver's license, which was a public record.

One July morning Bardo went to Schaeffer's West Hollywood apartment and pressed the buzzer. When she came to the door, he shot her in the chest.

Schaeffer's murder marked a turning point in the freedom-of-information debate. By encouraging a popular movement against open records, this crime was to have serious consequences for journalists—and the public's right to know—throughout the country.

It prompted the California Legislature to pass the country's first anti-stalking law, but more to the point it helped influence Congress to pass the Driver's Privacy Protection Act in 1994. The law prohibited states from disclosing a driver's name, address, photograph, Social Security number or telephone number without the driver's consent. (See "License Revoked," November 1995.)

Civil libertarians applauded the legislation. So did women's organizations, which were concerned about the stalking, assault and even murder of women by ex-husbands, ex-boyfriends and others, who often tracked down their victims through driver's license records. Sen. Barbara Boxer, D-Calif., a sponsor of the bill, argued that women "who move to escape an abusive relationship shouldn't have to choose between registering a car and maintaining their safety." The law was also seen as protection for reproductive health care providers and their patients. These people were sometimes harassed by antiabortion extremists who used license plate numbers to find out where they lived.

The state of South Carolina sued the feds over the new law, because South Carolina had been selling its database of driver's license information to mass marketers and didn't want to lose the revenue from those sales. In fact, many states were earning millions each year by selling this information to commercial databases.

By the time South Carolina's case reached the U.S. Supreme Court in 1999, there was a burgeoning public concern about stalking, identity theft, intrusive telephone solicitations from marketers and a host of other infringements on the peace and privacy of ordinary citizens.

The selling of private information—not just by governments but also banks, insurance companies, mortgage lenders and even medical facilities—was by then routine. Information from product warranty cards, credit cards, Web sites and other sources was assembled into lists of computerized dossiers, to be sold to marketers for target advertising, to government for law enforcement purposes or to private detectives.

No aspect of a person's life was off-limits. The assembled lists included people's addresses, phone numbers, Social Security numbers, credit card activity, shopping preferences, arrest records, credit history, income, race, ethnic background, hobbies, reading habits, Internet browsing habits, religion, political affiliation, drinking and smoking habits, gambling activities, charitable giving, clothing size, product ownership, pet ownership and health information.

The digital profiling industry had $10 billion in revenue in 1999, by one estimate, and was growing rapidly. One of the commercial profiling companies, Experian, claimed to have profiles on 98 percent of American households.

Predictably, stories of abuses began to appear. A man lost his job after his Social Security number was confused with that of a convicted felon. A woman had trouble getting health insurance because an information clearinghouse said, erroneously, that she had heart problems and Alzheimer's disease.

One profiling company was using prisoners to input personal information from surveys. This resulted in a stalking case in which a prisoner—a convicted rapist and burglar—harassed an Ohio woman based on the information she had submitted on a survey. The woman received threatening mail from the man, who knew everything about her, from the magazines she read to her preferred brand of bath soap.

A case in Florida, which came to light this summer, shows the kind of games marketers can play with people's medical and psychiatric records. A group of people with histories of mental depression received unsolicited free samples of Prozac in the mail along with this friendly message: "Congratulations on being one step to full recovery."

In response to such abuses, an army of privacy advocates appeared on the political battlefield. The more the public became aware of the problem, the stronger this privacy movement became. And it was in this climate that the Driver's Privacy Protection Act reached the Supreme Court.

The court surprised some observers by going against its recent strong tendency to favor states' rights, and in January of 2000 it ruled to uphold the DPPA. The vote of the justices was unanimous. The ruling required states to crack down on the dissemination of motor vehicle records.

AND JOURNALISTS—NOT TO MENTION THEIR READERS, viewers and listeners—are feeling the impact. Edward Seaton, editor in chief of the Manhattan Mercury, describes the difference this ruling has made in his state of Kansas. "Now," Seaton says, journalists "can't tell you if the school bus drivers in our region have any kind of driving record—DUIs, reckless driving. We can't do a story like that anymore."

Anders Gyllenhaal, editor of Minneapolis' Star Tribune, recently headed a study for ASNE on freedom of information. He sees the loss of driving records as a terrible precedent. "When we lose access to that, we lose a great deal," he says. "If driver's licenses are not public records, what about voter registration, births, deaths, all those fundamental databases?"

Voter registration lists are already a target. In Florida, as a privacy protection, the Legislature has already closed the state's voter lists to public scrutiny.

"I don't think you should discount the seriousness" of the driver's records precedent, says Rebecca Daugherty, director of the Reporters Committee for Freedom of the Press' Freedom of Information Service Center. "You're beginning to see the federal government, both Congress and the executive branch, come up with the idea that they can now require states to keep information confidential under some kind of a federal ruling."

A new health insurance law is having an even more damaging effect on health care information than the DPPA had on driver's license records. The main purpose of the federal Health Insurance Portability and Accountability Act, passed in 1996, was to give people easier access to health insurance. But it also included tough new privacy provisions, with guidelines to be established by the Department of Health and Human Services. In 1997, HHS Secretary Donna Shalala went before the National Press Club in Washington to explain why the government wanted to restrict the release of medical information.

"Until recently," Shalala said, "at a Boston-based HMO, every single clinical employee could tap into patients' computer records and see detailed notes from psychotherapy sessions. In Colorado, a medical student copies countless health records at night and sells them to medical malpractice attorneys looking to win easy cases. And, in a major American city, a local newspaper publishes information about a congressional candidate's attempted suicide—information she thought was safe and private at a local hospital."

Shalala made a compelling case.

After several years of preparation, the new rules are scheduled to take effect on April 14, 2003. But already, in anticipation, hospitals and other health care facilities have begun to comply.

"We have a running battle with our hospital here," Seaton says. "We can't get anything out of them." The Manhattan Mercury used to run a column listing the patients in the local hospital, but now, he says, the hospital won't cooperate. "They won't put out condition reports. They won't tell you whether someone's a patient. We historically ran all the births. We can't get the births from them anymore."

Several First Amendment organizations have asked HHS to revise its rules so the public and the press can get this kind of information. The rules, as now written, "effectively censor news reports on everything from basic hospital information about patients who are victims of violent crime, traffic accidents or natural disasters to investigative reporting concerning health-care fraud, patient abuse or environmental hazards," the Allied Daily Newspapers of Washington Inc., wrote in a commentary filed with HHS.

According to Charles Davis, writing in the July/August IRE Journal, the rules would also deny access to the kind of medical records that "tell us about poorly managed health care systems, the abuse of elderly in nursing homes, unethical research projects and abuse of children in foster care."

The rules apply not just to doctors, nurses and hospital employees but to any health care provider, even an ambulance driver. The law allows for massive penalties against anyone disclosing unauthorized information—civil fines of $100 per incident up to $25,000 a year and criminal penalties as high as $250,000 or 10 years imprisonment. Facing the threat of such punishment, Daugherty says, hospitals and their employees will surely play it safe and err on the side of secrecy.

The rules could provide stiff penalties for whistleblowers who tip off journalists to health care abuses. It isn't difficult to think of important stories that have been based on such insider tips. Daugherty cites a few, including the Orange County Register's revelations of fraud by University of California fertility doctors, which won a 1996 Pulitzer Prize, and the Seattle Times' recent series on the conflicts of interest of health care providers involved in experimental treatment programs.

"Those kinds of stories simply couldn't be done under these rules," she says. "And no one seems to care."

HHS has turned a deaf ear to the complaints of Daugherty's organization and others.

SURVEYS REPEATEDLY SHOW THAT MOST PEOPLE OBJECT strongly to the privacy abuses that became common in the 1990s. Politicians, lobbyists and law enforcement officers, seizing on this public mood, have made privacy a catchall excuse for keeping almost anything secret. When a reporter in Fond du Lac County, Wisconsin, asked for an arrest record, a deputy sheriff said, "If you were arrested, you wouldn't want your name released, would you?"

The Reporters Committee for Freedom of the Press has cited the case of an online news service in Texas that was denied information about a sheriff who pleaded guilty to drug charges. Federal agents seized the sheriff's horse trailer, which contained 2,500 pounds of cocaine, but the government contended that releasing information about the case would violate the sheriff's privacy.

And after September 11, as the federal government rounded up more than 1,200 people and held them in secret detention, Attorney General Ashcroft explained that their names could not be released because to do so "would be a violation of the privacy rights of individuals."

No matter how ridiculous these examples may seem, the question of privacy in the digital age presents serious challenges for journalists. Gyllenhaal calls privacy "a huge wild card" and says that, from now on, "if newspapers want to hold onto their access to public records, we're going to have to be a lot smarter than we have been."

"The FOI struggle," he says, "for a generation of journalists has been between the government on one hand and the media on the other. It's been a pretty evenly matched struggle. I think we can feel proud of some of the accomplishments we've made.

"But now, suddenly, there are so many more players and so many more forces out there—technology, public security issues—that FOI has blossomed into a much more difficult issue."

T O SEE HOW LAWMAKERS MIGHT RESOLVE THESE QUESTIONS, one state to watch is Florida. A classic case arose there last year, after the popular NASCAR driver Dale Earnhardt crashed into a concrete wall at the Daytona 500 and died.

One week earlier, writer Ed Hinton of the Orlando Sentinel had published stories explaining that the failure of NASCAR's drivers to use certain safety devices, including a Head and Neck Support (HANS) system, was causing unnecessary crash deaths.

Although NASCAR said a broken seat belt led to Earnhardt's death, the Sentinel thought he might have died from the kind of "head-whipping" injury that HANS is designed to prevent. The paper asked to have an independent expert examine the autopsy report, including autopsy photographs, to answer that question.

"The vast majority of NASCAR fans mistakenly believed that we wanted to *publish* the photos," Editor Tim Franklin says. "Very few had any idea that we had just spent six months investigating NASCAR driver safety." After Earnhardt's widow, Teresa, appeared on television declaring that she didn't want photos of her husband's body displayed in public, angry racing fans bombarded the newspaper with more than 15,000 e-mails, letters and phone calls. "Dozens of death threats poured in," Franklin says.

After reaching an agreement with Teresa Earnhardt, the newspaper's medical expert was allowed to view the autopsy photos. From this, the expert concluded that Earnhardt did not die of injuries resulting from a broken seat belt, as NASCAR had said, but from a head-whipping injury. Not only did the Sentinel have the satisfaction of being proved right, but late last year NASCAR mandated that all its drivers begin wearing the head and neck restraining devices.

However, while the controversy burned, the Legislature rushed to pass an exemption to the state public records law sealing autopsy photos from public view. In the emotional atmosphere, "Florida's open government advocates were overwhelmed in their efforts to conduct a rational debate," Lucy Dalglish, executive director of the Reporters Committee for Freedom of the Press, later wrote. Gov. Jeb Bush signed the bill into law with Earnhardt's widow by his side.

Jon Kaney, a lawyer who represents newspapers and other open government interests in Florida, says the prospect of the Earnhardt photos showing up on the Internet made all the difference. "The sole reason for passing that exemption," Kaney says, "was to prevent the operators of ghoulish Web sites from publishing photos of his mangled body." Apparently, the fear of Internet publication wasn't farfetched. During the struggle, Kaney says, the operator of an Internet site was lurking in the wings, trying to get his hands on the Earnhardt photos.

The state Legislature recently appointed a committee to recommend ways of dealing with such problems without sacrificing the state's commitment to open government. Some in Florida are beginning to argue that all public records should not be treated equally. As Barbara Petersen, president of the First Amendment Foundation in Tallahassee, says, "Information that is not sensitive when it is buried in a 20-page document could become very sensitive when put on the Internet."

Some therefore suggest a two-tier system, under which some records would be available in every form, including online, while others would be available only to those who took the trouble to visit a government office.

Lawyers in Florida now speak of sheltering public records from "jammies surfers." Kaney explains: "If your neighbor gets a divorce, you're not going to drive over to the courthouse and get the file. But in your jammies you can go online and look it up."

Most journalists would hate to settle for a two-tier system that sacrificed online access.

BUT JOURNALISTS FACE MORE THAN JUST A FIGHT OVER open records. They are being challenged to justify their very legitimacy.

Many people would agree with Bob Garfield of WNYC radio's "On the Media" when he said recently that the public "is mostly sympathetic with the government in its increasing restrictions. I think what they see is a knee-jerk reaction from the press, which wants to sort of compulsively have access to material that the public doesn't quite get why the press has to have."

The Bush administration encourages such thinking. In its not-very-subtle contempt for journalists, the administration sometimes appears to be saying that the press has no valid independent role to play in society. In a July 12 article in National Journal, White House correspondent (and AJR contributor) Carl Cannon wrote that reporters who cover the Bush White House "believe they are being not only used, but also disrespected—and prevented from doing their jobs properly." Cannon said this goes far beyond the usual gripes of White House reporters.

War correspondents in Afghanistan have not only been hindered in their work but sometimes bullied by the military (see "On Their Own," May). On January 10, the Pentagon ordered its troops not to allow photographers to transmit images of prisoners. On December 6, Marines herded a group of journalists into a warehouse so they couldn't see the effects of a stray bomb that had fallen on friendly troops near Kandahar.

When the federal government treats the press as an illegitimate presence, it is natural that some lower-level officials might do likewise. Oklahoma law enforcement officers provided a good example following the May 26 collapse of a bridge on Interstate 40, which killed 14 people whose cars plunged into the Arkansas River.

Sheila Stogsdill, a reporter for the Daily Oklahoman, was in a public park near the scene of the bridge collapse when officers tried to force her to leave. Like a good reporter, she refused. According to a story in the Oklahoman, John Hnath of the Tulsa medical examiner's office "ordered local police to arrest her."

"Officer Luke Morris handcuffed the reporter and took her to the nearby police station," the newspaper wrote. "Moments earlier, Johnny Pollard, a city councilman for eight years and a part-time police officer, had shouted: 'Arrest her! Arrest her! Handcuff her!'" Stogsdill said she was never told what crime she was supposed to have committed.

That same day, according to other news reports, state troopers tried to evict a Tulsa television station crew from private property where, with the landowners' permission, they had set up their cameras. Three reporters interviewing a relative of a victim on the town square were threatened with arrest unless they left immediately. A Muskogee County sheriff's deputy told yet another reporter he would be arrested for interfering with a federal investigation if he kept interviewing people on the street. And a number of print and broadcast journalists were corralled onto a convenience store parking lot nearly two miles from the scene of the accident.

A Dallas television reporter, Brett Shipp, recorded similar threats on tape. After National Guardsmen told him to leave, Shipp could be heard on the tape arguing that it was unconstitutional to order him off a public street. "I will go to jail if I have to," Shipp says on the tape, to which an official replies, "You will probably have to."

None of the harassed reporters was arrested or charged with any crime.

WHO WILL LEAD THE FIGHT AGAINST SUCH SECRECY, ignorance and contempt for the public's right to know? Although the giant media companies—AOL Time Warner, Disney and the like—are rich and powerful, their primary concern is not with journalism. The Center for Public Integrity reported this year that these media interests "lobby on issues ranging from protecting intellectual property to eliminating the death tax. They've fought against restrictions on tobacco advertising in print and alcohol advertising on the air, for eliminating the FCC's rules designed to prevent the concentration of the public airwaves and the press in too few hands, and to block any attempt to give candidates free air time."

As the challenge to open government has grown, many of the newspaper chains have responded by cutting the budget for newsroom training (an important element in any organized resistance effort) and by allowing the papers to downsize or eliminate state capitol bureaus.

The center's only reference to First Amendment issues was to note that lobbyists for Big Media "have consistently raised First Amendment freedoms as a carte blanche protection against any regulation of violent content broadcast over the airwaves."

Neither has the fight been taken up by leaders of the major newspaper chains. As the challenge to open government has grown, many of these companies have responded by cutting the budget for newsroom training (an important element in any organized resistance effort) and by allowing their papers to downsize or eliminate state capitol bureaus (see "Sad State," June).

Fortunately, at the grassroots level, one finds examples of editors and reporters fighting back in an effective way. This year, when it appeared that Florida lawmakers might pass scores of bills weakening the state sunshine law, a group of editors organized "Sunshine Sunday," a collaborative effort by 25 Florida newspapers and several radio and TV stations. All agreed to editorialize on the same day—March 10—about the threats to open government in Florida. By the end of the session, only 10 bills

had passed that would narrow public access to records, and most of those were deemed harmless by open government lobbyists.

After ordering more than 500 categories of information exempted from New Jersey's Open Public Records Law this summer, Gov. McGreevey backed down under withering criticism from newspaper editorial writers and good-government groups, keeping most of the records open.

Idaho's journalists also blocked an assault on public records this year. Press organizations and reform groups sprang into action after seven bills were filed in the Legislature aimed at restricting access. In the end, only one bill passed, after being modified to actually strengthen the open records law. "Idaho came through this nationwide assault on openness in government remarkably unscathed," Betsy Russell, president of the Idaho Press Club, wrote in the organization's newsletter.

These are not the only examples. Some of the FOI audits conducted in recent years have resulted in significant reforms. And in fact, it is worth recalling that practically every improvement in the open government laws since World War II—and every successful defense of those laws—has been due largely to the influence of the media.

However, in the present crisis, more is required. Members of ASNE's freedom of information committee are pushing for a nationwide campaign by journalists. The committee thinks this campaign should be led by newspaper editors.

The committee—composed of two dozen editors plus representatives of several nonprofit groups—has spent the last two years studying the problem and designing a plan of action. It has published a booklet, "The FOI Handbook," outlining its approach.

The committee's chairman, Doug Clifton, is now charged with implementing it. His goal is to form a unified front by coordinating his efforts with leaders of the Associated Press Managing Editors and forming closer ties with such like-minded groups as the Reporters Committee for Freedom of the Press, the First Amendment Center, the Society of Professional Journalists and OMB Watch, a government watchdog organization based in Washington.

Clifton's committee wants to help newspapers organize their newsrooms around freedom of information issues. This would mean much more training for reporters and editors, more frequent use of the sunshine laws and FOIA as newsgathering tools, and a more dogged insistence that officials stop withholding information. It would require spending the money to go to court whenever necessary. And it would mean much more editorializing on the issue, more news stories describing violations, more willingness to tell readers when they aren't getting all the facts. "Typically, you don't see stories in newspapers that such-and-such a record is unavailable," Clifton says. "You don't see many editorials in newspapers bemoaning the state of affairs."

He is putting together some public service ads on FOI issues that newspapers can run. And the committee is creating what he calls "a stump speech tool kit... that gives the busy editor the raw material to give speeches on behalf of freedom of information." Included would be specific examples of the harm that has been done because of government secrecy as well as the benefits that have flowed from transparency. The committee will also encourage newspapers to hold workshops to educate public officials on the sunshine laws.

Tim Franklin of the Orlando Sentinel is pulling together an FOI "strike force." This would be a network of editors with expertise, who could respond to problems as they arise by speaking at public forums, holding press conferences and appearing before legislative bodies. The strike force could also write op-ed articles geared to particular problems.

Clifton hopes the newspaper chains might be persuaded to underwrite some of the more costly aspects of this campaign.

MAKING ALL THIS HAPPEN, CLIFTON AGREES, WILL REQUIRE the cooperation of hundreds of editors. But are they up to it? Do they really have the stuff?

It isn't a good time to ask. Hodding Carter III, who heads the John S. and James L. Knight Foundation, came away from this year's ASNE convention with a sad assessment of editors' morale. "I've been going to ASNE for 52 years," he says. "I have never seen a time of more dispirit, more discomfort, more frustration, more fear, more resignation, more cynicism."

In an address to the organization, ASNE's outgoing president, Tim McGuire of Minneapolis' Star Tribune, sounded some of the same notes. He spoke of the fact that editors have been losing resources, respect and clout within their corporate organizations, and he described them and their newsroom staffs as feeling "scared," "powerless" and "isolated."

Last year, the ASNE committee tried to gauge editors' opinions on government secrecy and to gather a little basic information. For instance, it wanted to know how often newspapers had filed FOI requests and how successful those requests had been. The committee sent a questionnaire to the editors of 1,448 daily newspapers. One month later, only 247 papers had returned the questionnaire—a 17 percent response rate.

Even editors who aren't so apathetic—who care deeply about the problem—often hesitate to enter the political arena because they feel a conflict of interest in lobbying the politicians that their papers cover. "They are caught in a bind," the Freedom Forum's McMasters says. "There are those who agree this is a big issue and want to do something about it but are constrained by the ethical considerations."

Clifton sees "an instinctive reticence on the part of editors" even to write very much about FOI issues "for fear they'll be misinterpreted as self-serving. I don't think we've made enough of the reality that public access is just that—public access, citizen access." And so, says Clifton, the first crucial step in opening up the workings of government is not to persuade politicians or educate the public.

The first move, he says, is "to awaken editors to the threat."

Contributing writer Charles Layton, a former Philadelphia Inquirer editor and reporter, wrote about the decline in statehouse coverage in AJR's June issue.

From the *American Journalism Review*, September 2002, pp. 20-29. © 2002 by the Philip Merrill College of Journalism at the University of Maryland, College Park, MD 20742-7111. Reprinted by permission.

WEIGHING THE COSTS OF A SCOOP

How a Sniper Story Trapped the Press in an Ethical No-Man's Land

BY CHRISTOPHER HANSON

It's quiz time.

Question 1. Which of the following constitutes an ethical dilemma in journalism?

a. Reporter Bob fabricates a story about an eyewitness to one of October 2002's sniper attacks near Washington, D.C.

b. Competing reporter Carol plagiarizes Bob's fabrication.

c. Sniper beat reporter Ted sleeps with his intern, Alice, and sends her to accept his weekly payoff from the cops.

d. All of the above

e. None of the above

Some of my journalism ethics students would not readily grasp that the answer is e. An ethical dilemma is a conflict between two compelling principles, but some persist in thinking it's the absence of any principles whatsoever.

Question 2. Against the wishes of police brass, cops leak to a reporter a fascinating development: the sniper scrawled, "I am God" on a tarot card and left it at a shooting scene. Which of the following is the most promising path to resolving the ethical conflict faced by the reporter:

a. A news organization's duty is to provide the public with information, not to censor it. So print.

b. A news organization's duty is to minimize harm to the public. Police brass must think reporting the leak would impede the investigation and put more people at risk. Don't print.

c. A news organization should withhold information only for compelling reasons, like a clear risk to the investigation. But in a case like this one with lots of dead ends, the leak could help some citizen ID the killer. ("Check out the tarot card nut down the hall.") So print.

Of the three critiques, c. comes closest to resolving the ethical conflict between informing the public and minimizing harm.

But more than a few of my students would puzzle over this question, too. They forget that, when dealing with a conflict between two or more fundamental principles, a sound decision won't be reached by relying on just one of them.

What's surprising is that even seasoned journalists and press critics often make the same mistake and end up basing controversial news judgments on shallow "one principle" reasoning. For example, when Charles Moose, the police chief of Maryland's Montgomery County, began asking the press to convey information (toll-free tip-line numbers, messages to the sniper), some critics questioned whether journalists should comply. Independence from government influence, after all, is one of the key principles all journalists should follow.

Except when they shouldn't. Imagine the legitimate public outrage if TV crews turned off their cameras when Moose asked for help. Tempering one's independence to help stop a killing spree isn't exactly a tough call.

In the end, law enforcement news leaks unsanctioned by the brass led directly to capture of the sniper suspects. Fox News and rival CNN alerted the public to watch for a blue Chevy Caprice with New Jersey tags (NDA-21Z) and the pack followed their lead. A truck driver spotted the car at a rest stop and cops surrounded it as the suspects slept inside. Relief all around, to say nothing of glee among reporters, who now had a rejoinder to sniper coverage critics who had been calling them reckless opportunists: "The killers are behind bars because we put what we knew on the air. News competition serves the public."

Except when it doesn't. Suppose the sniper suspects had heard an urgent radio news bulletin identifying them. It is easy to imagine them rushing to ditch the Caprice, stealing a car and disappearing before the police closed in. Good fortune, not ethical deliberation, forestalls disaster during most media feeding frenzies.

Which brings us to our text for today: a *Washington Post* article, leaked by "law enforcement sources," reporting that suspect John Lee Malvo, seventeen, had confessed to being the trigger man in a number of the sniper killings and the shooting of a thirteen-year-old boy who survived.

The *Post* splashed its scoop across the front page on November 10 and 11, 2002. After chasing Fox, CNN, and local TV through much of the sniper spree, the paper was now squarely out front. Before this Malvo leak, legal experts had been raising doubts about a "murder one" conviction, arguing that it would be difficult to prove who pulled the trigger if both suspects denied doing so. A Malvo confession thus might have seemed like a big development—reassuring readers that justice would be done, as well as satisfying their interest in this gruesome case.

At the same time, however, the story raised more than a few eyebrows. The *Post*'s ombudsman, Michael Getler, asked in his November 17 column: "Are the police taking advantage of the

Post's competitive situation to saturate the public consciousness with the defendant's guilt?"

In defense of the article, which some critics claimed endangered Malvo's right to a fair trial, executive editor Leonard Downie Jr. made a statement that was quoted in the ombudsman's column. "We have reported suspects' statements under those circumstances routinely in the past," Downie said. "... Especially in this case, our responsibility is to report as much as we reliably know about these crimes and their commission as soon as we can."

In other words, because informing the public is a key principle of journalism, reporters should always disclose what the police tell them about a defendant's pretrial confessions.

Except when they shouldn't.

Again, merely citing a guiding principle of journalism—even one as basic as informing the public—is not sufficient to justify a news decision involving *conflicting principles*. The *Post* indeed had the duty to inform, but doing so risked harming news subjects, crime victims, public institutions, and its own credibility. (See below.)

To make its case for publication, *The Washington Post* would have had to demonstrate that the ethical imperative to inform readers trumped the potential damage of doing so. In that effort, the paper merits a grade of "Incomplete," at best, judging by the remainder of Downie's statement quoted by the ombudsman:

"The fact of Malvo's being a juvenile and the presence or absence of an attorney are not issues in decisions to publish or not," Downie said.

"... They are legal issues concerning the admissibility of his statements in court and will be adjudicated there. Our responsibility is to report fully and fairly on that legal process and debate.

"As to reporting statements made by Malvo or any other accused person to police, it does not matter whether such statements are revealed formally and publicly by authorities or by unnamed sources, so long as we believe those sources to be credible and to be accurately characterizing the statements. We clearly believe that to be so in this case. . . .

"The understandable clash between the *Post*'s constitutional responsibility [to report what it knows as soon as possible] and the constitutional requirement for a fair trial is the subject of the long-running 'free press-fair trial' debate between the media and lawyers.... I believe we have served our community well in this case."

Malvo's leaked confession in the *Post* raised more than a few eyebrows

This statement is less than persuasive.

First, how do we know the leaks accurately reflected what Malvo told the police? "No quotations from Malvo were made available," ombudsman Getler noted in his column, "so should the press be confident of the context in which these alleged confessions were made?"

The *Post*'s editorial board took the extraordinary step of casting doubt on the wisdom and accuracy of its own paper's scoop. "Sources told the *Post* that Mr. Malvo had confessed to

being the triggerman in some of the killings. Fairfax County Commonwealth's attorney Robert F. Horan Jr. stated yesterday that some of the reports concerning Mr. Malvo's interrogation ...'quite simply [weren't] true.' We do not purport to know what Mr. Malvo said ... [but] it seems particularly important to proceed carefully and make sure the facts are fully understood." (Editorial, November 13, 2002.)

A *Post* columnist, Courtland Milloy, declared that publicizing the alleged confession and other pre-trial evidence replaced "blind justice with this thinly veiled eagerness to execute." Others noted that juveniles in particular are prone to make false confessions under high-pressure interrogation. The infamous 1989 Central Park jogger case once seemed airtight. But the confession of a convicted rapist more than a decade later and subsequent DNA tests proved the teenagers' confessions false.

In fairness, the *Post* did note in its November 11 article that police were looking for possible discrepancies in Malvo's story and had found at least one. But the paper's focus was on the confession, not the discrepancy.

Second, Downie's statement equates the judiciary's constitutional obligation to ensure a fair trial with the press's constitutional *duty* to rush news into print. But no such duty exists. The press does have a First Amendment *right* to print, but that does not absolve it from making ethical judgments that might require withholding or delaying publication, as the *Post* has done at times.

Readers need some information quickly—dirt on candidates before Election Day, for instance. But because *Post* readers might *want* to know about Malvo's confession, it does not follow that the audience *needs* to know about it before trial. Quite the reverse.

The authorities often leak such stories as a form of insurance: if the judge refuses to admit the confession into evidence, there is still a chance that members of the jury will have been exposed to it through the back door.

"Unfortunately," writes the University of Texas criminologist William Black, "police and prosecutors now seem to commonly believe that executing a defendant is so important that it justifies acting unethically—e.g., by leaking information with the intention of prejudicing potential jurors.

"... Even if the confession turns out to be inaccurate, jurors will 'know' that Malvo confessed to murder ... [but] the courts are reluctant to overturn a conviction. The result is that governmental 'crime' pays. Leaks are common because they work." (*The Washington Post*, November 24, 2002.)

Investigating a source's misconduct is the last thing on the mind of a reporter reaping its benefits

This essentially makes the *Post* and other news outlets that use such information accomplices in the "crime." Given that pre-trial disclosure of interrogation leaks under such circumstances can encourage future police misconduct, it's hard to buy Downie's contention that "it does not matter" whether such information is leaked or released officially.

Which brings us to point three. By printing its Malvo scoop, *The Washington Post* had thrust itself headfirst into a conflict-of-interest honey bucket. Consider the following developments, reported in the November 16 *Post*:

- Citing the paper's Malvo confession article, a defense lawyer asked a Virginia Circuit Court judge to impose a gag order barring the police from talking to the press about evidence in the case.
- A Fairfax County prosecutor retorted that a gag order would have a "chilling effect" on the police, who need to share evidence with other agencies in an investigation.
- The judge, M. Langhorne Keith, said he was outraged by the leaks but could not impose a gag order. He had no evidence that leaks had come from county police, and no jurisdiction over federal authorities from whom the leaks might have come.

Talk about a newspaper becoming part of the story!

So did the *Post*'s editors deal with the conflict by using only wire copy, much as Bloomberg News did for the New York mayoral campaign coverage after its owner became a candidate? Far from it. The paper *assigned a reporter whose byline was on the original two confession stories* to cover the gag-order controversy. Read the following excerpt closely:

"Fairfax County police internal affairs officers said yesterday that they are still investigating the leaks. Maj. Audrey M. Slyman, commander of the internal affairs bureau, and Lt. Mike Kline said after the hearing that investigators are considering interviewing more than 150 officers as part of the probe. They asked one *Washington Post* reporter to reveal information about sources yesterday; the reporter declined." (*The Washington Post*, November 16, 2002, page A10.)

It's unclear from the article whether the reporter the police grilled was this particular story's own author, Josh White, confession scoop co-authors, Sari Horwitz or Allan Lengel, or some other *Post* writer. What is clear is that the *Post* was interrogating police internal affairs officers on their leak investigation at the same time internal affairs officers were interrogating the *Post* as part of the very same leak investigation.

What's more, the *Post*'s conflict of interest could easily continue as the sniper prosecutions unfold. Malvo's lawyers are likely to cite the *Post* scoop prominently in any request for a change of venue or appeal on grounds of pre-trial publicity. (LEAKS ON STATEMENTS MAY HURT SNIPER CASE, Associated Press article in the Bergen County, New Jersey, *Record*, November 12, 2002.)

Fourth, there is the problem of the distracted watchdog. The *Post* seemed to be an effective monitor of official conduct just one day before it broke the Malvo confession story. It reported on page A1 that detectives had "grilled" Malvo for more than seven hours without a lawyer, ejecting the defendant's court-appointed guardian when he showed up at police headquarters to demand that the questioning stop and that he be allowed to talk to Malvo. This was only the latest in a chain of dubious police moves exposed since the arrests.

Then came the Malvo confession leak, which immediately diverted the paper to the red meat of solving the case and advancing this riveting narrative. Investigating a source's alleged misconduct is the last thing on the mind of a reporter reaping the benefits of that very alleged misconduct.

To "serve the community well" when manipulative sources are serving up leaks to the press would require that journalists come clean about how news is plotted behind the scenes. It would require a candid assessment of the anonymous source's motivation for leaking, as ombudsman Getler suggested in his column. A Malvo truth-in-packaging box might go something like this:

"Since the arrests of the sniper suspects, the Post *and other news organizations have been reporting how the police stumbled badly during the manhunt. Just yesterday, this paper exposed how officers had grilled the seventeen-year-old sniper suspect John Lee Malvo for seven hours with no lawyer present, which raised questions about whether the authorities had violated his constitutional rights.*

So certain law enforcement sources have broken department rules to reveal how Malvo allegedly confessed during that interrogation. They hope the accompanying story you are about to read will predispose you to see Malvo as an evil predator, despite his tender years—especially if you are a potential juror, wavering on the issue of executing minors. At the same time, the police are hoping to divert your attention from their record of embarrassing sniper case miscues, to wit:

- *Cops had been on the lookout for a white man in a white van, getting the race of the perpetrator(s) and the color and type of the vehicle wrong.*
- *They played down eyewitness reports of a blue Caprice speeding away from one crime, even though this turned out to be the car.*
- *As a result, the suspects slipped through their fingers many times.*
- *The roadblocks and dragnets that ate up resources and snarled traffic became a mammoth waste of effort. The special Pentagon surveillance plane lent with fanfare to the local police was just a useless gadget when looking for the wrong car.*
- *Several clueless "tip line" operations hung up on the suspects, who evidently called hoping to negotiate a payoff for ending the killings.*
- *The arrest seemed like a lucky accident, hardly a police tour de force. The suspects finally got a hot-line call through and, to prove their bona fides, bragged about an earlier killing, which turned out to be in Alabama. With prints from that crime scene, investigators were finally able to identify the suspects. But in effect the alleged killers trapped themselves through reckless stupidity.*

The Malvo leak is thus aimed at convincing you, the responsible newspaper-reading public, that law enforcement has everything under control. You be the judge."

Of course, printing such a confession about a confession poses ethical conflicts, too. The need to be accountable butts against the need to inform the public. After all, how many potential law enforcement leakers would drop a dime if they knew their acts would require full disclosure?

Well, no one said this ethics thing was easy. Ombudsman Getler says, "It would be hard to argue that this was a case where the *Post* should have engaged in self-censorship." But it's even harder to argue convincingly that the newspaper should have printed what it did.

And so to a final quiz question, for extra credit:

Suppose *The Washington Post* had considered options other than running its Malvo exclusive in the form that appeared. Which of the following is the best alternative?

a. Use a sexier headline—MALVO GUILTY—EXCLUSIVE: INSIDE THE DEATH CAR. Include news-you-can-use come-on: "Read now and avoid jury duty."

b. Recast the story as one on overzealous police jeopardizing a case using all juicy confession details without seeming to exploit them.

c. Print a story only if reporters get access to full interrogation transcripts for context or if reporters see corroborating evidence that convinces them Malvo did what he claimed.

d. Hold the story until the last jury in the last sniper trial has been sequestered.

e. Write in your own.

Explain your reasoning. There is no certain right answer, although there are a couple of wrong ones. But don't worry. If you avoid those dangerous one-principle arguments, you're already a step ahead of many old pros.

Christopher Hanson was a print reporter for twenty years. He teaches journalism ethics at the University of Maryland.

Reprinted from *Columbia Journalism Review*, January/February 2003, pp. 34-37. © 2003 by Columbia Journalism Review, Columbia University. Reprinted by permission of Columbia Journalism Review and the author.

"We Mean Business"

In the wake of Jayson Blair, Jack Kelley and numerous other instances of fabrication and plagiarism, the nation's newspapers are scrutinizing their operations and stiffening their defenses against ethical lapses.

By Jill Rosen

With a Sharpie in his left hand, David House flips through the pages of the Fort Worth Star-Telegram, scribbling a number onto each local bylined story. At the end of the week, he's tagged more than 100.

So he goes to find a big roll of tickets, the kind you might get at a fair. For every marked story, House rips off a ticket, then dumps the whole lot into the lid of the box that came with his ombudsman stationery. Stirring them up a bit, he carries the package into the editor's office, announcing, "OK, we're ready for a drawing."

House lifts the lid high over his head as Editor Jim Witt reaches up, fishes around and pulls out—ta-da!—No. 41. But for this chosen one, there's no prize waiting, unless your definition of "prize" involves having David House put your page-one story about Lockheed Martin under a post-publication microscope, scrutinizing every fact, every quote.

Grim, but such is life these days at a paper that's been burned. And the burn victims are mounting.

With dismaying regularity, papers across the country are realizing that they've been had by cheating reporters. Jayson Blair's bamboozling of the New York Times, the most headline-grabbing example, is among the reasons we've since heard of sin after sin after sin. (See "All About the Retrospect," June/July 2003.) That's because the Times' stark mea culpa, which publicly detailed not only Blair's lies but how the paper missed them, set a new standard for burned papers: You confess, you're contrite, and then you clean house.

Lest editors thought Blair a fluke, along came USA Today's revelation that its anointed star correspondent, Jack Kelley, had been playing the paper for years—in ways even more outrageous than Blair's. (See "Who Knows Jack?" April/May.) Then smaller papers chimed in, owning up to plagiarizers here, fabricators there, to the point where this spring it was getting a bit hard to keep track of it all.

Though flamboyant and well-publicized cases give the past year's crimes a particularly egregious feel, it's not the industry's first ugly breakout. In 2001, editors were having fits after, in a span of just a few months, publications including BusinessWeek, the Detroit News, the San Jose Mercury News, Myrtle Beach, South Carolina's Sun News and Bloomsburg, Pennsylvania's Press Enterprise offered embarrassed apologies. (See "Ethically Challenged," March 2001.) Three years earlier witnessed the Chiquita, Tailwind and Patricia Smith/Mike Barnicle episodes.

As each new case chipped away at the news industry's already fragile credibility, most newsroom leaders this year heard a call to action. Knowing that wiping out plagiarism and fabrication is pretty much a pipe dream, editors started having at it just the same, tightening ethics policies, having heart-to-hearts with their staffs, monitoring corrections, tracking expense reports and learning about software that detects plagiarism.

In this spring's cacophony of confessions was Fort Worth's. Editors there had fired a reporter in 2001 for plagiarizing once. But after hearing that same reporter had racked up at least 40 plagiarism counts in Georgia at the Macon Telegraph, appalled Star-Telegram editors realized they, too, probably had more than a one-time transgression on their hands. Checks revealed that to be true.

So, with a magic marker, a roll of tickets and a box lid, Star-Telegram Senior Editor/Reader Advocate David House is out to win back his paper's credibility. By randomly choosing a story a week to fact-check after it's published, the paper wants to simultaneously dissuade potential corner-cutters while proving to readers its commitment to honesty.

"We mean business," House says. "There's such a cloud over the profession, we've got to take pretty drastic steps."

"I am so sick of this angst filled handwringing, like this has not been an issue in ours and every other business since the first disciple got paid for his notes about 'Adventures on the Shores of Galilee,'" writes Mike Lloyd, editor of Michigan's Grand Rapids Press, responding to an AJR survey tapping editors for their thoughts about preventing fabrication and plagiarizing. "Journalism is no more nor no less vulnerable to the weaknesses of human beings than any other. We just think we're above the fray and love to self-flagellate.

"Jayson Blair was and is a sick puppy. Jack Kelley had the morals of a dime-store shoplifter. In both cases, their frailties led to huge abuses because they put more energy into deception than they did honest work. There is no cure for that in any business—except jail."

In an April column for Washingtonian magazine's Web site, National Editor Harry Jaffe also scoffed at the notion of journalism in crisis. "At the American Society of Newspaper Editors convention in Washington this week, there was much handwringing and self-flagellation about ethics problems in American newsrooms," Jaffe wrote, suggesting that the industry would do well to trade in the angst for some celebration about how well it's "ferreting out fakers."

But upon receiving the same survey that the Michigan editor pooh-poohed, about 25 other top editors bluntly stated how seriously they're taking the problem. And at the same ASNE/Newspaper Association of America convention where Jaffe noticed all the wringing of hands, New York Times Publisher Arthur O. Sulzberger Jr., urged the hundreds of editors and publishers in a session on ethics and standards to work with the assumption that someone in their organization is cheating. "Get ahead of this curve," he warned. "Until your newsroom grapples with it and it feels in its soul it came up with answers, it's probably not going to stick."

Jack Fuller, president of Tribune Publishing, followed that up, adding: "Anyone who says this is not happening in my newspaper is not seeing clearly."

Though journalism certainly has its share of navel-gazers and doomsayers, the people taking the recent spate of ethical transgressions seriously hardly come off as hysterical Chicken Littles.

Peter Bhatia, executive editor at Portland's Oregonian, a paper without any recent plagiarism or fabrication incidents, says that all newsrooms suffer side effects from the recent cases. "This is a real crisis. The public sees it," he says. "We're kidding ourselves if we don't think it's had an impact on our credibility."

Kelly McBride, an ethics expert at the Poynter Insitute, believes the problems are rampant in the industry. In high school and in college, she says, students are plagiarizing and cheating as a matter of course. Why would everything change once these students hit the real world?

McBride recently spoke to a convention of Florida high school journalists. Asking their teachers to leave the room, she asked the kids if they drop chunks of copy from published sources into their reports. Yeah, they told her—and, yeah, they know that's bad. "They know it's wrong, but they equate it to speeding rather than drunk driving," McBride says.

"The problem is that when they do it for a school paper, once they've established a habit, it's hard not to do it in their publication," she says.

Coke Ellington, a former reporter who now teaches journalism at Alabama State University, has caught his less- erudite students turning in work that includes words like "doyenne" and "maven." He's heard about cheathouse.com, a site filled with thousands of papers on hundreds of topics. And he's confronted plagiarizers who immediately ask for a do-over. "They don't get it," Ellington says. "When someone is caught robbing a bank, they don't just give the money back and walk away.

"I hope I can keep some people out of the field who don't belong in it," he says. "I hate to think I'd have to check reporters the way I check my Intro to Mass Communications students."

"I t sounds funny, but the wall is my rock," went the first quote in the story David Zeeck, editor of Tacoma, Washington's News Tribune, was reading. Funny indeed is how it sounded to Zeeck.

The November 2002 story by reporter Bart Ripp was a front-page feature about a historical cobblestone wall in town. The day before, when Zeeck saw the piece slated for A1, he asked that the archives-based stroll down memory lane be freshened with quotes from real people who have something modern and relevant to say about the wall.

"He went out and got them in a nanosecond," Zeeck says. "It was just too easy." So reading the story in the paper, getting to the quote by a "Lynn Kim of Lakewood," Zeeck got "the little flag in your gut that goes off as an editor."

Zeeck marched into the office, pulled another editor aside and told her he thought the quote was bogus. Searches through phonebooks and directories revealed no Lynn Kim; another quoted appreciator of the wall, a Brian Wellisch, wasn't listed either.

But with only suspicion rather than proof, Zeeck decided that he'd just keep an eye on Ripp, a 32-year reporting veteran who'd been at the News Tribune for 15 years. Flash forward a year-and-a-half to this spring. Ripp's editor on the features desk, Linda Dahlstrom, is reading his Q&A column on area dining. Though Ripp had been told to include the name and hometown of questioners, and call them for permission to use their names, these questioners were anonymous. When Dahlstrom demanded the names, Ripp said he'd add them—that is if a computer crash hadn't erased the file where he kept them.

Ripp soon provided the names, mentioning nothing more about the computer issue. But, suspicious, Dahlstrom asked him if he'd gotten permission to use them—Ripp responded with an all-too-quick yeah, yeah, yeah. At that point, her editor alarms blaring, Dahlstrom grabbed some phonebooks and started hunting down Ripp's names. No matches.

In the year-and-a-half since Zeeck looked for Lynn Kim in Tacoma area directories, the paper had invested in a database called Accurint, a tool for finding people and information about them. According to Accurint, only one of the six people in Ripp's column appeared to exist. Meanwhile, every adult quoted in nine stories by other reporters appeared in the database.

Dahlstrom called the one woman in Ripp's column Accurint turned up. As the woman readily confirmed sending the letter, Dahlstrom apologized for having to bother her about it twice. The woman said this was the first call about it she'd gotten. When Dahlstrom asked Bart about the discrepancy, he replied: "I'm sorry I lied to you."

When it all came to a head in Zeeck's office, Ripp insisted he never made up a thing and quit on the spot. He claimed he had e-mails from those people, though he couldn't produce them.

After Ripp left, the paper checked his sources from the last 18 months of stories, everything back to the feature about Lynn Kim and the wall. Another 20 people in them are probably made up, Zeeck says.

"It's sad because Bart had real talent, he was kind of a star in town," Zeeck says. "It's so frustrating, so maddening."

Bart Ripp seems cut from the mold of USA Today's Jack Kelley who, even when filing from the world's most dramatic locales, felt compelled to add blood to already graphic war scenes and make up people in despair when, perhaps, real people in despair didn't emote to his liking. Zeeck says that Ripp would go out to cover an event, quote plenty of real people, then fill out the story with fakes.

In Ripp's case, the official sources would be legitimate—the booth-owners at an ethnic festival, the purveyors of a butcher shop. But the strolling festival-goers or the butcher shop customers that Ripp supposedly caught up to in the parking lot were apparently figments of his imagination. "These are the easiest interviews in the world. Why would you make these things up?" Zeeck asks. "Jack Kelley is making things up in Israel and Bosnia. There real life is good enough. Great storytelling is there for the asking—why embellish? I can't comprehend what this is about. It's very frustrating."

Frustrating and near-impossible to catch until you suspect something. After Jayson Blair was defrocked last year, the News Tribune started sending question-naires each week to six or nine randomly chosen sources. Only two or three of several hundred have come back revealing any factual problems in stories. And only sources with easy-to-find addresses would get mailed one—so chances are, if oblivious to Bart Ripp's transgressions, the paper tried to send one to Lynn Kim, she would simply be passed over in favor of some of the story's more accessible, official sources. And since he probably quoted the official guys accurately, a questionnaire about a Ripp story would probably leave him looking like a great, thorough reporter.

W hen Khalil Abdullah came to work for Lois Norder in her suburban bureau of the Fort Worth Star-Telegram in

February 2000, she thought she'd hired a young, enterprising reporter with a bright future. He'd interned at the Dallas Morning News, he'd worked at Charleston, South Carolina's Post and Courier, and he seemed to possess real enthusiasm for writing.

Which is why, even though his primary responsibility was covering cities and school districts, she chose him to team up with the paper's more experienced immigration reporter on a project about the "lost boys" of Sudan who had settled in Texas. Abdullah seemed to throw himself into the project, spending a lot of time with the young men as they adjusted to their new lives. But as the deadline approached for a first draft, Abdullah's partner on the story came to Norder in tears. She said she thought Abdullah had stolen parts of his section from two other papers. Having read the other pieces, she recognized the writing.

Unquestionably, the passages were verbatim lifts. When Norder asked Abdullah about it, he claimed he hadn't plagiarized. Rather, he was on deadline, in a hurry, so he used other papers' copy to hold space for reporting he wanted to do later himself. "He said he would never have let it get into the paper that way," Norder says. But then an assistant at the paper revealed that she had once taken a message for a former editor, a complaint from a Dallas Morning News reporter that Abdullah was plagiarizing her. "We fired him," Norder says.

And that was that until Norder started getting reference calls—by 2002 Abdullah wanted back in newspapers.

When Abdullah first sent his résumé to the Macon Telegraph, Executive Editor Sherrie Marshall says the plagiarism in his past turned her and other editors off. But when the reporter reapplied months later, seeming persistent, driven and reformed, Marshall gave in. She talked to colleagues and to Norder in Fort Worth—no one ruled out the idea of a second chance.

It seemed to Marshall as if Abdullah's transgression was a one-time, stupid, young reporter's mistake. He admitted it and was willing to work at a smaller paper to get back in the game. "He [wanted] to earn his way back," she says.

That was September 2002. By this spring, Marshall knew better.

In March an editor from the San Diego Union-Tribune called her to say that an article Abdullah had written a few months back about the enrollment decline for high school shop classes was "remarkably similar" to a piece reporter Alex Lyda wrote for the California paper in July 2003.

All of the national context, the meat, for Abdullah's story, which ran on the front page, came from San Diego's A1 story. The lead in San Diego, "When cars had no computers and power steering was a luxury, high schools had a shop class where students with gritty nails lingered over engines and mingled with friends content to turn wrenches, not pages," pops up verbatim as Abdullah's nut graph.

Seeing the pieces side by side, there was really no question for Marshall—Abdullah had stolen the words. She fired him immediately, but first asked him for an explanation. "We got more or less the silent treatment," she says, though Abdullah told a Telegraph reporter writing the paper's story about his firing, "I certainly would want to say that I knew better."

Abdullah left the Telegraph on a Friday. Editors started exhuming his other stories that Saturday. They found that more than 40 of the approximately 200 stories Abdullah wrote for the paper included cribbed material. Abdullah plagiarized consistently for more than a year, the Telegraph says, taking passages from, to name a few, the Baltimore Sun, the Washington Post, the Oregonian and, ironically, the Fort Worth Star-Telegram.

These days, neither Norder nor Marshall is too keen on second chances for supposedly rehabilitated journalism convicts. "I hate to think one strike and you're out," Norder says wryly. "Though I've since changed my mind on that."

While Fort Worth is counting on the post-publication fact-checking to get out from under Abdullah's shadow, in Macon, where the sting is fresher, they're in debate mode, talking and trying to get a handle on what, if anything, might stop their next problem. They're feeling vulnerable.

Obviously, for starters, there's the hiring issue. More careful checks on candidates and a zero tolerance for plagiarism are on the table. "As an editor who's now faced this situation, I can't imagine I would ever take the chance again," Marshall says. A committee the Telegraph convened to think about how to protect the paper from unethical journalists has recommended having more seminars and discussions about accuracy and ethics and random post-publication fact-checking like at Forth Worth. The paper is also considering buying plagiarism detection software and possibly using it to check the clips of job candidates.

Norder incredulously learned that a recent Star-Telegram job candidate applied with plagiarized clips. "This is much more pervasive than I ever imagined," she marvels. "To apply for work with plagiarized material?"

Just the existence of her paper's fact-checking program will deter reporters tempted to cheat, Norder guesses. "You can gamble on it," she says. "But your number might come up some time."

These wayward journalists leave trails, says Philip Meyer, the Knight Chair in Journalism at the University of North Carolina at Chapel Hill. With Jayson Blair, there were the expense reports that didn't match his whereabouts. With Jack Kelley, absurd quotes, outlandish scenarios and claims to have witnessed more death gasps than some emergency room nurses. Khalil Abdullah had a habit of plagiarizing graphs with national perspective to elevate his locally based stories. With Bart Ripp it was quoting average Joes oddly absent from powerful databases. "You could go back and find clues," Meyer says. "If you have a scam, an editor could at least find a way to figure out how to prevent the scam."

If anything can stop plagiarizers or fabricators, common sense seems to dictate, it's aggressive questioning by shrewd, skeptical editors and creating a newsroom environment where concerns raised by readers and staff are dignified with responses. Those two concepts, editors say, form the foundation for a protected organization—and while extras like fact-checking or plagiarism software can supplement them, they can't substitute.

"There's no pill we can take," says the Oregonian's Bhatia. "Every newsroom has to look deeply at itself and say, 'These are our points of vulnerability.'"

Turning up the heat on story editing is an amorphous proposition—who's to say when one's doing enough? But the idea, editors say, is to just consciously try harder. USA Today editors who read Jack Kelley's filings say at the time nothing struck them as odd, though looking back on individual stories, some of them have said they wonder why they didn't ask more questions.

"Editors, assignment editors, copy editors, top editors need to be especially questioning," Boston Globe Editor Martin Baron says. "With too many assignment editors, with too many copy editors, things are getting through that shouldn't be getting through." If something looks too good, he says, it may well be, and editors shouldn't give a pass to blockbuster quotes and anecdotes—particularly if they involve anonymous sources.

As journalists digested the news of Jayson Blair last year, David Zeeck reminded his editors how critical it is to trust their instincts—if something seems wrong, by all means, check it out. "He told us to pay attention to the little feelings in the pit of your stomach," says Dahlstrom, who used that very tactic to help stop Ripp.

To set the stage for solid editing, newsrooms might have to rethink the traditional editor-to-reporter ratio. Often, top editors say, there are so many reporters per supervisor that an editor just doesn't have enough time in the day to give copy the attention it deserves, let alone know exactly what each reporter is up to.

"The editing process takes more time than we've traditionally given it," UNC's Meyer says. And Denver Post Editor Greg Moore told his peers at the NAA/ASNE convention that the editor/reporter ratio is a "potential for calamities." "Any assigning editor who has to handle eight reporters, that's too many," Moore said.

Though most of the Blair-Kelley disaster clean-up efforts focus on assignment-editor questioning, at the Baltimore Sun, the copy desk chief knows that his team, which already catches a lot of mistakes, can catch cheaters. Last fall John E. McIntyre, the Sun's assistant managing editor for the copy desk, revamped the desk's guidelines to specifically deal with plagiarism and fabrication.

Every copy editor now knows of the "danger signs" of plagiarized copy—abrupt shifts in vocabulary or syntax, aspects to a story that don't seem like the writer's usual work, single-sourced stories.

One Sun copy editor recently found plagiarism in a staff-written story, McIntyre says. When checking the spelling of a place name online, the copy editor noticed a sentence on a Web site identical to what the Sun reporter had written. It turned out the story included six passages taken verbatim from two different Web sites. The story was spiked.

McIntyre says: "We want copy editors to be aware that this might crop up in virtually anything they handle."

When USA Today released its 28-page report explaining how Jack Kelley deceived his newsroom and his readers for years, the authors, veteran editors John Seigenthaler, Bill Kovach and Bill Hilliard, levied particularly harsh criticism on newsroom personnel who ignored or brushed off complaints about the reporter and criticisms of his work. According to the report: "One formal, written complaint received from a foreign source, bluntly and specifically challenging the accuracy of Kelley's work, was not responded to by anyone at USA Today for more than two years. We were told that the letter, 'somehow had been lost.'" The report lists time after time that editors did nothing when confronted with issues about their ace correspondent.

To make sure that bosses at the Charlotte Observer hear all concerns that need to be aired about the paper, they've laid down a little law. "Our main rule here," says Deputy Managing Editor Cheryl Carpenter, "is the only sure way to get yourself in real trouble is to blow off a reader or blow off a colleague that has a concern about your story." Some Observer reporters have even been disciplined for ignoring a reader. "We were trying to show the staff that not having a conversation about a reader's concern is a higher sin than publishing a correction," she says.

Globe Editor Baron told his staff after Blair that they should not only feel com-

PLAYING DEFENSE

To get a handle on how top editors are reacting to and dealing with the recent spate of cheaters in journalism, AJR e-mailed a survey to a number of them. Here is how some editors responded:

Has a reporter in your newsroom ever fabricated or plagiarized? If so, how did you find out about it?

- **Steve Smith, editor, Spokane, Washington's Spokesman-Review**: "We had an incident late last year. The plagiarism was identified by our city editor, who read our story in the paper and remembered a nearly identical report from another paper in the region published the previous day. Subsequent investigation showed that our report married lifted grafs from the other paper and entire sections of an Internet-posted press release."
- **David Green, managing editor, Nashville's Tennessean**: "The most recent … involved a freelance book reviewer. He lifted material from book jackets. A staffer noticed it when he was looking at a book jacket."
- **Stu Wilk, associate editor, Dallas Morning News**: "We had a situation in which an editor was unable to verify the existence of individuals quoted in a column. That led to further inquiry. It turned out that numerous names in numerous columns by this author were unable to be verified. The author insisted it was not plagiarism but rather reportorial sloppiness caused by illness."

If you answered no to the first question—no one in your newsroom has been found fabricating or plagiarizing—how confident are you that your newsroom is free of those things?

- **Smith, Spokesman-Review**: "Up to the point of this incident, I was absolutely confident the risks here were minimal … This was a clear wake-up call and reminder."
- **Frank Denton, editor, Tampa Tribune**: "Such behavior is so abhorrent, unthinkable in my mind, that I—probably naïvely—would put myself in a 'pretty confident' category."
- **Joe Worley, executive editor, Oklahoma's Tulsa World**: "Fearful."
- **Douglas C. Clifton, editor, Cleveland's Plain Dealer**: "I am fearful, not because I suspect that it is going on, but I recognize how difficult it is to detect."
- **Carole Leigh Hutton, editor, Detroit Free Press**: "I think anyone who says they're completely confident of that is dreaming or living in denial."

Do you have any newsroom systems in place to guard against fabrication or plagiarism? If so, what are they—and did the Jayson Blair or Jack Kelley or other publicized incidents inspire you to set them up?

- **Greg Moore, editor, Denver Post**: "We really don't have systems, but we have become adept at spot-checking stories, especially if we have received a complaint. But we are now looking into obtaining plagiarism software that will assist us in vetting stories. As far as fabrication goes, one thing we are thinking about is spot-checking stories against expense accounts from time to time. But there is no surefire way to guard against that sin except good aggressive questioning."
- **Jack McElroy, editor, Tennessee's Knoxville News-Sentinel**: "I think live fact-checking would be difficult for a daily paper, but I think after-the-fact accuracy checks are a good idea."

- **Mike Connelly, executive editor, Sarasota Herald Tribune**: "At the moment, we don't do spot checks. That may change. I suspect in the past that editors have sometimes downplayed complaints about reporters they trust. I can't imagine that happening any more."
- **Clifton, Plain Dealer**: "I send out approximately 10 accuracy letters a day to people quoted in stories. That device is a better vehicle to detect fabrication than it is plagiarism, but it does increase the chances that it might be noticed."
- **Hutton, Detroit Free Press**: "I asked our public editor to look into anti-plagiarism software after the Jack Kelley story, but it seems too cumbersome and inefficient. We certainly talk about this more in the newsroom than we did before the Blair story came out."
- **Vickie Kilgore, executive editor, Olympia, Washington's Olympian**: "We have an ethics policy that newsroom staff sign each year as a condition of employment … I send letters to at least five people each week who have been quoted in the paper. These letters include a questionnaire that asks about fairness, accuracy, balance, professionalism and a stamped, addressed envelope."
- **Wilk, Dallas Morning News**: "We spot-check names of people quoted in stories to make sure they are actual people."

Do you think that instituting fact-checking could curb these reporting transgressions?

- **McElroy, Knoxville News-Sentinel**: "We are considering launching accuracy checks later this year."
- **Don Wycliff, public editor, Chicago Tribune**: "To be frank, fact-checking is what I have always thought reporters do.... It strikes me that, if you're to do something effective, it has to be substantively different from what you already do. That suggests to me something like post-publication verification by contacting sources named in stories and asking if they were properly represented."
- **Thomas Mitchell, editor, Las Vegas Review-Journal**: "Sometimes, but there is always a way to game a system."
- **Ken Bunting, executive editor, Seattle Post-Intelligencer**: "I am not certain if a more elaborate system of fact-checking might catch more journalistic transgressions. If we were to institute a more elaborate fact-checking system, however, I would aim most of its resource at pre-publication fact-checking, not post-publication fact-checking. I recognize that is not always possible with breaking news. However, the objective should be to make publications better, and to catch errors or transgression before they happen."

Would you consider a fact-checking system at your paper? If not, why?

- **Tom Eblen, managing editor, Lexington Herald Leader:** "I would consider it if I had sufficient staff. However, if I were to gain back some of the staff I have lost in recent years, or even get more, I would add reporters rather than fact-checkers. I think the payoff for readers would be greater."
- **Dennis Ryerson, editor, Indianapolis Star**: "It could help, but again, a foolproof system would be virtually impossible to develop."

- **Clifton, Plain Dealer:** "Spot pre-publication fact-checking is possible and would certainly be worth talking about. The accuracy letters are an excellent post-publication practice."
- **Paul Anger, editor, Des Moines Register**: "Fact-checking would help. The question is whether fact-checking is an appropriate response to the amount of risk and whether it outweighs some of the negatives—the practicality of doing it at a daily newspaper, the doors that open to a source diving into a story before it is published. A rogue employee will be able to get around almost any system."

Do you think that reporters in your newsroom might feel pressure to come up with "wow" stories in order to be considered a star? If not, do you have any newsroom "stars" that don't come up with "wow" copy?

- **Eblen, Lexington Herald-Leader**: "I think that's always a danger. An editor must communicate two messages: I want 'wow' stories, but only, if they are accurate, truthful and ethical You can't have one without the other."
- **Moore, Denver Post**: "I think reporters feel the pressure to be successful. That does not mean necessarily getting 'wow' stories. But I am sure they feel pressure to be on page one and to do stories that their colleagues marvel at from time to time. Our stars tend to be people who get exclusives, get their stories right and are great at source development. If they are working their beats so they can do those things, the wow stories seem to come."
- **Kilgore, Olympian**: "There's not enough 'wow' copy."

Do you think that the recent spate of fabrication and plagiarism incidents indicates a growing industry problem, or is it just that we're hearing more about them now thanks to the Internet?

- **Reed Eckhardt, managing editor, Cheyenne, Wyoming's Eagle-Tribune**: "I think the problem always has been there. We just are catching it more and hearing about it more. We also, as an industry, are more concerned about our credibility and are willing to wear our mistakes on our sleeves."
- **Smith, Spokesman-Review**: "I 'think it's a growing problem with numerous factors to blame. Staffs are smaller. Pressure never more intense. And basic ethics training simply is not happening at the university level and in most newsrooms. J-School deans report that more and more students, including graduate students, don't understand that lifting material from the Internet is plagiarism. Students are being taught research techniques in K-12 that confuse the line between research and plagiarizing. The instructional burden" has fallen to the newsrooms and we need to do a better job in response."
- **Tom Brooker, editor, Wisconsin's Green Bay News-Chronicle**: "I think there are actually fewer instances, but our ethical standards are much higher, our mistakes much more publicized, the punishment meted out much more severe and, thus, also much more publicized."

Do you think editors, in general, are skeptical enough?
- **Denton Tampa Tribune**: "Apparently not all."
- **Smith, Spokesman-Review**: "Yes, Skeptical to the point of harmful cynicism. But relentless skepticism is impossible and unhealthy.... Still, we have to develop generations of front-line leaders who'd rather be aggressive editors who ask tough questions than well-liked editors who blindly support their reporters."
- **Karen Hunter, reader representative, Hartford Courant**: "I think the Courant's editors trust that their reporters are ethical and hardworking until something makes them think otherwise."
- **John Burr, assistant managing editor, Jacksonville's Florida Times-Union**: "No. That's one of the dangers of down-sized newsrooms—people tend to get in a production mode just to get the paper out, and have less time to step back and question stories and sources."
- **Connelly, Sarasota Herald Tribune**: "[O]ne of the great lessons of the past year is that even when an editor trusts a reporter, the editor must never stop saying, 'Prove it.'"
- **Hutton, Detroit Free Press**: "I think we all want to believe in our colleagues, and it's hard to imagine someone in your own newsroom violating such a fundamental rule. So maybe loyalty and familiarity get in the way of skepticism sometimes. But I wouldn't want to create an environment that cast a shadow over the entire newsroom and treated everyone with suspicion."

—Compiled by Jill Rosen

fortable bringing editors suspicions that something is off-kilter about another staff member's work—they should feel obligated. "We depend on our staff to alert us to unethical behavior," he says.

At the Sun, McIntyre says he's never taken an issue to a ranking editor without getting a serious hearing. "A paper that doesn't take copy editors' questions seriously," he says, "is like checking out of a hospital against medical advice.... You might be OK."

McIntyre says the Sun has caught sneaky reporters more than once because of calls from outside the paper. Once, he says, a veteran reporter was fired after inventing a bereaved person for an obituary. "It was ingenious," McIntyre says.

"Who is going to call up to complain about a favorable quote in an obituary?" But a family member of a deceased surgeon did—she wanted to get in touch with this stranger who had all the nice things to say. Alas, not possible.

Once the editor of another paper called the Sun to say that although one of the Sun's suburban reporters quoted an official, that paper's reporter was present when the official made the remark and the Sun's wasn't. Questioned about it, the Sun reporter claimed he caught the official at home later. When the Sun asked said official, he said there had been no call.

Some papers aren't just listening harder for complaints, they're actively encouraging readers to bring them on.

The Boston Globe invites—and actually uses the word "welcomes"—readers to comment by fax, by e-mail or by ordinary phone call. They've got special numbers and addresses for these comment outlets and someone monitors them daily, looking for concerns that might lead to corrections. The box listing the numbers is on Page 2A, which is also home to the corrections themselves.

The move to the prominent 2A location was yet another action taken in the aftermath of Jayson Blair. No New York Times readers had called in, even when Blair, writing about places he never visited, got scenes and events completely wrong. Baron says the relocated box has sparked a "sharp increase" in public response. "We get a lot of calls—some readers seem to have an avocation of letting us know mistakes," he says. "We've been alerted to many errors in the paper that we wouldn't have known about previously."

The Globe then monitors the corrections, keeping an eye on the nature of the errors and who's making them. In April, the paper began auditing reporters making more than their share of mistakes. An audit means that sources in those reporters' stories will be asked, after publication, to verify information.

That might not be the most popular move in the newsroom, but Baron really doesn't care. "I don't think reporters involved will be that pleased, but that's too bad," he says. "The accuracy of the newspaper is critical to the credibility of the paper."

For years, newspapers wanting to toughen their corrections policies turned to the Chicago Tribune as a model. They still do. In the '90s, the Tribune was among the first to realize that a correction isn't necessarily an isolated mistake—it could be part of a pattern, so a paper that tracked and analyzed its corrections could illuminate systemic deficiencies. And, by requiring that reporters fill out a form after each error, the unspoken message is that accuracy and credibility are paramount, says Don Wycliff, the Tribune's public editor. "To be sure, if there is a perpetual, helpless, relentless maker of errors, that person will be gotten rid of," Wycliff explains. "But the main point of this is that it allows us to identify where errors are being made and what circumstances lead to them."

At the Charlotte Observer, where the motto is ignoring a complaint is worse than admitting an error, management also requires reporters to fill out a form each time they incur a correction, forcing them to think about how they could have prevented the mistake. Like the Globe, the Observer moved its corrections box to 2A and then had a special staff meeting to explain why—a grab at the elusive brass ring of credibility.

"The pain at the New York Times and USA Today have given us all reasons to talk about [these problems] more and think about it more," Carpenter says. "It's a constant conversation that has gotten louder."

Pamela Luecke was editor of Kentucky's Lexington Herald-Leader in 1998 when the Cincinnati Enquirer ran a front-page correction that essentially retracted its damning investigation of Chiquita Brands International, not because the story was wrong but because the reporter used unethical means to get his information (see "Bitter Fruit," September 1998). "It really shook me to the core," says Luecke, now a business journalism professor at Virginia's Washington and Lee University. "It made me realize you could not assume every reporter working for you shared your values."

She went to work on a statement of ethics, not another dusty irrelevancy for the back shelf, but something in black and white that her staff would discuss, know and use. "It's something you need to infuse through the culture," she says. "What is our expectation? What is our standard? These are not simple conversations. But it creates a sense of shared values in a newsroom. And it sends a message that newsroom leaders are committed to a high standard."

After reading the New York Times' report last year about how it was deceived and USA Today's version this spring, the Sun's McIntyre understands that the right message must emanate from the corner office, then settle into the minds and practices of everyone from the investigative gurus to the editorial assistants. "If the top-level editors aren't serious about this and don't push for accuracy and integrity," he says, "there's not much a copy editor can do."

But even as editors realize that something of a crackdown is needed, they dread even using a word like that. Karen Brown Dunlap, president of the Poynter Institute, as strong a believer in the need for more robust editing as anyone, cringes a bit when she hears colleagues talking about "prosecutorial editing."

"Prosecution comes to bear when there is a crime, and I don't think an editor should proceed as if a crime has been committed," Dunlap says. She also doesn't like the image of the nation's editors as a panicky SWAT team, searching for the bomb as it ticks away at their pa-

per. "I don't buy that," she says, adding that though some newsrooms are "disasters waiting to happen," having a newsroom philosophy of "which one is the nut?" will only make things worse.

"You have to trust your folks and you have to know some will abuse that trust."

Baron, who will put mistake-ridden reporters on an audit track and encourage colleagues to reveal errant peers, tightens the reins very aware that going too far is possible. "We're doing what we need without turning our reporters into suspects, which I don't want to do."

While editors puzzle through this problem, weighing their possible courses of action, the one ignored option is doing nothing. Most editors agree that the ethics crisis is real. Even if there isn't another Jayson Blair or Jack Kelley, odds seem huge that less spectacular perpetrators are out there with the ability to do a paper's credibility great harm.

It's now a matter of figuring out how much good cop to mix with the bad, thinking about how people operate in a given newsroom, and maybe turning some conventional wisdom upside-down. Like, is trusting reporters really the soul of journalism? Maybe skeptical editors should be the soul.

At a burned paper in Fort Worth, Reader Advocate David House is willing to do anything to keep it from happening again. He talks about "avoiding" and he talks about "fixing." Whatever it takes. Magic markers and movie tickets.

And as for trusting reporters, House puts it like this: "You have to trust your folks and you have to know some will abuse that trust."

These days, when he considers the Star-Telegram's newsroom, House sees a "splendid" staff. He says he'd be "shocked" if there was another Khalil Abdullah lurking in the mix. "I just don't believe it would happen," he says. But then, a beat later, he adds with a little ironic chuckle, "But see? There's that vulnerability coming out."

IMPORTANT IF TRUE

**Despite periodic spasms of concern over discredited
stories relying on unnamed sources, the practice
of granting anonymity has survived and thrived.
Will the Jayson Blair episode
reverse the momentum?**

By Jill Rosen

It was that Sunday morning in May when the New York Times landed at people's doorsteps with a bit more of a resounding thud than usual. Rocky Mountain News Editor John Temple was at his Denver home and, like many in the news business, mesmerized by that edition with its promised account of what exactly happened with story thief and fabricator Jayson Blair, an infamous and overplayed tale now, but then, still a jaw-dropping stunner with a back story worth getting up early on a Sunday to read about.

With appalled fascination, Temple delved into the entire saga that morning, the inventing of details from locations Blair never visited, the outrageous lying, the seeming obliviousness of management. At times the editor said to himself, "I can't believe what I'm reading." But Temple hadn't even gotten to the part about how Blair, already an employee with something of a Times rap sheet for disturbing corrections and erratic behavior, contrived anonymous sources for reports about the D.C.-area sniper. Blair's editors hadn't asked for the identity of those sources even though the story was controversial—they didn't even ask after officials involved with the case questioned the accuracy of Blair's information.

The next day, his shock still fresh, Temple dialed the New York Times when he got to work. He wanted to get Editor Howell Raines on the line, hoping the top Timesman could explain how the nation's most esteemed daily could play so loose with sourcing. "I said, 'I'm John Temple, editor of the Rocky Mountain News and a subscriber. I want to talk with Howell Raines about anonymous sources. I'm concerned as a subscriber and for what I put in my paper.'" Not surprisingly, Raines, who shortly thereafter resigned, was a tad busy that day and didn't get on the phone. But a Times spokeswoman did, telling Temple that the paper's anonymous source policy was essentially that it didn't have one. In other words, Times editors and reporters don't necessarily discuss anonymous quotes before they're published, a well-worn practice at many smaller papers.

As someone who makes his own staff jump through hoops before allowing a nameless quote into print, the Times' anything-goes approach didn't sit well with Temple. Right then he decided that if the Times couldn't guarantee that anonymous material was at least as checked and double-checked as his own reporters', then anonymous Times stories weren't automatically going into his paper Already the Rocky has passed on Times copy that, pre-Blair, would have run.

"Blair's a fraud. I'm not worried that reporters at the New York Times in general are frauds," Temple explains. "To me the discussion is central not because people would act out of malice—not like Jayson Blair—but because newspapers are better when they're discussed, weighed and critiqued."

Along with the thousand and one other Blairisms editors have since lost sleep over, the young reporter's abuse of anonymous sourcing, though arguably not the worst of his sins, left certain journalists nervous about their own papers' standards. The could-it-happen-here factor. So much talking has begun—policy talk in newsrooms, ombudsman talk aimed at reassuring dubious readers... even some talk about cracking down on anonymity.

Though plenty of people have long felt anonymity is overused, if not abused, it's only become a more popular reporting tool through the years. Some think that if anything can temper the trend, Jayson Blair's shenanigans might be it.

Trusting information from dubious sources has always given editors pause. When Moses tumbled down the mountain with his breaking Ten Commandments news, no doubt when he reached the bottom, some editor probably wanted a bit more proof that the information actually came from God. Unquestionably, it was Watergate that gave anonymity such allure. After the Washington Post's Bob Woodward and Carl Bernstein toppled the Nixon Administration in the 1970s with tips from the mysterious "Deep Throat," it was not only acceptable to drop secret sources into copy, it was almost desirable—every Lois Lane at every Daily Bugle wanted the cachet that comes with the feeling that a source is dispensing critical information only to them.

But bit by bit, incident by incident, reality began tarnishing the anonymity facade. There was fabricator Janet Cooke in 1980, who, by using unnamed sources as the foundation for a made-up Pulitzer winner about an 8-year-old heroin addict, singlehandedly deflated the anonymity legend her paper had built. Anonymity, for a while, seemed to conjure risk rather than glow. But by 1994, journalists squawked anew over O.J. coverage (see "Judgment Calls," September 1994). The "trial of the century" hit a roadblock after a TV reporter broadcast a report from an anonymous source that blood on a sock in the former football star's Brentwood mansion matched that of his murdered ex-wife. Judge Lance Ito threatened to ban TV cameras and called the reporting "outrageous" and "irresponsible." The station later admitted parts of the story were wrong.

After O.J., not unlike after Cooke, journalism declaration-makers heralded the end of an era for unnamed sources (see "Anonymous Sources," December 1994). Not so. Fast-forward to the torrential Bill Clinton-Monica Lewinsky newsstorm (see package of stories, March 1998). Anonymous was the Everysource in that affair, and the hand-wringing resumed in earnest. In the thick of things, the Committee of Concerned Journalists examined more than 2,000 statements reported by TV, newspapers, magazines and the Associated Press as well as some tabloid publications and shows. The group found that six in 10 anonymous utterings were characterized about as vaguely as possible, and it basically concluded that this sort of lax reporting was bad for business. Yet still no end to the era. More fast-forwarding brings us here, to Jayson Blair, wondering how things got this bad. Or, how bad they are.

Because for all the times anonymity has backfired, there have been countless instances of its benefits. It's revealed truths of wrongdoings that almost certainly would

WHO SAID THAT?

For an industry supposedly trying to cut back on anonymous sources, we've apparently got a ways to go. Not that it's scientific, but a Lexis-Nexis check of news outlets in the first 10 days of June shows nebulous "officials" are getting more than a little ink. Here's how many times certain anonymity catchphrases appeared during that period as well as a few examples of how reporters categorized their nameless sources:

Phrase: *"Who requested anonymity"*
Appearances: 48
Who said it: "High level staffers" (Milwaukee Journal Sentinel); "A hospital worker" (Boston Globe); "Another council member" (Seattle Post-Intelligencer).

Phrase: *"Who declined to give his name"*
Appearances: 32
Who said it: "One delivery man" (Washington Post); "a Carpet Mart shopper" (Pennsylvania's Harrisburg Patriot-News); "a jeweler out on the street" (New York Times).

Phrase: *"Sources close to"*
Appearances: 155
Who said it: Sources close to the ACC expansion (Charlotte Observer); a source close to Janeane Garofalo (New York Post).

Phrase: *"Sources say"*
Appearances: 140
Who said it: "A diplomatic source" (Christian Science Monitor); an "inside" source at Ricky Martin's record label who's also referred to as "our snitch" (New York's Daily News); "sources close to the family" (Washington's Tacoma News Tribune).

never have come out had a nervous whistleblower not been offered the security and sanctity that anonymity provides.

Love them or hate them, anymore anonymous quotes are standard—in D.C., any fashionable source wouldn't be caught dead without them. Much of the time many officials simply won't speak on the record. Tom Rosenstiel, director of the Project for Excellence in Journalism, says we're at the point where the media's anonymity standards have slipped and sources are taking advantage. "In the last 25 years, anonymous sources have gone from a tool journalists used to coax reluctant sources into speaking to a condition that those who would manipulate the news media are using," Rosenstiel says, adding that you can tell things are out of hand when you call spokespeople to speak and even *they* decline. "When paid mouthpieces are granted anonymity, that's ridiculous."

What gives Blair's offense extra sting is that it comes at a time when journalists are realizing that readers, even on good days, are taking their reportage with a few grains of salt. An Associated Press Managing Editors survey after

Jayson Blair found that many readers, even if they spotted an error, wouldn't call it in because they think journalists don't care. Worse yet, some of them think that the mistakes are done purposefully for embellishment.

Society of Professional Journalists President Robert Leger thinks anonymous sources contribute to the industry's low credibility figures. "Jayson Blair," he says, "only gives readers more ammunition. People are going to say, 'If they blew it on that one, why should we believe this?'"

It didn't take long after John Temple's declared crackdown on New York Times wire copy for the new law of the land to come into play. It happened the very next day. The Times sent out a piece about the United States military announcing it would shoot Iraqi looters on sight. The reporting included nary a name, citing only "officials." And though it had run above the fold in the Times, Temple said no way it was going in the Rocky. The stuff wasn't being reported elsewhere and, Temple decided, "If they shoot a looter, I figured we'd know about it soon enough." The following day many other media outlets quoted officials *with* names denying the Times report.

Since Rocky Mountain News Editor John Temple found out that New York Times editors don't always discuss the identity of anonymous sources with reporters, he has his editors carefully weigh Times pieces with unnamed sources before running them.

Since then, Temple guesses he's said no thanks to at least two other Times stories with iffy sourcing. He's careful to point out that his stand has nothing to do with contempt for the Times and everything to do with maintaining the highest standards for his paper and protecting its integrity. "I stress that I'm not a New York Times basher," Temple says. "I have tremendous respect for that paper, but there still is an issue, no matter how good a [reporter] is, when you're dealing with anonymous sources."

At the Syracuse Post-Standard, Executive Editor Mike Connor isn't certain that using anonymous sources makes readers doubt the news. But, he figures, if his own reading habits are any indication, it certainly doesn't help—after Jayson Blair to be sure. "Blair makes it really clear," he says. "You can see the value of rigorous and high standards."

Connor likes the idea of being able to give his readers such conclusive information in a story, such "scientific proof," that the accuracy is beyond doubt. "Ideally newspaper reporting is built on a solid foundation of fact that any reader could go out and gather the same facts," he says. "When you have unnamed sources, that's impossible."

Which is why, Connor, too, is now keeping a closer eye on wire copy with unnamed sources. He's asked his news and sports desks to look "very carefully" at wire offerings before using them—though there's so much anonymity in major national stories these days, playing hardball to keep his pages free of it isn't easy. "If we hold [wire] to the same standards [as local], would we still have an A-section? Would we still have a Washington page?" he half-jokes.

So now if, say, a Washington Post story quotes a "top military official," Post-Standard editors will decide whether to run the story, and if so, how. They could cut the nameless quote or, they could leave it and try to explain to readers that the stuff in the story can't be vouched for, but "it's news we can't ignore." Not long ago someone showed Connor a Civil War-era edition of his paper that had a battlefield gossip section called "Important if true." Maybe, he jokes, they can revive that section to house the anonymous wire copy.

The Times has recently gotten complaints and questions from its wire clients about the paper's use of anonymous sources. According to a Times spokesman, sourcing is one of the topics in-house investigators are looking into in the aftermath of Jayson Blair. After the committee makes recommendations, "[W]e will be able to discuss any changes in our sourcing policy," Toby Usnik, the Times' director of public relations, wrote in an e-mail to AJR. "That said, in light of recent events, it would be accurate to say that there has been increased vigilance by our newsroom staff with regard to sourcing."

In a May column headlined "According to Someone," Washington Post Ombudsman Michael Getler said that since the New York Times' problems surfaced, readers have sought him out, worried about the Post's credibility—and he's worried, too. He wrote that people's skepticism "is being reinforced by a lack of confidence caused by the extent of anonymous sourcing."

Getler explained that the Post has sourcing rules and that, sometimes, the need for sensitive information trumps that for names. Still, he continued, the Post asks reporters to try everything to get material on the record before going off of it, and if they must, then they should tell readers why and try to describe who spoke and their motivations to do so. But, Getler concluded, "My impression is that these rules have largely fallen by the wayside, along with demands by editors to know sources' identities, because the use of unnamed sources has become so routine. The administration wins simply by refusing to allow the use of any attribution other than 'senior administration officials.'"

Deborah Howell, who runs Newhouse News Service's Washington bureau, acknowledges that anonymous quoting runs amok in D.C. "They're very overused in Washington," she says. "It's gotten to be such a culture that everybody expects to be anonymous." That said, she works hard to make sure that her people don't hang with the pack. Though the major papers say allowing anonymity is the only way to stay competitive, Howell's reporters avoid the device, even in the thick of D.C., because they generally don't cover breaking news—they're concentrating on enterprise and analysis.

Howell's approach is "You can hide a source from readers, but you don't hide a source from me." When the issue does come up, as it does from time to time, she's got rigid rules. "We do not let them negatively slam someone in a story. I don't like them high up in a story. I don't like a whole story based on anonymous sources," she says, ticking off a few of her guidelines.

Guidelines are also on the mind of Jack McElroy, editor of Knoxville's News-Sentinel. At the head of the Tennessee paper for about a year and a half, McElroy decided after Blair that now was the time to put the News-Sentinel's anonymity rules in writing—basically, he says, the paper had a "strict" policy, but it was word of mouth and some "people knew the rules, but some might not have." "What I wanted to do," he says, "was shut the barn door before the horse got out."

Mike King, the Atlanta Journal-Constitution's public editor, says that in the current climate of public distrust, "There's an assumption…that we [use anonymous sources] all the time and it's not a big deal. But we don't and it is a big deal."

McElroy doesn't believe the Jayson Blair case indicates a new wave of sourcing trouble or even that the debacle will substantially diminish the New York Times' credibility. However, he does think it's oh-so-indicative of major gaps in the industry's standards, particularly when it comes to the media outlets dispensing the nation's wire copy. "I think people realize that bad or rogue people can arise in any industry," he says. "Whether this points out a problem in quality control of the New York Times, that's the larger issue."

Though McElroy strives to bolster his paper's sourcing etiquette, he hasn't found a good way to address the wire issue. Not that he's unaware of the risks. Handling wire copy, he says, is "a little bit of a crack in the dike."

"You can set standards for local, but you get wire copy and you just have no idea," he laments. "You have to hope they have good judgment and are adhering to high standards."

In the immediate aftermath of Blair, editors by the dozen felt obligated to offer their readers some sort of assurance, some sort of promise that despite the disturbing New York Times tales they heard about on TV, read about in national magazines and laughed about with David Letterman, the news business wasn't all bad—in fact, they desperately wanted to note, they were doing their best. Most often these pleas for understanding and respect manifested themselves in columns to readers. And often these columns pointedly mentioned anonymous sources.

GOING NAMELESS

For almost every paper, there's a different policy on anonymity. Here are how some daily newspapers approach a few key aspects of many anonymity policies:

1. *How they boil it down.*
   San Francisco Chronicle: The use of confidential sources should be the exception rather than the routine.
   The Washington Post is pledged to disclose the source of all information when at all possible.
   Tampa Tribune: It's sometimes necessary, but seldom a good idea, to quote an unnamed source.
   San Antonio Express-News pledges to make every effort to tell our readers the source of all information we publish.
   Norfolk's Virginian-Pilot: Anonymous sources should be rare and reasoned.

2. *Requires or recommends editor/reporter discussions before printing a quote from an unnamed source.*
   Arizona Republic
   San Jose Mercury News
   Wilmington, Delaware's News-Journal
   Champaign, Illinois' News-Gazette
   Kansas City Star
   Nebraska's Lincoln Journal Star
   Salem, Oregon's Statesman Journal
   Dallas Morning News
   San Antonio Express-News
   Richmond Times-Dispatch

3. *Includes an anonymity "test," a set of questions that must be answered before the paper uses an anonymous quote.*
   Orlando Sentinel
   San Francisco Chronicle
   Bergen County, New Jersey's Record
   Salem, Oregon's Statesman Journal
   Norfolk's Virginian-Pilot
   Virginia's Roanoke Times

4. *Specifically alludes to the concept of "credibility."*
   Orlando Sentinel
   San Francisco Chronicle
   Newport News, Virginia's Daily Press ("A newspaper risks its credibility each time it bases a news report on the word of unnamed sources.")
   Kansas City Star
   Nebraska's Lincoln Journal Star
   Bergen County, New Jersey's Record
   Virginia's Roanoke Times
   Tampa Tribune ("When we do so, we in effect tell readers: 'Trust us.' The more we ask for trust, the less we seem to deserve it.")

Adapted from an American Society of Newspaper Editors compendium of news organizations' policies on anonymous sources

Under headlines like "Building, maintaining readers' trust is vital" and "Unnamed sources not part of our routine," many editors publicly aired what's usually much more private soul-searching. Mike King, the Atlanta Journal-Constitution's public editor, told readers of an editor/reporter heart-to-heart after Blair on ethics and credibility. He described how the staff talked about their error count, when to credit other news organizations, and not only how much they should trust wire stories that rely on nameless sources, but how they should handle anonymity in-house. He wrote: The Blair scandal has "everything to do with how seriously we guard our credibility and police ourselves. The issues it raises are the bedrock of the relationship we have with readers."

That could be a lot of inside baseball for a comics-and-coupons sort of subscriber. But King thinks that because Jayson Blair exposed average Joes to the seamy side of news, showed them a host of appalling ways reporters could trample their trust, readers have a better view of the game than ever. "Jayson Blair has opened up for readers the inside world of editing," King says, adding that after the Blair story broke, calls from concerned readers "increased phenomenally"—and almost two months later had not let up. "The result of Jayson Blair is we have to articulate [our policies] for the public as opposed to just the journalists."

Despite the current climate of distrust—King says, "There's an assumption out there that we [use anonymous sources] all the time and it's not a big deal. But we don't and it is a big deal."—he thinks readers will believe stories with anonymous sources if they are skillfully presented. "It depends on how good we are at being able to explain ourselves," he says. "They think we do it too often. They think we do it too lazily. I think there's some truth to that. But when we fight this ship a little bit, our credibility will come back."

In Cleveland, Plain Dealer Editor Douglas C. Clifton has noticed that since Jayson Blair, even readers who'd never paused to consider ink-stained mainstays like attribution and sourcing are suddenly budding media analysts. "This isn't just an issue in the hothouse journalism press," he says, adding that readers normally skeptical of unnamed sources have less faith in the tactic than ever. It's an extreme case of "everyone's a critic."

Readers, never shy about missing a dig at the media—it's almost as fun as lawyer-bashing—have added New York Times cheap shots to their repertoire. "Like, if you run a New York Times story, they'll say, 'It's not like the New York Times has an unblemished record,' or something like that," Clifton says, describing something that happened to one of his features columnists. A couple days after the Times' Blair mea culpa, the writer did a piece on dignity—how people in menial jobs don't get treated with it. She talked about two cabbies in Washington and didn't name them. The day it ran, she got a dozen nasty e-mails challenging the existence of the cabbies.

ONE PAPER'S POLICY

Here's an example of a newspaper's policy regarding the use of anonymous sources. From the Orlando Sentinel:

The use of anonymous sources should be avoided because it undermines the newspaper's credibility. Those readers who are suspicious of what we have to report have greater reason to distrust information when we can't tell them where we got it. Writers should make every effort to get information on the record—that is, with the source willing to be quoted by name. The use of anonymous sources is considered legitimate in some cases. But they ought to be used sparingly, and not just because someone "asked to remain anonymous." To determine which cases are legitimate, the following four-part test should be applied in each instance:

Is the information being attributed to the anonymous source NECESSARY to the article?

Can the information be had ON THE RECORD from any other source?

Does the anonymous source have a LEGITIMATE REASON for remaining unidentified?

Can we EXPLAIN that reason in the article?

The required responses should be yes, no, yes and yes. We need to explain in the article—unless it is patently obvious from the context—why the source can't be identified.

Whenever possible, use a term other than source to describe people providing us with information. It's too cloak-and-dagger. Partial identification should be included whenever possible; it allows the reporter to circumvent source and lends more credence to the information being reported. For instance, a high level EPA official said, a congressional aide said, a department official said, even persons familiar with the negotiations said are better than the source said or sources said....

No reporter can promise a source absolute confidentiality because at least one editor will need to know the source's identity before the newspaper will publish information provided by an anonymous source. Cases where confidentiality means a reporter's possibly going to jail to protect a source require the prior approval of the managing editor or editor.

"It's a reminder that for artistic reasons, you can elect not to use a name," Clifton says. "But if a reader is going to be suspicious about it, maybe we really ought not to."

Clifton says that immediately after Blair, the newsroom had a leadership meeting, "asking ourselves if something like that could happen here," and the idea of tightening the anonymity policy came up. As it stands, at the very least, a reporter who wants to use a quote without a name must tell his editor who said it. "The Times took it as a matter of policy that you don't ask—that really encouraged corner-cutting and slovenliness," Clifton says. "That was a shocker."

But Clifton has no plans to transform his newsroom policy or to fortify the paper's gates against errant wire copy. "I don't believe [Blair] represents the norm of journalism any more than the behavior of the Enron executives represented the practices of corporations." Neither does Mark Seibel, managing editor/news at Clifton's former paper, the Miami Herald. Seibel thinks journalism shouldn't be getting into a sweat over sourcing. "You can think about attribution and think about anonymous sources—it's easy to get all caught up in Jayson Blair, a horrifying incident," he says. "But let us not forget we have committed inaccuracies in much broader kinds of stories—are we thinking about that?"

Seibel, who in September becomes managing editor/international at Knight Ridder's Washington bureau, theorizes that if we did away with all unnamed sources, that would be one way to deal with Blair-esque risks. "But we quote lots of named sources and never question what they say to us," he counters. "You can't get rid of anonymous sources to solve your problem. Just because someone said something doesn't mean it's true."

Just the same, Seibel, like lots of newsroom managers, took the opportunity to send his staff a reminder of the Herald's anonymous sources policy. Across the state in Sarasota, staff at the Herald-Tribune got a similar e-mail refresher. However, unlike Seibel, Diane Tennant, Sarasota's managing editor, sees danger in anonymity, at the very least, the danger of losing credibility with readers.

"This is something important for newsrooms and journalists to be discussing," she says. "Readers already suspect papers of making things up and being sensational and of cutting corners, and so it's our job to reinforce to our readers [what we do], making our processes transparent." In the name of transparency, Herald-Tribune Executive Editor Janet Weaver's post-Blair column explained that because of her paper's strict sourcing policy, some of Blair's sniper stories didn't make it past the wire editor. "One of my first editors told me that if you can't know information on the record... it is not worth knowing," Weaver wrote to readers. "I still believe that. Showing readers where we get our information is an important part of preserving our credibility."

Mike King at the Atlanta Journal-Constitution senses that in the wake of perhaps the industry's classic embar-

rassment, things just might be looking up. Anonymity abuse is out of the closet and hence, he says, "This will chill us a little on that. It's a price we ought to be able to pay for overusing these things."

Still, he knows there's only so much he and the editors who sit near him can do. So they create the best set of sourcing rules in the country—any reporter hell-bent on cheating could still dodge them. So they police their local reporters to the nth degree—there's still the wire copy that they'll never be able to stand behind yet can't do without. As Rosenstiel of the Project for Excellence in Journalism says, "the norms of journalism are set at the top." King must wait for a move, then, from the top.

He can't stop D.C.'s elite from reporting anonymous whispers. He can't force the New York Times to change its policies. "That's going to have to be dealt with on a more cultural level," King says. "We can choose or not choose to run things from wire sources." And though on the surface all those options sound great, in reality, in the heat of deadline, there might not be so much choice—and King knows that, too. "It's tough for a national editor to get a story from the Times at 9 p.m. and to call New York and say we need to get some information," he says. But they're going to try.

"The reality," says Seibel, "is that the New York Times might get things wrong. While we're sitting here selecting a New York Times story for page one as the end all and be all, we should remember it's not always right—even the best can be wrong.... We should all be aware of that and make our own judgments."

"All of us are going through this right now," King says. "Every major paper in the country is examining this.... It's just gonna be a new day for American newspapers."

So by scaring editors silly, maybe Jayson Blair scared them straight. "That was a frightening experience what happened, to editors around the country," King says. "The legacy here could be a good one for the paper, even though [Blair] doesn't deserve that legacy."

Assistant Managing Editor Jill Rosen wrote about the Jayson Blair affair in AJR's June/July issue.

From the *American Journalism Review*, August/September 2003, pp. 46–51. © 2003 by the Philip Merrill College of Journalism at the University of Maryland, College Park, MD 20742-7111. Reprinted by permission.

Who Knows Jack?

For years USA Today star Jack Kelley filed amazingly vivid reports from virtually every major international scene. And for just as long, doubts simmered around his work. But to many who thought they knew him, Kelley seemed above such questions, the last person they'd suspect in a lie.

By Jill Rosen

Editor's Note: Since this article was written, USA Today revealed at AJR's deadline that Jack Kelley fabricated major stories and plagiarized at least two dozen times. The paper said Kelley's "journalistic sins were sweeping and substantial." This story demonstrates the doubts that surrounded the reporter for years, and the depth of loyalty he inspired in some colleagues that possibly allowed his acts to go uncovered.

The phone is ringing too early in the morning. Reporter Matthew Fisher, who had been sleeping, answers, annoyed and ready to give whoever it is what for. But it's his friend Jack Kelley, out of breath and practically shouting into the receiver, "They're going to kill me!" They being the Chechen mafia.

Kelley was running from them through the streets of Moscow. He'd made it to a pay phone. He needed Fisher to call Kelley's editor at USA Today, tell her that he was in trouble. She had to get the U.S. Embassy to open its gates so that he could run in. If he had to stand at the locked gates, Kelley said, he'd be dead.

Fisher knew Kelley had been working on a story about an assumed mafia hit on an American businessman. The two had just talked about it over lunch at a Moscow diner. In fact, the day after that lunch, Kelley told Fisher that "he'd been shown" photos of the two of them eating and now the mafia men were trying to figure out who Fisher was. They beat him up in the hotel elevator, Kelley told Fisher. He feared for his life.

And now the call. Fisher got ahold of Kelley's editor. Kelley made it to the embassy and was escorted safely back to the United States. It all worked out. But to Fisher, it didn't all add up.

"I'll tell you, I've lived in Russia," says Fisher, who's been reporting overseas for 20 years and now is based in Moscow for the Canadian CanWest News Services. "If they want someone dead in Russia, they're dead. It's their country, they don't fuck around. Jack was staying at their hotel.

"That to me doesn't have the ring of truth."

The ring of truth and Jack Kelley. To some, those concepts are intertwined, exchangeable, a given. Others, however, wonder just how many times the one has abandoned the other. Especially after Kelley, a 21-year USA Today veteran, with the paper since its very first issue, lied to editors during an investigation last year into the veracity of his work. He had one of his former translators pose as someone who could vouch for a story, admitting it only after editors figured out the scam. Given the choice between being fired and resigning, Kelley quit USA Today in January.

As the most prominent foreign correspondent for the nation's largest newspaper, Kelley filed hundreds of stories from all over the globe. For about the last decade, he had a hand in nearly every major international news event, hitting A1 constantly with his trademark vivid accounts of violence and strife.

He was newspaper legend. With the interviews no one else could match, the hair-raising tales from the front, the marvelous eyewitness accounts. And now, with the lie. And plagiarism claims. And a power committee examining every last thing he ever wrote because none of it, anymore, is a given.

Kelley implores that his lie was a one-time deal, a mistake made under pressure that has nothing to do with his stories, all of which he stands firmly behind. Reporting the truth, he says over and over and over again, is his passion. And, he adds, those who know him know that's the case. But the thing is, who really knows him?

Some know him as a fresh-faced kid, eager, naïve and enthusiastic, willing to do anything to make his mark at the fledgling newspaper where he started on the ground floor. Others know a swashbuckling foreign correspondent with an almost cinematic blend of fearlessness and sensitivity—he'll dodge bullets and sidestep landmines, then, somehow, find the words or the tone to let people know they can trust him with their secrets.

But quite a few others, particularly these days, only know that they doubt the whole package. They see a reporter who's just too damn lucky. And one who's clearly not above a lie. "Jack is a complex individual," says Fisher, just one of Kelley's longtime colleagues struggling to figure out what is knowable.

"The people who knew me and knew my work and trusted me," Kelley says, "they knew then as they do now that I've never fabricated or plagiarized a story.... People who know me know I didn't do this."

So, who really knows Jack?

Jack Kelley is waiting in a nearly empty Panera Bread restaurant out behind a suburban shopping plaza in Maryland. It's February, mid-morning, and the former foreign correspondent has the place to himself, aside from some moms and coffee-sipping retirees. Exactly a year ago his marquee byline assumed its expected front-page position over a story about terrorism. Fresh from a trip to the border of Jordan and Iraq, the globetrotting Kelley was about to head back to the region to document the impending war. From mayhem to muffin shop.

Kelley settles into a booth near the back. Pale and gaunt, he looks nothing like the vibrant head shot that's been running with all the scandal stories. He's unassuming almost to the point of apologetic—sorry to have to meet all the way out here, trying to pay for the coffees. He's hoping that this talk will somehow lead to his vindication. On the table in front of him he places a briefcase full of proof.

In a subdued and earnest voice, he starts at the beginning, telling the synopsized story of his life, the same one that he seems to tell anyone who's writing something about him. There's the part about how he knew, even at age 8, that he wanted to be a reporter; how he started a neighborhood newspaper to investigate such scoops as what Mrs. So-and-So was planting or why the guy on his corner was taking his dog to the vet. This part of the story sometimes comes with a vignette about how his young self broke news about a neighbor having an affair with the widow down the street, but he's stopped telling that part—the alleged offender still lives in the region.

Continuing, there's the writing for the PTA newsletter, editing his high school paper, attending college at the University of Maryland where he reported like crazy for the campus paper, the Diamondback. When his journalism professor required 18 published stories to get an A, he left 18 in the dust.

Though Kelley is 43 now and it's been more than 20 years since college, that teacher with the 18-things-for-an-A hasn't forgotten one of her favorite overachievers. "I remember his first assignment—an obituary," says Maurine Beasley, who still teaches at Maryland. "He screwed it up. I gave him a D. After class he came up to me and said he wanted to do it again. He said, 'Dr. Beasley, I just don't make Ds.' "

Barbara Hines, assistant dean of the journalism school when Kelley was a student, clearly recalls the young Kelley as tireless, passionate and self-disciplined. "He had the highest standards that he set for himself," says Hines, who's now a journalism professor at Howard University.

It was Hines who encouraged Kelley to apply to USA Today. And she might be the reason he got the job, even after an apparently flat initial interview. After that session, "He came back to see me, and he looked crestfallen," she says. "I asked how it went and he said, 'They told me I don't have enough experience.' And I said, 'And you accepted that?' He just looked at me. Then he turned and walked out of my office. And he went back there."

Kelley replays on autopilot his early USA Today days like he does his childhood. After his start in July 1982 as a news assistant, there was much photocopying, occasional pantyhose-buying—all kinds of minutiae he had to attend to before he could get to any actual reporting. So he'd stay late and come in on weekends to try to make it happen. He says he felt honored to be there, amid the buzz and optimism of starting something from scratch that could be great.

He got his name into the first issue. And four years later he was officially a staff reporter, establishing himself and earning his editors' trust on big stories like the explosion of the Challenger space shuttle and the transgressions of evangelist Jim Bakker.

Steve Davis, now a journalism professor at Syracuse University, edited some of Kelley's first stories. Kelley's work ethic blew him away. All reporters work hard, he says, "but not as hard as Jack."

"He produced stories on time, he worked like a dog, he never let me down," Davis says. "I saw in Jack something I didn't see in very many reporters—he was just totally committed to the story."

A few editors and reporters suppose that rather than cutting his teeth on national coverage, Kelley should have first covered cops or a city council. If you work a local beat "and you misspell someone's name, you're going to hear about it," says former USA Today World Editor Timothy Kenny, who worked with Kelley and is now a media consultant. "The whole value system of how-well-did-you-do becomes evident; you understand it immediately."

But Kelley says starting in the spotlight only made him work harder to be "100 percent accurate." "Rather than hearing from the city council president, you'd hear from sources all across the country," he says, adding about his swift ascent: "I'm so thankful. I've been blessed. I never took it for granted. I tried to approach each and every story like it was my first and last."

"I never saw myself as being ambitious," Kelley says. "I saw myself as being in love with the profession. I'm a people person. I love to get to know different kinds of people." And the people, they love him right back. "He's a Clintonesque figure," his friend Matthew Fisher says. "He's got a fantastic personality like Bill Clinton. People are besotted by him and want to do things to help him."

Except unlike Clinton, Jack Kelley is rated G. He's polite and clean-cut. There's no smoking and certainly no drinking. His ardent churchgoing is no secret, nor was his desire to save himself for marriage. Even the guy's desk was spotless. When he smiles, people half-expect one of those gleaming pings like in a toothpaste commercial.

"He's someone who seemed they would never, never lie. He's like an altar boy. . . . Some of the foreign staff were like cowboys. But Jack was pure as the driven snow."

"He's someone who seemed they would never, never lie," says a USA Today reporter. "He's like an altar boy. He's pure almost to the point of naïveté. I never heard Jack curse, not ever. Some of the foreign staff were

like cowboys. But Jack was pure as the driven snow."

Helen Kennedy, a politics writer for New York's Daily News, was a war-zone newbie whom Kelley took under his wing in Macedonia. His ease in the chaos impressed her, as did his bravery—she recalls him as the type who would traipse through areas that were supposed to be mined.

Some say Kelley believes God is protecting him.

In describing his brush with the Chechen mafia to Christian Reader magazine, Kelley talks of praying as he ran through the streets, and then of an image coming to him "of an apartment building with the number 925 on it and an elderly man next to a door up one flight of stairs." Next thing he knows, there's building 925 and an old man beckoning him in. He told the magazine he waited in an apartment there with a blue sofa and a stocked refrigerator until his pursuers passed. When his interpreter went back the next day to thank the old man, she found the apartment had been vacant a year. Kelley told the magazine: "This was just one of many times God has spared me."

Tony Mauro, a former USA Today reporter who now covers the U.S. Supreme Court for Legal Times, remembers that when he'd bring his daughter to work, Kelley was the one staffer who'd go out of his way to fuss over her. "Just being with him in the office, or walking with him on the street, you could see he was the kind of guy people would just walk up to and talk to," Mauro says. "What you could perceive of him, it matched how he was then able to get these amazing stories."

Says reporter Jim Cox: "Jack knew the janitors by name and the ladies who pour the coffee by name...and all their kids by name."

Cox, who's traveled on assignment with Kelley more than any other USA Today reporter, to places including Israel, Kuwait and Hong Kong, has witnessed his friend getting some of his famous gets. In Ku-

wait, Cox remembers coming back to the hotel room he and Kelley shared and finding a half-dozen Filipino maids there, many of them crying, telling Kelley about being raped. That resulted in Kelley's attention-getting report about the mistreatment of foreign housekeepers in Kuwait.

"He had an incredible rapport with people, especially people who were somehow victimized by violence or corruption or who happened to be very poor," Cox says. "Maybe it was his body language or the tone of his voice or what he actually says, but people tend to be very open in his company, even if they'd have dark and horrible experiences that they wouldn't be comfortable talking to their own family members about."

Doug Stanglin, one of Kelley's editors, says that when Kelley travels, he's the kind of reporter who befriends the person behind the hotel desk, the doorman, the taxi driver—the everyday folks. "He'd very quickly plug into the people in a country," Stanglin says.

A frequent knock against Kelley's reporting is skepticism about how he drops into countries where he doesn't speak the language and immediately mines brilliant quotes. Stanglin, who reported overseas for United Press International, Newsweek and U.S. News & World Report, says, "I'm a little put off by these very naïve kinds of charges. Anybody who's spent any time overseas knows if you're a good solid foreign correspondent, you've made contacts—you have a fixer, you have a driver. You can immediately start working when your plane lands."

Former Time magazine correspondent David Aikman agrees, after seeing Kelley get "a remarkable handhold on some very difficult reporting" in Moscow even though he didn't speak Russian. "I have met reporters here and there—just very good reporters—and the fact that they didn't know the local language is not a bar to them getting stories," Aikman says. "I put Jack in that category."

Stanglin remembers Kelley phoning in with news about a skirmish in Kosovo during the lead-up to war there in 1999. "No one else was reporting that," Stanglin says. "Here's Jack, one guy and a phone. And every time something like that happened, the next day or within hours there would be reports about exactly that. It showed me he wasn't sitting in a hotel room in Belgrade making stuff up."

"**Y**ou know what's amazing?" Jack Kelley asks. "I've always sat back and said I've tried to do two things in journalism. One is report stories that no one else could report and develop contacts that no one else thought to develop. I worked around the clock to do that. It's those two things that caused suspicion among those who don't know me."

On top of the table Kelley has arranged a neatly stacked pile of photocopies, mostly of news stories. He reaches for one stapled packet to illustrate his point. The top sheet is a printout of a BBC story headlined "Mystery over 'Musharraf interview.' "

"I got one of the first print interviews" with Pakistan President Pervez Musharraf, Kelley says. "The day the story was published, the Pakistani foreign ministry denied an interview even took place. The BBC wrote a story implying I fabricated the entire thing." But there was an interview, a coup Kelley got thanks to a plugged-in fixer who got him into a Musharraf family gathering, something the foreign ministry didn't even know about. "One of Musharraf's family members took a picture of me with the president," he says, eagerly leafing through the packet to a photocopy of that snapshot. "Musharraf himself even called me on my cell phone" to apologize.

Gregg Jones was reporting out of Pakistan for the *Dallas Morning News* when the Musharraf brouhaha hit and also when Kelley broke an-

other big story that was initially doubted—that U.S. Special Forces had moved into Afghanistan to hunt Osama bin Laden. "It was a frustrating situation in Islamabad," Jones says. "It was just hard to get information as to what was going on. Everyone was scrambling. It was an incredibly competitive atmosphere, and obviously this was a big scoop.

"It's precisely illustrative of the type of aggressive reporting Jack was known for," Jones continues. "Jack was out to break stories. That sort of became his stock-in-trade."

Jones worked out of Kelley and Jim Cox's room in Pakistan a bit that trip because he got to town too late to score his own room. On a later trip, he heard that Kelley was living in the home of his fixer's family, Jones says, still impressed. "The mother just loved him like a son."

"I routinely would pick up the paper and read a Jack Kelly story, and I'd scratch my head and say, 'How did he get that access?' And I don't mean that in a questioning way."

Knight Ridder Moscow Bureau Chief Mark McDonald also worked around Kelley in Pakistan—they even shared some sources "in the various intelligence communities, in ministries and embassies, in the field, even in the most dangerous border areas," McDonald writes in an e-mail. "He sure wasn't a lobbysitter."

Though they'll deny it, Matthew Kalman says, most parachuters—correspondents who drop into a region to report and then leave—are lazy. "They sit in hotel rooms and file the story off CNN. You'd be amazed." The former Jerusalem correspondent for USA Today, who now reports from that region for the *San Francisco Chronicle* and Toronto's *Globe and Mail*, says Kelley used a "fantastic" network of fixers to get into places most parachuters couldn't touch.

Kalman adds: "He has been taken to places here by people I know who would not take me there."

"**I** routinely would pick up the paper and read a Jack Kelley story, and I'd scratch my head and say, 'How did he get that access?' " says reporter Tony Mauro. "And I don't mean that in a questioning way."

But plenty of people do. Questions have simmered around Jack Kelley's reporting for more than a decade. When he got quotes from infamously tight-lipped people, his colleagues doubted them. When he wrote of jaw-dropping scenarios he'd witnessed firsthand, they'd roll their eyes. As one USA Today staffer says, "Pretty much anything Jack came up with, [people] would say, 'Oh yeah? Bullshit.' "

After Kelley's controversial 2001 Special Forces piece, Linda Mathews, USA Today's front-page "cover story" editor, heard the questions herself. "A Gannett reporter called me up and he said, 'Linda, have you ever talked to Special Forces people? I just don't believe Jack was able to interview Special Forces…. It's inconceivable to me that this could happen.' I said I would pass it on to other people, and I did. But within a week or so it was clear Jack was right. Confirmation came from other sources," says Mathews, a former Los Angeles Times foreign correspondent and foreign editor for ABC News. "Does that mean he had personal contact with them? I don't know. It's still an open question in my mind."

Months after the Special Forces story, when Kelley was still reporting from Pakistan, staffers back home he was collaborating with on a piece about the hunt for bin Laden lost confidence in the information he was providing. Reporters told their editor they couldn't trust the anonymous quotes Kelley had sent, so they asked Kelley to name his four sources. They could only confirm that one of four people existed so, a

THE RISE AND FALL OF JACK KELLEY

July 1982 ➤ Jack Kelley is hired as a news assistant at startup USA Today, just after graduating from the University of Maryland.

September 15, 1982 ➤ USA Today launches. Kelley has a story in the first issue.

1986 ➤ Kelley becomes a reporter; the Challenger space shuttle explosion is among his first assignments.

1988 ➤ Kelley joins USA Today founder Allen H. Neuharth on JetCapade, his heralded reporting tour of 32 nations.

November 25, 1992 ➤ A 568-word Kelley story from Berlin describes Germany's hatred of Gypsies. (A significant portion of Kelley's story is similar to parts of a 3,500-word Washington Post piece on Gypsies from earlier that month.)

November 1996 ➤ Kelley writes about an American businessman gunned down, supposedly by the Chechen mafia. Kelley says the mafia wanted to kill him and he literally ran for his life out of town.

May 2, 1997 ➤ Kelley attributes a spokesman's quote to the president of the International Committee of the Red Cross. The misattribution was not corrected.

September 2, 1998 ➤ A 658-word Kelley story from Pakistan describes Darra Adam Khel, a village that exists to sell guns. (A significant portion of Kelley's story is similar to a 1,300-word Washington Post piece that ran July 9, 1998.)

April 26, 1999 ➤ After Kelley returns from a trip to Macedonia, USA Today runs his vivid account of trekking for two-and-a-half days with Kosovo Liberation Army fighters as they searched for Serb forces, at one point ambushing some Serbs in a deadly battle.

July 14, 1999 ➤ Kelley files a 417-word scoop from Belgrade about how he "examined" a notebook that contained a direct order from the Yugoslav army to "cleanse" a Kosovo village.

March 10, 2000 ➤ In a dramatic A1 story from Cuba, Kelley is apparently a witness on a beach as Cubans get onto a boat, trying to make it to Florida. Some of them die in a storm at sea and Kelley gets play-by-play details of their demise from survivors.

August 9, 2001 ➤ Kelley happens to be walking by a Jerusalem pizza shop as a suicide bomber detonates a bomb. His A1 story the following day details how he saw the bomber enter the restaurant and how, later, arms and legs "rained down onto the street."

September 1, 2001 ➤ An A1 Kelley story from the West Bank describes how he observed a group of Jewish settlers as they set out to kill "blood-sucking Arab" taxi passengers. The settlers' wives and children helped as they fired upon a taxi, Kelley wrote.

September 28, 2001 ➤ Kelley breaks news of U.S. Special Forces being inside Afghanistan hunting Osama bin Laden. Controversy flares inside and outside USA Today about the validity of the story. Eventually, other news outlets confirm it.

April 2002 ➤ Kelley is named a finalist for the Pulitzer Prize in beat reporting.

May 2003 ➤ New York Times reporter Jayson Blair resigns after being caught plagiarizing. Later the Times reveals that Blair lied, fabricated and plagiarized in dozens of cases. USA Today editors solicit staffers for concerns about the accuracy of USA Today stories. Just before that happens, someone sends an anonymous letter questioning Kelley's work.

May-June 2003 ➤ The paper begins trying to verify some of Kelley's more controversial stories. A staffer tells a top editor of a complaint at the time about Kelley's 1999 Belgrade story.

September 27, 2003 ➤ Under increasing pressure to find sources to verify the 1999 Belgrade story, Kelley tells investigators that he found a translator who helped him report the piece.

October 22, 2003 ➤ Kelley's last story runs in USA Today. He had only written two others since August.

November 2003 ➤ Kelley hires attorneys, ceases to cooperate with the investigation.

January 6, 2004 ➤ Given the choice between resigning or being fired, Kelley resigns.

January 13, 2004 ➤ USA Today issues a statement detailing how Kelley deceived the newspaper during the internal investigation by having a friend pose as a translator who could validate the 1999 Belgrade story. About a week later, after reports surface alleging Kelley plagiarized two Washington Post stories, USA Today announces a prestigious trio of journalists will lead a review of everything Kelley has written for the paper during his 21-year career there.

March 19, 2004 ➤ The inquiry team reports Kelley faked major stories, lied and plagiarized. It says his "journalistic sins" were "sweeping and substantial."

reporter says, the story ran with just one of Kelley's quotes.

Were the other three people real? Hard to know. That's the way it is when it comes to most complaints about Kelley's reporting. Vague suspicions rather than gotcha, experienced people asking what are the chances that this or that could have happened, especially after that last crazy thing and the one we all couldn't believe the time before that. What are the chances all this happens to one guy? Small, surely. But small isn't nonexistent.

"He always seemed to be in the center of attention, which is theoretically possible but hard to imagine on virtually every big international story," one reporter says. "It's hard to have confidence when so many things happen." Another adds: "You get lucky like that, but not all the time."

Reporters point to how Kelley is always alone when he gets his most dramatic material. A former USA Today reporter says, "When he was in Washington, he seemed incapable of doing routine journalism. Then he'd go abroad, and it was like Clark Kent emerging from the phone booth."

The Kelley stories most notorious among skeptics showcase not only the shocking access Kelley achieved to report them, but the high drama that ensued once he was on the scene.

Matthew Fisher recalls being at the Rogner Hotel in Albania with two tables of journalists just after a Kelley story ran in April 1999 detailing how he trekked for two-and-a-half days through the snowy mountains of Yugoslavia with a group of Kosovo Liberation Army fighters. (See "Suicide Mission," June 1999.) "They were going absolutely berserk," Fisher remembers. "They were shouting, 'How was this possible?' " That Kelley had been allowed along for the mission was stunning enough, but then Kelley's KLA group actually ambushes a convoy of Serbs: Bullets whistle by people's heads, Serbs chase them, mortars and grenades land all around them. Kelley hears bones break, sees shrapnel cut into someone.

Then, in March 2000 Kelley travels to Cuba as the country and the United States brawl over rights to the 6-year-old Elián González, who floated into Florida waters on an inner tube. Kelley apparently gets invited to watch on the beach in predawn as a group of Cubans tries to escape their homeland on a small aluminum boat. The boat sinks in a storm, and Kelley is on the beach days later when the Cuban Coast Guard hauls in the survivors, who vividly tell Kelley how their boat mates perished.

In August 2001 Kelley is walking by a Sbarro pizza shop in Jerusalem at lunchtime with an Israeli official just as a suicide bomber blows it up. Kelley's first-person account tells how he saw the bomber fight his way into the restaurant through the crowds, then of the burst of heat that accompanied the detonation, and how when three men "catapulted" out of the restaurant, their heads "separated from their bodies and roll[ed] down the street."

A month after the Sbarro bomb, just before the September 11 terrorist attacks, Kelley is allowed along as Jewish West Bank settlers, with their wives and children, set out to kill "blood-sucking Arab" taxi passengers. Complaints from a settlers' group that it never happened vanished in the shadow of 9/11.

"He gave them the 'wow' type of copy that everyone wanted," a reporter says of Kelley. "Someone should have questioned why he came up with 'wow' copy all the time…. When something doesn't seem right, it almost never is."

As suspicions about Kelley's work festered at USA Today and elsewhere, his star only rose. He spoke at events on behalf of the paper. The powers that be were telling reporters to be more like Jack, such a go-getter. Some colleagues tended to be either jealous of the attention and plum assignments he got, or bitter that the goal they were supposed to aspire to was being set by a guy whose achievements they didn't even believe.

"*When he was in Washington, he seemed incapable of doing routine journalism. Then he'd go abroad, and it was like Clark Kent emerging from the phone booth.*"

"I always thought his reporting was sort of a joke," says Don Kirk, a former USA Today foreign correspondent who since has written several books and reported for the New York Times and the International Herald Tribune. Even Kelley's casual chitchat seemed farfetched, says Kirk, remembering how Kelley told him in Kuwait in the aftermath of the Persian Gulf War that he'd helped carry bodies of Kuwaitis or Iraqis killed in the fighting. "It seemed unlikely to me. You couldn't exactly disprove it, but you just sit there and say, 'Wow.' "

Kirk never contested Kelley's claims. He didn't take Kelley seriously, he says, adding in an e-mail, "Had anyone suggested I 'emulate' Jack…I would have viewed the request as hysterical—that is if I weren't overcome by rage."

At the Maryland restaurant Kelley mentions his "enemies." He doesn't want to get too much into it—he'd rather other people explain

the situation. But the enemies are the harping doubters, the newsroom nonbelievers who wouldn't shut up through the years about problems in his copy. An enemy must have sent the anonymous note to Executive Editor Brian Gallagher last May, comparing Kelley to notorious New York Times fabricator and liar Jayson Blair, Kelley says. And when Gallagher and his fellow top editors decided to follow through on the note and look into Kelley's work, it was apparently the enemies who saw to it that the investigation wasn't fair.

Kelley admits, however, that his decision to lie during the investigation was no one's fault but his. He's his own worst enemy there.

Like many news executives haunted by Jayson Blair, last May Gallagher sent a mass e-mail to his staff asking anyone who doubted the accuracy of anything in the paper to come forward. Coincidentally, just before he sent it, an anonymous letter arrived through USA Today's internal mail system raising doubts about Kelley. According to reports and a description by Kelley, the letter-writer called Kelley a highly paid "golden boy" and pointed to his "obviously fake" quotes, in particular ones in a March 2003 story from Pakistan in which a Pakistani intelligence official who thought Osama bin Laden was being cornered says, "Jesus, this could be it, this could really be it."

Gallagher shared the note with USA Today Editor Karen Jurgensen and Managing Editor for News Hal Ritter. After discussing it, the three decided to see, "very quietly," if other concerns existed, Gallagher says, adding, "We found a few." So they decided to review a body of Kelley's work. From that they culled a few stories to look at more closely. "Our assumption from that was not that Jack was guilty—just the opposite," Gallagher says.

Kelley says Gallagher told him of the note, saying, "I have something to show you that's going to make you angry." (Kelley also remembers

Gallagher telling him at the time, "I believe this is all a case of envy." Gallagher says he didn't say that, but "I certainly told him I didn't regard the note as proof of anything.") Kelley eagerly endorsed the editors' plan to verify his stories to remove the doubts. He wanted to start that very night.

According to a USA Today statement, during the ensuing investigation, a reporter told editors that after Kelley wrote a story in July 1999 out of Belgrade about a document linking Serbs to war crimes, an official from the War Crimes Tribunal in The Hague questioned "the existence of a notebook at the heart of the story." The reporter said nothing of the complaint at the time.

Kelley replayed to editors how he got that story, in which he says he "examined" a notebook that included a direct order from the Yugoslav army to "cleanse" a Kosovo village. But Kelley and the main investigator, reporter Mark Memmott, ran into trouble verifying Kelley's account. Kelley's main source, Natasa Kandic, the human rights investigator who purportedly showed him the notebook, told Memmott she didn't remember an interview with Kelley and that she never had such a notebook. And the translator Kelley said witnessed the Kandic interview was unreachable. Kelley then told Memmott that two translators actually attended the interview, not just one.

Memmott reached the second translator. She remembered an interview with Kelley and Kandic but said Kelley wasn't shown any documents. She also said she was the only translator there. According to USA Today's statement, eight days later, on September 27, Kelley called Memmott to say he had reached the original translator and that she'd be calling him.

The woman called in October to vouch for Kelley's story. Kelley showed the investigators a photo of her in November. But the paper, which had taped the woman's calls and hired a voice expert, matched her phone number and voice to that of a Russian translator Kelley had used before.

In December Kelley admitted his deception to USA Today's publisher.

Terence Sheridan, a former reporter for Cleveland's Plain Dealer, has written extensively about the Balkans for his former paper, the International Herald Tribune and Pacific News Service. Sheridan says he encountered plenty of journalists there who, due to inexperience in the country or unreliable fixers, misrepresented the complex conflict. But Kelley, he writes in an e-mail, didn't have that excuse.

"He wasn't a rookie or a blockhead. He was a well-traveled, experienced star working for a rich and powerful organization," Sheridan says. "In the end, his Belgrade piece was a calculated but laughable lie, the scoop that came apart like a breakaway suit when barely touched."

Another journalist, who has closely followed the war crimes tribunal against former Yugoslav President Slobodan Milosevic, says if a document such as Kelley described in his story existed, those prosecuting Milosevic surely would have brought it up.

"Kelley basically described a direct order from the Yugoslav army high command to attack civilians, that is, to commit a crime," the journalist writes in an e-mail. "But as far as I know, no order of this magnitude has ever emerged in any of the war crimes trials in The Hague, which is one reason the prosecution is having such a tough time convicting Milosevic of genocide. If such a 'smoking-gun' document actually existed and was in the hands of the UN prosecutor, we would know about it."

Kelley stands resolutely behind the Belgrade story, as he does everything he's ever written. When he lied about the translator, he says it was an act incongruent with everything he is. Because the investigation "was not being conducted in good faith," he says, he panicked.

"I've replayed this in my mind sooooo many times," Kelley says. "I thought, you know, you've been shot at overseas, you didn't panic there. Because there I knew I had a job to do, and I was confident in my ability. In this investigation I was not confident that it was conducted in good faith and I panicked.... I didn't trust the system. They didn't give me reason to trust them. They refused to interview editors who edited the stories, reporters who were with me in the field, researchers who worked with me on the stories from back here."

Kelley says the desperation overtook him the day before he told his editors about the phony second translator, the day "Brian Gallagher told me I had better come up with the interpreter or else."

Gallagher says, "Any suggestion that there was a threat along those lines is not accurate." Kelley's deception was already in play by then, he adds. As far as not contacting people Kelley suggested, Gallagher says though they went to great lengths to keep the months-long review quiet to avoid damaging Kelley's reputation, they interviewed the people who needed to be interviewed. "It was very important to us that this investigation be kept secret so someone who was innocent would not be tarred," Gallagher says. "We succeeded in that, but it constrained the investigation."

As Kelley sits in the restaurant talking about the investigation and about his lie, he's at times quick to blame himself, appearing ashamed and quietly frustrated at not being able to pinpoint exactly what made him step so far outside his character. Like a tape looping back on itself time and again, he repeats things like, "I knew it was wrong. It was against everything that I believed in but I panicked.... For the rest of my life I'm going to regret it.... I understand I caused them to question 21 years, I do."

And then he calls what he did a "mistake," suggesting that those in the USA Today newsroom who've always been against him primed the climate that led to this situation, saying, "It's open season on me."

"When they say I engaged in an elaborate deception, they're giving me way too much credit," Kelley says at one point. "They imply that I set up this entire thing with the interpreter. All I did was make one phone call. She's known me very, very well and she told me flat out, 'I know you and I worked with you and I know you've never fabricated a story.' She said, 'Let me pose as the interpreter because you're never going to find her.'"

Ultimately Kelley concedes that whether the investigation was fair or not doesn't matter, only his lie. After that, he says, he didn't deserve to work at the paper anymore. But before he resigned, he only wanted to know one thing: Would USA Today correct or retract any of his stories? It didn't.

"I...leave knowing I stand behind every story," he says. "And that I never fabricated or plagiarized."

In 1992 Marc Fisher, now a Washington Post metro columnist, was the Post's Berlin bureau chief. Not long after he'd written a 3,500-word feature about the plight of Gypsies in the country, he was reading USA Today's international edition, which he'd picked up for the baseball box scores.

Fisher, an AJR contributor, wasn't surprised to see that Jack Kelley, who he knew had been in the country, had also written something about the Gypsies, a big issue in Germany at the time. "But what was unusual," Fisher says, "was the number of elements that were virtually identical to mine. It struck me as particularly strange because there were quotes I'd gotten in one-on-one conversations with people I'd gone to great lengths to find. They're word for word in Kelley's piece to mine."

Especially odd, Fisher thought, Kelley had quotes from a man named Alfred Erdolli, someone without a phone who was not only difficult to locate but who, Fisher believes, didn't speak English because he interviewed him in German for just that reason. "It's incredible enough to find the guy," Fisher says, "and then to get precisely the same words, the same sentences in the same order."

Fisher told his editor, Michael Getler, about it, he recalls, and Getler then wrote a letter to the editor of USA Today. Getler, now the Post's ombudsman, doesn't remember sending a letter to USA Today but says it could have happened. USA Today's editor at the time, Peter Prichard, doesn't recall ever getting any complaints about Kelley's reporting. Though Prichard doesn't recall it, Fisher remembers him writing back a note to Getler defending Kelley. And Kelley remembers hearing about Fisher's complaint at the time.

Kelley's short Gypsy story includes significant portions in which phrases or entire sentences are identical to Fisher's story. For example, Kelley wrote: "Gypsies, a dark-skinned people who arrived in Central Europe from northern India in the 10th century, are arguably the most hated people in Germany, if not all of Europe." Fisher wrote: "Gypsies are dark-skinned people.... They are descendents of a northern Indian tribe that wandered to Europe in the 10th century.... That the Gypsies are Europe's most despised ethnic group is unquestionable."

Kelley called Germany "homogenous." Fisher called Germany "homogenous." Kelley wrote: "Gypsies recently canceled their annual memorial services at the former Bergen-Belsen concentration camp after organizers received threatening phone calls." Fisher wrote that exact sentence except for the word "recently." Kelley wrote: "More than 500,000 Gypsies were killed in the Holocaust. Nazis chose them as a first target, characterizing them as 'Oriental-West Asian bastard mixtures.'"

Fisher wrote: "The Nazis chose them as one of their first targets, officially characterizing them as 'Oriental-West Asian bastard mixtures.' More than 500,000 Gypsies were murdered in the Holocaust."

And then there are the Erdolli quotes. Kelley quoted him as saying, "'We're Germany's scapegoats again. And no one helps us. This is the hardest fight we've ever had.'" In Fisher's piece Erdolli says, "'We're Germany's scapegoats again.... And no one helps us.... This is the hardest fight we've ever had.'"

Kelley was reporting in Moscow when his Gypsies piece ran and he heard about Fisher's charge. He had the Post story faxed to him, he says, and then called Fisher to explain his reporting. "At the end of our call," Kelley writes in an e-mail, "[H]e said he believed that I had not seen a copy of his story before I wrote mine or plagiarized his story in any way."

Continuing, Kelley writes: "Several months later, I heard he was at a dinner party in Washington and repeated the same concern. I then...met with him for nearly 30 minutes. At the end of our conversation, he said, 'I believe you. I believe you didn't plagiarize me.' As I told Marc, I never saw a copy of his story and my 'fixer' in Berlin could verify all the interviews I had done there on the topic. I also told him that plagiarism is against everything I believe."

Fisher insists he never told Kelley he believed him. "That's patently false," he says. Fisher does, however, remember a middle-of-the-night call from Kelley in Moscow and then meeting with him in Washington. "He said I'd done terrible harm by in any way questioning his truthfulness," Fisher says of the call. "He defended the piece and said he'd done the interviews. He said he may have read my piece but did not remember. I told him what I thought of the piece and that was the end of that."

After news broke of Kelley's resignation from USA Today, the Washington Post reported another possible plagiarism incident involving a story Post reporter Kevin Sullivan wrote in July 1998 about a village in Pakistan known for its gun market, Darra Adam Khel.

As with the Gypsies story, the Post's piece was lengthy, and Kelley's much shorter piece, written in September, includes significant similar portions.

For instance, Kelley wrote: "The small family-owned shops that line the road through the village are filled with Russian Kalashnikovs, American M-16s, Italian Berettas, Israeli Uzis, cannons, grenades, guns hidden in walking sticks…. A few U.S.-made Stinger missiles, sent to help the Afghan Mujaheddin fight the Soviets…also are available." Sullivan wrote: "The main street—the only street—is lined with tiny shops and stalls filled with every kind of firearm: Russian Kalashnikovs, American M-16s, Italian Berettas, Israeli Uzis, even guns hidden in walking sticks…. Darra's merchants also sell cannons, antiaircraft guns and grenades. A few U.S.-made Stinger missiles, sent to help the mujaheddin fight the Soviets, are said to be still available…."

Kelley wrote: "An AK-47, captured from the Soviet army in Afghanistan, sells for $320. But a near-identical Darra copy starts at $50." Sullivan wrote: "an AK-47 captured from the Soviet army in Afghanistan goes for about $320, but almost identical copies made in Darra start at about $50." Kelley wrote: "Pakistan's national and provincial governments are exploring ways to regulate the gun trade in Darra." Sullivan wrote that exactly except for the word "Pakistan."

Also, in describing when people test-fire the wares in the street, Sullivan wrote, "not even the dozing dogs flinch." In describing the same apathy to the constant gunfire, Kelley wrote: "The dogs didn't even flinch."

Kelley says he didn't see a copy of the Post's story before he wrote his. He stopped in Darra spontaneously as he worked his way through the region, he says, at the suggestion of a BBC cameraman. He says the place is

so small, it's not strange that two reporters there would describe the same things. Many of the details in his story, such as the type of guns for sale at the market, came from the Pakistani government, Kelley says, adding that when he listed the types of guns, he just went by size.

"When a foreign reporter shows up to cover a story like that, you all tend to use the same fixers, and because there are so few people who speak English, you all tend to interview the exact same people," Kelley explains. "And when you look at this town, there is nothing but men firing guns in the middle of the road, donkeys and dogs sleeping that don't wake up….

"You go up there…and if somebody shoots a gun and the dogs continue sleeping, they don't flinch, for lack of a better way to say it. They don't flinch. That doesn't mean you've plagiarized, you're seeing the exact same things some of the other reporters did….

"I know in my heart I didn't plagiarize a Washington Post story. I would never do anything like that. It goes against everything I believe in."

"I knew this guy had this tendency," says reporter Don Kirk. "Why didn't they get him for 20 years?"

Kirk describes what he calls an "underlying contempt for reporting" that permeates USA Today. When he was there, he says, editors regularly inserted wire copy into his stories without telling him and would second-guess his take on international events in favor of what they'd see on TV. "That's no doubt one of the reasons why Jack was taken so seriously when he should have been viewed as an overeager neophyte and curbed at the onset from a tendency to tell tall tales," he says.

Gallagher says that's "ridiculous," adding that USA Today is "built on the assumption that the most important aspect of the paper is the relationship between" editors

and reporters. As for whether or not the USA Today culture might have contributed to the Jack Kelley situation, he says that's part of what the inquiry committee is considering.

But some USA Today staffers say though there were most certainly longstanding doubts about Kelley, such thinking wasn't all that pervasive in the newsroom. "There was a relatively small group of people talking about this," one reporter says. "There was not a buzz across the newsroom, though you might get that impression from those who are consumed by it."

Since the news of Kelley's deception broke, Linda Mathews, the cover story editor, says people have called her to say they wondered about this and that. "I'd say, 'Then why didn't they say something?' The answer was always, 'I couldn't prove it.'"

Timothy Kenny, a USA Today world editor who was with the paper until 1993, says he never had a problem with Kelley's work and, in fact, thought his Persian Gulf War reporting was particularly good, especially his stories about Filipinos in Kuwait. "There was no reason for me to question anything, and if I did, he had the answers," Kenny says.

Because of his own experience overseas, Kenny says he was equipped to know if a reporter was playing loose with the facts. But, he says, "Were [his editors later] able to ask the questions of people you sometimes have to ask? If you're working overseas and you're not really a good professional, you could make stuff up…and [an editor would] never know."

But even if Kelley did take some liberties, Kenny believes the reporter's work was more often legitimate. "Even if these questions prove to be true," he says. "I'm sure a lot of stories were absolutely accurate and good."

If Kelley did anything wrong, many suppose it was more likely along the lines of plagiarizing and embellishing rather than full-scale fabricating. Like the time in 1997 when he attributed the quote of a Red Cross spokesman to the president of the International Committee of the Red Cross. In that case, Kelley didn't just put the words of the spokesman in the official's mouth, he wrote the lead-in to the quote to make it seem as if the president was responding directly to a question, "shouting" his answer back.

When Mathews edited Kelley, it never occurred to her that he made things up. Relying too heavily on a source? Sure. Being naïve? Maybe. But not making things up. "It's not as if anyone here lived in a cave and didn't think about these issues," she says. "If you've done any foreign reporting you know there are pipe artists out there."

USA Today is indeed "light on foreign experience," she says. But even if the paper could boast all the overseas brainpower in the world, she's not sure that would have made a difference. "If Jack really was making stuff up, would anyone necessarily have known that, even if they had 20 years of experience?" she asks. "There were experienced people on the metro desk of the New York Times and it took them a long while to figure out Jayson Blair was making stuff up. Ben Bradlee had a lot of experience and he didn't find out about Janet Cooke....

"If editors can be blamed for anything here, it's being too busy.... When I beat myself up at night over this, I ask myself, 'Why didn't I pay more attention?' The answer, I swear to God, is that I had a hundred other things to do.

"I don't think a newspaper can protect itself from a wily and creative fabricator.... I hope that's not what he is."

Jack Kelley *knows* his stories were above board. He *knows* he didn't plagiarize. And above all else, he *knows* that the people who know him best know these things, too.

But those people who know him best, the ones he's counting on to prove his case, are sick and sad that they can't do that. They want to. And maybe before his lie they would have. But not after the lie. They can't.

"Were [his editors later] able to ask the questions of people you sometimes have to ask? If you're working overseas...you could make stuff up...and [an editor would] never know."

Gregg Jones, who was so impressed with Kelley's work during the war in Afghanistan, would be shocked to learn that Kelley engaged in "wholesale journalistic fraud." "But," he says, "I'm troubled that he'd go to such elaborate lengths to thwart the investigation—I don't know what to make of that. I racked my brain and tried to put myself in that situation, like you knew your body of work was being looked at and you had to point to one story on which your whole career hinged and you couldn't find an interpreter.... I find it difficult to understand that leap."

Mathews was once one of Kelley's most stalwart newsroom defenders. Then Kelley didn't just lie to the investigators, he lied to her. Very upset to catch wind of the investigation last fall, she asked him about it. Kelley told her about his Belgrade reporting, about the two translators. "Of course the truth turned out to be very different than that," she says. Then once the whole thing broke, he called her at home to own up about the lie. "He told me how he 'instantly' realized this was a mistake. Even that confession turned out to be a lie," she says with undeniable disgust. "He didn't own up to it for two months. Two months!

"At that point I'd gone to bat for him, I'd yelled at people here. I felt kind of like a fool, left out to dry.

"I don't know what that tells you about the quality of the rest of his

work," she says. "It's hard to argue with where we are now."

And where we are now is with a team of USA Today journalists, led by some of the industry's most esteemed editors, continuing to comb through each and every story Kelley filed. It's a daunting pile to ponder, accumulated over nearly 22 years. They're looking to conclude once and for all if Jack Kelley's reporting was solid and also how to ensure that the newsroom is better protected from such questions in the future.

Jim Cox is hoping hard that the inquiry provides answers. Though he's supposed to know Jack Kelley best, having spent more time overseas with him than anyone in the newsroom, he just doesn't know what to think.

"How could colleagues of mine who I like and respect have such a different view of someone who I like and respect?" Cox asks. "I've heard people chalk it up to envy and professional jealousy, or maybe because he's a born-again Christian and there was hostility about that among the reporters. I heard it suggested there was resentment because he was a pet of [USA Today founder Allen H.] Neuharth's or [former Publisher Tom] Curley's.... I don't think my colleagues are that small and petty, at least I hope they're not. Which leaves me with no answer."

Cox thought Jack Kelly was an exemplary reporter. But he's also a liar, and that's "extremely disappointing." So which is it? Who has he been working side by side with all these years? It's all down to the inquiry.

"I hope they put a punctuation mark on this, a definitive punctuation mark," Cox says. "Either tell us we worked with the real deal, or tell us we worked with a fraud. Don't leave us with gray."

Assistant Managing Editor Jill Rosen wrote about coverage of Kobe Bryant and Michael Jackson in AJR's February/March issue.

From the *American Journalism Review*, April/May 2004, pp. 29-38. Copyright © 2004 by the Philip Merrill College of Journalism at the University of Maryland, College Park, MD 20742-7111. Reprinted by permission.

UNIT 4
A Word From Our Sponsor

Unit Selections

Key Points to Consider

- What is the difference between television programming that will appeal to older versus younger adults? Males versus females? What specific programs would you place in each category? Why?

- Is it worth it to you to pay more for television, magazines, newspapers, movies, and/or Internet access with fewer advertising messages? Why or why not?

 **Links: www.dushkin.com/online/**
These sites are annotated in the World Wide Web pages.

Advertising Age
  http://adage.com
The Cable Center
  http://www.cablecenter.org/history/index.cfm

Advertising is the major source of profit for newspapers, magazines, radio, and television, and advertising tie-ins are a common element in motion picture deals. While media writers may have the potential of reflecting their own agendas and social/political viewpoints as they produce media messages, they depend largely upon financial backing from advertisers, who have their own interests to protect. Advertisers use media as a means of presenting goods and services in a positive light. They are willing to pay generously for the opportunity to reach mass audiences but unwilling to support media that do not deliver the right kind of audience for their advertisements.

Mass advertising developed along with mass media; in fact, commercial media has been described by some as a system existing primarily for the purpose of delivering audiences to advertisers. The income from selling commercial space is determined by statistical data on how many and what kinds of people are reached by the media in which the ad is to appear. American Association of Advertising Agencies and Association of National Advertisers statistics report 16 minutes of each hour (27%) during prime time television is devoted to non-programming content, 18 minutes (30%) during early-morning, 21 minutes (35%) during daytime TV. In 2001 the value to NBC of retaining the *Today* show's 5.1 rating (versus competitor *Good Morning America* at 3.6 and the CBS morning show at 2.1) put an estimated value of $150 million per year in ad revenue on Katie Couric's charisma. The February/March 2001 issue of *Bride's* magazine carried 1,108 pages of advertising (out of 1,286 total pages), weighed 4.9 pounds, and set a Guinness record for the most pages of advertising to appear in a single issue of a periodical. Thirty-seconds of advertising time sold for $2.3 million for the 2004 Super Bowl, $2 million for the last episode of *Friends.*

However, as the number of media choices increases and audiences diffuse, advertising agencies have largely adjusted their media-buying focus from quantity to quality of potential consumers who will be exposed to a single ad. According to a recent study by Marian Azzaro, professor of marketing at Roosevelt University in Chicago, advertisers would need to buy 42 percent more time on the three major networks than they did 10 years ago to reach the same number of consumers. The current focus of many agencies is niche advertising, with particular interest in ratings/circulation data split by age, gender, ethnic background, and income factors that determine how a given consumer might respond to a product pitch. The outgrowth of niching is seen in media products from the Food Network and Home & Garden Television to the diversification in magazine titles, this is the topic of "Finding a Niche." "The Myth of '18 to 34'" discusses (and refutes) the premium advertisers place on attracting young consumers. Internet advertising is largely targeted to this demographic. "America Untethered" suggests that cell phones are the newest advertising frontier.

Sometimes product pitches creep directly into entertainment media, where they can strike below the level of consumer awareness. In the fall of 1998, *Chaos! Comics* began offering to weave commercial products into its comic book story lines, charging advertisers up to $100,000 for the service. Video games have grown into a $28 billion business through attracting product placement revenue. In the summer of 2003, Mirimax shopped a contract asking $35 million from car makers to get their brand into a new film version of *The Green Hornet,* projected release 2005. The product placement deals were to be in place before negotiating for screenwriter or director. BMW donated 32 Mini Coopers to be demolished in production of *The Italian Job,* and reported a 20% spike in Mini Cooper sales following the movie's

2003 release. Products or logos may be inserted into already filmed movies and television programs—not a new practice, but one attracting new attention as technological advances make it easier to do so, and as VCRs and TiVo allow consumers to bypass traditional commercial messages.

Advertisers are subject to federal agency rules regulating their content. For example, until recently, the Federal Drug Administration tightly restricted advertising of prescription drugs. The Federal Trade Commission monitors deceptive advertising. Among its policies: a celebrity who endorses a product and implies he or she uses it must actually use it; an ad cannot mislead consumers to their detriment; objective claims must be supported with competent studies; and advertisers are responsible for "reasonable implications" of their ads to consumers. The FCC investigates about 150 deceptive advertising complaints each year. However, from a media literacy standpoint, analyzing truth and values communicated by advertisements themselves is only part of the picture. It is important to understand the gatekeeping role financial backers have in overall media content.

The dependent relationship between those who make decisions regarding media content and those who underwrite the production and distribution of that content has long been an issue of concern among media critics. As described in "Trial and Error," producing media messages is expensive. "Going Long, Going Deep" profiles editorial versus business decisions at The Atlantic, a critically acclaimed but historically unprofitable magazine. "Pay for Play" discusses cross-ownership influence on radio music programming. Some advertising account executives admit, and others deny, that one consideration in buying advertising space is whether their brands or companies are featured favorably in photo spreads and feature stories in magazines. Most admit to unwillingness to be associated with television shows that create negative publicity. All recognize that target marketing puts a premium on reaching certain advertiser-desirable groups; media targeted to the interests of those audiences proliferate while those attractive to other audiences do not. In light of such trends, critics contend that in the future true "mass" media may be obsolete.

The Myth of '18 to 34'

Since the day an ad exec came up with the notion of the targeted demographic, advertisers' fetishizing of this audience block has transformed our culture. But the business premise behind it is bunk.

By Jonathan Dee

Who says Shakespeare doesn't matter to young people anymore? On a recent episode of "Gilmore Girls," the hourlong flagship drama of the Warner Brothers television network, Rory Gilmore's high school English class performed scenes from the Bard. Rory, cast as Juliet opposite the handsome and frequently suspended Tristan as Romeo, fretted that the heat of their on-stage kiss would expose to her current boyfriend, Dean, the fact that Rory had once kissed Tristan at a party when she and Dean were temporarily broken up. Still, the performance had to be convincing, because it counted for 50 percent of her grade. "People who fail Shakespeare don't get into Harvard," admonished the group's alpha female, named Paris—who, upon seeing that their rehearsal space has not yet been vacated by an adult aerobics class, remarks, "What's with the cast from 'Cocoon'?"

Tough stuff for older folks to identify with, to be sure, but we've all had a generation or more to grow accustomed to the fact that, while we ourselves may age, popular culture remains a kind of garden of attenuated youth. And while we may not like it, we all think we understand the reason for it: youth is where the money is. The WB, after all, is not run by a bunch of teenagers bent on self-expression; it's part of a multibillion-dollar entertainment conglomerate whose programming decisions are based on sober business acumen. So if they took the risk of launching a new broadcast network in 1995—when the network TV audience overall was shrinking—then they must have a pretty good idea of who that audience is and what it wants. Right?

Well, if you assume that a TV show's "audience" consists of the people who watch it when it's on, your first conclusion might be that the folks at the WB are laboring under a gross misconception. Nielsen ratings for "Gilmore Girls," when considered as raw numbers, are horrible. Somewhere around five million people watch an average episode, which puts it in 121st place among the 158 shows broadcast in prime time this past season.

But if you consider that a TV network's true audience is advertisers, then you're on your way to understanding why Tuesday night is, in fact, a big moneymaker for the WB. The network more than makes up for its abysmal ratings by charging an inflated ad rate for those few viewers its shows manage to attract. A 30-second commercial spot on "Gilmore Girls" costs about $82,000—nearly three quarters of the fee for advertising on an episode of, say, "Law and Order: SVU," an NBC program that regularly has about three times the number of viewers. The WB gets away with this because its overall ratings, poor as they appear, were up 5 percent in the 18-to-34-year-old category last season, and while "Gilmore Girls" may be among the least-watched series on television, it's also No. 2 in its time slot among viewers aged 18 to 34.

Down to their level: TV networks continue to court the youth market despite dwindling numbers and reduced spending power.

Eighteen to thirty-four: for decades, conventional advertising wisdom has attached the adjective "coveted" to this slice of the viewing audience. According to an analysis by the former NBC News president Lawrence K. Grossman, advertisers pay an average of $23.54 to reach 1,000 viewers in that age bracket, versus $9.57 per 1,000 over the age of 35. And since commercial television, whatever else it may be, is fundamentally a system for delivering audiences to advertisers, network executives lose a lot of sleep trying to figure out what will hold fast the slippery attention of people in their late teens, 20's and early 30's. It is, as it has been for 40 years, the principle by which a great deal of our popular culture—not just TV, but music, movies, radio—comes into existence.

The odd thing is, there's no real reason for it anymore.

People over the age of 50 account for half of all the discretionary spending in the United States. Proportionally speaking, there are more of them than there ever were, and they are voracious cultural consumers. They watch more television, go to more movies and buy more CD's than young people do. Yet Americans over 50 are the focus of less than 10 percent of the advertising.

What makes advertising an entertaining field of study is that its twin natures—pop art and dismal science—are never really reconciled. If the notion of the "target demographic" lives on well past the point where it stopped obeying any kind of economic logic, it may be worth wondering how much sound, unsentimental business sense was ever behind this juggernaut to begin with.

Brand loyalty: this was the concept that turned the minds of young people into an advertising battleground, before television was even invented. Get them early, the thinking went, and if your product isn't junk, then you'll have that customer's fidelity for life. And, of course, advertising aimed at the young has always had a secondary target as well: those who aren't young but want to appear so, who believe that purchased commodities have the power to stave off time.

But in the earliest days of television, when the popularity of network programming was measured mostly by the sales of TV sets themselves, there was no question of "targeting" anything but the broadest possible audience. It wasn't until the 1950's that the A.C. Nielsen Company started breaking down its crude data on the TV audience by age as well as income, geography and other categories—at which point advertisers began to develop more of an interest in some TV viewers than in others.

"Embedded within the 18-to-34 cliché is a lot of social and economic history," says Stuart Ewen, author of "Captains of Consciousness" and several other books on the history of advertising. "The development of that group coincided with the dramatic expansion of the American middle class in the years right after World War II. The notion was that these young people coming out of the war were going to be the engine that drove the American economy."

The history of Pepsi's advertising campaigns—from the era of "Pepsi Refreshes Without Filling" and Polly Bergen in the early 1950's to Britney Spears in 2001—typifies the transition from selling the product to promising the lifestyle.

It would be giving advertisers of the late 40's and 50's too much credit, though, to say that they got onto the demographic bandwagon right away. The work of such Eisenhower-era ad barons as Rosser Reeves and David Ogilvy relied almost smugly on simplicity and repetition, on what Reeves termed the Unique Selling Proposition drilled mercilessly into the public consciousness: "Wonder Bread Helps Build Strong Bodies 12 Ways," "Pepsi Refreshes Without Filling" and so on. Indeed, Reeves's famous Anacin ad featuring an animated hammer pounding inside one's head could function as a metaphor for both the intent and the effect of late-50's advertising in general. The very idea of targeting some demographic niche would have been unknown to Reeves; his own ad-spending mantra was characteristically drab and concise: "the most people at the lowest possible cost."

By 1960, though, when Bill Bernbach, the man generally credited as the father of Madison Avenue's "creative revolution," placed a photo of a Volkswagen just above the large-type word "Lemon" (an event that had roughly the effect on advertising that the 1913 Armory Show had on the history of American art), the pendulum had begun its long swing from paternalistic notions of brand loyalty to exuberant iconoclasm. The advertising industry ushered in its own version of the Age of Aquarius, in which youthfulness—being young, thinking young, speaking young, buying young—was all.

TO BE SURE, there was a hard-numbers aspect to the initial explosion of youth-targeted advertising in the 1960's and early 70's. By 1966, 48 percent of the U.S. population was under the age of 25. Failure to speak their language meant kissing off half of the market.

Still, this is advertising, in which numbers never tell the whole story. Thomas Frank, in his brilliant study of 60's advertising, "The Conquest of Cool," offers the example of automobile ads; in the 40's and 50's they preached reliability and endurance (a typical ad might picture a happy nuclear family out for a Sunday drive), but in the 1960's they suddenly aspired to the symbolism of revolution: Oldsmobiles were rechristened "Youngmobiles," consumers were exhorted to join the "Dodge Rebellion" and as staid a make as Buick promised consumers "Now We're Talking Your Language." This all seems understandable enough in the context of the times, until you consider that in the mid-60's young adults accounted for only 9 percent of all new car sales. So why would the car business bother to target them?

The business world, it seems, was going through its own generational insurgency, and the old model of customer relations was tossed gaily out the window. In a society in which young people predominated numerically and were acknowledged as the vanguard of change, the idea of brand loyalty was turned upside down. What advertisers prized in American young people was their disloyalty, their insistence upon the new. The notion of "revolution" (i.e., fashion) could be applied to any and every commodity—and common sense was no obstacle: when Pepsi adopted its wholly metaphorical slogan "Join the Pepsi People Feelin' Free," sales soared.

Such ads were never designed to extract riches from the nation's youth—"youth" simply became their new subject matter. They posited a plain-speaking friendship between the advertisers and the young, a friendship that was entirely fictional but seemed really cool, and the way to get in on it was to purchase the product being advertised. The genuine counterculture was, of course, tiny in comparison to the legions of people who admired it and wanted to be a part of it in some small, risk-free way—by, for instance, joining the Pepsi Generation. It was a seductively undemanding model, for advertisers and consumers alike, and it kept the business world's focus squarely on the 18-to-34 bull's-eye for the next three decades.

HOW DID THE TV networks satisfy their advertisers' demand for this newly calibrated audience? Well, if they couldn't always bridge the gap between themselves and the bona fide counterculture, they could certainly attract the attention of those who wanted at least to feel that they could lay some claim to membership in it by watching TV.

"That period—the end of the 60's, the beginning of the 70's—was really an extraordinary moment in our culture," says Robert Thompson, director of the Center for the Study of Popular Television at Syracuse University. "In one fell swoop, CBS canceled a whole bunch of programs that were still fairly high-rated—'Mayberry, R.F.D.,' 'Hee Haw,' 'Gomer Pyle'—and replaced them with a very different kind of show."

The highest-rated show for the 1970–71 season was the decidedly unrevolutionary "Marcus Welby, M.D."; No. 2, though, was "The Flip Wilson Show," and other programs like "The Mod Squad" and "Rowan and Martin's Laugh-In" sneaked into the Top 20. These hybrids of old forms (sketch comedy, the cop show, the family sitcom) and young subject matter became the entree into the cycles of hip for millions of viewers, and the advertisers who paid for those programs gave their viewers a way to make the idea of permanent revolution not just a philosophy but something they could take home and put on a shelf, or in their closet, or in the fridge.

"TV definitely became more research-driven and more demographically self-conscious in the 60's and 70's," says Mark Crispin Miller, director of the Project on Media Ownership at New York University. "I think one can safely say that entertainment generally is research-driven now, but television, being the most directly responsible to advertisers, was the first to take the plunge."

The first, but not the last. Hollywood discovered, somewhere around the release of "Star Wars," that movies could also profit by functioning as advertisements for their own merchandise; whereupon they, too, started pitching their work to a younger audience. Commercial radio, determined to lead rather than follow music's fruit-fly-like cycles, undertook the ghettoization of programming intended for anyone above the age of 29. Thus the cultural productions of what Variety magazine, in its inimitable style, calls the Zitgeist continued to snowball. By the early 80's it had grown into the self-fulfilling prophecy (Why are movies designed to appeal to people in their teens and 20's? Because those are the people who go to the movies.) that we're still living with today.

IT WAS A LONG TIME before anyone cared to notice that the target demographic itself, and its status in American society, had gone through some profound changes. The population bubble caused by the baby boom kept floating up; whereas in 1940 only 6.8 percent of the population was 65 or older, as of 2000 that number was 12.4 percent. And the economic news wasn't bullish either. Between 1973 and 1990, median real income for families with children headed by persons under 30 fell an amazing 16 percent. And in 1990, three out of four men between the ages of 18 and 24 were still living at home, the largest proportion since the Depression.

"Young people's hopes and prospects for the future have in very real terms become diminished," says Stuart Ewen, "and in a situation like that, obviously you have to rethink whom you're selling to."

And what of the theory of brand loyalty—the idea that winning over the young consumer means winning him or her over for life? There the big change has come about not so much in the young but in the old. The baby-boom generation, raised in front of the TV, just never became brand-loyal in the way their parents were. Everyone is pretty malleable these days: 67 percent of female heads of household between 18 and 34 were willing, in a Nielsen study, to try a new brand even if it went against their customary buying habits; the corresponding number in the 35-to-64 age bracket was 70 percent.

Even the argument that most pop culture is for young people because young people consume the most pop culture has begun to fall apart. ESPN's highly promoted X Games, a kind of "alternative" Olympics featuring skateboarders, BMXers and the like (referred to by The Wall Street Journal as "the Holy Grail of youth marketing") was outperformed this summer on the network's primary channel by the bargain-basement Great Outdoor Games, a decidedly non-youth-oriented event featuring lumberjack contests and the talents of various sporting dogs. Over the last decade, the proportion of the national moviegoing audience between the ages of 50 and 59 doubled, while the proportion of teenagers shrank steadily. The percentage of CD's sold to consumers over 45 doubled as well.

And yet the romanticization of youth persists: the adjective "coveted" has been joined by the phrase "hard to reach" as a justification for the premium advertisers continue to pay to speak to the 18-to-34 crowd. Put aside for the moment the fact that these so-called hard-to-reach young adults spend an awful lot of time with the TV on—men between 18 and 24 watch more than 20 hours a week, according to the Nielsen people; put aside the fact that those young X Games rebels come plastered head to toe with corporate logos. What logic suggests that, because there are proportionally fewer young people than there used to be, because they have less money than they used to and because it's harder to separate them from that money than ever, advertisers should spend more money trying to court them? It would make as much sense to say that advertisers really ought to pay top dollar for viewers who don't have any spending money at all.

IF YOU ASK the agencies themselves about the relevance of the target demographic, they're likely to tell you that numbers-oriented research of any kind is so last year. Forty years after creative advertising's Big Bang, the study of demographics is a "science" many now scorn as outdated and crude. "Now they call it psychographics," Thomas Frank says. "They hire sociologists, anthropologists—it's very elaborate." The methodology of today's market research often approaches the mystical.

So who's willing to pay the WB extra to reach today's young adults? The ads featured on "Gilmore Girls" themselves paint a portrait of the coveted youth audience. Apparently, they spend as if they still get an allowance. Wendy's, Snickers, Cover Girl makeup, chocolate milk—there was hardly a product advertised on "Gilmore Girls" that would cost a consumer more than $10. With one glaring exception: new cars. Ford and Honda advertised throughout the Tuesday-night lineup.

"These younger folks may not be big-ticket purchasers now," says a Ford spokesperson, "but they may one day be. Ford wants to form a relationship with these younger buyers now and grow them up into our various brands." As for Honda, it has, according to a company representative, "pretty much one of the youngest buying demographics of any car company out there. The Civic in particular—almost all the ads on the WB are for Civics. And we're on MTV all the time."

And how many of these youth-oriented Civics, sticker-priced at a minimum of $14,000, are actually sold to people under the age of 26? One in five. Not so different from the 60's.

They'll catch on eventually. But advertising is a vast mechanism, risk-averse and inertia-driven, and like most multibillion-dollar industries it changes course with all the agility of an oil tanker. And so, for now, the polestar of the target demographic endures. It has gone from an ecstatic confluence of societal change and economic opportunity to a fusty business institution.

Of course, it's more than that as well. No matter how many dollars might be squandered in the process, you see in modern TV advertising what you see in, say, Greek statuary: a cultural key, a worldview whose increasing irrelevance to cold economic models only testifies to how compelling it remains for us.

In the meantime, the Fox network, eager to reassure advertisers made restless by its drop last year to second place among 18-to-34-year-olds, has just announced that this fall it will become "bold, younger, more noisy." The network's new motto? "It's Good to Be Bad."

Jonathan Dee is the author, most recently, of the novel "Palladio."

From the *New York Times* Magazine, October 13, 2002, pp. 58-61. © 2002 by Jonathan Dee. Distributed by The New York Times Special Features. Reprinted by permission.

Finding a Niche

From ferrets to tattoos: *Specialization is the name of the game in today's crowded magazine world.*

BY JILL ROSEN

At Yale University's law school, in a campus recruiting center, staring at a job board busy with postings for corporate law gigs, none distinguishable from the last, Steven Brill had something of a career epiphany. These firms weren't identical, he thought, and the jobs hardly were—but how was anyone to figure that out? There was no place to just look that stuff up, word of mouth wasn't exactly reliable, and magazines, the few that had anything to do with law, weren't any help—they "just weren't speaking" to any of my classmates, Brill says. "They wanted to know which firms offered the most opportunities, which firms offered the most money, which firms offered the most exciting work."

And it wasn't just students. Any corporate lawyer, he figured, would love to know the deal on these places. They might even pay to know the deal. Could he provide the deal?

Two years later, in 1978, Brill unveiled The American Lawyer, an irreverent, hard-nosed magazine dedicated to giving attorneys from big firms that very deal, or, as the magazine's own material boasts, giving subscribers what they "want, and need, to know."

Nearly 25 years later, The American Lawyer is still speaking to its once unspoken-to audience. That audience, from day one, was the magazine's bread and butter. Brill knew that and knows now that the title didn't make it because it targeted lawyers. It made it because it targeted *corporate* lawyers. Just a niche of the law world. A fragment. Readers of The American Lawyer, Brill says, feel like they're part of a community, even part of the magazine. "The way to do it," he matter-of-factly adds, "is to talk to people about something they're interested in."

In the swinging '70s, as Brill was starting that talk with attorneys, across the country similarly embryonic magazines were striking up intimate conversations with eager audiences. In 1977, Entrepreneur made overtures to those who wanted to be their own boss. That same year a pub called Mix reached out to recording industry sound aficionados, and, not long before that, Offshore invited Northeastern boating enthusiasts to drop anchor and subscribe.

These magazines and hundreds like them were coming into the world not long after such stalwart titles as Life, Look and the Saturday Evening Post took their deathbed gasps. But none of the new pipsqueaks had designs on the grandeur and scope of those granddaddies; they weren't shooting for staggering mass appeal. The newbies aimed lower, circulationwise, yet much, much truer. They had no need to talk to all of America. Just corporate lawyers or audio junkies.

"Magazines became like cable, serving a specific audience willing to pay for that product," says Samir Husni, a University of Mississippi journalism professor known in the trade as "Mr. Magazine." "For every mass audience magazine to die, we saw the birth of five or six little specialty titles. In 1978 we had a magazine about pets. Now we have cats, dogs, horses, ferrets, goldfish. We took areas of interest and dissected them further."

Publishers were clearly turning from titles meant to be all things to all people to a more clubby approach, but it wasn't as if they had a choice—a magazine in the 1970s couldn't have carried out a national conversation if it tried. TV, which bullied its way onto the scene in 1947, had sucker punched the general interest titles, taking not only their mass appeal but their advertising. By the 1960s, TV lured twice as many ad dollars as magazines. And there was no going back. Come the '70s, the only way for a magazine to get the attention of the so-called Me Generation was to appeal to them personally and individually.

That need for niching only intensified through the cable '80s and Internet '90s, as media choices multiplied faster than you can say Home & Garden Television, everything pushing and crowding for a little face time with the public. It's harder to be a magazine now than it was in 1977, says Steve Cohn, editor in chief of Media Industry Newsletter. "The number of media is infinite, but the number of ads are finite. Then the biggest fear was TV. Now it's competing with everything."

And with each other. Last fall there were more than 17,690 titles. In 1975 it was a mere 9,657. And the new-magazine death rate could rival that of a Quentin Tarantino movie—for every success, every Maxim or Oprah's O, 100 or 200 go down in slick paper flames.

Back when Life and Look reigned, says David Abrahamson, an associate professor of journalism specializing in magazines at Northwestern University, we were a conformist society, and relatively poor. But by the '60s, Americans were feeling flush, more financially secure than their parents ever were and ready to kick back and spend some quality time on, well, themselves. As magazine titles flowered during the 1970s, plenty focused on things to do with that newfound time and money—skiing, boating, photography.

To look at magazines over the last 25 years reveals much about America's changing vibe—a story that wouldn't crystallize quite so clearly by studying other media. Magazines mirror, and the most vital ones dictate, the signs of the times, Abrahamson says.

Like, in the late 1970s the counterculture could compare its excesses with Hunter S. Thompson's in Rolling Stone, and empowered women venturing into the workplace could stuff Savvy into their briefcases. A decade later it was boomers artfully arranging Architectural Digest in their mauve living rooms, and by the 1990s, Maxim and Men's Health affirmed for men that it was OK to spend as much time in front of the mirror as their girlfriends did.

And as 24-hour cable and the high-speed Information Highway taught us that information seems better the faster it comes, magazines reflected that, too, by becoming less newsy—why read it a week or a month later when it's online two minutes after it happens?—more graphic and increasingly individualized. "There are fewer and fewer words in each issue," says Peter Carlson, who writes about magazines for the Washington Post. "Attention spans are shorter; there's just more media around. People don't want to nestle in and read a 10,000-word magazine piece."

But while TV grew to dominate, there was an Achilles' heel, one that magazines quickly learned to nip at. "TV became the No. 1 information source," says Clay Felker, who founded New York magazine in 1968 and now directs the Felker Magazine Center at the University of California, Berkeley's Graduate School of Journalism. But "the one thing [TV] couldn't do was give you the specialized information."

"I went to the newsstand the other day and counted 22 tattoo magazines," Husni says. "Tattoo magazines for men, for women, skin and ink—you name it, it's out there. If you're an Asian American gay male between the ages of 18 and 30, there's a magazine for you… Name a specific part of the human body. There are at least three titles devoted to that part."

When a magazine falls behind in this ceaseless cultural morphing, or misses society's beat, readers seldom tolerate it, Felker says. "Rolling Stone is an example of a magazine that had an enormous impact because Jann Wenner had a particular view that a broad audience shared: He said the music will set you free at a time that was important," Felker says, adding that when that message grew stale, so did Rolling Stone's icon status. "Now the kids don't want that. They want music you *get* for free, they want Napster.

"You have a generation of young people, who I teach, who grew up reading Spy magazine, or Mad, and watch 'The Simpsons' and 'South Park.' They get news from Jon Stewart. Magazines that don't understand that can't appeal to young people today."

To look at magazines over the last 25 years reveals much about America's changing vibe— magazines mirror, and the most vital ones dictate, the signs of the times.

What appeals anymore? What do people now want out of a magazine that they didn't want back in the '70s? For one, says Stephen Koepp, deputy managing editor of Time, a magazine that has undergone big-time adaptations in the last 25 years, they want it easy. The days of struggling through a rambling piece, patiently awaiting the point, are history. Readers, Koepp says, want their information useful, and they want it delivered in an easily digestible, yet stylish and compelling, form made even more enticing with splashy photography and helpful graphics. And, oh yeah, they also want stories they haven't read elsewhere and pieces about what's on their mind.

It's a quest that Koepp says the magazine can't forget for a second. He uses the phrase "respect for a reader's time." When Koepp joined Time's business desk in 1981, "We used to say, 'What should people read?' " he says. "Now we spend more time thinking about...satisfying the reader." Then readers came easy. "It was an oil well then," he says. "Now we need to keep it steadily pumping. Nowadays you have to earn the readers' attention week after week."

In the 1970s, people bought a newsweekly for news, to find out what happened last week. Time traded in its news roundups for, among other things, photo essays that run 14 pages, with photos that play across two pages, intricate graphics and health and fitness pieces that boomers lap up like reduced-fat cheese curls.

As Husni says, "Anyone who refers to Time, Newsweek, U.S. News as newsmagazines is out of their mind... The term 'news' has expanded from what's happening in D.C. or in Tel Aviv to this is what's happening in your home."

Ben Fong-Torres, a former Rolling Stone editor immortalized in the movie "Almost Famous," says magazines were always designed to sell, with covers as sensational and provocative as a publisher allowed. Yet, never as much as now, he says. "It's more flagrant in the sell, sell, sell approach," he says. "Back then, things were more straightforward."

Or, as Felker says about the early New York magazine days, "We didn't have enough money for a focus group. We sat around and thought of stories about our lives. We were the people who wanted to live in Manhattan; we put our enthusiasm and passion for living in New York City in the magazine. That's all we had in mind. And that resonated with our audience."

That attitude made a big difference in what a magazine decided to cover—or not cover, Fong-Torres says. "We didn't have the same kind of pressures to focus on what makes a magazine sell. We had the luxury to pretty much build a magazine off the cuff. In a story meeting, if you had a notion and other editors nodded their head, and Jann nodded, you had a story. Now magazines are driven by other priorities," mainly which stars have handlers willing to let you have a piece of them. "That leads to looking at a newsstand and seeing Tom Cruise on five covers, and it leads to an entire category of women's magazines having the same headlines, styles and promises...314 fat-busting secrets, 107 vacation spots, 3,000 money-saving tips."

Fong-Torres remembers suggesting Ray Charles as a story subject. At the time he didn't have a hit record or a major tour on the horizon. He wasn't even particularly hip. "I just raised my hand and said Ray Charles. They asked why. And I said because he helped set the foundation for all the stuff we're covering at Rolling Stone. They said sure, so we followed him around, he told us things about his times with drugs—the story was a triumph for me personally and for Rolling Stone... Just sticking your hand up and just suggesting something, that wouldn't be done that way today. It's usually only the hottest subject available."

Despite laments that magazines ain't what they used to be, like just about anything that's moved on from what it once was, the changes aren't necessarily for the worse. In a Darwinian way, magazines over the last 25 years have become what they need to be to survive. And it's not as if the industry is merely hanging on by a thread—it's rather hearty. Sure, total circulation is dropping now after years of steady rise, mainly because of dramatic declines at industry leviathans like TV Guide and Reader's Digest. Yet, readership is up overall, thanks to the continual swell of new titles and red-hot ones like Maxim, O and Real Simple.

"Americans still want magazines," Felker says. "They're not going to be replaced with information technology or Web magazines. They'll just be part of the menu. They're too convenient and brilliantly designed for a modern, fast-paced life." Despite the competition, and in a way, because of it, magazines have a pretty secure foothold heading into the 2000s. "They provide something that other places don't—a point of view, a version of the world," Felker says. "As the country grows, there will be more and more subcultures, more and more opportunities to segment audiences. It's just a matter of figuring out what an audience wants."

Despite laments that magazines ain't what they used to be, the changes aren't necessarily for the worse. In a Darwinian way, magazines...have become what they need to be to survive.

Steven Brill, back in the late '70s, figured that an audience would want the real deal on the country's biggest law firms. Fortuitous figuring. Less on the money was Brill's 1998 stab at a title on the media, Brill's Content. That one had just a three-year ride. But if he had to start a magazine today, Brill has an idea on the tip of his tongue: homeland security. "For people in the business of doing corporate security or domestic security," he says. In post-9/11 times, it's not only a topic on people's minds, but something companies and government agencies will be spending a lot of money on in coming years. In other words, a niche waiting to be exploited.

He's been beaten to the punch.

Just hours after Brill threw out the security concept, professor Abrahamson in Illinois noticed the first issue of a magazine that had just landed on his desk, a title that struck him as a rather savvy way to tap into one of the country's current fetishes.

Its name? Homeland Protection Professional.

Jill Rosen is AJR's assistant managing editor. Though Rosen was unemployed for a few weeks after the niche publication she worked for went under in 2001, she bears the magazine genre no ill will. In fact, she subscribes to quite a few.

Pay for play

Why does radio suck? Because most stations play only the songs
the record companies pay them to. And things are going to get worse.

By Eric Boehlert

March 14, 2001

Does radio seem bad these days? Do all the hits sound the same, all the stars seem like cookie cutouts of one another?

It's because they do, and they are.

Why? Listeners may not realize it, but radio today is largely bought by the record companies. Most rock and Top 40 stations get paid to play the songs they spin by the companies that manufacture the records.

But it's not payola—exactly. Here's how it works.

Standing between the record companies and the radio stations is a legendary team of industry players called independent record promoters, or "indies."

The indies are the shadowy middlemen record companies will pay hundreds of millions of dollars to this year to get songs played on the radio. Indies align themselves with certain radio stations by promising the stations "promotional payments" in the six figures. Then, every time the radio station adds a Shaggy or Madonna or Janet Jackson song to its playlist, the indie gets paid by the record label.

Indies are not the guys U2 or Destiny's Child thanked on Grammys night, but everyone in the business, artists included, understands that the indies make or break careers.

"It's a big f---ing mudball," complains one radio veteran. At first glance, the indies are just the people who grease the gears in a typical mechanism connecting wholesaler with retailer. After all, Pepsi distributors, for example, pay for placement in grocery stores, right?

Except that radio isn't really retail—that's what the record stores are. Radio is an entity unique to the music industry. It's an independent force that, much to the industry's chagrin, represents the one tried-and-true way record companies know to sell their product.

Small wonder that the industry for decades has used money in various ways to influence what radio stations play. The days are long gone when a DJ made an impulse decision about what song to spin. The music industry is a $12 billion-a-year business; today, nearly every commercial music station in the country has an indie guarding its playlist. And for that right, the indie shells out hundreds of thousands of dollars a year to individual stations—and collects a lot more from the major record labels.

Indeed, say many industry observers, very little of what we hear on today's radio stations isn't bought, one way or another.

The indie promoter was once a tireless hustler, the lobbyist who worked the phones on behalf of record companies, cajoling station jocks and program directors, or P.D.s, to add a new song to their playlists. Sure, once in a while the indies showed their appreciation by sending some cocaine or hookers to station employees, but the colorful crew of fix-it men were basically providing a service: forging relationships with the gatekeepers in the complex world of radio, and turning that service into a deceptively simple and lucrative business. If record companies wanted access to radio, they had to pay.

In the 1990s, however, Washington moved steadily to deregulate the radio industry. Among other things, it removed most of America's decades-old restrictions on ownership. Today, the top three broadcasters control at least 60 percent of the stations in the top 100 markets in the U.S.

As that happened, indie promoters became big business.

Drugs and hookers are out; detailed invoices are in. Where indies were once scattered across the country, claiming a few dozen stations within a geographic territory, today's big firms stretch coast to coast, with hundreds of exclusive stations in every major format.

In effect, they've become an extraordinarily expensive phalanx of toll collectors who bill the record company every time a new song is added to a station's playlist.

And the indies do not come cheap.

There are 10,000 commercial radio stations in the United States; record companies rely on approximately 1,000 of the largest to create hits and sell records. Each of those 1,000 stations adds roughly three new songs to its playlist each week.

The indies get paid for every one: $1,000 on average for an "add" at a Top 40 or rock station, but as high as $6,000 or $8,000 under certain circumstances.

That's a minimum $3 million worth of indie invoices sent out each week.

Now there's a new and more ominous development. There are rampant industry rumors that Clear Channel Communications, the country's largest radio station owner, is on the verge of formalizing a strategic alliance with one of the biggest indie promotion firms, Tri State Promotions & Marketing. The Cincinnati indie company has been closely aligned with the radio chain for years; now, sources suggest, Clear Channel will be using Tri State exclusively for the company's hundreds of music stations.

If the talk proves to be true, the move would dramatically alter radio's landscape in several ways—and raise new questions about the effect of the nation's payola laws at a time when the Federal Communications Commission has seemingly given up on regulating radio.

According to the FCC, there's nothing wrong with a radio station's accepting money in exchange for playing a song. The payment only becomes payola—and illegal—if the station fails to inform listeners about the cash changing hands.

But stations, of course, are reluctant to pepper their programming with announcements like "The previous Ricky Martin single was paid for by Sony Records." Besides that, stations want to maintain the illusion that they sift through stacks of records and pick out only the best ones for their listeners.

The secretive, and at times unseemly, indie system has been in place for decades. Rock radio pioneer Alan Freed was convicted in 1960 for accepting bribes in exchange for playing records. (What became known as the payola laws were passed as a response soon afterward.) More recently, legendary indie heavyweight Joe Isgro battled prosecutors for nearly a decade over payola-related charges before they were dismissed in 1996.

Isgro's tale of money, drugs and the mob was told in "Hit Men," Fredric Dannen's revealing 1991 book about the world of independent promoters and the extraordinary power they wielded over record companies.

Amazingly, says one radio veteran, "nothing's changed since 'Hit Men.' The cast of characters is different, but nothing's really changed."

One major-label V.P. agrees: "It's only changed color and form, but in essence it's the same. It's nothing but bullshit and operators and wasted money. But it's very intricate, and the system has been laid down for years."

Some in the increasingly sophisticated and global music business wonder if the time has finally come to break free from the costly chains of independent promotion. After all, no other entertainment industry vests so much power and pays so much money to outside sources who do so little work. Yet just-released figures indicate music sales were soft last year. Will record companies have the power, or the nerve, to walk away?

"Labels claim they're trying to cut back on indies, but everybody just laughs," says one radio veteran, who has both programmed stations and done indie promotion work. (He, like most of the people interviewed for this story, asked that his name not be used.) Adds another veteran: "Labels are pissed off and want to cut back, but they're powerless to do anything about it."

"The labels have created a monster," agrees longtime artist manager Ron Stone. Nevertheless, Stone views indies as an important insurance policy for his clients. "I never want to find out after the fact that we should've hired this indie or that indie. I want to cover all the bases.

"Because you only get 12 weeks for your record to get any traction at radio. After 12 weeks the next wave of record company singles come over the breach and if you don't have any traction you get washed away. But now it's become even more complicated and expensive because of consolidation. It's a high-stakes poker game."

Playing off record industry insecurities, indies have been winning this poker game for decades.

The Clear Channel/Tri State move would be a watershed. Arguably the most powerful force in the music business, Clear Channel's multibillion-dollar assets include 60 percent of the United States' rock-radio business and the leading Top 40 stations in major markets across the country, including KIIS Los Angeles, WHTZ New York, WJMN Boston, WKSC-FM Chicago, KHKS-FM Dallas and WHYI Miami. The company also has extensive holdings in concert venues, concert production firms and outdoor advertising companies, stemming from its merger with the SFX conglomerate last year.

In that arena, Tri State would appear to be a minor player. But by maintaining a close relationship with Clear Channel as the conglomerate mushroomed and bought hundreds of new radio stations in recent years, Tri State has become synonymous with Clear Channel in the industry.

That relationship has translated into power and wealth. "Tri State's billings are probably up more than 1,000 percent since deregulation, considering how many more stations they have influence over," says one indie promoter.

Tri State's chiefs, Lenny Lyons and Bill Scull, did not return phone calls seeking comment.

Clear Channel stations not already using Tri State exclusively are likely to have to terminate their contracts with indie competitors, such as longtime powerhouse Jeff McClusky & Associates. That already may be happening. "They're clearing the decks," says one person who works at a major-label radio promotion department. (McClusky declined to comment.)

The move could mean higher indie fees for record companies. Tri State was charging labels $1,000 an add at some stations, but sources say those rates could jump considerably if Clear Channel and Tri State join forces.

Indeed, particularly in this deregulatory era, Clear Channel can basically charge whatever it wants. Why? Because record companies realize they can't create a hit without help from the conglomerate.

With that kind of clout, Clear Channel, through Tri State, could institute national buys for new singles. "Labels would pay $100,000 or $200,000 to get a single added to all the Clear

Channel format stations one week," suggests one radio source. "And if they don't pay, there is no chance in hell they're getting that song on the radio without Tri State. If it's not on the list, it's not on stations."

And if the song isn't played on the radio, chances are it's not going to make the record company any money.

That raises real red flags at the record companies. "Tolls go up if there's only one road into town. And today you cannot have a hit record without Clear Channel or Tri State," says one record company president whose label recently scored a top-five hit on pop radio with the help of indie promoters. "That allows for an abusive type of toll collections. It seems to be getting out of hand. It's creating burdensome costs and it's screwing with the economics of the music business."

And perhaps most important, any long-term deal between Clear Channel and Tri State would essentially eliminate the all-important middleman. Record companies would instead be paying Tri State for airplay on Clear Channel stations. "That would put it into the realm of payola," says one record company promotion exec.

Clear Channel CEO Randy Michaels recently told the Los Angeles Times that the company does want a piece of the promotional pie, but only through an odd new twist: It plans to sell promotional packages to record companies that would identify the artist after each song is played.

But in a business swimming in money, some doubt things could become that cut and dried. For instance, what Clear Channel is proposing is something stations usually do for free; it's called "back-announcing," letting listeners know which artist they just heard. Will Clear Channel stations now only I.D. songs if the labels pay for the service?

"It sounds like extortion to me," says a former programmer. (Clear Channel executives were not available for comment.)

If the practice takes hold, look for competing groups, like Viacom's Infinity Broadcasting, to start hitting up labels for similar commercial buys. "It will throw the whole system into chaos," fears one indie.

The indies' power illustrates just how crucial radio, especially Top 40, is in generating CD sales. (U.S. consumers bought more than 700 million CDs last year.) Steady touring, an Internet presence, glowing press and MTV help, of course, but mainstream radio play is still the engine that drives the music business.

Yet radio has traditionally been a brood of literally thousands of sometimes spatting siblings, each typically run by a P.D. with high self-regard.

The problem for record companies has always been that there are too many radio stations—and too many egos—nationwide for label staffers to keep close tabs on. So they need to hire indies, people with close business relationships in different markets. (Third-party indies have traditionally insulated labels from direct involvement in any payola activity as well.)

Here's how the game is played today:

The reality is, disc jockeys were cut out of music-making decisions at stations many years ago. Virtually all commercial radio airplay is determined by program directors, who typically construct elaborate schedules directing the DJs what to play and when.

Today, thanks to consolidation, even station program directors often get their playlist cues from above—from general managers, station owners or, in this age of consolidation, regional program directors.

So many indies no longer bother to target the P.D.s. Instead, they go straight to the general managers or owners and cut deals, typically guaranteeing a station in a medium-sized market roughly $75,000 to $100,000 annually in what is termed "promotional support." The station claims that the money goes to buying new station vans, T-shirts or giveaway prizes; in reality, the station spends the cash any way it wants.

That payment makes the indie the station's exclusive point man, the only one (or at least the first one) its programmers will talk to about adding new singles. Once that indie has "claimed" a station, he (there are very few shes in the business) sends out a notice to record companies, letting them know he will invoice them every time the station adds a song to its playlist.

"The truth is, you could [be] making a handsome living, and have a gigantic house in Greenville, S.C., for instance, if you have just six exclusive stations there," explains one industry veteran. (Arbitron ranks Greenville as the 61st largest radio market, with a metro population of 750,000.) "You could gross between half a million and 1 million dollars each year. That's with no staff—just a couple of phones and a fax machine. Because somebody is going to pay you $1,000 every time one of those Greenville stations adds a song. And that $1,000 is just the average. Columbia records may be dying to get a single on, so they say, 'We'll pay you $2,500 for this add.'"

Do the math: six stations in a market like Greenville adding three songs a week, 50 weeks of the year. That represents about $900,000 worth of invoiced adds. If the indie is paying each station $75,000 a year in "promotional support," that leaves him with $450,000.

But that's just the beginning. There are additional sources of indie income, including retainers, "bill-backs" and "spin maintenance." Along with being paid on a per-add basis, some indies earn a retainer (roughly $800 a week) just to call stations on behalf of a song. Bill-backs are essentially second invoices—to cover "promotional purposes"—that indies send to record companies on top of the one for the add. If the add cost $2,000, the indie often sends a $1,000 bill-back invoice as well.

Meanwhile, the cost of the add covers just that: getting the song added to the playlist. If labels want to increase the spins (or number of times a song is played each week), that costs money, too. "There are spin programs you can buy," explains one record company source, such as "$4,000 to make the song top 15 at the station."

In the past, if indies wanted to increase their billings by getting stations to add more songs, they could employ "paper adds." Stations would notify labels that a song was on the playlist so the indie got paid, but in reality the single never got spun. Today, however, all key radio stations are monitored electronically by a company called Broadcast Data Service, which gives labels a detailed readout of actual airplay. Paper adds no longer pass the test.

The solution? A so-called lunar rotation.

"I've got one station that during crunch time in September and October, when every label is desperate for fourth-quarter adds, will do eight adds a week for four weeks in a row at $2,000 a pop," says one label source. That's 32 added songs—and $64,000 in indie invoices—for just one month. But the station's playlist could never support that many new songs. (With today's tightly controlled playlists, any new song is a risk that can cause listeners to switch to a channel with an older and more comforting hit.) Most of these new "adds" are played only in the early-morning hours, or in the "lunar rotation." They are detected by BDS, but don't really affect the station's playlist or ratings.

For record companies, indie costs can be staggering. Just to launch a single at rock radio over several weeks can cost between $100,000 and $250,000 in indie fees. What exactly do labels get in return? "I'll be damned if I know," says artist manager Stone. "It's bizarre." (Labels can sometimes get artists to pay the indie promotion costs, but not always.)

Regardless, the No. 1 rule of radio promotion is that the indie always gets paid. Even if rock programmers discover a good song by a new band on their own, and add it to their playlists because they like it, the station's indie gets paid for it.

Even if someone at Universal Records persuades a pop station to play Nelly's new single "Ride Wit Me," the indie gets paid. Even if the song is a sure hit that needs almost no promotion, like Aerosmith's latest, "Jaded," the indie gets paid. "Ei-ther way the invoices arrive and you pay, in the interest of keeping everybody happy," says one former programmer.

The fear is that if a label tangles with an indie over billing, he could torpedo the label's next project by bad-mouthing a new single or keeping it off the air until his previous invoice is paid. As messy as the relationship can be, the third-party arrangement between labels, indies and stations is crucial for appearance' sake. Today, indies pay stations for "access," not airplay. At least in theory.

"Everyone says indies don't force stations to add records. That's ridiculous," says one rock programmer who has worked in a Top 10 market. "Because [if there is friction] the indie will get on the phone with the station G.M. and say, 'Look, your P.D. has not been cooperative over the last few months on adds I need.' The G.M. either says to the indie, 'Our relationship is about access, not influence,' or he caves. Most G.M.s cave and have a word with the P.D.: 'Look, we have $100,000 a year riding on this relationship with our indie.' Then suddenly—bam—a song you know the P.D. hates shows up on the air."

"Record companies say, 'We're not doing anything illegal; we're just paying indies to promote the records,'" says another programmer. "And indies say we're not doing anything wrong; we're just helping market a radio station. Everybody toes the company line on this.

"But indies are like money launderers; they make sure record company money gets to radio stations, but in a different form."

The big money guys

Educational TV can't exist without marketing tie-ins. But some toys teach better than others.

By G. Jeffrey MacDonald
Special to The Christian Science Monitor

Hundreds of first-graders in rural Mississippi have learned to read in recent years, thanks in part to award-winning public television programs and a host of enticing books and toys like Leona Bean Bag.

At $9.99, eight-inch Leona helps finance "Between the Lions," a programming innovation where cuddly musical lion muppets bring children into contact with the latest findings on how children best learn to read. The show builds on concepts introduced on "Sesame Street," the 34-year-old classic television show that now depends on revenue from the Tickle Me Elmo doll and other merchandise to pay for about 50 percent of its $15 million budget.

GENTLE NEIGHBOR: Fred Rogers set a high standard with "Mr. Rogers' Neighborhood." He was also selective about endorsements and did not pursue tie-in merchandise.

With the death of Fred Rogers in late February, the children's television industry said good-bye to one of the last creators who didn't sell merchandise to finance his show. Today, more than 20 programs draw on his pedagogical legacy to educate the preschoolers he gently welcomed to "Mr. Rogers' Neighborhood," but with one big difference: Unless kids buy the goods, their favorite shows and characters disappear.

Few observers would argue that the possibilities for merchandising have sparked robust competition and injected fresh offerings to the daily lineup of educational television. But on the question of whether merchandising leads to programming in the best interest of children, the industry's trusted voices are far from agreement.

Among those most wary of merchandising are public broadcasting purists and James Steyer, a Stanford University education professor and author of "The Other Parent: The Inside Story of the Media's Effect on Our Children" (Atria, 2002).

"In the days of 'Mr. Rogers' and 'Captain Kangaroo,' they just wanted to put on the best stuff," Mr. Steyer says. Now networks are "not thinking about children as little beings to love and nurture. They're thinking about them as little consumers to sell plush toys to."

But other makers of educational television programs beg to differ, saying well-chosen merchandise can enhance a child's learning experience while attending to bottom-line realities.

"If given the choice between the system we have now and a system where there were deep public resources set aside for quality-driven programming, I'd probably prefer the latter," says Joe Blatt, a lecturer at the Harvard School of Education and producer of children's programs. "But we don't have that in this country, and we never have had that.... If a merchandising tie-in goes with the show's mission, then it's not such a bad way to finance it."

Financing educational television never posed the hurdle for Fred Rogers that it does today. Because he wrote the scripts and songs himself, and because public sources dutifully supported his low-tech, low-budget, iconoclastic show, he didn't need to sell toys in order to keep cameras rolling.

Children's shows face marketing quandary

Those days are long gone, however, as competition among myriad stimulating programs gives networks ample choices for what to distribute. Result: Networks pay less and less for any given show, or else produce their own shows in-house. Either way, virtually every show needs lucrative licensing contracts

When you've outgrown PBS

By April Austin

My family has reached an uneasy truce with the commercial kids' TV networks. Despite our best intentions, we couldn't stay a PBS-only household.

The problem: Our kindergarten-age son has lost interest in public-television staples such as "Clifford the Big Red Dog" and "Arthur." Instead, he begs to watch such commercial network fare as "He-Man and the Masters of the Universe" and "Samurai Jack."

As we do each time the TV status quo is about to change, my husband and I watch the shows in question. While I'd like to say that we select highly educational programs, the reality is that we're choosing shows on the basis of at least one redeeming factor, or, failing that, ones that seem relatively harmless.

In the last go-round, "He-Man" and "Samurai Jack" were rejected (too much fighting) in favor of "Time Squad" (about a group of goofy time-travelers with some history and literary references thrown in) on Cartoon Network. Nickelodeon, another commercial network for kids, remains the middle ground between staid PBS and anarchic Cartoon Network. Nick shows such as "Hey, Arnold!" have a slower pace and a hero with more brain than brawn.

Marketing plays a role in what our son pleads to watch. Despite the fact that we videotape the shows and fast-forward past commercials, he still wants the latest action figures and gizmos. Merchandise feeds interest in the show, and the show creates story lines for the toy.

In this environment, parents serve as gatekeepers, and it's not easy to make compromises you can live with.

E-mail **austina@csps.com**.

for related books, toys, and CD-ROMs to cover production costs.

Such pressures to sell merchandise inevitably come to bear upon those whose goal is to make television educational. In balancing dual needs to meet bottom lines and also make trustworthy programs, all seem to agree on this principle: An educational show should never exist or unfold for the sake of selling an item. Instead, the product should somehow emerge organically from a show's story line to advance or reinforce what children are learning from the show.

"We don't like to sell to kids," says Brigid Sullivan, vice president of children's programming at WGBH in Boston, where "Between the Lions" is produced. "We start from a societal need in developing our shows and we build from there."

"Elmo [the character] was not invented to become 'Tickle Me Elmo'," says Gary Knell, CEO of Sesame Workshop. "Elmo was invented to become a great character. The question is, how far do you want to push characters so they're not exploiting a relationship with a preschooler?... If something happens to enter the marketplace and it's consistent with our educational package, fantastic."

An example from Mr. Knell of such consistency: a for-sale video of the character Zoe dancing with performer Paula Abdul. The video helps build girls' self-esteem by showing female role models, Knell says, and by promoting physical activity.

Merchandising to children was of central concern to Peggy Charren, founder and president of Action for Children's Television, when she led the charge in 1990 to pass the Children's Television Act. The law requires broadcasters to air at least three hours of educational programming per week. She had been "nauseated," she says, to find 70 programs on the air with a primary purpose of selling toys. Example: "G.I. Joe" became a "whole little war show for children," she says, in order to sell the action figure.

Regulators never enforced the law, Ms. Charren says, because it purposely didn't define what constitutes educational television.

"You can't have legislation that says what's good," Charren says. "The problem with television for children is that everything educates.... If the leading character didn't hit the other one in the eye, then [networks said] it was educational programming."

Charren had hoped the law would encourage networks to feel a duty to air high-quality shows. Some such shows, she says, have in fact emerged—ironically with help from merchandising opportunities.

Charren praises, for instance, "Between the Lions" for employing multiple theories and approaches in teaching literacy. On the show, Muppets and live actors sing upbeat songs as children learn spelling and pronunciation. Charren also likes "Arthur," an animated PBS series that "deals with all the problems of childhood" and "wants children to feel safe." And she commends "Dora the Explorer," a Nickelodeon program featuring a young Latina role model and heroine. All three rely largely on the sale of books, featuring the shows' characters, for revenue.

Helpful as merchandising revenue can be, its accompanying pressures force frequent dilemmas for creators. At Nickelodeon, for instance, a consumer-products division regularly pitches merchandising ideas to those who decide what characters will do on screen. Such meetings can lead to "big struggles when they ask for something we're not comfortable with," says Brown Johnson, executive vice president of Nick Jr., the network's block of shows for preschoolers.

In one example of accommodation, staffers in consumer products wanted Joe, host of "Blue's Clues," to start appearing in five different colored shirts to get viewers to buy more shirts. At first, creators balked. But then they asked, "Can't Joe have more than one favorite color?" They decided he could, and the show would not sacrifice educational value by doing so.

When working with merchandisers, Johnson speaks of "marinating our partners in the 'Blue's Clues' way," which means the product "allows kids to play... when the TV is off." Offering magazines, books, and on-line games, she says, means "characters [from shows] have a bigger sandbox to play in."

All those toys add up!

Producers, even of the two respected children's shows here, say they can't afford to make programs without a merchandising element.

SHOW: Sesame Street

First broadcast: 1969 **Network**: PBS
Producer: Sesame Workshop
Educational value: Teaches social and cognitive skills with a mix of live characters and Muppets
Products include: books, puzzles, videos, CD-Rom, apparel, home and school accessories, plush toys
Annual production cost: $15 million
Revenue from merchandise sales & licensing: $7.5 million

SHOW: Arthur

First broadcast: 1997 **Network**: PBS
Producer: WGBH-TV (Boston)
Educational value: Offers encouragement and coping skills for everyday situations
Products include: books, videos, two character dolls
Annual production cost: $4 million
Revenue from merchandise sales & licensing: $1.4 million

Source: PBS

Yet not everyone sees the merchandising dynamic as a promising one.

"We're finding it harder and harder to get our new shows on public television," says Ms. Sullivan, who develops shows for Boston's PBS affiliate. Other producers offer their shows, such as "Teletubbies," at no charge to a network because they can count on merchandising revenue. Those at WGBH, who focus more on research and curriculum development than on marketing strategy, find themselves pounding the pavement to find distributors who will pay for programming.

Such an environment means experimental shows might not be developed. Knell describes one idea in which sofa crumbs come to life to discuss "what really happened on that show." The goal is to help children become media literate, but without a merchandising angle, the show would have to depend on grant money. And because online projects attract more grant money than do proposals featuring the long-familiar medium of TV, production seems a long way off.

Another neglected area, say Knell and Blatt, is that of educational programming for children ages 9 to 14. Because, as consumers, this group can't "nag" parents as effectively as preschoolers can, Knell says, producers devote few resources to shows for this age group.

Charren sees a glimmer of hope in the arrival of digital television. Distributors will have so much spectrum from which to make money, she says, that they can more easily afford to make educational television. And perhaps they will.

"It's a world," Charren says, "where the excuses don't exist."

This article first appeared in *The Christian Science Monitor,* April 8, 2003. © 2003 by G. Jeffrey MacDonald.

GOING LONG, GOING DEEP

BY SCOTT SHERMAN

The *Atlantic*, one of the few American magazines that still dares to publish high-quality, complex narratives, sits in Boston's Little Italy, a slightly raffish neighborhood with narrow, twisting streets and filled with comfortable little restaurants, espresso bars, and cheese shops. The office has a charm of its own: there are hardwood floors, exposed brick walls and ceilings, and cozy sitting areas with easy chairs and coffee tables. Framed minutiae from the *Atlantic*'s long history line the walls. The immaculate corner office belongs to the dapper, red-haired managing editor, Cullen Murphy, who, a few weeks ago, replaced Michael Kelly at the top of the masthead. He is not the editor, however: the magazine's owner, David Bradley, is trying him out for the top job.

Murphy is responsible for one of the greatest coups in the history of the *Atlantic*. A few days after the collapse of the World Trade Center towers, Murphy dispatched a letter to Kenneth Holden, the commissioner of the New York City Department of Design and Construction, the agency responsible for cleaning up Ground Zero. Murphy asked if he could send one of his most distinguished correspondents, William Langewiesche, to the site. To Murphy's astonishment, Holden said yes. The commissioner had subscribed to the *Atlantic* for twenty years, during which time he had devoured most of Langewiesche's articles, along with several of his books. Holden knew instantly that Langewiesche was the ideal journalist to chronicle the story of the cleanup. "He is very interested in how things work, and how people relate to processes," commissioner Holden said recently. "Obviously I'm not an editor; I run a construction agency. But it seemed like it would be a very good fit."

Holden went to bat for Langewiesche with Mayor Giuliani's office, which, for a variety of reasons, was eager to restrict media access to Ground Zero. "Let's just say I had to use up quite a number of chits in order to secure the kind of access that William was looking for," Holden says. In the end, Holden got his way, and Langewiesche got the journalistic opportunity of a lifetime.

He made the most of it. For five months, Langewiesche (pronounced long-gah-*vee*-shuh) showed up at Ground Zero virtually every day, and often stayed there for sixteen hours at a time. "When I went down to see him on a few occasions," Cullen Murphy recalls, "he was indistinguishable from the people there. He was wearing overalls and hardhat, respirator slung around his neck, and had an easy relationship with everybody on the pile that I saw. Engineers and construction people would come up and talk to him. He knew everybody there."

The fruit of Langewiesche's labor was an extraordinary 70,000-word series entitled "American Ground," which ran in three consecutive issues of the *Atlantic*, and which has just been published as a book by North Point Press, a division of Farrar, Straus and Giroux. The series, which flew off the newsstands, focused attention on the *Atlantic*—a magazine that, under the leadership of the unusual new owner, Bradley, is experiencing something of a renaissance. *The Boston Globe* recently called it "the magazine of the moment." *The Washington Post* referred to the July/August issue, which contained the first installment of "American Ground," as "probably the best issue of any magazine published in America this year" for "people who actually like to read." "It's the hot book right now," says Hendrik Hertzberg of *The New Yorker*.

The magazine's current success owes much to the deep pockets of Bradley, who has invested a great deal of money in a publication that, since its founding in 1857, has drained a fortune from its owners. When Bradley purchased the magazine in 1999, he promised to guide and protect it, and to honor its history. If he reneges on that promise, the *Atlantic* will probably return to the kind of economic instability that has burdened it for much of its history. If Bradley keeps it, years from now it can be said that he safeguarded and revitalized one of the great American magazines.

William Langewiesche came to the *Atlantic* through the slush pile. "Enclosed are two pieces on Algeria," he wrote in a blind query to the magazine. The year was 1990. The Algeria pieces didn't quite work, the editors felt, but the writing was graceful and evocative, and something about Langewiesche's sensibility impressed them. Eventually they let him write about North Africa, and the result was a 1991 cover story on the Sahara. In the 1990s, Langewiesche—a professional airplane pilot whose only writing experience had been for aviation magazines—would turn out a series of remarkable pieces for the *Atlantic*, including "The Shipbreakers," a stunning report from Alang, India, a place where massive ships are torn apart by hand and turned into scrap metal; "The Crash of EgyptAir 990," which showed how a pilot's intentional act led to the deaths of 217 people; and "The Profits of Doom," a parable about pollution and urban renewal in Butte, Montana. In an eerie way, much of Langewiesche's work for the magazine—on the unmaking of colossal ships, on suicide pilots, on massive pits in old mining towns—foreshadowed his report from Ground Zero.

WILLIAM LANGEWIESCHE
Grace under pressure, an unsentimental approach to tragedy, a certain cockiness served him well at Ground Zero.

Langewiesche's has been a most unusual career. His father, a distinguished pilot, wrote a classic text on aviation, *Stick and Rudder*. The son decided to become a writer in high school, after devouring the books of John McPhee. Following his graduation in 1977 from Stanford, where he majored in anthropology, Langewiesche spent a few years in Manhattan working for *Flying* magazine. But he recoiled from the New York magazine world, and for the next fifteen years earned his living as a pilot—flying cargo planes, air ambulances, air taxis, and corporate jets—while writing on the side, with "great determination" and "many rejections." In those years, he also worked as a flight instructor. "He teaches students how to fly into storms," explains Cullen Murphy. "He'll wait for a storm front to come across the country, and then when he sees it getting close to

where he is, he'll call up his students and say, 'OK, we've got an ice storm coming over Denver, and class is ready.'"

Langewiesche's technical expertise, and his unruffled manner, enable him to move with unusual ease in hostile environments. In 1996, when ValuJet 592 plunged into a Florida swamp, killing 110 people, the *Atlantic* dispatched Langewiesche to the Everglades. The press was confined to an area seven miles from the accident site, but Langewiesche persuaded investigators to give him access. (In a fraternal gesture, the pilot even let him fly the helicopter to the crash site.) Langewiesche moved effortlessly among the rescue workers, who sat in the shade, chatting and sipping cold drinks. He would later write:

> They were policemen and firemen, not heroes but straightforward guys accustomed to confronting death. Not knowing who I was, they spoke to me frankly about the gruesome details of their work, and made indelicate jokes, but they seemed more worried about dehydration than about "taking the job home" or losing sleep. I relaxed in their company, relieved to have escaped for a while the expectation of grief.

The same reporting qualities—grace under pressure, an unsentimental approach to tragedy, a certain cockiness—would serve Langewiesche well in his assignment at Ground Zero.

Some print reporters, despite only intermittent access, wrote well about the structural and technical aspects of Ground Zero—Eric Lipton and James Glanz of *The New York Times* are in this category—but only Langewiesche got the whole story from the inside, and told it in a single, expertly constructed narrative. The piece consists largely of mini-profiles of the men who toiled on the site, and it's a superb cast of characters—bureaucrats, collapsed-building experts, barge operators, construction executives, and Port Authority engineers, many of whom are brought to life with quick, powerful strokes. In Langewiesche's hands, the pieces of heavy equipment, too, become characters: "The stars of the show were the machines themselves, and particularly the big diesel excavators, marvels of hydraulics and steel, which roamed through the smoke and debris on caterpillar tracks and in the hands of their operators became living things, the insatiable king dinosaurs in a world of ruin."

Some of the best (and most controversial) pages of "American Ground" concern the "tribal" conflicts on the pile between construction workers, cops, and firemen, about whom Langewiesche writes with a cold eye. We read about a "muscular and charismatic" field superintendent for one of the major construction companies who grew weary of the "moralistic airs" of the firemen—who, in their determination to find their own dead, kept shutting down his cleanup efforts. One day, reports Langewiesche, a fire truck was found underneath the ruins—its crew cab "filled with dozens of new pairs of jeans from The Gap, a Trade Center store." Construction workers began to jeer; a fire chief tried to calm them down, arguing that the jeans had been blown into the truck by the force of the collapse. Writes Langewiesche: "The field superintendent, seeming not to hear, asked the fire chief to repeat what he had said. When he did, the construction workers only jeered louder." It's those kinds of details that give the piece its unique tone and texture, its insider's perspective.

Langewiesche composed the entire piece in a frenetic five-month burst, from various locations in Massachusetts, California, and France. In writing about Ground Zero, Langewiesche says, he wanted to chronicle a "grand experiment in American-ness that was growing up" on the pile, a unique mixture of cooperation and contestation. He also wanted to "break through the maudlin emotionalism that was surrounding this subject."

Despite a brief flirtation with *The New Yorker* in 2000, Langewiesche has decided to remain at the *Atlantic*, where he recently became a national correspondent, a title he shares with James Fallows. "I'm very happy there," Langewiesche says. "The *Atlantic* right now is *the* place to be for this kind of writing."

The *Atlantic* was born at two successive dinner parties in May of 1857, in the luxurious confines of Boston's Parker House Hotel. The guests—who included Ralph Waldo Emerson, Henry Wadsworth Longfellow, and Oliver Wendell Holmes Sr.—dined on steak and oysters. "By the time the wine had run out and the brandy supply was dwindling," the former *Atlantic* editor Robert Manning wrote in his 1992 memoir, "the guests… reached a judgment: America needed a new magazine devoted to literature, art and politics."

What America got was emphatically not a magazine for the masses. Edward Weeks, who edited the *Atlantic* from 1938 to 1966, once wrote that "our aim from the first has been to reach thinking people and to entertain them or make them think harder." Wrote Manning, "from its beginning the *Atlantic* was an obviously if not avowedly elitist periodical" whose purpose was "'to inoculate the few who influence the many.'"

From the start, the *Atlantic* endeavored to both enlighten and entertain. Its archives constitute a Who's Who of American literature—from Harriet Beecher Stowe to John Sayles—and the magazine also published the work of public figures like Theodore Roosevelt and Woodrow Wilson. Yet it wasn't all seriousness: the *Atlantic* takes leisure seriously, and its pages have always been filled with articles about travel, dogs, food, sports, and manners.

No one seems to know for sure, but it is doubtful the *Atlantic* ever made a great deal of money for its owners. Still, until the 1960s, it survived in a journalistic landscape congenial to general-interest magazines. That didn't last. Poetry editor Peter Davison, who arrived at the *Atlantic* in 1956, explains that during certain years in the 1950s, under the ownership of Marion Campbell, the magazine made "a profit—a small profit, sometimes a large profit—and it was undone in the early 1970s by sudden raises in postal rates and paper costs because of the petroleum crisis. And it knocked out all kinds of magazines, and it put us into the red considerably."

In 1980, the magazine was sold to the real-estate developer Mortimer Zuckerman, who, in many respects, turned out to be a model owner: he paid the bills and left his handpicked editor, William Whitworth (who had been a top deputy to William Shawn at *The New Yorker*) to his own devices. Still, after heavy initial investment, Zuckerman kept the magazine on a tight financial leash for most of his tenure, so Whitworth had to make do with relatively scarce resources. Calm, mannerly, fond of bowties, Whitworth was a workaholic. One evening, a former *Atlantic* staff member, Nicholas Lemann, returned from dinner to find him in the office at a late hour; the editor would frequently stay until 11 P.M. "Tell me, Nick," Whitworth remarked. "What is Boston like?"

The hours paid off. Whitworth played a major role in discovering writers like Eric Schlosser, Nicholson Baker, Witold Rybczynski, and Holly Brubach; he published a torrent of fine humor writing and he oversaw major pieces like William Greider's "The Education of David Stockman," which blew the whistle on Reaganomics; James Q. Wilson's "Broken Windows," which influenced police departments all over the country, and Robert Kaplan's "History's Cauldron," which helped to lay the groundwork for the preventive deployment of UN peacekeepers in the Balkans. Whitworth's *Atlantic* was in no sense a trendy or "hot" magazine, but it was a consistently good one for twenty years.

And then, in 1999, Zuckerman sold the *Atlantic* to David Bradley, and Whitworth was dismissed. He was immediately replaced by a very different kind of man—the pugnacious Michael Kelly.

The career paths of David Bradley, a wealthy businessman, and Michael Kelly, a journalist, converged in 1997. What propelled Bradley there was a sense of malaise, a kind of midlife crisis. He was born in 1953 to parents who were devout Christian Scientists; he didn't discover Tylenol until he was twenty-four. Politics interested him from an early age. He became an intern in the Nixon White House, and later enrolled in Harvard Business School. Starting in 1979, he created a pair of corporate consulting firms, which eventually brought him more than $300 million. But Bradley's first love was ideas and politics, and for years he aspired to be a United States Senator. Instead, in 1997, he purchased the National Journal Group, and in 1999 bought The *Atlantic Monthly*. "For twenty years, I worked a pretty quiet, pretty earnest terrain of research for banks, corporations and hospitals," Bradley says. "My best friend threatened, if he outlives me, to have 'a man of fine research' chiseled onto my tombstone. By comparison, even a magazine as serious as the *Atlantic* is a popular, public, glamorous affair. By my late forties, I was ready for a change."

MICHAEL KELLY
Kelly's open-minded attitude toward unknown talent has proved beneficial to the magazine.

In the rough-and-tumble world of Washington, Bradley has a reputation for kindness and decency, and his new colleagues at the *Atlantic* seem to agree. "The week the magazine was sold we were all numb and in shock," says senior editor Jack Beatty. "David Bradley came to the office and the second or third thing he said to us was, 'I just want to assure everybody here that their health insurance is not going to change, that there will be complete continuity.' That told me volumes about this man."

At the time he met Bradley, Michael Kelly was enjoying an extraordinary career. He had started at *Good Morning America* as a researcher, then associate producer, and later worked for the Baltimore *Sun*. Kelly covered the 1991 gulf war for *The Boston Globe, The New Republic*, and *GQ*, and then produced a much-admired book about the conflict, *Martyrs' Day: Chronicle of a Small War*. After a stint at *The New York Times* and *The New Yorker* (where he wrote the "Letter from Washington") he became editor of *The New Republic* (see "The New *New Republic*," CJR, March/April 1997). When Bradley met Kelly, the latter had just been fired from *The New Republic*, largely as a result of his angry, emotional columns lashing Al Gore and Bill Clinton, which infuriated *TNR*'s owner, Martin Peretz.

Right from the start, there was a special chemistry between Kelly and Bradley; when they met they talked for a dozen hours over two days. Bradley wanted to build a magazine empire, and Kelly soon became his chief editorial adviser in that expansive venture. Bradley—who claims to be centrist and nonpartisan in his politics—admired what Kelly had done at *The New Republic*: "I did sense a ramping of velocity when Michael moved into the editorship," says Bradley. There was "huge narrative drive in Michael's own writing but a nice edge and speed in the magazine as a whole."

When Bradley installed Kelly as Whitworth's replacement, after a period in which Kelly ran *National Journal*, some media watchers expressed concern that the *Atlantic* was being handed over to an ideologue. Writing in *The Nation*, Eric Alterman worried that "this cultural treasure" was now entrusted to "the alarming Michael Kelly, a reporter and editor with no literary background, a volcanic temperament and history of colossal bad judgment." There were indeed reasons for concern. When Kelly became editor of *The New Republic*, he took over the weekly "TRB" column, which also appeared in *The Washington Post*, thereby launching his career as a syndicated columnist. As a reporter and book writer, Kelly's voice varied widely in tone, but it remained generally civil. As a columnist, however, he showed a preference for venom and invective: His columns, by and large, are swashbuckling compendiums of abuse directed at liberals, radicals, and left-leaning intellectuals of all stripes and colors. In 1997, Kelly spent a weekend in Vermont and wrote about it for *The New Republic*:

> The place is stuffed with verdant vistas, mountain views, bosky dells, bubbling brooks and limpid lakes. But then there is man, and he is vile. You cannot swat a black fly in Vermont without disturbing the vacant-eyed rest of a pallid, hairy, and purposefully ugly white person. Hippies are everywhere, in every variety and of every age: ancient bedspring-scarred veterans of the summer of love, dreadlocked ingénues still

plowing through the mire of their first Chomsky, pre-schoolers with names like Cypress and Che.

Yet, in his first months at the *Atlantic*, it became clear to his new colleagues that there were two Michael Kellys: There was the fire-breathing columnist, who called to mind some brutally contemptuous Irish-Catholic synthesis of Tom Wolfe and Taki Theodoracopulos. But another side soon emerged. Colleagues saw a man who could be generous and open-minded, who said "please" and "thank you" to fact-checkers, and who listened carefully to young free-lancers and human rights lawyers and left-leaning professors of economics. Fears that Kelly would change the tone of the *Atlantic*—as he changed the tone of *The New Republic* with his anti-Clinton screeds—were soon dispelled. As Kelly remarked recently, "There are certain writers I love—I won't name names—who, because of their ferocity, I would not put in the *Atlantic*, because we're not that ferocious."

What makes a serious magazine take off and fly? Money and editorial talent are the crucial factors, but money always matters more. William Whitworth, for most of his editorship, had fewer financial resources than Kelly had. Thanks to David Bradley's largess, the editorial budget doubled, which meant that Kelly was able to offer contracts to twenty-five new writers (at what he calls "competitive rates") and the magazine itself grew, with ten or so extra pages each issue for editorial copy. Kelly ordered a complete redesign, and the magazine's paper stock was upgraded. But most of the spending went toward editorial quality. The Langewiesche series, for example, cost nearly $200,000 when all expenses were tallied.

Kelly's first hire was James Fallows, who had served as the *Atlantic*'s Washington editor from 1979 to 1996, and then left to work at *U.S. News & World Report* and Microsoft. It was Whitworth who said to Kelly, "Fallows is the best reporter we ever had and we should get him back," and Kelly agreed.

Another key hire was Robert Vare to the position of senior editor. Vare, a gifted editor who specializes in narrative journalism, had worked at *Rolling Stone, The New York Times Magazine*, and *The New Yorker*, where he had clashed frequently with Tina Brown, but was admired by his writers. When Ron Rosenbaum sent *The New Yorker* a fifteen-thousand-word article that later formed part of his book *Explaining Hitler*, he recalls being bowled over by Vare's first edit: "Covered with tiny inscribed comments and questions," says Rosenbaum, "it looked like a manuscript illuminated by a mad monk, but his queries were all on target."

One of Kelly's major achievements was the revitalization of the *Atlantic*'s books section. He immediately hired a thirty-eight-year-old polymath, Benjamin Schwarz, to do the intellectual heavy lifting. Schwarz, in turn, hired writers like Christopher Hitchens—who now writes every month for the *Atlantic*, mostly on literary matters—and Caitlin Flanagan, who, with virtually no journalism experience, has produced a series of lively, much-noticed essays on manners, mores, and domestic life. Schwarz himself had worked for nine years at the Rand

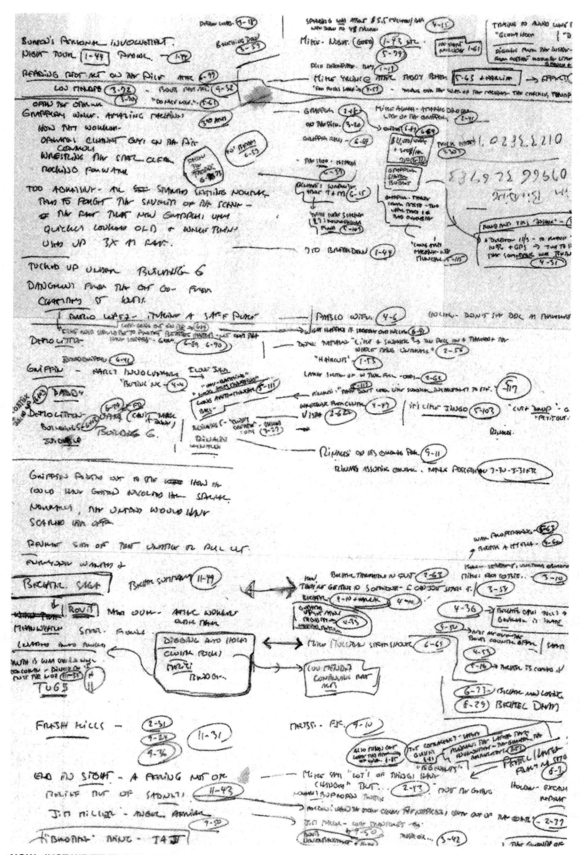

NOW, JUST WRITE IT: A 70,000-word narrative requires a plan. For his "AmericanGround: Unbuilding the World Trade Center," William Langewiesche mined his notes for weeks, then created an outline on several feet of butcher paper. This is a piece of the outline for Part III. © 2002 William Langewiesche.

Corporation and joined the *Atlantic* in 1997 as a correspondent. With his encyclopedic knowledge of U.S. foreign policy, military history, and English literature—he reads two books a day—he serves as the magazine's in-house intellectual, though he claims his only true political passion is animal rights.

Much of the credit goes to Kelly himself. Before his arrival at the magazine, Kelly's editing experience was fairly limited. But friends say his mind has always worked like an editor's. Robert Vare, when he was working at *The New Yorker*, would get frequent calls from Kelly. "He would say, 'You should have Susan Orlean do this, or Peter Boyer do that, or Larry Wright do this,'" Vare says. "He was always thinking like an editor, even when he was a writer."

The *Atlantic*'s feature well has always contained a mixture of policy pieces and narrative journalism. Under Whitworth, the magazine leaned in the direction of policy. Whitworth, who wrote many profiles at William Shawn's *New Yorker* in the 1960s, wanted to inspire his readers to rethink the major issues of the day; he felt there was something indulgent about pure narrative. Kelly leaned in the other direction, toward storytelling, and some *Atlantic* writers rejoice in that emphasis. William Langewiesche is blunt about what he sees as the shortcomings of Whitworth's regime. "A lot of times," Langewiesche says, "they were writing stuff that amounted to predicting the future. It sometimes lacked a connection to the world."

Kelly has certainly run his share of policy pieces—David Bradley is fond of them—but he seems to prefer the narrative efforts, many of which have shined: Mark Bowden on the private life of Saddam Hussein, Mary Gordon on nuns, David Brooks on Ivy League yuppies, Byron York on the demise of *The American Spectator*, David Grann on the Haitian thug Toto Constant, and Christopher Hitchens on Winston Churchill, to cite just a few examples from the last two years. Kelly's open-minded attitude toward unknown talent has proved beneficial to the magazine. When Trevor Corson, a young writer (and former lobsterman) cornered Kelly at the magazine's Christmas party and told him he wanted to write a long narrative on Maine's lobster industry, Kelly gave him the green light. When Samantha Power, a Harvard-based human rights lawyer, sent Kelly a thick stack of material about Rwanda and U.S. indifference to mass slaughter, he was quick to see the possibilities. The resulting piece, "Bystanders to Genocide," which ran at eighteen thousand words, won a National Magazine Award and helped to lay the groundwork for Power's important book, *A Problem from Hell: America and the Age of Genocide*.

Has the *Atlantic* become more conservative under Kelly? Under Whitworth, the magazine leaned left on poverty, foreign policy, and defense spending; it tilted right on multiculturalism, immigration, and crime. A truly conservative editor would probably not have signed off on David Grann's piece on Toto Constant, which illuminated CIA chicanery in Haiti, or on Byron York's article on the death of Emmett Tyrrell's *American Spectator*, a piece that made the Right look rather foolish. On the other hand, the magazine's new "Agenda" section—short essays on current political subjects—seems stacked in favor of conservatives like David Brooks, P.J. O'Rourke, and

Kelly himself. *Atlantic* watchers differ about the political shift under Kelly. "He is extremely conservative," says Robert Manning. "I disagree with a lot of what he writes in his syndicated column. But I don't think that he has injected his politics harmfully in any way into the *Atlantic* so far." Others have a different view. Nicholas Lemann insists that Whitworth and Kelly are both conservative, but in different ways. "In both cases, though, the liberal articles can have a perfunctory, ticket-balancing feeling—the conservative articles are more passionate and heartfelt." Still, it was never Kelly's job to produce a magazine that reflected a perfect political balance. It *was* his job to put out a good magazine, and he did it.

But Kelly grew restless in the editor's chair. Beginning with the November issue, he appears on the *Atlantic* masthead as "Editor at Large," a position that he says will enable him to work on his columns, on a book about the American steel industry for Random House, and on various editorial projects for the company. Kelly insists that he will remain deeply involved in editorial decision-making, but some *Atlantic* staff people see a diminishing role for him in the future.

CULLEN MURPHY
His colleagues admire his Zen-like editing skills, calm demeanor, and efficient administration.

Murphy, sometimes described as the magazine's "heart and soul," was the obvious choice to take over from Kelly. Colleagues admire his Zen-like editing skills, his calm demeanor, and his efficient administration. *Atlantic* readers know Murphy primarily as a writer. Over the years, he has produced a large number of witty, quirky essays, each of which imparts a nineteenth-century feel; they are wry, whimsical ruminations on the small movements of life, and they reflect his personality: self-effacing, calm, inquisitive. In the introduction to a collection of those essays, *Just Curious*, Murphy wrote:

> We are all doomed to inhabit a tiny wormhole of familiar space amid an unimaginably vast and growing unknown. At the same time, the situation offers opportunities: one's chances of bumping into interesting and unfamiliar things by accident have never been better. In recent days, for example, I have learned through utter happenstance that the number of birds killed by domestic cats in the United States in a typical year exceeds the population of China; that modern cooking practices are reducing human tooth size at an estimated rate of one percent every thousand years; that Richard Nixon left instructions for 'California, Here I Come' to be the last piece of music played at his funeral ('softly and slowly') were he to die in office....

Along with his short essays, Murphy has written widely on religion for the *Atlantic*. He is the author of a well-reviewed book, *The Word According to Eve: Women and the Bible in Ancient Times and Our Own*, a personal journey through the world of feminist biblical scholarship, and he is currently writing a book about the Catholic Inquisition. On top of his duties at the *Atlantic*, Murphy has managed to find the time to write the syndicated *Prince Valiant* comic strip. *Prince Valiant*, which is set in medieval England, is a family affair: His father, John Cullen Murphy, has drawn it since 1970; Cullen has written it since the late 1970s. The strip, which appears weekly, goes to 350 newspapers around the world.

While Murphy's name now sits at the top of the masthead, he still has the title of managing editor. David Bradley is clearly taking his measure. Bradley explains, "With Michael stepping back from day-to-day management, I decided to slow us down, see how the magazine develops and then seek the right editor for the assignment. Please know this does not reflect unfavorably on Cullen in the least. Cullen carries the enterprise and has for twenty years." Concludes Bradley, "He may well succeed to the editorship, if he wants that outcome."

T wo years ago, Lawrence Weschler, a longtime staff writer at *The New Yorker*, published a little-noticed essay in *ARTicles*, the annual publication of the National Arts Journalism Program at Columbia University, entitled "The Long Goodbye: Trying to See Past the Increasingly Harrowing Plight of Longform Nonfiction in General Interest Magazines." "Over the past decade," Weschler began, "a certain kind of writing—and with it, a certain tenor of attentiveness—has been disappearing from the world." He was referring to prose in the tradition of A.J. Liebling and Joseph Mitchell, Jane Kramer and John McPhee, Tom Wolfe and Norman Mailer. In Weschler's view, "the magazine universe today is increasingly niche-slotted, peg-driven and attention-squeezed," a situation he likened to "the death of the soul—or, at any rate, the successive parching of the staging ground of any sort of idiosyncratic readerly-writerly communion of souls."

Bradley clearly understands that tradition. But he also understands that revitalizing the *Atlantic* will not be easy. The magazine lost $3 million a year in the Zuckerman era, and last year, under Bradley, it lost more than $5 million. Indeed, Bradley insists that finding a viable business model for the *Atlantic* is the most arduous challenge of his entire career—"as taxing of intellect as any I've faced."

To meet that challenge, Bradley has installed top members of his corporate consulting firm, the Advisory Board, to the *Atlantic*'s business side. For instance, the magazine's new publisher, Elizabeth Baker-Keffer, has no experience in the magazine business; she spent eighteen years working alongside Bradley on the corporate research and consulting beat. Bradley thinks his people can bring fresh eyes to old, vexing questions pertaining to magazine advertising and business strategy. Says John Fox Sullivan, who is the *Atlantic*'s president, "From an advertising standpoint, and to some extent from an editorial standpoint, the *Atlantic* has been kind of out of the game, off people's radar. We have brought it back editorially, and we are in the process of doing the same in terms of reaching advertisers." So far, that strategy has yielded results. With regard to the magazine's long pieces, Bradley notes, "I was not, but now am, a complete convert. The 'American Ground' series is also the best-selling piece in a decade. It is transforming to the reputation of the magazine." Bradley's business team has so far convinced certain larger advertisers to attach themselves to specific editorial features. The Langewiesche series, for instance, was sponsored by UPS, Legacy, and the American Stock Exchange. (Sullivan insists that advertisers "do not have *any* involvement as to content of pieces or series.")

DAVID BRADLEY
He holds a delicate treasure in his hands, a magazine that has deliberately sidestepped odious trends and lived to tell about it.

Bradley and Co. are preparing a bold, risky move: to raise the subscription price, which for years was in the $10-$15 range. "Our goal, quite literally," says Sullivan, "is to double our prices over the next year." His logic is simple: "Most consumer magazines are, in my view, way underpriced." Bradley and Sullivan are betting that readers will pay more money for a better product—much in the same way that readers of *The New York Review of Books, Granta, The Economist*, and *The New Republic* pay high subscription prices for those publications. But it's not a sure bet. Admits Bradley: "There is not much precedent for so dramatic a price shift."

One person who shares Bradley's concern is Mortimer Zuckerman, the former owner, who is enamored of what Bradley and Kelly have done. "I think they have done an *excellent* job editorially in maintaining and enhancing the magazine," Zuckerman says. But he is not sanguine about the magazine's future. Can the *Atlantic* break even? "I don't know," Zuckerman replies. "I can only tell you that I tried for twenty years and didn't succeed. If Bradley can do it, good luck to him. It's not going to be easy." Is raising the subscription price a wise decision? "I don't think that's the solution. The vast bulk of the revenues in print still come from advertising. Without advertising, you can't make it work." Zuckerman knows this firsthand. Asked how much he lost during his twenty-year ownership, he groaned loudly and then replied, "tens and tens of millions of dollars."

Those who directly compete with the *Atlantic* see a fundamental flaw in the magazine's business strategy—its reliance on an expensively inflated circulation, which is now about 500,000. When John R. MacArthur took over *Harper's* magazine in 1980, he deliberately reduced spending on circulation-building, and allowed the numbers of subscribers to fall to a more "natural" level. The result, says MacArthur, is a smaller, healthier magazine with a circulation of roughly 220,000. By spending to remain above its "natural" circulation level, the *Atlantic*, MacArthur insists, is fighting a losing battle—since, in his words, "advertising agencies are not impressed by 450,000; they want millions." Says MacArthur: "If they are serious about making it a going business proposition, they're going to have to bring the circulation down." Raising the *Atlantic*'s subscription price may bring about that result.

These days, Bradley's ambitions are larger than the *Atlantic*. He dreams of creating a new weekly magazine, something as authoritative as *The Economist*, which would appeal to elite readers. "There is almost nothing I would rather do in journalism than start a weekly magazine from scratch," says Bradley. "Michael and I have talked about this for the whole of our relationship. I think the prudent position for the moment, however, is to turn the fortunes of the *Atlantic* first before taking on so large a next endeavor."

In a recent obituary for *Lingua Franca* in the *Los Angeles Times Book Review*, the critic Russell Jacoby wrote, "After 11 years, a backer of *Lingua Franca* decided enough was enough and pulled out. Nearly 280 million Americans did not notice." If the *Atlantic* perished tomorrow, it seems likely that 270 million Americans wouldn't notice. Of course, those who would notice are its readers, who tend to be movers and shakers, people like Kenneth Holden of the New York City Department of Design and Construction—people for whom, as Edward Weeks, a former *Atlantic* editor, wrote in 1957, "the printed word is still the most powerful medium for imparting the truth and for penetrating to the heart."

To his credit, Bradley understands that he holds a delicate treasure in his hands, a magazine that has deliberately sidestepped odious trends in the magazine industry and lived to tell about it; a magazine that remains, in Lawrence Weschler's words, a staging ground for an "idiosyncratic readerly-writerly communion of souls." Bradley cares about the *Atlantic*, and he frets that he is not doing enough on its behalf. "I've not done any of this work before—circulation, direct mail, newsstand promotion, magazine positioning—and worry I'm performing still to B-standard," he says. "I'm glad I own it outright, or surely I would be terminated." It's vintage Bradley—self-effacing, modest, understated.

But for how long will a money-losing magazine hold his interest? "I am on the *Atlantic* watch for the long haul," Bradley says. "This is, of course, what every corporate CEO says right up to the moment he bails out. I simply don't see that here. The *Atlantic* is very much the thing I do every day when I get up. It is the largest share of my thinking. It is the largest share of my professional purpose. Deeply, deeply I do not want this to remain a vanity possession for a succession of wealthy men. My purpose, though evidently not my gift to date, is to reset the *Atlantic* as a successful, profitable magazine. This will require a good deal of time."

It may indeed. There are two hard questions facing the *Atlantic*. If David Bradley, a man who earned $300 million as a corporate consultant, insists that bringing the *Atlantic* to profitability is the most taxing challenge of his entire career, one wonders if it can be done. And if the *Atlantic* continues to bleed money, will Bradley—a man of fine research and fine character, but also a man who played by corporate rules for a long time—still feel so charitable down the road?

Scott Sherman is a contributing editor to CJR. *His article about Donald Graham's* Washington Post *appeared in the September/October issue.*

From *Columbia Journalism Review*, November/December 2002, pp. 48-57. © 2002 by Graduate School of Journalism, Columbia University. Reprinted by permission of Columbia Journalism Review and the author.

America Untethered

Wireless communication is beginning to have a notable impact on our social behavior. A look at what ethnographers have observed about our changing social habits, thanks to the rise in cell phone use.

BY HASSAN FATTAH

As they sat on a train headed toward Washington, D.C., two women called home on their cell phones and were struck by the same thought. On a Virginia highway about 200 hundred miles south of their location, a 30-year-old man picked up his cell phone to set up meetings and had a similar epiphany. Thousands of miles away in San Francisco, a man long reluctant to carry a cell phone stopped to ponder the same question: How did we ever live without cell phones?

Since the early days of the Dick Tracy comic strip, Americans have envisioned a world of anywhere, anytime communication. That vision came to life when the first commercial cell phone hit the market in 1984. Almost two decades later, slightly more than half of all Americans—about 150 million people—tote mobile phones, feeding a $94 billion industry (not including hardware) that's growing 15 percent each year. But the telecom business isn't the only area revolutionized by America's wireless transformation. As cell phones reach deeper into our lives, they're beginning to create a deeper impression on the American psyche. To hear researchers and ethnographers tell it, wireless communication is beginning to have a notable impact on our social behavior—one that could have a long-lasting effect on our society and the world around us. "We're at a transitional point where a lot of new rules are being set," says Robbie Blinkoff, principal anthropologist and managing partner at Context-Based Research Group in Baltimore. "The basic metaphor of the phone is changing. What [it] does today is connect you to an informal network."

At least four ethnographic studies in the U.S. and Europe released in 2001 and 2002 have detected signs of changing habits due to wireless communication. Thanks to mobile phones, the researchers found, Americans and Europeans may be becoming more independent and spontaneous. But they may also be growing prone to planning at the last minute and arriving at meetings late. They're sharing more of their personal lives in public but are also forcing a redefinition of basic etiquette. This in-

creasing accessibility is allowing work to impinge even more on family lives even as it enhances social lives.

What makes these empirical findings important now is the sheer numbers of people who have cell phones in this country. By the middle of 2002, the legions of Americans carrying cell phones were each spending an average of $53 a month to talk 442 minutes on their mobile phones—about 100 minutes more per month than they did in 2001. All in all, Americans log more than 53 billion minutes chatting, getting directions and letting someone know they will be a little late. (See sidebar.)

Ethnographers and social scientists had long wondered what the portability of cell phones would engender, but they didn't have much data to go by. Until recently, most studies about wireless phones focused on design and technology issues. The latest ethnographic studies, however, have yielded significant clues about cell phone users' communication habits. Almost all observed changes in how cell phone customers form relationships and define a sense of time and place. Whether here in the U.S. or in other countries, the clearest changes were in the social networks people were creating.

The latest ethnographic studies yield clues about cell phone users' communication habits. Most observed changes in how these people form relationships and define a sense of time and place.

One of the first of this new crop of studies, conducted in 2000 by Leysia Palen, assistant professor of computer science at the University of Colorado at Boulder, focused on new cell phone users. Palen's team followed 19 people in Colorado who had never owned a cell phone but had recently ordered one. The researchers watched newly wired users at work and play, and found that one of the

Mobile Phone Universe

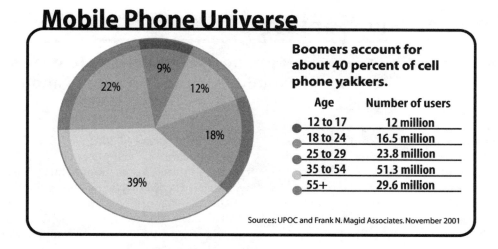

Boomers account for about 40 percent of cell phone yakkers.

Age	Number of users
12 to 17	12 million
18 to 24	16.5 million
25 to 29	23.8 million
35 to 54	51.3 million
55+	29.6 million

Sources: UPOC and Frank N. Magid Associates. November 2001

biggest differences was that they became more accessible to their social network. Palen and her team observed that mobile phones supported entire social networks and relationships. The researchers interviewed participants regularly and watched their habits change over a six-week period. Consistently, Palen found participants more flexible in how they arranged their schedules and gradually more willing to speak on a cell phone in public.

Take "Matthew," a study participant and full-time pastor who began managing his social network between Sunday services with his mobile phone. His congregation leased meeting space on Sundays only, requiring him to be on a flexible schedule and accessible outside of regular working hours. "Having programmed all 60 of his parishioners' numbers into his phone, Matthew calls anyone and can be reached anywhere," Palen notes. "A mobile telephony benefit implied in this account is the ability to manage multiple roles simultaneously, possibly keeping one's location ambiguous."

Palen also found that mobile phones help sustain social ties for purely psychological and emotional value. For instance, "Elizabeth," a meteorologist in Colorado, began to use her mobile phone to maintain social ties with her large family. The phone's portability and the financial advantages of her family calling plan made it possible for her to stay in close contact with them, Palen writes. Moreover, by regulating who had her mobile number, Elizabeth knew that incoming calls were most likely from a relative or good friend, and she no longer had to screen her calls when the phone rang.

The Wireless Lifestyle

That same kind of active participation in wireless life was a central theme in an ethnographic study by Context-Based Research Group released in January. Blinkoff and his team of ethnographers found mobile phone users integrating wireless into their lives. Ironically, the more they integrated it, the more juggling they had to do.

"Consistently, we can say it's a lifestyle, and point after point, we see people changing their lifestyles because of [mobile phones]," says Blinkoff. "But a lot of time people are also using [wireless] as a crutch."

The new study is a follow-up to a 2000 survey in which Blinkoff and his team spent time with mobile phone users in Europe, Asia, Latin America, New York and San Francisco to get a picture of the cultural dynamics of wireless life. Back then, the Context researchers found Americans still new to wireless communication, tending to have "device fascination" but not knowing how to use the phones to their full extent. When they returned to many of the same locations last summer to study 144 phone users in seven cities, the researchers observed changes in how the subjects related to mobile life. In the U.S., says Blinkoff, people were far more concerned with wireless as an enabler than as a toy, and they had learned to use the wireless features they needed while ignoring those they didn't.

To be sure, Context's sample cell phone users tend to represent a far more technology-savvy bunch than other researchers have chosen. Even in the U.S., for example, they chose to study several Europeans who were more familiar with mobile phones than the average American. "We weren't necessarily looking for average Americans—we were looking for people who are mobile and invested in the lifestyle," notes Kit Waskom, project director at Context.

Nonetheless, Context's researchers concluded that most mobile users give a taste of things to come. Their findings, including the predilection of cell phone users to be late and to micromanage time, mirrored those of other researchers.

If wireless is encouraging people to gab, it's also giving them newfound spontaneity. With cell phones in hand, both Palen and Blinkoff's research subjects could change their plans at the last minute more easily, deciding to meet at a different location, say, or inviting others to join their group. "Pietro," for example, an engineer in Italy for

Equal Opportunity Gabfest

Just a few years ago, the average cell phone user was likely to be wealthy and white. Today, women, African Americans and teens are the hot markets.

Cell phones were once all business, but these days, they're all in the family. In a 2002 survey of 221 Americans between the ages of 18 and 64, conducted by Knowledge Networks, the vast majority of respondents underscored family as the top reason to go wireless. Respondents—the young ones more so than older ones—cited reaching friends as their second leading reason to go wireless. They ranked work-related calls the third most important reason to have a wireless phone.

And though the world of wireless is split 50-50 between men and women, men tend to make more calls on cell phones than women, and they tend to use them for business more than women do, according to Knowledge Networks, a market research consultancy in Cranford, N.J.

On average, men made or answered 8.3 calls per day, while women said they made or received about 5.5. Although both put family first, women were more partial to calling friends than men, whereas men were three times as likely to use their phones for work.

But the real story behind mobile phones is the demographic shift that has occurred as prices for service have fallen and providers have added more features. Just a few years ago, the average cell phone user was more likely to be wealthy and white. These days, African Americans and teens figure far more prominently. In 1999, Knowledge Networks found 37 percent of African Americans and 32 percent of Hispanics had cell phones, while 42 percent of whites had

them. By the spring of 2002, however, 65 percent of African Americans had cell phones, compared with 62 percent of whites. Hispanics remained well behind, with just 54 percent penetration.

Kids, too, have gone mobile fast. By February 2002, half of all teenagers between 12 and 17 had cell phones, according to a study by UPOC and Frank N. Magid Associates. In 2000, an estimated 11 million cell phone users were between the ages of 12 and 24; by the end of 2002, that number was estimated to be closer to 29 million. Here again, African Americans have taken the lead: According to Magid, almost three-quarters of African Americans between 12 and 34 now tote mobile phones, compared with 57 percent of whites and 56 percent of Hispanics.

There are crucial reasons to pay attention to cell phone users. For one, cell phone penetration has surpassed Internet penetration in American homes. According to the Pew Internet and American Life Project, while 59 percent of Americans were logged on to the Net, 62 percent were punching the buttons on their cell phones. That could have major implications for cell phone providers racing to add Internet and data functionality. And just as important, there are strong correlations between the adoption of wireless and of other high-tech gadgets and services. According to Pew, cell phone users are more likely to have broadband cable access: 16 percent of all wireless users have broadband, compared with 12 percent of the general population. And though wireless Internet use is just a trickle today, 44 percent of wireless Net users have college degrees, versus about one-quarter of the general population. —HF

whom wireless is his lifeblood, was among those who were chronically late. Blinkoff and his team noticed that Pietro's frequent calls to say he would be delayed dramatically eased his relationships with clients and colleagues.

In Brazil, Australia and the U.S., cell phone users repeatedly admitted that they now often call friends and colleagues to tell them they're running behind schedule. In turn, being late is becoming more acceptable than it used to be, Blinkoff and Palen conclude. "Mobile technology is starting to remove a strict adherence to a schedule. It's a loss in respect for calendar time," says Palen. "And that's happening across the board in all sorts of interactions."

Indeed, a 2001 study by Rich Ling, a researcher at Norwegian telecom firm Telenor, and by Leslie Haddon, a research associate in the media and communications

department at the London School of Economics, found "micro-coordination" to be the backbone of mobile phones. Unlike the traditional telephone, the mobile phone has none of the strictures of location and therefore "softens" time, enabling people to merely suggest a time and place to meet, and to pin down a location as they approach the meeting time. Perhaps not surprisingly, as users of mobile phones leave more planning to the last minute, they also tend to overshoot the final arrival time as well.

Palen and Blinkoff both found that greater accessibility has brought work even deeper into the home—where it's often least wanted. For many recent wireless subscribers, that is often the greatest concern, though workers are growing increasingly used to the change. Blinkoff says that at least some of the concern is overblown.

Send a Message

This year, 33 million Americans (21 percent of all U.S. wireless subscribers) will use the sort message service feature—also known as text messaging—on their wireless device, but by 2007 nearly 100 million individuals (51 percent of wireless users) are expected to use the service.

Category	2003	2007
Total U.S. subscribers	157	194
Sort message service subscribers	33 (21%*)	99 (51%*)
Wireless Internet subscribers	31 (20%*)	117 (60%*)
Instant message subscribers	16 (10%*)	77 (40%*)
Multimedia message subscribers	2 (1%*)	43 (22%*)

● 2003
● 2007

*Percent of all wireless subscribers   Source: ICD

"As the new mobile technology pervades life, it's more difficult to separate work from personal life," Blinkoff says. "The reality is that work and home have been overlapping faster anyway, but what the mobile phone does is highlight the effect."

Public and Private Lives

What the mobile phone has really demarcated is the shifting boundary between public and private lives. Discussing private matters in public has become a habit in Europe and the U.S. For years, Americans have complained about cell phone users who gab in public. But Palen found that as people acquired cell phones, their resistance to chatting in public ebbed and they often found themselves guilty of the same act. Because of their portability, phones now appear in places they never did before. But because cell phones are relatively new, social norms about their proper use, especially in public, are just being formed. Palen, for example, found most of her newly unwired subjects gradually accepted using their phones in public.

"[Mobile phones] are a cultural menace. People are talking all the time, and they obviously aren't saying anything," one respondent told Palen. Yet just weeks after decrying the practice, the same respondent ventured outside with his phone and saw the value of talking on the go. He soon admitted to being less judgmental about how important people's public calls were.

Kids Speak

By far the clearest effects of wireless are being seen in kids, a naturally media-savvy group whose lives are being shaped by this technology. Kids are the fastest-growing mobile demographic, with half of all teenagers between 12 and 17 carrying cell phones in 2002, according to a study by Frank N. Magid Associates. By the end of 2002, 29 million kids were expected to be toting cell phones. Much of that growth is being driven by parents who are giving their kids phones so they can keep tabs on them. Yet three studies found kids gaining more independence and developing new ways of connecting once they became wireless. "For parents, [cell phones are] a matter of security," says Jay Melican, senior research associate at the Illinois Institute of Technology's Institute of Design. "For kids, however, it's a matter of coming of age."

Melican's research entailed observing and filming cell phone users in Chicago, London, Shanghai and Recife, Brazil. In each city, the team of filmmakers and ethnographers met with families in their homes, followed them to work and school, and recorded the impact of mobile communication on their everyday lives. Melican was at first interested in the work/home segmentation issues of cell phones. But he says the team soon realized "that we were hearing equally interesting stuff from our younger subjects. Of course, few of the teens we spoke with have jobs, but they are confronted with their own interesting boundary issues—issues involving their roles as members of a family, their emerging social identities and their interactions with their schools and with school officials."

Consistently, Melican and other researchers found that cell phones offer kids privacy and independence while serving as primary connectors to their community. Kids can use these phones without being monitored by snooping family members. The ease of accessing friends with cell phones makes them an ideal community builder. And as with a driver's license, the cell phone has become a rite of passage. "You turn 16, you get a car and now a cell phone," says Andrew Pimentel, marketing director at wireless community portal and marketing firm Upoc.

Kids told Melican and Blinkoff that talking on a cell phone is a more personal form of communication. "It's like your own personal belonging. It's like your diary," said one teenager interviewed by Melican. And even as parents grow more accustomed to their children being

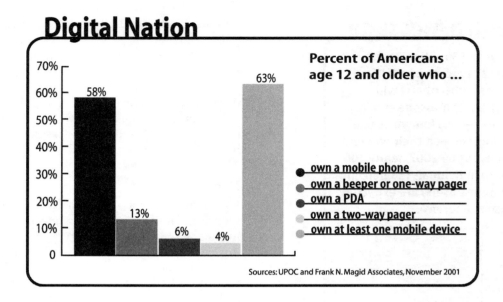

Digital Nation

Percent of Americans age 12 and older who ...

- own a mobile phone — 58%
- own a beeper or one-way pager — 13%
- own a PDA — 6%
- own a two-way pager — 4%
- own at least one mobile device — 63%

Sources: UPOC and Frank N. Magid Associates, November 2001

reachable, the cell phone is becoming a symbol of independence. "I can get in touch with [my parents] more and I talk with them more, but in a way, it doesn't really help bring us closer together because it enables me to ... get farther away," another teenager told Melican.

Similar reactions were uncovered by University of Surrey professor Nina Wakeford and Annenberg Research Fellow Nalini Kotamraju in a study done in late 2001. Kotamraju and Wakeford found that kids treat their cell phones like watches—always keeping their mobile phones within reach. One 17-year-old girl said she sometimes wears her cell phone around her neck when she sleeps.

If the cell phone helps kids get farther away from parents, it also helps them get closer to friends. In several instances, the researchers found kids organizing impromptu parties thanks to their cell phones. The cell has also become the first point of contact in dating, offering privacy and a certain level of anonymity. And when kids want to introduce themselves to someone new, Blinkoff's and Magid's research found, they're increasingly turning to text messaging.

Yet surprisingly, young people communicate with their parents as often as they do with their friends, Kotamraju and Wakeford discovered. Teens in the U.S., especially, expressed little resentment with the seeming "family surveillance" of parents checking up on them. As one 16-year-old boy in the U.S. explained it to Kotamraju, "She's my mom. I have to [answer] her calls, or if I miss her call, then I'll call her right back."

Making the Pitch

Opportunities for businesses exist because of these new habits, as countless marketing firms have realized. Never before have businesses had a chance to reach so many people individually and in context. Unlike idle Web surfers, cell phone users are out in the real world. And their increased tendency to be spontaneous could lead to sales when they're near a store, for example.

There's been a lot of dabbling with wireless marketing schemes, such as sending customers coupons and offering special wireless promotions over their cell phones. Stores and theme parks have experimented with wireless ordering and payment systems. At one golf course in Georgia, golfers can order food and beverages using their mobile phones and have it all caddied straight to them. At some Schlotzsky's Deli locations, cell phone users can order and pay for food directly over their phones using "digital wallets." And AvantGo, a Hayward, Calif., provider of mobile software, is hoping to turn its successful PalmPilot city guides into wireless portals supported by advertising. "Wireless allows a more targeted approach to reaching people," says Scott Searle at Lockstream, a Bellevue, Wash., developer of security software for wireless services. "But it's a different way of thinking."

> **Never before have businesses had a chance to reach so many people individually, yet business continue to search for ways to reach wireless customers without annoying them.**

So different that so far, it has been a nonstarter for most marketers. For all the opportunity, businesses continue to search for ways to reach wireless customers without annoying them. That, in part, has to do with the fact that Americans pay for calls they make as well as receive. Understandably, most consumers have resisted the idea of paying for messages from marketers.

Still, some firms think they have an answer to this dilemma. New York-based Upoc has focused on the community aspect of cell phones to let marketers tap in to various demographics. The company builds subscription communities, allowing users to instantly contact each other through their phones, primarily through text messaging. People can sign up for communities like Killer Mike, about the latest happenings in music, or the Alias Channel, for the latest scoop on the popular TV program *Alias* and to keep in touch with other fans wherever they go. Customers can also vote in polls and take part in special offers. They have been known to immediately contact each other whenever they spot stars or to get together with each other at events. Upoc offers up the agreeable communities to marketers for targeted messages.

Meanwhile, a service called Zingy enlists companies to advertise in an unusual way: by sending jingles as ring tones for mobile phones. Pepsi, Atlantic Records and Columbia Pictures have all used the service. In one instance, Zingy released rings based on singles from Wu-Tang Clan's *Iron Flag* and Mobb Deep's *Infamy* albums some weeks before they were released, to build buzz. According to Zingy, several hundred thousand fans chose the sound bites from these artists for their cell phones.

To be sure, there is a risk in going for gimmicks. But at least one critical lesson can be learned from marketers who have been successful on the Web: Give people what they want. "All this means that now's the time to create what people need," says Context-Based Research Group's Blinkoff. "People need mobility in their lives and are willing to accept certain sacrifices to get it."

UNIT 5

The Shape of Things to Come

Unit Selections

Key Points to Consider

- What attributes do new media forms need to win mainstream adoption?

- It has been argued that spectrum scarcity, the driving force behind FCC regulation of electronic media, is no longer an issue. Is there a need for regulation of Internet access? Of Internet content? Why or why not?

 **Links: www.dushkin.com/online/**
These sites are annotated in the World Wide Web pages.

Citizens Internet Empowerment Coalition (CIEC)
http://www.ciec.org
Educause
http://www.educause.edu

In 1926, U.S. inventor Lee De Forest, the "father of the radio," noted, "While theoretically and technically television may be feasible, commercially and financially I consider it an impossibility, a development of which we need waste little time day dreaming." In 1946, Darryl Zanuck, head of the 20th Century-Fox motion picture studio, predicted that "[Television] won't be able to hold onto any market it captures after the first six months. People will soon get tired of staring at a plywood box every night." Contrary to their predictions, television established itself as a mass medium with unexpected speed.

The articles in this section provide their own predictions of changes to come. Advertisers are taking new media increasingly seriously and are particularly intrigued with the target marketing potential of the Internet. It is estimated that today's typical Internet user will spend a million minutes, or 23.5 months, online during her or his lifetime. "Searching for Online Gold" discusses the attraction of user registration to gain access to online newspaper sites, balancing the potential of customized advertising against concerns about privacy, identity theft, and intrusiveness.

The eminent media theorist Marshall McLuhan proposed four questions that help predict how new media invariably affect the form and content of old media: (1) What does a new medium enhance or amplify in the culture? (2) What does it make obsolete, or push out of a position of prominence? (3) What does it retrieve from the past? and (4) What does a medium "reverse into" or "flip into" when it reaches the limits of its potential? Network television, for example, added visual to auditory communication and pushed radio out of prominence in broadcasting serial dramas, comedies, and soap operas. Television retrieved those formats from the past, while radio flipped into talk and music programming. "Low Power, High Intensity" describes another niche flip of radio aimed at serving localized audiences with "voices that have either been pushed out of the radio spectrum or were never invited into it." DVD players have flipped the way movies are made and marketed.

Not surprisingly, change in the media landscape has been viewed from varied perspectives. Some foresee an exciting evolution that turns today's passive media forms into a two-way, interactive information highway offering endless variety, convenience, and flexibility. Others fear the impact of consolidated corporate structures on independent news reporting. Some voice concern over misguided target-marketing schemes and consumer privacy. Some wonder whether digital recorders, which can strip broadcast advertisements and insert their own as they download programming for replay, will mark the end of commercial television as advertisers withdraw their willingness to pay for program production. Jamie Kellner, chairman of Turner Broadcasting System, has argued that folks who have DVR players that can skip over advertisements should pay a fee of $250 a year for ad-free TV. Some futurists predict media consumers' increasing selectivity may erode shared national identity and compromise informed decision-making (see "Exposure to Other Viewpoints Is Vital to Democracy").

Most media futurists admit that one important factor in the picture of media to come is the evolution of business and technological linkages that set the stage for widespread adoption: alliances between AOL Time Warner and its media industry rivals; agreements between Sony, Philips, Kohji Hase/Toshiba, IBM, and Warner Brothers on a single DVD format; deals involving programmers, carriers, hardware manufacturers, and advertisers necessary to make interactive television attractive, reliable, and profitable. Another factor is the direction of government regulatory policy. Movie studios and broadcast networks are lobbying Congress to mandate transmission protection that will block digital HDTV signals from being copied or redistributed over the Internet; consumer electronics manufacturers contend that such protection will infringe on legitimate home recording. Media companies that fought VCRs on copyright infringement grounds in 1984 have headed to court again over digital video recorder (DVR) technology. A third factor is cost—of both media services and of equipment and infrastructure. Still, converting to digital transmission at an estimated cost of $3,000,000 per facility is a challenge for small-market broadcasters. PBS, operating without commercial revenue, faces a transfer cost of $1,800,000,000.

Technology is the conduit through which mass media messages move between senders and receivers. Its development is a scientific experiment, but its use is a social endeavor. Mass media shape the form and content of mass messages, of who communicates what to whom, with what intent, and what effect.

Searching for Online Gold

Newspapers are trying a variety of methods to wring money from their Web sites. One increasingly popular approach is requiring visitors to register, in order to amass data to help boost advertising. But the paid-subscription model is losing favor.

By Doug Brown

Reading a print newspaper every day involves a standard exchange: Before wading through the stories, customers buy the paper. There's nothing standard, however, about reading news online.

Everybody who wants to read the Wall Street Journal's cyberspace edition (online.wsj.com/public/us) must pay, whether or not they're print subscribers. At the Albuquerque Journal (www. abqjournal.com), print customers get memberships to the online version, but everyone else must fork over a fee to see Journal stories. But at Albuquerque's other newspaper, the Albuquerque Tribune, anybody can glide into www.abqtrib.com and surf themselves silly, without registering or spending money. Those who want to peruse the New York Times (www.nytimes.com) can do so for free, but first must register and adopt a user name and password.

Why the diversity? The drive for revenue. Online publishing is still a big experiment, and papers around the country are trying just about anything to beguile advertisers and persuade them to open their wallets. For years, newspapers dumped money and resources into their blossoming online operations without seeing profits. The frenetic pace of newspapers' spending for online dropped, however, after the dotcom collapse. At the same time, newspapers grew more adamant about squeezing profits out of their electronic offerings. It's now an industrywide standard, for example, to charge customers for access to news archives. The practice, however, doesn't funnel much money to the bottom line—less than 5 percent of total online revenue, according to Peter Krasilovsky, a partner with the media consultancy Borrell Associates Inc. in Virginia.

In some cases, the hunt for elusive advertising dollars is starting to pay off. This year, for a change, newspaper publishers are trumpeting the money their online operations are raking in. Some, like the Tribune Co., Knight Ridder and Scripps Howard, are calling their cyberspace efforts profitable.

But the trend will not necessarily culminate in a revenue fiesta.

Of 246 newspapers surveyed during 2002, between half and two-thirds claimed their online arms were profitable, according to a study by Borrell Associates Inc. Profitability, however, is hard to measure with online sites, says company President Gordon Borrell, because they depend on the print publications for content and, in many cases, free advertising.

Borrell, in fact, is troubled by online publishing trends for newspapers. The average newspaper Web site gets 70 percent of its revenue from classified advertising, he says. "There is great fear that the business model of charging for classified advertising is going to dissipate or disappear on the Internet, because classifieds are as much content that draws traffic as they are advertising on the Internet, and the cost of delivering that content is cheap on the Internet," he says. "So we believe there will be some downward pressure on online classified listing revenue, and if newspapers are overly dependent on that they're in real trouble."

At the same time, Borrell champions how aggressively newspapers have pursued cyberspace. In 2002, newspapers harvested $655 million in online revenue, according to a Borrell study. That's much better than the number for local television news Web sites, which raked in only $55 million in revenue during the same year. The Internet was an opportunity for television news to get some of the classified advertising dollars that newspapers have long feasted upon, but only now are broadcasters exploring classified ads on their Web sites, says Krasilovsky.

One thing is certain: As newspapers' online outfits stumble across moneymaking formulas, expect to see a burgeoning uniformity among their Web sites, experts say. Reading online will increasingly come with strings attached. And for now, those strings will largely be tied to free registration requirements at newspaper sites—not paid online subscription schemes.

Online publishing at the E.W. Scripps Co. newspaper chain turned a profit for the first time last year, says Bob Benz, Scripps' general manager of interactive media.

When the company started launching Web sites in the 1990s, the cyberspace operations were kept separate from print editorial and advertising. The advantage, Benz says, was a "fresh culture" online. But by keeping that sharp demarcation, the Web sites lost the community connection, the tentacle reach that took newspapers as much as 100 years to build.

Registration gives the advertising staff detailed demographic data, which they can use to build the reader portraits that clients demand. The level of detail, combined with the ability to customize ads, is the online publishing advantage.

"When we disassociated ourselves from that online," Benz says, "we created an uphill battle for ourselves to become profitable."

The corporation abandoned that approach about two years ago, melding print with electronic and broadcast. The change, Benz says, transformed the online ventures from struggling editorial sideshows to increasingly muscular profit centers. Benz declined to elaborate on the extent that the digital side was bleeding prior to the union of offline and online, but he did say the digital side would not be profitable if not for the merger.

E.W. Scripps' Bob Benz says the chain will nudge its newspapers toward registration models, where customers must provide personal information and open a free account before accessing online news.

"We aren't going it alone anymore," he says. "We're pushing multimedia sales, multimedia content. I think we're finally turning the corner, where people realize they don't just work for a newspaper anymore, they gather and disseminate news. It may be the newspaper, it may be online, it may be broadcast."

Benz says the next step is nudging the chain's more than 20 newspapers toward registration models, where

customers must provide personal information and open a free account before accessing news. The chain will probably introduce such models this year, with each publication deciding for itself whether to try it. Benz, however, is a big registration booster.

"Online should not be free," he says. "You shouldn't be able to just come in and take that information. You may not have to pay money for it, but you might need to hand over information and see some advertising."

Gordon Borrell, president of Borrell Associates, fears newspapers depend too much on classified advertising to make money from their Web sites. "If newspapers are overly dependent on that they're in real trouble."

Registration can reveal loads about online readers. It gives the advertising staff detailed demographic data, which they can use to build the reader portraits that clients demand. The level of detail, combined with the ability to customize ads, is the online publishing advantage.

"I have a base of registered users, and I know what they are interested in," Benz says. "Over time, I gather information about them and they trust me to use that information intelligently and not abuse the information. I can do some pretty powerful things for advertisers and my readers."

Steve Yelvington, vice president of strategy and content for Morris Digital Works, a corporate arm of the media company Morris Communications, says the company plans to adopt registration at the Web sites of its 26 small and midsize daily newspapers even though the online outfit hit the black last year.

Registration will let the newspapers fine-tune their advertising pitches, he says, and show readers ads that match their demographic. Morris isn't too worried about the inevitable post-registration erosion of traffic.

"There is traffic, and then there is good traffic, and there are users and then there are good users," Yelvington says. "You are going to lose some traffic by putting barriers to usage in place.... But the traffic you will lose is largely not interesting traffic, it's people who aren't going to come more than once in a blue moon anyway. They aren't in your community, they are following some search engine link. That's not the sort of audience we need to be building."

Imposing registration schemes on readers is "a really smart thing to do," says University of California, Berkeley, adjunct professor Paul Grabowicz, an online publishing specialist. "There doesn't seem to be as much resistance as we once feared," he says. "I think part of that is people are feeling a little more comfortable with the medium, so some of the concerns about privacy and identity theft and having your personal information peddled to marketers has dissipated a little."

But the whole model could crumble if media companies abuse their online relationships with readers. If companies sell readers' registered data, opening the floodgates to spam, then people won't sign up and online publishers will fail to capitalize on the Internet's commercial possibilities.

The balance between customized advertising and intrusiveness may be delicate, but it's worth striving for, Grabowicz says. After all, he adds, delivering custom ads is the "value proposition" of online publishing.

For now the Internet is "an unproven commodity," with big advertisers like Procter & Gamble and Coca-Cola hesitating on the sidelines. Nobody quite understands, yet, how to make cyberspace work for huge businesses, but Grabowicz thinks the answer is wrapped up with registration. "If ads can be personalized," he says, "then I think you'll start to see more of a shift in advertising dollars."

Only a few dozen newspapers now charge for online access, says Krasilovsky, of Borrell Associates. At the end of 2001, analysts were predicting that newspapers in much greater numbers would force people to pay for online content, he says, but after flirting with subscription models, "most papers have reevaluated, and while they might want special premium [content] tiers, they are better off finding out who their users are and selling advertisers on their reach."

Morris' Steve Yelvington isn't worried about the loss of visitors registration will bring. "[T]he traffic you will lose is largely not interesting traffic, it's people who aren't going to come more than once in a blue moon anyway."

"Registration is the drumbeat of 2003, rather than firewalls," he says.

Both Benz and Yelvington dismiss the subscription tactic. Morris experimented with a paid-content model at its Juneau, Alaska, paper several years ago, but abandoned it because "it wasn't working," Yelvington says.

At Morris, one of the company's overarching aims is to bring in younger readers, those under the age of 35. Yelvington calls the Internet "a powerful tool to win that audience back, and we want to be aggressive about pulling that audience in." Making them pay for access, he reasons, seems counterproductive.

"If you look at the curve of Net usage by age group, it's pretty much the reverse of the curve of the readership of newspapers," Yelvington adds. "Younger people simply go online more often. They're not necessarily going online and reading news, and that's something we need to change."

Says Benz: "The demographic that might be coming to you online but not getting your paper may be your most valuable demographic. If we drive them away, we've

missed a huge opportunity. Most younger readers are marginal in their interests in the paper to begin with. When they come online, it may be our chance to reel them in and tell them, 'You know what? A paper is relevant to your life. As you buy a house, as you get ingrained in a community, you need to know what the zoning board is doing, what the city council is doing.'" The Tribune Co. started requiring registration for the Los Angeles Times and the Chicago Tribune Web sites last year, and it's headed toward the subscription concept, says David Hiller, senior vice president of Tribune and president of Tribune Interactive. "I think that the totally free, complete open-access Web site model is pretty flawed, and we're going to be working on a better mousetrap," Hiller says. "Elements of subscription will definitely be a part of it."

"I think that the totally free, complete open access Web site model is pretty flawed, and we're going to be working on a better mousetrap," says David Hiller, president of Tribune Interactive.

Tribune Interactive became profitable in the second quarter of 2002, Hiller says. Cutting expenses and building the advertising from $50 million in 2000 to $77 million in 2002 brought the division past the break-even point. Classifieds in particular, he says, have been a boon for the interactive division, accounting for about 75 percent of all ad revenue.

Tribune's next goal is targeted advertising, which, Hiller says, "was one of the primary reasons for getting into registration." "With those 2.5 million people who have registered [at the Los Angeles Times and the Chicago Tribune Web sites], we're able to target on-site advertising as well as develop targeted specialized e-mail programs that are very popular with advertisers and something for which they are willing to pay considerably."

Most newspapers aren't embracing subscription models, says Neil Budde, founder of the Wall Street Journal Online and now a consultant. Advertising executives at papers don't want to scare off clients just venturing into cyberspace; they don't want to rattle them with the loss of traffic that subscriptions bring. But longer term, he says, where newspapers "have a franchise for local news, you will see some level of subscription imposed."

Michael Zimbalist, executive director of the Online Publishers Association, an industry trade group, echoes Budde, saying that smaller newspapers will likely lead the subscription battle cry. "In a funny way," he says, "they are more indispensable to their market than the big metros."

The Albuquerque Journal did exactly what Benz and Yelvington warn against—it forced readers to pay to read. The guy in charge of the paper's online division, Donn Friedman, isn't blinking.

How Stand-Alone Sites Cope

Newspapers are forcing readers to jump through hoops before they can get to Web stories, but the situation can get even more complicated at stand-alone online news sites.

For instance, nearly everything is free at the financial news Web site CBSMarketWatch.com, and anybody can click with abandon through Slate.com. Want to read a story on the National Journal's Technology Daily Web site? You'll have to pay as much as $4,700 for a year's subscription. And as of April, readers who want to zip through online People, Entertainment Weekly, Teen People and a host of other AOL Time Warner titles have to pay for either AOL memberships or magazine subscriptions. For now, Time, Sports Illustrated, Money and Business 2.0 will remain accessible to anyone online.

And that's all easy compared with the system at Salon.com, where readers have choices: They can drop $30 for the "premium" subscription and get Salon without advertisements for a year as well as free magazine subscriptions, discounts and MP3 downloads; or pay $18.50 but see ads and get some but not all of the premium advantages; or go for $6 a month for the access with ads and even fewer perks. Also in the mix of possibilities is a seven-day trial, in which people first pay any of the annual fee options and then keep or cancel the membership, and a free "day pass," which comes larded with full-page advertisements that capture the screen before delivering the stories.

As at newspapers, the divergent approaches to cultivating both readers and advertisers are symptomatic of an industry in flux. Online publishing is less than a decade old, and companies are picking their way through a buffet of models to see what formula best delivers profits.

CBS MarketWatch, where all is free, this year proudly announced its first profitable quarter. In March, Salon's chairman, founder and editor, David Talbot, praised the subscription gambit, calling it "the key reason Salon is in business today." Slate is "on a path to profitability" with a "dramatically" growing audience, says Publisher Cyrus Krohn. "Television is down, print is down, but online is growing." Slate and Salon, online newsmagazines of sorts, specialize in irreverent news commentary, arts and entertainment coverage and feisty columnists.

Advertisers like to plug their products online because they can reach people during the day, says Larry Kramer, chief executive officer of CBS MarketWatch.

The hook online Web sites are nabbing advertisers with is access to those elusive consumers who historically might have read the paper or watched a little TV in the morning and listened to the radio on the way to work, but were then largely inaccessible until the end of the workday. With Internet-wired computers on the desks of so many desirable consumers, the time between commutes is no longer an advertising wasteland.

"TV is primarily a prime-time media, but for us prime time is daytime," says Larry Kramer, chairman and chief executive officer of CBS MarketWatch (cbsmarketwatch.com). "That's how we're going after the biggest advertisers. They are on our site because they can reach that audience during the day that they are reaching at night. It's a big deal when you are trying to deliver a message."

Kramer credits the site's editorial niche, extensive licensing deals and cost-cutting for its financial success. "Financial news is perfect for the Internet," he says. "It has a short shelf life, it has a need to be paired up with historical data, and it in some ways needs to be both customized and not customized—you need a front-page mentality to help people know what is important.... But there is value in giving them customized news, based on what stocks they own."

The online Wall Street Journal "did us a big favor" by charging for information, Kramer adds. People interested in financial news, but not in paying for it, came to CBS MarketWatch, Kramer says, and haven't left.

About half of the site's revenue comes from licensing. The company licenses content—stories written by MarketWatch staffers—to more than 200 Web sites, Kramer says, including all of the major financial brokerages. It also bought a technology company specializing in financial software called BigCharts a few years ago, and it licenses BigCharts services to other Web sites. BigCharts software lets Web sites, for example, offer their clientele customized maps, graphs and other information about financial data.

The online magazine Slate is "on a path to profitability" with a "dramatically" growing audience, says Publisher Cyrus Krohn.

"When advertising was cut in half from 2000 to 2001, licensing grew about 75 percent," Kramer boasts.

Slate toyed with paid subscriptions in 1998 before abandoning the approach after 11 months and letting readers surf the site for free (see Free Press, March 1999). "We had 30,000 subscribers," says Publisher Krohn. "It became apparent that advertising would be the better approach." Revenue has grown every year during the past five years, he says, and "we're on a path to profitability."

Krohn adds, however, that Slate, which has the deep pockets of Microsoft behind it, may simply have been ahead of its time. "We may want to revisit that in the future," he says.

"At the moment we're having a good deal of success with advertising, and we're getting Fortune 500 companies with six-and seven-figure marketing campaigns," he continues. "Ultimately, I think we made the right decision, and whether or not we choose to pursue a subscription model in the future with some content, or put the entire site behind a subscription model, those are all avenues we will consider taking."

Technology Daily (nationaljournal.com/pubs/techdaily/) started publishing during the height of the Internet boom, in January 1999, and it's still up and running, supporting five reporters and other editorial staffers all focuses on one thing: intersections of government and technology.

continued

How Stand-Alone Sites Cope (continued)

Washington is dense with rarefied print publications like Technology Daily, which is essentially a newsletter for lobbyists and other creatures of the capital who obsess over government minutiae. Information is vital to these people, about 350 of whom are willing to spend big bucks on Technology Daily.

"You're talking about people who are very well informed, and you're trying to tell them something they don't know already," Says Editor in Chief Louis Peck. He says Technology Daily has been "marginally profitable" for the first time this year.

Salon received "lots of snide and skeptical" comments when it started "charging for access," says Chairman David Talbot. But the subscription revenue "has kept us going."

No online publication has been subject to as much scrutiny, praise and ridicule as Salon, founded in San Francisco in 1995 by Talbot, a former arts and features editor at the San Francisco Examiner. News of Salon's imminent demise has appeared persistently since the collapse of the dotcom bubble, fluttering through Weblogs and newspapers as regularly as government consumer spending reports. The site has in deed come close to shuttering several times, but injections of cash from investors have allowed Talbot & Co. to escape from every dance with death.

The company has tried a range of different money-making strategies. For the most part, however, it lives thanks to the wallets of investors.

"Talbot says the company continues to examine deals with print publishers and broadcasters to further cement the Salon brand, but it's mostly focusing on the Internet. The company received "lots of snide and skeptical" comments when it started charging for access. But the subscription revenue "has kept us going," he says, explaining that the rise in subscription revenues convinced investors that Salon was viable, and that's one reason they hung in there.

The company achieved its first week of profitability in February, Talbot says. About 60,000 people have bought subscriptions, accounting for about half of the company's revenue. The other half, advertising, fell "considerably during the past year or so," Talbot says, partially blaming the constant Salon deathwatch.

"The economy has been terrible," Talbot laments. But in the wake of the war in Iraq, he predicts, "advertising will come back. It can't be down forever."

—Doug Brown

The independent, family-owned paper first published an online edition in 1996, keeping the site free and open until July 2001 when it launched what Friedman calls "our print-retention model." "There was enough anecdotal evidence of people saying, 'I've stopped getting the paper because I can get it online for free,'" he says. The cannibalization cost the company only 2 or 3 percent of its circulation, he says, about 4,800 subscribers out of about 160,000. But that loss wasn't worth it.

All print subscribers get the online edition for free. Everybody else pays $8 a month or $60 a year. When the paper switched to the new model, traffic plummeted by between 20 percent and 40 percent and the office was flooded with calls from angry New Mexicans.

In 2000, the Web site enjoyed about 133,000 unique visitors a month. That dropped to 106,000 users in 2001, but has now rebounded to 130,000, Friedman says. About a quarter of the paper's print subscribers signed up for free online memberships. Another 1,600 people have paid for online-only access.

At first Donn Friedman, head of the Albuquerque Journal's online division, wasn't enthusiastic about making visitors pay, but now he embraces the concept.

Friedman was not thrilled, at first, about making everybody pay. He liked the freewheeling environment of the Internet, where so much information is free and the reigning ethos ridicules anything involving forking over money for service. He was also leery of the drop in advertising that he predicted would follow the change.

The ads did fall off immediately after the switchover. But now, he says, ad sales people "have found it easier to sell ads, in the same way it's easier to sell ads in papers that are paid."

"We know the people who are entering our site, who took the time to register," he says. "They will spend more time with the content. They are members, they are readers, and if they've taken the time to log in, they will spend more time at the site as well."

Clickshare Service Corp. designs systems that let publishers sell content. Newspapers are a big client. "I would say it's dramatically different from a year ago, it's picked up a lot," says Vice President Dirk Swart.

At Clickshare Service Corp. in Massachusetts, business is brisk. The company designs systems that let publishers sell content. Newspapers are a big client.

"I would say it's dramatically different from a year ago, it's picked up a lot," says Dirk Swart, the company's vice president of customer technology. "There clearly is an understanding that this is a need."

Clickshare works with about 15 newspapers, including the Worcester Telegram & Gazette, which offers a variety of pay-as-you-go plans. Want to read a story on the Web site? If you subscribe to the print edition, you can surf for free. Otherwise, you could pay 50 cents for a day's worth of access, or choose from other options: $1.99 a week, $6.75 a month, $69 a year.

Clickshare allows publishers to introduce registration schemes, which Swart champions as a good interim step on the march toward paid subscriptions. By starting with a registration model, "you move your readers gradually in that direction," he says.

The Wall Street Journal has charged for access to its Web site since August 1996. The model has worked and the folks at Dow Jones aren't going to fiddle with it, says Scott Schulman, senior vice president of sales and marketing of Dow Jones Consumer Electronic Publishing. People who don't subscribe to the print edition are charged $79 a year to get online while print subscribers pay $39.

Dow Jones' Scott Schulman says the Wall Street Journal's online health edition "has dramatically increased traffic."

"Our strategy is about premium content and premium audience, meaning we have a very desirable audience that advertisers want, and a premium environment, because we have a clean, less cluttered environment on our site compared to the others that only depend on advertising for their revenues," he says. "All of the pieces support each other."

The Internet business unit, Consumer Electronic Publishing, has been profitable since the third quarter of 2002. The business unit includes more than WSJ.com, but the Journal's Web site is the largest of the roughly 10 businesses within the division, according to spokeswoman Karen Miller Pensiero. As a "corporate practice," she says, the company does not break out profitability levels for any individual products.

The Journal this year launched a new online product, Health Industry Edition, which telescopes content around the health care industry. The site—essentially a trade magazine carved out of the online Journal—costs the same as the regular online Journal, and once readers sign up, they can tap into the rest of the electronic Journal, and vice-versa.

The health edition generates new subscriptions, Schulman says, and it "has dramatically increased the traffic to our health content." "The Wall Street Journal has always done a fantastic job of health coverage, and this was a way to elevate it and highlight it," he says. "It's a way to get incremental subscribers who might not subscribe to the Wall Street Journal, but view this as very valuable."

The journal has launched another so-called "vertical site" on media and marketing aimed at professionals in advertising, public relations, media and entertainment.

After the collapse of the dotcom economy, some advertisers went away, or their budgets withered, and the site did lose revenue. But display ads were up about 20 percent in 2002 over 2001, Schulman says, and the trend seems to be continuing this year. Subscriptions continue to rise, too, up about 9 percent this year over last, hovering around 700,000.

Only six papers, according to Schulman, have more paid subscribers than Wall Street Journal online.

The challenge ahead is all about size, says Zimbalist of the Online Publishers Association. Newspaper online ventures are finally turning profits, but can they grow into revenue leviathans?

"If today the online channel is contributing 3 or 4 percent, how can it get to 10 or 20 percent in the next five years, and where will it reach the point of equilibrium?" he asks. "Everyone feels we are just ramping up now."

Doug Brown, a regular contributor to AJR, is a writer based in Baltimore.

EMERGING ALTERNATIVES

LOW POWER, HIGH INTENSITY

Building Communities on the FM Dial

They bought their equipment on e-Bay. Their antenna is attached to a water pipe on the roof. They have only two staff members, but more than fifty people volunteer in the studio on their time off from jobs as factory workers, busboys, and grocery clerks. Few at the station speak English. Some are illiterate. No one has any previous experience in radio. It's WSBL-LP in South Bend, Indiana, and it's low-power FM.

BY LAURIE KELLIHER

In the increasingly corporate world of radio, low-power FM isn't about how far your signal reaches but how near. These are neighborhood stations with 100-watt signals that travel single-digit miles. They are run by civil rights organizations, by environmental activists, by church groups and school districts. They are voices that have either been pushed out of the radio spectrum or never invited into it, and the appetite for them speaks to a growing need in this country for community. And with a recent technical study providing leverage in low-power's struggle with big radio, there just might be more of them on air.

Low-power FM licenses were introduced in January 2000 under William E. Kennard, then former Federal Communications Commission chairman. The move was partly a strategy to control the proliferation of unlicensed pirate channels, partly a reparation for the Telecommunications Act of 1996, which deregulated

radio and set the stage for media consolidation. The idea was simple: low-power FM stations would be small enough to fit between the frequencies of existing full-power stations, and their licenses would be granted to noncommercial organizations for educational purposes. "When hundreds of stations are owned by just one person or company," Kennard said in March 2000, "service to local communities and coverage of local issues lose out."

On the west side of South Bend, losing out meant a Hispanic community with no Spanish-language radio station. When WSBL-LP began its Spanish-language broadcast in September 2002, the community not only heard traditional and contemporary Hispanic music but also received English-language vocabulary lessons during the breaks. The station raises money for a local scholarship fund and helps collect corn flour for the local food bank. WSBL-LP regularly runs public service an-

nouncements for early-childhood vaccinations, prostate cancer testing, and HIV screenings, and can measure the results. "The statistics at local clinics jumped from last year to this," says Eliud Villanueva, director of WSBL-LP. "We have really made a difference, and that surprised us more than anyone else."

For Villanueva, an electrical inspector with no previous radio experience, the road to WSBL-LP began with a 700-mile drive to Maryland. That's where the Prometheus Radio Project was holding a "radio barn-raising" seminar at the site of another low-power FM station, WRYR-LP in Sherwood, Maryland. Prometheus, a nonprofit organization devoted to the growth of noncommercial community radio, offers legal and technical support to communities that want to build a low-power station—something that can realistically be done for about

$10,000. The barn-raising offers three days of classes (including "Intro to Radio Engineering," "Running an All-Volunteer News Operation," "How the FCC Works") and concludes with the raising of a transmission tower and the station's first broadcast. "Once these stations were just a glint in the eye of the village wacko," says Pete Tridish, technical director for Prometheus. "People would say, 'You can't build a radio channel, only Clear Channel can build a radio channel.'"

Clear Channel, based in San Antonio, Texas, now owns more than 1,200 radio stations in 230 cities and has become Exhibit A for opponents of media consolidation. Many of its broadcasts originate in locations other than the cities where they are heard, saving Clear Channel considerable money. Low-power FM is technically and philosophically the opposite, originating locally and focusing tightly on local needs and concerns. "The purpose of low-power FM isn't profit," says Tridish. "The purpose is to rethink how we use media to bring communities together."

Mike Shay was a member of a Maryland environmental group battling to prevent a Chesapeake Bay wetland area from being developed into a supermarket when his organization applied to the FCC for a construction permit to build WRYR-LP. "We thought of it as a way to fight billionaire developers and corporations on a playing field that was not level," says Shay. WRYR-LP identifies itself as the first radio station owned and operated by an environmental group. Amid a mix of gospel, jazz, and alternative music, the station runs programs dedicated to local and national environmental issues. WRYR-LP also offers coverage of county council meetings and local elections, with particular emphasis on land-use and zoning issues. The programs on the station feature local musicians and writers, and are hosted by local residents. "We thought if we could celebrate our community, we would make it stronger," says Shay.

As with most low-power FM stations, WRYR-LP is funded through the donations of local residents and businesses. Running the station is a challenge for a volunteer staff with other full-time jobs, but the difficulties haven't deterred them. Shay, who traveled to Richmond, Virginia, to deliver a statement at the FCC's public hearing on broadcast ownership rules there last February, says he is disgusted with media deregulation and the buildup of media conglomerates: "Everything is going in such a wrong direction. Low-power FM is the one bright spot."

The birth of the low-power FM movement is generally attributed to DeWayne Readus, later renamed MBanna Kantako, who in 1987 began a 1-watt broadcast out of his apartment in Springfield, Illinois. "Kantako was the Johnny Appleseed of micro-radio," says Peter Franck, a San Francisco lawyer who advised Kantako on behalf of the National Lawyers Guild when the FCC fined Kantako for broadcasting without a license. Kantako was broadcasting to the African-American community in the John Hay Homes housing project where he lived, and his shows discussed the issues concerning that community, particularly issues related to police brutality in Springfield at the time. "People with alternative concerns of all kinds want to speak to their community," says Franck. "They want media that is not mediated by the government or by corporate advertisers."

But with limited spectrum space, radio has always necessitated some sort of regulation. And it is the apportionment of that spectrum space that is at issue in the low-power FM movement. When the FCC opened its first window for low-power construction permits in May 2000, 720 applications were filed. At the same time, the National Association of Broadcasters, joined by National Public Radio, raised concerns with Congress about the potential interference low-power FM channels might cause to existing full-power channels, and asked that the prescribed minimum dial distance between the two be increased. More distance meant fewer low-power channels. Though studies done by FCC engineers showed that the low-power signals were too small to cause interference at the designated distance, Congress complied with the NAB and NPR request for further study in December 2000. This effectively knocked out of contention more than half the original applications and all but excluded low-power stations from congested urban markets.

Low-power advocates were appalled. "It has never been appropriate policy in this country for Congress to make engineering decisions," says Cheryl Leanza, deputy director of Media Access Project, a public-interest telecommunications law firm based in Washington, D.C. "They were persuaded by incumbent broadcasters."

The results of the independent study requested by Congress were released in July and concluded what low-power FM advocates and FCC engineers had always maintained: that the majority of interference issues voiced by the NAB and NPR were not legitimate. A public comment period will now be open until September 12, when the FCC will prepare its recommendation to Congress. "Right now is a very important time for media policy," says Leanza. "Low-power FM is one step we can take on a national level that says we support diversity and localism in media."

While the study is potentially good news for low-power FM, conceivably adding hundreds of new channels to the existing 220, the movement is still mired in bureaucracy with many applications filed more than a year ago still awaiting approval. Chairman Michael K. Powell announced in a press conference on August 20 that the FCC would expedite the approval process but the agency is not currently accepting new applications for licenses and has not said when it will start again.

Which makes a station like Radio Bird Street grateful it has its license. "I would have been a pirate station if it weren't for low-power FM," says Erv Knorzer, general manager of KRBS-LP in Oroville, California. When KRBS-LP moved into an abandoned laundromat, its goal was to bring community radio to Oroville. In the process it brought some life back to a downtown area that had been deserted years ago for outlying strip malls. The station runs public service announcements for the local library, community theater, and senior center. It broadcasts the independent news program *Democracy Now!*, offering an alternative to the nearby commercial stations, five of which are owned by Clear Channel. Knorzer's daughter, Marianne, serves as the station manager and arranges a programming schedule that includes Hmong-language news broadcasts for the Oroville Laotian community and a labor issues show that keeps local hospital workers up to date with news of the local Steelworkers Union. The station's youngest deejay is ten, the oldest seventy-two. The board of directors includes members of the local Mexican-American, Native-American, African-American, and Hmong communities. The studio on Bird Street is often crowded with people from the sixty-five-member staff of volunteers who make the station run. "This station gives hope to a lot of people," says Marianne.

Editor's note: A Q&A with Pete Tridish of The Prometheus Radio Project can be found on www.cjr.org.

Laurie Kelliher is an assistant editor at CJR.

From *Columbia Journalism Review*, September/October 2003, pp. 31-33. © 2003 by Graduate School of Journalism, Columbia University.

The Myth of Interference

Internet architect David Reed explains how bad science created the broadcast industry.

By David Weinberger

There's a reason our television sets so outgun us, spraying us with trillions of bits while we respond only with the laughable trickles from our remotes. To enable signals to get through intact, the government has to divide the spectrum of frequencies into bands, which it then licenses to particular broadcasters. NBC has a license and you don't.

Thus, NBC gets to bathe you in "Friends," followed by a very special "Scrubs," and you get to sit passively on your couch. It's an asymmetric bargain that dominates our cultural, economic and political lives—only the rich and famous can deliver their messages—and it's all based on the fact that radio waves in their untamed habitat interfere with one another.

Except They Don't.

"Interference is a metaphor that paints an old limitation of technology as a fact of nature." So says David P. Reed, electrical engineer, computer scientist, and one of the architects of the Internet. If he's right, then spectrum isn't a resource to be divvied up like gold or parceled out like land. It's not even a set of pipes with their capacity limited by how wide they are or an aerial highway with white lines to maintain order.

Spectrum is more like the colors of the rainbow, including the ones our eyes can't discern. Says Reed: "There's no scarcity of spectrum any more than there's a scarcity of the color green. We could instantly hook up to the Internet everyone who can pick up a radio signal, and they could pump through as many bits as they could ever want. We'd go from an economy of digital scarcity to an economy of digital abundance."

So throw out the rulebook on what should be regulated and what shouldn't. Rethink completely the role of the Federal Communications Commission in deciding who gets allocated what. If Reed is right, nearly a century of government policy on how to best administer the airwaves needs to be reconfigured, from the bottom up.

Spectrum as color seems like an ungainly metaphor on which to hang a sweeping policy change with such important social and economic implications. But Reed will tell you it's not a metaphor at all. Spectrum is color. It's the literal, honest-to-Feynman truth.

David Reed is many things, but crackpot is not one of them. He was a professor of computer science at MIT, then chief scientist at Software Arts during its VisiCalc days, and then the chief scientist at Lotus during its 1-2-3 days. But he is probably best known as a coauthor of the paper that got the Internet's architecture right: "End-to-End Arguments in System Design."

Or you may recognize him as the author of what's come to be known as Reed's Law—which says the true value of a network isn't determined by the number of individual nodes it connects (Metcalfe's Law) but by the far higher number of groups it enables. But I have to confess that I'm biased when it comes to David Reed. I first encountered him in person three years ago at a tiny conference when he deftly pulled me out of a hole I was digging for myself in front of an audience of my betters. Since then, I've watched him be bottomlessly knowledgeable on a technical mailing list and patiently helpful as a source for various articles I've worked on.

It doesn't take much to get Reed to hold forth on his strong, well-articulated political and social beliefs. But when it comes to spectrum, he speaks most passionately as a scientist. "Photons, whether they are light photons, radio photons, or gamma-ray photons, simply do not interfere with one another," he explains. "They pass through one another."

Reed uses the example of a pinhole camera, or camera obscura: If a room is sealed against light except for one pinhole, an image of the outside will be projected against the opposite wall. "If photons interfered with one another as they squeezed through that tiny hole, we wouldn't get a clear image on that back wall," Reed says.

If you whine that it's completely counterintuitive that a wave could squeeze through a pinhole and "reorganize" itself on the other side, Reed nods happily and then piles on: "If photons can pass through one another, then they aren't actually occupying space at all, since the definition of 'occupying' is 'displacing.' So, yes, it's counterintuitive. It's quantum mechanics."

Surprisingly, the spectrum-as-color metaphor turns out to be not nearly as confounding to what's left of common sense. "Radio and light are the same thing and follow the same laws," Reed says. "They're distinguished by what we call frequency." Frequency, he explains, is really just the energy level of the photons. The human eye detects different frequencies as different colors. So, in licensing frequencies to broadcasters, we are literally regulating colors. Crayola may own the names of the colors it's invented, and Pantone may own the standard numbers by which digital designers refer to colors, but only the FCC can give you an exclusive license to a color itself.

Reed prefers to talk about "RF [radio frequency] color," because the usual alternative is to think of spectrum as some large swatch of property. If it's property, it is easily imagined as finite and something that can be owned. If spectrum is color, it's a lot harder to think of in that way. Reed would recast the statement "WABC-AM has an exclusive license to broadcast at 770 kHz in NYC" to "The government has granted WABC-AM an exclusive license to the color Forest Green in NYC." Only then, according to Reed, does the current licensing policy sound as absurd as it is.

But if photons don't interfere, why do our radios and cellphones go all crackly? Why do we sometimes pick up two stations at once and not hear either well enough?

The problem isn't with the radio waves. It's with the receivers: "Interference cannot be defined as a meaningful concept until a receiver tries to separate the signal. It's the processing that gets confused, and the confusion is highly specific to the particular detector," Reed says. Interference isn't a fact of nature. It's an artifact of particular technologies. This should be obvious to anyone who has upgraded a radio receiver and discovered that the interference has gone away: The signal hasn't changed, so it has to be the processing of the signal that's improved. The interference was in the eye of the beholder all along. Or, as Reed says, "Interference is what we call the information that a particular receiver is unable to separate."

But, Reed says, "I can't sign on to 'It's the receiver, stupid.'" We have stupid radios not because we haven't figured out how to make them smart but because there's been little reason to make them smart. They're designed to expect signal to be whatever comes in on a particular frequency, and noise to be everything on other frequencies. "The problem is more complex than just making smart radios, because some of the techniques for un-confusing the receiver are best implemented at the transmitter, or in a network of cooperating transmitters and receivers. It's not simply the radios. It's the systems architecture, stupid!"

One of the simplest examples of an architecture that works was invented during World War II. We were worried that the Germans might jam the signals our submarines used to control their radio-controlled torpedoes. This inspired the first "frequency-hopping" technology: The transmitter and receiver were made to switch, in sync, very rapidly among a scheduled, random set of frequencies. Even if some of those frequencies were in use by other radios or jammers, error detection and retransmission would ensure a complete, correct message. The U.S. Navy has used a version of frequency-hopping as the basis of its communications since 1958. So we know that systems that enable transmitters and receivers to negotiate do work—and work very well.

So what architecture would Reed implement if he were king of the world or, even less likely, chairman of the FCC?

Here Reed is dogmatically undogmatic: "Attempting to decide what is the best architecture before using it always fails. Always." This is in fact a one-line recapitulation of the end-to-end argument he and his coauthors put forward in 1981. If you want to maximize the utility of a network, their paper maintained, you should move as many services as feasible out of the network itself. While that may not be as counterintuitive as the notion of photons not occupying space, it is at least non-obvious, for our usual temptation is to improve a network by adding services to it.

That's what the telephone companies do: They add Caller I.D., and now their network is more valuable. We know it's more valuable because they charge us more for it. But the end-to-end argument says that adding services decreases the value of a communications network, for it makes decisions ahead of time about what people might want to do with the network. Instead, Reed and his colleagues argued, keep the network unoptimized for specific services so that it's optimized for enabling innovation by the network's users (the "ends").

That deep architectural principle is at the core of the Internet's value: Anyone with a good idea can implement a service and offer it over the network instead of having to propose it to the "owners" of the network and waiting for them to implement it. If the phone network were like the Internet, we wouldn't have had to wait 10 years to get caller I.D.; it would have been put together in one morning, implemented in the afternoon, and braced for competitive offerings by dinnertime.

For Reed the question is, What is the minimum agreement required to enable wireless communications to be sorted out? The less the system builds into itself, the more innovation—in ideas, services and business models—will arise on the edges.

There is active controversy, however, over exactly how much "hand shaking" protocol must be built in by the manufacturer and required by law. Reed believes that as more and more of radio's basic signal-processing functions are defined in software, rather than etched into hardware, radios will be able to adapt as conditions change, even after they are in use. Reed sees a world of "polite" radios that will negotiate new conversational protocols and ask for assistance from their radio peers.

Even with the FCC removed from the center of the system so that the "ends" can dynamically negotiate the most efficient connections, Reed sees a continuing role for government involvement: "The FCC should have a role in specifying the relevant science and technology research, through the NSF [National Science Foundation]. There may even be a role for centralized regulation, but it's got to focus on actual problems as they arise, not on theoretical fantasies based on projections from current technology limits."

It's clear in speaking with Reed that he's frustrated. He sees an economy that's ready to charge forward economically being held back by policies based on the state of the art when the Titanic sank. (That's literally the case: The government gave itself the right to license the airwaves in 1912 in response to the Titanic's inability to get a clear help signal out.) Key to the new generation, according to Reed, are software-defined radios. An SDR is smart precisely where current receivers are dumb. No matter how sophisticated and expensive the receiver in your living room is, once it locks on to a signal it knows how to do only one thing with the information it's receiving: treat it as data about how to create subtle variations in air pressure. An SDR, on the other hand, makes no such assumption. It is a computer and can thus treat incoming data any way it's programmed to. That includes simultaneously receiving two signals on separate frequencies from the same source, as demonstrated by Eric Blossom, an engineer on the GNU Radio project.

Of course, an SDR doesn't have to treat information as encoded sounds at all. For example, says Reed, "when a new Super-Frabjoulous Ultra-Definition TV network broadcasts its first signal, the first bits it will send would be a URL for a Web site that contains the software to receive and decode the signals on each kind of TV in the market."

But SDR addresses only one component. Reed sees innovation all across the spectrum, so to speak. He and his fellow technologist, Dewayne Hendricks, have been arguing for what they call "very wide band," a name designed to refer to a range of techniques of which "ultra-wide band" (UWB) is the most familiar. Ultra-wide band packs an enormous amount of information into very short bursts and transmits them across a wide range of frequencies: lots of colors, lots of information. Reed says: "The UWB currently proposed is a simple first step. UWB transceivers are simple and could be quite low-cost. And UWB can transmit an enormous amount of information in a very short burst—for example, a whole DVD could be sent to your car from a

drive-through, fast movie-takeout stand." Other very-wide-band techniques, not yet as well developed as UWB, spread energy more smoothly in time and, Reed believes, are more likely to be the basis of highly scalable networks.

Given Reed's End-to-End commitment, it should be clear that he's not interested in legislating against older technologies but in helping the market of users sort out the technology they want. "Our goal should be to enable a process that encourages the obsolescence of all current systems as quickly as economically practicable. That means that as fast as newer, better technology can be deployed to implement legacy functions, those legacy functions should go away due to competition." In other words, you'll be able to pick up NBC's "West Wing" signal on your current TV until so many people have switched to the new technology that broadcasters decide to abandon the current broadcast techniques. "People didn't have to be legislated into moving from the Apple II. They did it voluntarily because better technology emerged," Reed says.

But ultimately Reed isn't in this because he wants us to have better TVs or networked digital cameras. "Bad science is being used to make the oligarchic concentration of communications seem like a fact of the landscape." Opening the spectrum to all citizens would, according to him, be an epochal step in replacing the "not" with an "and" in Richard Stallman's famous phrase: "Free as in 'free speech,' not free as in 'free beer.' Says Reed: "We've gotten used to parceling out bits and talking about 'bandwidth.' Opening the spectrum would change all that."

But surely there must be some limit. "Actually, there isn't. Information isn't like a physical thing that has to have an outer limit even if we don't yet know what that limit is. Besides advances in compression, there's some astounding research that suggests that the informational capacity of systems can actually increase with the number of users." Reed is referring to work by researchers in the radio networking field, such as Tim Shepard and Greg Wornell of MIT, David Tse of UC-Berkeley, Jerry Foschini of Bell Labs, and many others, as well as work being carried out at MIT's Media Lab. If this research fulfills its promise, it's just one more way in which the metaphor of spectrum-as-resource fails and misdirects policy.

"The best science is often counterintuitive," says Reed. "And bad science always leads to bad policy."

David Weinberger is the coauthor of "The Cluetrain Manifesto" and the author of "Small Pieces Loosely Joined."

Your Next Computer

There are 1.5 billion mobile phones in the world today. Already you can use them to browse the Web, take pictures, send e-mail and play games. Soon they could make your PC obsolete.

By Brad Stone

ONE HUNDRED NINETEEN HOURS, 41 MINUTES AND 16 SECONDS. That's the amount of time Adam Rappoport, a high-school senior in Philadelphia, has spent talking into his silver Verizon LG phone since he got it as a gift last Chanukah. That's not even the full extent of his habit. He also spends countless additional hours using his phone's Internet connection to check sports scores, download new ringtones (at a buck apiece) and send short messages to his friends' phones, even in the middle of class. "I know the touch-tone pad on the phone better than I know a keyboard," he says. "I'm a phone guy."

In Tokyo, halfway around the world, Satoshi Koiso also closely eyes his mobile phone. Koiso, a college junior, lives in the global capital of fancy new gadgets—20 percent of all phones in Tokyo link to the fastest mobile networks in the world. Tokyoites use their phones to watch TV, read books and magazines and play games. But Koiso also depends on his phone for something simpler and more profound: an anti-smoking message that pops up on his small screen each morning as part of a program to help students kick cigarettes. "Teachers struggle to stop smoking, too. You hang in there," the e-mail says one day.

Another few thousand miles away, in Frankfurt, Germany, Christoph Oswald is winding his way through his favorite nightclub, busily scanning for women who are his type: tall, slim and sporty. The 36-year-old software consultant is doing this by peering into his cell phone. Before he reaches the bar, Oswald's Nokia starts vibrating, and a video of an attractive blonde appears on the color screen. "Hi, I'm Susan, come find me!" she says. Oswald scans the crowd and picks out the blue-eyed financial adviser he'd glimpsed in the video. She has seen his picture, too. The proximity of their two phones has activated a service called Symbian Dater, which compared their profiles and decided they were compatible. Soon they are laughing, and Christoph is buying Susan drinks.

Technology revolutions come in two flavors: jarringly fast and imperceptibly slow. The fast kind, like the sudden ubiquity of iPods or the proliferation of music-sharing sites on the Net, seem to instantly reshape the cultural landscape. The slower upheavals grind away over the course of decades, subtly transforming the way we live and work. The emergence of mobile phones around the world has been slow but overwhelmingly momentous. AT&T rolled out the first cellular network in 1977 for 2,000 customers in Chicago. The phones had the approximate shape and weight of a brick.

Those phones sit in museums now, and half a billion sleeker, colorful new mobile sets are sold each year. Sales of mobile phones dwarf the sales of televisions, stereos, even the hallowed personal computer. There are 1.5 billion cell phones in the world today, more than three times the number of PCs. Mobile phones are so integral to our lives that it's difficult to remember how the heck we ever got on without them.

As our phones get smarter, smaller and faster and enable users to connect at high speeds to the Internet, an obvious question arises: is the mobile handset turning into the next computer? In one sense, it already has. Today's most sophisticated phones have the processing power of a mid-1990s PC while consuming 100 times less electricity. And more and more of today's phones have computerlike features, allowing their owners to send e-mail, browse the Web and even take photos; 84 million phones with digital cameras were shipped last year. Tweak the question, though, to ask whether mobile phones will ever eclipse, or replace, the PC, and the issue suddenly becomes controversial. PC proponents say phones are too small and connect too sluggishly to the Internet to become effective at tasks now performed on the luxuriously large screens and keyboards of today's computers. Fans of the phone respond: just wait. Coming innovations will solve the limitations of the phone. "One day, 2 or 3 billion people will have cell phones, and they are all not going to have PCs," says Jeff Hawkins, inventor of the Palm Pilot and the chief technology officer of PalmOne. "The mobile phone will become their digital life."

Parlez-Vous Wireless?

It's unfortunate that the inventors of most new technologies aren't as good at naming them as they are at designing them. A little help:

WI-FI	Also known as 802.11, an increasingly popular way to connect devices to the Net and each other.
BLUETOOTH	About one fifth the range of Wi-Fi, used to connect devices like printers to PCs, earpieces to phones.
GPS	The Global Positioning System provides highly accurate navigation using data from 24 satellites.
3G	A mobile-phone standard that can beam data at 144 kilobits per second, perfect for music and video.
SMS	The Short Message System is basically e-mail for mobile phones. Also known as texting in Europe.
WIMAX	Ultrafast and long-range wireless intended to connect homes and businesses not reachable by cable.
VOIP	Voice Over Internet Protocol is slowly replacing regular telephone service in broadband homes.

PalmOne is among the firms racing to trot out the full-featured computerlike phones that the industry dubs smart phones. Hawkins's newest product, the sleek, pocket-size Treo 600, has a tiny keyboard, a built-in digital camera and slots for added memory. Other device makers have introduced their own unique versions of the smart phone. Nokia's N-Gage, launched last fall, with a new version to hit stores this month, plays videogames. Motorola's upcoming MPx has a nifty "dual hinge" design: the handset opens in one direction and looks like a regular phone, but it also flips open along another axis and looks like an e-mail device, with the expanded phone keypad serving as a small qwerty keyboard. There are also smart phones on the way with video cameras, GPS antennas and access to local Wi-Fi hotspots, the superfast wireless networks often found in offices, airports and cafes. There's not yet a phone that doubles as an electric toothbrush, but that can't be far away.

The smart-phone market constitutes only a slender 5 percent of overall mobile-phone sales today, but the figure has been doubling each year, according to the Gartner research firm. In the United States, it's the business crowd that's primarily buying these souped-up handsets. "What makes [the smart phone] so much better than the computer is that it's always with you, always up and always ready," says Jeff Hackett of Gordon, Feinblatt, an 80-member law firm in Baltimore that recently started giving its lawyers Treo 600s instead of laptops.

In Asia, it's not the boring professionals driving the newest innovations in the mobile market but what the Japanese call *keitai*-crazy kids. Teens sit in Tokyo's crowded plazas, furiously messaging each other, reading e-mail magazines and playing fantasy games like Dragon Quest. In South Korea, phones are so cherished by youngsters that in a recent survey of elementary-school kids, half said they wanted a phone as their gift for Children's Day, a national holiday. Dogs got 22 percent of the vote, PCs a meager 10 percent. Many Asian phone manufacturers think the next killer app for all these kids is actually 75 years old: television. In May Samsung announced it would launch a phone that receives 40 satellite TV stations.

In the near future, at least, new phones won't look anything like PCs. "The industry is figuring out that a wireless handheld is a different beast," says Mark Guibert, marketing director of Research in Motion, maker of the popular BlackBerry e-mail device. Mobile-phone watchers say that handsets in the next few years will pack a gigabyte or more of flash memory, turning the phone into a huge photo album or music player and giving stand-alone iPods a run for their money. For several years the industry has also talked about "location-based services," built around a phone's ability to detect its exact location anywhere in the world. With this capability, phones will soon be able to provide precise driving directions, serve up discounts for stores as you walk by them and expand dating services like the one Christoph in Frankfurt enjoyed.

BUT NOT ALL MOBILE technologists think the ultimate promise of the mobile phone ends there. Could your phone one day actually perform many of the functions of the PC, like word processing and Web browsing? PalmOne's Hawkins thinks so. The inventor of the Palm Pilot and the Treo keeps a desktop PC and a thin Sony Vaio laptop in his office. Yet he waves at both dismissively, as if they were heading for the dustbin of history. Within the next few decades, he predicts, all phones will become mobile phones, all networks will be capable of receiving voice and Internet signals at broadband speeds, and all mobile bills will shrink to only a few dollars as the phone companies pay off their investments in the new networks. "You are going to have the equivalent of a persistent [fast] T1 line in your pocket. That's it. It's going to happen," Hawkins predicts. The computer won't go away, he says, but it might fade to the background, since people prefer portability and devices that turn on instantly instead of having to boot up.

Defenders of the PC react with religious outrage to this kind of prophecy. Laptops allow another kind of mobile computing, they point out, particularly with the emergence of thousands of Wi-Fi networks around the world over the past four years. By the end of this year half of all laptops shipped will be Wi-Fi-equipped, allowing laptop owners to set up temporary offices in the local café or public park. Then there's the matter of simple practicality: mobile phones are small and getting smaller. Humans are not. "Hundreds of millions of people are not going to replace the full screen, mouse and keyboard experience with staring at a little screen," says Sean Maloney, an executive VP at chipmaker Intel, which is investing heavily in both Wi-Fi and mobile-phone technology.

Yet mobile-phone innovators are working to solve that tricky problem, too. Scientists are continuing decades of research into speech-recognition systems and have recently introduced the technology into PDAs. Users can control these gadgets with simple voice commands. Phones don't have enough processing power for speech recognition yet, but Moore's Law—the inevitability of annual improvements in computing power—will help phones get there soon, provided that battery life can keep up. Other innovators are working on improving the keyboard instead of scrapping it altogether. Canesta, a five-year-old firm in San Jose, Calif., is working on a product called a "projection keyboard." A laser inside the phone emits the pattern of a large keyboard onto a flat surface, and the phone's camera perceives the user's finger movements. Canesta's first products for phones will be available as plug-ins later this year, but one day they could be cheaply integrated into handsets.

Cell phones aren't likely to take the fastest road to this bright future. Innovation in the mobile industry is full of zigzags and wrong turns, often because no single company completely controls the device in your pocket. Carriers like Sprint and AT&T sell the phone to customers, provide billing and run the phone network; device makers like Sony, Nokia and Samsung design the phone itself and outsource the actual manufacturing to factories in China. Another challenge is that, unlike the Internet, the phone world has no open and single set of protocols for programmers to build around. Software written for one kind of phone won't work on all the others. The uncoordinated, noncommercial programming that led to the quick evolution of the Internet hasn't taken hold in the world of mobile phones.

Handsets will pack a gigabyte of memory, turning phones into huge photo albums or music players that give iPods a run for their money

But what if you could sidestep those business barriers and, limited only by your imagination and by the feasibility of existing technology, design the Phone of the Future from scratch? NEWSWEEK wondered, and asked Frog Design, a 34-year-old Silicon Valley firm that helps build phones for companies like Motorola and Nextel, to work on the problem. Over the course of a month, four professional tech designers produced the specifications for the "petfrog," a sleek, enticing prophecy of things to come. The phone's touch screen can display any interface, from keypad to keyboard to mouse pad or game console. A second, higher-resolution screen can slide out of the unit for video chats and Web surfing. Thin, insertable cartridges can turn the phone into an MP3 player or a camera, or add extra memory or a large keyboard. "This phone will be your alter ego," says Frog founder Hartmut Esslinger.

The only drawback is that the petfrog doesn't really exist—yet. But Esslinger says it would take only two or three years to build. "The challenge is to get companies to think beyond the boundaries of their businesses," he says. Incongruously, he is demonstrating the petfrog on his ultra-thin Vaio laptop, exactly the kind of personal computer he believes we will all one day leave behind. But for now, that doesn't matter. In this vision of the next frontier, we are all phone guys.

With EMILY FLYNN, in London, KAY ITOI in Tokyo and B. J. LEE in Seoul

Index

Index

Test Your Knowledge Form

We encourage you to photocopy and use this page as a tool to assess how the articles in *Annual Editions* expand on the information in your textbook. By reflecting on the articles you will gain enhanced text information. You can also access this useful form on a product's book support Web site at *http://www.dushkin.com/online/*.

NAME:

DATE:

TITLE AND NUMBER OF ARTICLE:

BRIEFLY STATE THE MAIN IDEA OF THIS ARTICLE:

LIST THREE IMPORTANT FACTS THAT THE AUTHOR USES TO SUPPORT THE MAIN IDEA:

WHAT INFORMATION OR IDEAS DISCUSSED IN THIS ARTICLE ARE ALSO DISCUSSED IN YOUR TEXTBOOK OR OTHER READINGS THAT YOU HAVE DONE? LIST THE TEXTBOOK CHAPTERS AND PAGE NUMBERS:

LIST ANY EXAMPLES OF BIAS OR FAULTY REASONING THAT YOU FOUND IN THE ARTICLE:

LIST ANY NEW TERMS/CONCEPTS THAT WERE DISCUSSED IN THE ARTICLE, AND WRITE A SHORT DEFINITION:

We Want Your Advice

ANNUAL EDITIONS revisions depend on two major opinion sources: one is our Advisory Board, listed in the front of this volume, which works with us in scanning the thousands of articles published in the public press each year; the other is you—the person actually using the book. Please help us and the users of the next edition by completing the prepaid article rating form on this page and returning it to us. Thank you for your help!

ANNUAL EDITIONS: Mass Media 05/06

ARTICLE RATING FORM

Here is an opportunity for you to have direct input into the next revision of this volume.
We would like you to rate each of the articles listed below, using the following scale:

1. **Excellent: should definitely be retained**
2. **Above average: should probably be retained**
3. **Below average: should probably be deleted**
4. **Poor: should definitely be deleted**

Your ratings will play a vital part in the next revision.
Please mail this prepaid form to us as soon as possible.
Thanks for your help!

RATING	ARTICLE	RATING	ARTICLE
_____	1. A Defense of Reading		
_____	2. Parents or Pop Culture? Children's Heroes and Role Models		
_____	3. Media Violence and the American Public: Scientific Facts Versus Media Misinformation		
_____	4. The Whipping Boy		
_____	5. Crime Scenes: Why Cop Shows Are Eternal		
_____	6. We're Not Losing the Culture Wars Anymore		
_____	7. Spirit TV: The Small Screen Takes on Eternity		
_____	8. The Triumph of the Image		
_____	9. The Pentagon Is Fighting—and Winning—the Public Relations War		
_____	10. Baghdad Urban Legends		
_____	11. Re-Thinking Objectivity		
_____	12. Across the Great Divide: Class		
_____	13. High Anxiety		
_____	14. Journalism Without Profit Margins		
_____	15. Et Tu, "Nightline"?		
_____	16. The Next Generation		
_____	17. Do Media Monsters Devour Diversity?		
_____	18. Tripping Up Big Media		
_____	19. Media Money: How Corporate Spending Blocked Political Ad Reform & Other Stories of Influence		
_____	20. Children, Entertainment, and Marketing		
_____	21. The Information Squeeze		
_____	22. Weighing the Costs of a Scoop		
_____	23. We Mean Business		
_____	24. Important if True		
_____	25. Who Knows Jack?		
_____	26. The Myth of '18 to 34'		
_____	27. Finding a Niche		
_____	28. Pay for Play		
_____	29. The Big Money Guys		
_____	30. Going Long, Going Deep		
_____	31. America Untethered		
_____	32. Searching for Online Gold		
_____	33. Low Power, High Intensity		
_____	34. The Myth of Interference		
_____	35. Your Next Computer		

(Continued on next page)

BUSINESS REPLY MAIL
FIRST CLASS MAIL PERMIT NO. 551 DUBUQUE IA

POSTAGE WILL BE PAID BY ADDRESEE

McGraw-Hill/Dushkin
2460 KERPER BLVD
DUBUQUE, IA 52001-9902

NO POSTAGE
NECESSARY
IF MAILED
IN THE
UNITED STATES

ABOUT YOU

Name   Date

_____

Are you a teacher? ☐   A student? ☐
Your school's name

_____

Department

_____

Address   City   State   Zip

_____

School telephone #

_____

YOUR COMMENTS ARE IMPORTANT TO US!

Please fill in the following information:
For which course did you use this book?

_____

Did you use a text with this ANNUAL EDITION?   ☐ yes ☐ no
What was the title of the text?

_____

What are your general reactions to the *Annual Editions* concept?

_____

Have you read any pertinent articles recently that you think should be included in the next edition? Explain.

_____

Are there any articles that you feel should be replaced in the next edition? Why?

_____

Are there any World Wide Web sites that you feel should be included in the next edition? Please annotate.

_____

May we contact you for editorial input?   ☐ yes ☐ no
May we quote your comments? ☐ yes ☐ no